JOHN CATT'S

Which London School? & the South-East

2022/23

33rd Edition
Editor: Jonathan Barnes

JOHN
CATT

Published in 2022 by
John Catt Educational Ltd,
15 Riduna Park,
Melton, Suffolk IP12 1QT UK
Tel: 01394 389850   Fax: 01394 386893
Email: enquiries@johncatt.com
Website: www.johncatt.com

Designed and typeset by John Catt Educational Limited

**A CIP catalogue record for this book is available from the
British Library.**

ISBN: 978 1915261 22 9

Contacts
Editor
Jonathan Barnes

Advertising & School Profiles
Tel: +44 (0) 1394 389850
Email: sales@johncatt.com

Distribution/Book Sales
Tel: +44 (0) 1394 389863
Email: booksales@johncatt.com

Contents

Preparing today's students for the jobs of tomorrow

Brendan O'Keeffe, Head of Digital Learning at Fulham School, explains how the school has reimagined the role of IT (Information Technology) in education through its Vision2025 programme

According to the World Economic Forum's "The Future of Jobs" 2020 report, by 2025 the time spent on current tasks at work by humans and machines will be equal. As smart technology continues to transform every corner of our lives, it's clear that schools have a huge task ahead to equip children with the skills they'll need to thrive in an ever-digitised workplace.

Recognising how the Fourth Industrial Revolution is ushering in new ways of working, last year Fulham School decided it was time to radically shift the way we deliver our Information Technology curriculum education to keep up with the rapid pace of advancements and emerging technologies.

In Autumn 2020 we therefore introduced our bold new Vision2025 programme to 200 students across years three to eight; an initiative designed to reflect emerging technology trends and help prepare the workers of tomorrow as best we can for the digital shift.

Whilst no one can predict the new wave of careers that Industry 4.0 may give rise to over the coming years, we have identified three key areas that we believe will give students the knowledge and skills to succeed in the future jobs market.

As part of our quest to support the development of the digital natives of the future, pupils aged seven to thirteen are learning to build robots, code and use design

software. Through our programme of vertical learning, each year will build on the previous one to compound their earlier knowledge and ensure a clear linear educational pathway throughout their time at our school. And, whilst Vision2025 currently focuses on our Preparatory students, our goal is to expand our forward-thinking curriculum further to create an integrated programme that runs from Reception right through to Sixth Form.

Whilst the three core strands of our Vision2025 initiative - coding, robotics and exploring the digital world - will remain constant throughout the programme, the curriculum content will be regularly reviewed and adapted in line with new emerging technologies to ensure we keep it relevant.

As long-term advocates of the value of experiential learning, we recognised that creating opportunities for hands-on learning would be key to developing both confidence and understanding in our students. We have therefore invested significantly in LEGO® Education equipment – a brand already known by the students and associated with fun – to ensure they have the freedom to experiment, put theory into practice and build technological confidence along the way.

And we know from our students that this is an approach they appreciate, with one student explaining: "I love LEGO, and I love that one of my favourite subjects is mixed with one of my favourite things to do."

By supplying home kits during the pandemic and encouraging students to learn by trial and error, we've been delighted to see how our reimagined approach to digital learning has igniting a new passion for STEM-oriented skills equally across girls and boys.

What's more, our after-school Robotics clubs – which give students the chance to work on projects individually as well as in small groups - are already over-subscribed. Interest in our sessions has grown 200% since we launched the new curriculum last September, and we've been delighted to see how these sessions – formally more popular with male students – now attracts all genders equally.

The interactive programme has gone down equally well with parents. Many of them have fed back how much they've welcomed the way the practical-based learning has helped reduce the amount of time their children were spending in front of their screens, while also boosting their engagement levels with their studies.

During lockdown parents told us the practical kits were "a welcome respite from online lessons, and allowed creativity and fun," with one adding "we all loved it as it took them away from their screens and meant they had

to think logically and methodically – it was a creative idea using concepts they had been learning online."

The world is more connected than ever, and over the last decade we've seen how evolving technologies and digital globalisation have made it easier than ever to work overseas. Recognising that many of our pupils may also go on to study across different countries and continents, we also created an international robotics competition which is hosted by Fulham School but open to Inspired schools across the world. The competition has encouraged students to showcase their new skills and adopt a global citizen mindset by sharing ideas with their counterparts across Europe, Asia Pacific, Africa and the Middle East and Latin America.

Critically, as part of Inspired Education's global network of premium schools, we are always looking for ways to share best practice to ensure Inspired schools are always at the forefront of new educational approaches. We're therefore exploring the possibility of broadening our Vision2025 project to roll the concept out to our wider group of global partners.

As teachers, one of our jobs is to ensure our students have the right range of skills to succeed in the workplace. We hope that, by shaking up the traditional approach and shifting our focus onto where technology trends are heading rather than where it has been, we can inspire the next generation of engineers.

For more information about Fulham School and its Vision2025 curriculum, visit Fulham.school. You can also read Fulham School's profile on page 51

How to use this guide

Are you looking for...

Help and advice?

If so, take a look at our editorial section (pages 5-40). Here you will find articles written by experts in their field covering issues you may well come across when choosing a school for your child.

A school or college in a certain geographical area?

Then you need to go to page D109 to find the directory page reference to a particular area. We suggest that you look first in the directory for basic information about all the schools in each region, complete with contact details, so that you will be better informed about the choices

available to you. From this section you will be directed to more detailed information in the profile section, where this is available.

A certain type of school or college in a particular area?

Look in the directories for the area you want (again, you can find the directory page reference on D109). Underneath each school listed you will find icons that denote different types of schools or qualifications that they offer. You can find a key to these icons on the following page; this key is repeated at the front of each section of the directory.

Schools featured in this guidebook are also profiled on its accompanying website: www.whichlondonschool.co.uk and www.schoolsearch.co.uk

School profiles include embedded Twitter feed and YouTube/Vimeo video, direct links to email, website and social media. Users can search by region, county, or postcode; and by age, gender and day/boarding.

A specific school or college?

If you know the name of the school or college but are unsure of its location, simply go to the index at the back of the guide where you will find all the schools listed alphabetically. You will find that some page numbers are prefixed with the letter D, this denotes that the school appears in the directory section. Schools with page numbers not prefixed by the letter D are those that have chosen to include a fuller school profile, which will provide you with much more extensive information.

Maps?

See pp 42, 79 and 85 for maps of London, Greater London, and the South-East. There are also maps within the directory sections on D111 (Central London), D131 (Greater London) and D137 (South-East).

More information on relevant educational organisations and examinations?

Look in the examinations and qualifications section and the useful organisations section, both located towards the back of the guide.

Key to directory

County	**Wherefordshire**
Name of school or college	**College Academy**
Indicates that this school has a profile	*For further details see p. 12*
Address and contact number	Which Street, Whosville, Wherefordshire AB12 3CD
	Tel: 01000 000000
Head's name	**Head Master:** Dr A Person
School type	**Type:** Coeducational day & boarding
Age range	**Age range:** 11–18
Number of pupils. B = boys G = girls	**No. of pupils:** 660 B330 G330
Fees per annum. Day = fees for day pupils. WB = fees for weekly boarders. FB = fees for full boarders.	**Fees:** Day £11,000 WB £16,000 FB £20,000
	(ii) Ⓐ (≜) Ⓔ (✎) (16)

Key to directory icons (abridged)

Key to symbols:
- (♂) Boys' school
- (ii) Coeducational school
- (♀) Girls' school
- (✿) International school

Schools offering:
- (Ⓐ) A levels
- (≜) Boarding accommodation
- (Ⓔ) Bursaries
- (16) Entrance at 16+

- (IB) International Baccalaureate
- (✎) Learning support
- (16) Tutorial/sixth form college
- (✿) Vocational qualifications

Building a sense of belonging within our schools to help nurture self-belief and empower children to make a difference

Claire Murdoch, Head of Maple Walk School, talks about how prep schools can inspire positive change by focusing on citizenship and community

Maple Walk has always been a nurturing, affordable prep school with a big heart. Fees are lower than most so that as many families as possible can join us and become a part of our supportive and dynamic community. It is a place where the children are at the centre; with parents and teachers working together to ensure they feel loved, understood, challenged and inspired. Most importantly it is a place where the children learn that they can make a difference.

Over the past few years, many of us have realised the huge benefit of being a part of a community, having a sense of belonging and working together to support each other and our environment. But the power of

citizenship has long been a part of what makes Maple Walk special and it is this 'togetherness' that has helped the school to forge a unique path. Becoming socially aware local citizens helps children to see how their actions impact those around them and they can see the benefits of efforts; singing at local care homes, collecting food for those in need, litter picking in the local area all form a part of this process and we have found it to be wonderfully inspiring.

Each morning the 'Walking Bus' meet at the fountain in Roundwood Park and stroll through the park to get to school. This small but magical start to the day really helps to bind the children to their local park, gets them outside and appreciating their surroundings, and also reduces the traffic and pollution around school with the inevitable surge of vehicles during morning drop off. Using the park has become ever more important to us in recent years and, with a lovely new 'forest school' on our doorstep, the can enjoy nature, as well as the sports pitches, courts and ample outdoor space.

So taking sketchbooks to the park to draw the birds in the aviary or the wild flowers on the grass has is becoming more of a regular occurrence. For practical maths, science experiments and circle time, the park becomes an outdoor classroom in which the children can use the skills they are taught in 'real life'. In fact, there is not a subject that you can't manage to take outside – mapping, music, creative writing, and design technology – all of it can be explored and developed in the great outdoors at the end of the road.

More and more we find that children are looking wider, deeper and further afield, wanting to learn about how they can be global citizens, and make a difference in the world by using their voices to make positive changes in their future. Nurturing this and showing the children how they can keep their horizons open – building upon their knowledge of the past but looking ahead to the future – allows the curriculum to continuously grow and adapt around the children's interests and the changing world. Having Eco and Travel Ambassadors hard at work with new initiatives is the perfect way to get the children involved in caring for and looking after our environment and builds on our existing eco credentials including our pioneering new build, complete with solar panels, a ground source heat pump and Cedam roof.

This year the children at Maple Walk have helped to develop the playground and spaces within school; more trees, more interactive play equipment, more space for creativity and imagination have all formed an important part of our recent growth as a school. For us, the success of a community approach is bound up in the involvement and investment of parents and teachers. We have such a kind, caring and incredibly dedicated staff team and that coupled with a dynamic, proactive parent body mean that ideas come off the ground and positive change is made to ensure the school is developing and growing, looking to the future and ensuring that we forge ahead in an era when anything is possible.

For more information about Maple Walk School, see page 60

Quaker schools are hidden gems

Leighton Park is one of 10 Quaker schools in the UK – open to students of all faiths and none

You don't seem to hear very much about Quaker schools but then grandiose self-promotion isn't very Quakerly.

A little research reveals some interesting facts. The Obama family sent their daughters to a Quaker school in the US and Sixth Form leavers at UK Quaker schools achieve some of the best academic progress in the country (the measure that UK Government uses to assess schools), with two in the top 0.5% in England. Quaker schools in the UK are open to students of all faiths and none, with the emphasis being on the Quaker values rather than religion.

For some families this will be exactly what they are looking for – a focus on values and personal development at a school that achieves excellent academic results

without the pressure and conformity of an academic hot house. Academic success has to be important in any school, but as Matthew Judd, Head at Leighton Park, identifies, there is more than one way of achieving this:

"A student's academic development cannot be understood in isolation but must be considered in conjunction with their emotional and physical wellbeing, confidence, maturity and happiness."

There are ten Quaker schools in the UK including three which are located close enough to London to offer a viable weekly boarding option.

- Leighton Park in Berkshire
- Sidcot in North Somerset
- Sibford in Oxfordshire.

So what is a Quaker approach to education? This varies subtly between the different Quaker schools, but an academic study from Bristol University, characterised the approach as follows:

"Quaker schools are distinguished by a value system and an ethos that is characterised by an emphasis on mutual respect, social justice and the pursuit of peace." Broadfoot et al (2016).

Evidence of a commitment to social justice can be seen from Sidcot School's Centre for Peace and Global Studies or Leighton Park's focus on Ethical Enterprise. The latter builds on the heritage of successful Quaker businesses, such as Rowntree, Cadbury and Barclay's Bank that sought to create social good as well as profit, as well as Quakers' involvement in founding organisations like Oxfam, Greenpeace and Amnesty International. Headmaster at Sidcot School, Iain Kilpatrick expanded:

"Since their formation in the Seventeenth Century, Quakers have always focused on social justice and held the vision of a more just and equal world. These qualities are alive in Quaker schools today. Sidcot is an Ashoka Changemaker School, one of only fifteen in the UK and 300 across the world. Ashoka's mission is to support a new generation of social entrepreneurs who have the skills and determination to see the world as it could be rather than accepting it as it is. The confidence this builds in our students means that they leave school determined to make a difference in society."

A website that represents Quaker Schools in the UK & Ireland, www.quakereduction.co.uk, identifies the following Quaker values in education:

- Silent reflection helps students and staff develop as individuals
- We promote truth and integrity in all that we do
- All learning should promote social responsibility and global sustainability
- We encourage positive and peaceful resolutions to conflict
- Everyone is of equal worth and diversity is celebrated
- Students develop open-mindedness and confidence without arrogance
- Academic study should be rich, challenging and free from anxiety.

Talking to some of these Quaker schools it is clear that these values are genuinely lived out in the schools, giving them a distinctive character developed over hundreds of years. School assemblies, for example, include time for quiet reflection – where the whole community come together to sit in silence – similar to mindfulness. Any member of the community can stand up and say what is on their mind during these silences, reinforcing the importance the schools place on equality.

The schools also share a significant focus on the development of character, particularly through co-curricular activities and off-curricular projects. As well as the usual sport and arts clubs, there is a noticeable emphasis on social responsibility and global citizenship, with clubs like Amnesty International and Model United Nations very much in evidence. Off-curricular projects often have an international dimension, such as Leighton Park's Global Mindedness week. Iain Kilpatrick, Headmaster at Sidcot, reflects on the benefits of a values-led education:

"The time for a Quaker education is now. The world is a complex and complicated place and needs young people with both academic and emotional intelligence to help tackle the big issues facing contemporary society. A Quaker education is values-based and so encourages intellectual curiosity around the principles of peace, equality and sustainability. Whether you apply these principles to a FTSE 100 company or an NGO working in the Third Sector, the drive to made their lives speak and use their education for good runs deep through the consciences of all our students long after they leave school."

Toby Spence, Head at Sibford School added:

"Quaker Schools offer a unique pathway. Schools shape young people and their communities by their ethos, culture and values. The distinct blend of values encompassing peace, equality, tolerance, social justice, simplicity and stewardship help to frame a community where the individual is known and valued, indeed celebrated for who they are rather than which box society might like to place them in."

The schools seem to imbue gentle, civilised values – where students can develop and grow in a kind and supportive environment – with inspiration to encourage them to play an active role – or 'Live Adventurously' as Quakers would term it, all while achieving some of the best academic progress in the country.

With Quaker schools not predisposed to shouting about themselves too much, one is left with the distinct feeling that these schools are something of a hidden gem.

For more information about Leighton Park School, see page 94

Why choose an international school?

The Lycée Français Charles de Gaulle in London is a fine example of cultural inclusion with a strong anchoring in a national heritage.

The benefits of a bilingual education have been repeatedly evidenced by numerous studies pointing to improved mental health, enhanced cognitive skills and amazing communication abilities opening up global opportunities. At international schools, the target is even more ambitious: multilingualism.

When families are monolingual and sedentary, the most efficient way to achieve this is through school. When families are multilingual and mobile, the most efficient way to perfect multilingualism is through school.

Multilingualism – At international schools, multilingualism is the norm. Within the school community, many nationalities and native tongues coexist, making up a rich cultural environment to grow up in. At these schools,

languages are as much study topics as they are vehicles for informal communication. In London, the Lycée Français Charles de Gaulle is a fine example of cultural inclusion with a strong anchoring in a national heritage. With its main setting located in a very French London area, it welcomes over 40 nationalities and delivers various curricula to its 3,450 pupils spread over 4 sites. As part of a global network of 552 French schools in 138 countries, the AEFE (*Agence pour l'Enseignement Français à l'Etranger/* Agency for French Education Abroad, run by the Ministry for Europe and Foreign Affairs), the Lycée offers a wide range of languages beyond French and English. Most pupils learn at least another one to choose among Spanish, German, Italian, Arabic, Russian and Ancient Greek or Latin.

Multicultural – Another strong suit of international schools is the ability they have to combine the best in each education system: their native one, the local system and international features. Enriching a national curriculum with different approaches allows pupils to develop more skills in terms of adaptation and cultural awareness. For example, pupils at these schools will not only study the history of one country, but at least that of two, thereby learning about various perspectives, traditions and rituals. At the Lycée, Remembrance celebrations thus involve both British and French symbols (i.e. poppies and cornflowers). This fusion of cultures is palpable at all levels from school meals to lessons content and teaching methods. Not only do pupils come from very diverse backgrounds, but also teachers and other staff, which brings variety and open-mindedness.

Excellence – This ambition of delivering rich curricula, of broadening horizons and of combining the best of each system naturally leads these schools to uphold high academic standards. As at any independent school, each pupil receives the best support and enjoys an ideal environment to thrive and progress at their own pace. Success is fostered from the start, avoiding counter-productive pressure or stress with pastoral care being as important as state-of-the-art facilities or inspiring teaching.

Strong values – With excellence and diversity at their core, international schools promote robust values of tolerance, effort and above all insatiable curiosity. Charitable work, community engagement, peer representation, mutual support are all encouraged so pupils can develop personal skills which are not taught as school subjects. At the Lycée, pupils take part in all decision-making bodies, representing their peers as elected members of all committees and boards to voice their opinions and take an active part in improving school life and pupil experience. They also have a charity supervised by adults where mainly pupils carry out actions and fundraising operations.

Beyond the classroom – Offering a wide range of "traditional" academic topics including all humanities and science, these schools also have a strong focus on the arts and sports as well as on extra-curricular activities helping pupils become well-rounded citizens. There are many opportunities for international sport competitions, connections with performers, artists, intellectuals and other inspiring individuals willing to share their experience.

Worldwide opportunities – Different curricula lead to different degrees and diplomas: national ones, such as A-Levels, German *Abitur* or French Baccalaureate, hybrid ones including the French International Baccalaureate, as well as fully international ones, such as the International Baccalaureate, generally with exceptional results and amazing outcomes. This allows pupils to continue into the most competitive universities and further education settings worldwide.

Seamless mobility – The global opportunities open to all multilingual pupils start from their first years at school. By definition, international schools can be found everywhere. Families who occasionally or regularly relocate abroad are seeking stability for their children. International schools can offer that where the curriculum and many aspects of its delivery will be quite similar from one international school to the other, allowing for swifter and smoother transition and adaptation without borders.

Global alumni networks – International school means international pupils who create worldwide alumni networks. A strong sense of belonging, a common language (which usually combines several!), and the need for roots unite these schools' alumni through space (and time) building everlasting connections and shaping limitless opportunities.

For more information about the Lycée Français Charles de Gaulle see page 55

Developing transferable skills is key to unlocking the world of work

Amanda Glubb, Head of Careers at Mayfield School, looks at the qualities that equip students for their future careers

In years to come it will be interesting to see how the pandemic is presented. Despite being a period without precedent, many positives have materialised: the speed at which people of all generations upskilled their use of technology to maintain communication; team working and academic excellence creating vaccines in record time; and the care and support people have shown for each other, whether through small local acts of kindness, or national campaigns to ensure children

do not go hungry during school holidays. People have demonstrated creative responses to problem-solving, the flexibility to adapt, and resilience in the face of ongoing adversity. It is not surprising perhaps that not only are these the skills we need to survive and thrive as humans, but they are also the transferable skills employers look for in their workforce.

When you consider that, fundamentally, the role of schools is to educate and prepare children for the transition into the adult world – which for most is the world of work – it seems strange that some schools have not always given careers education the focus it deserves. Now more than ever, all young people need to be able to make informed choices about their future. Now more than ever, educators have a duty to ensure their students leave their establishments not only with good qualifications, but career-ready as well.

Careers education plays an important role at Mayfield. Pupils are encouraged to be aspirational, to challenge stereotypes, to build on their strengths and to use their skills in the service of others, on both a local and global stage. The soft or transferable skills they acquire and develop through co-curricular activities are as important as hard knowledge. Involvement in sport clubs, drama productions, art shows, musical concerts, Model United Nations conferences, the Duke of Edinburgh's Awards Scheme, or Mayfield's own 'Actions not Words' programme, all help young people to learn about themselves and develop valuable transferable skills.

At Mayfield, careers knowledge and understanding is built using a collaboration of teachers, parents, alumnae, employers, representatives from business, UK and overseas universities, and careers professionals. The thinking behind the approach is three pronged: to engender self-awareness, opportunity awareness and an agile mind-set. Coined by businesses to encapsulate what they need in their workforce, employees with an agile mind-set are those who are open-minded, learning oriented, willing to reflect on strengths and weaknesses, and have a positive attitude towards change and development. These attributes are useful for budding entrepreneurs as well as employees, of course.

Academic or vocational attainment is, as ever, the knock on the employment door; but an agile mind-set and strong transferable skills will get you through it and into the role you want.

For more information about Mayfield School, see page 97

Developing skills for the future

Philippa Ireton ponders what awaits the next generation of the workforce and how Dallington School is preparing the children of today for the jobs of tomorrow

Much has been written in recent times about the future world of work, and the kinds of careers we need to prepare our children for. We know that many of the jobs of tomorrow have not yet been invented, and that the next generation's workforce may well have as many as twelve different careers in their lifetime. They are going to need to be flexible, quick-thinking and fast on their feet. It begs the question – what does this really mean for the schools and universities of today? How can we best prepare children at school today for the world they will be facing in a decade?

There is much talk, and even concern that soon robots will be able to do everything that a human can do, and technically it's hard to deny this assertion, but a robot will never be able to emulate the human skills which are often called "soft skills": having high emotional or social intelligence, adaptability, flexibility, good judgment, resilience, an ability to communicate. All these skills categorise our human strengths and define our competitive edge over robots.

Human skills require practice and it seems that just as they are becoming key to people's economic value, young people are abandoning these skills in favour of digital communication. The question is, what can schools do to help develop the very skills that employers are desperately seeking?

These skills can start to be learned from the moment a child enters school. By putting the child at the absolute centre of the educational journey, by expecting them to think for themselves, to develop enquiring minds and to conduct research into the topics that excite them most, children start to develop those very skills that they will need for the rest of their lives. They will learn to work in teams, work collaboratively, be flexible and adaptable, and develop the confidence to present to each other. Children will make mistakes but are encouraged to reflect on them and learn from them.

At a school like Dallington in Clerkenwell in London, traditional education has been turned on its head: a fully integrated curriculum allows the children to make connections between different discrete subjects; to see the world in a more connected way. Topic based learning encourages them to explore real-world problems and challenges, conduct meaningful research and link knowledge gained in different areas. There is a balanced approach to work, integrating the use of digital tools to enhance their work. Themes are further contextualised through the performing arts, which offers them a deeper understanding of the topics. Children can demonstrate their own capabilities whilst working independently, and they develop the art of working in teams, listening to each other's point of view, and learn to be flexible and adaptable in their work. Large, airy open-plan classrooms, often shared with other year groups, encourage respectful use of the environment, and offer many opportunities to collaborate, and to model good behaviour. A holistic, integrated approach to education, teaching the whole child, will equip them with the natural skills they will need for success in the rest of their lives.

These are all skills which employers reportedly are crying out for. They understand that technical skills can be learned along the way, on the job, or can be acquired in order to take on a certain job. What employers also recognise is that they need people to join their workforce who have the fundamental human skills and strengths outlined earlier, which will enable them to turn their hand to any task presented to them. Children at Dallington School become self-regulated learners and

innate skills are fostered and developed and become standard. This gives them the fundamental tools needed to complement any technical skills they will be required to learn for a particular job.

The concept of lifelong education is something that we are beginning to understand will be vital for the workforce of the future: the ability to dip in and out of education to learn the technical skills required for the next career. The idea that education is shoehorned into school, and then in some cases, 3 years of university study – and then stops – is absurd. We never stop learning and increasingly it is clear that the next generation not only has to prepare itself for jobs that don´t yet exist, but needs to be armed with a strong suite of human skills which will complement their technical skills.

Dallington School, situated in the heart of the City, is perfectly placed to start children on their journey of discovery, and to equip them with the skills vital to a variety of successful careers in the future.

For more information about Dallington School, see page 46

Values are more valuable than ever

Headteacher Sam Gosden explains why Dolphin School is 'a greenhouse, not a hothouse'

Love. Wisdom. Truth.

These three words are our school motto and define our values at Dolphin School. Love – having and showing love for one another – being outwardly encouraging towards anyone and everyone. Wisdom – a love for learning and academic excellence, mental and spiritual growth. Truth – having the courage to be honest with yourself, understand your thoughts and mobilise your sense of self worth to motivate, aspire and dream.

In recent years children have been, and continue to be, put through the mangle in their global, local, online and offline worlds. For our older pupils and teenagers at secondary school, these worlds have already merged – the noise from the news, social media, parents and friends can be deafening at worst, confusing at best.

We are not long out of a global pandemic where pupils learnt new words such as self-isolate – the idea that humans have to choose or are told to withdraw from society and not see our grandparents, our friends or do something as simple as go to a supermarket or a cafe. Some children I've worked with in previous schools enjoyed wearing masks as it gave them the security from the world – allowed them to internalise and control their self-expression. We won't know the visceral effect of the pandemic on children for a long time. If ever. Now, they are faced with words such as invasion, shelling, violence, nuclear, refuge or shelter – words which conjure the real and terrifying images of being forced to withdraw from your world, to run, escape and seek sanctuary.

As parents and educators we face the challenge (and opportunity) of supporting our children through this fast paced and ever changing world. The additional layers of understanding our children have embraced has been inspirational to watch – the agility they show in accepting and dealing with change, their compassion and foresight to tackle discrimination and bias, accepting that the world isn't perfect. They seem to navigate their way through the challenges with an entirely different mindset than perhaps we may have done. They know the world has complexities from a young age.

At Dolphin School, it's clear that the very thing that binds us together in adversity are values.

Values create standards of care, human connections, respect and support for each other.

Values ensure that not only do teachers stop and support the children and each other, but children also do this for each other and the staff. Parents are outwardly encouraging and support each other, their children and our staff. Values create relationships and uphold the very thing we yearn for in society; positive and meaningful contact and connections with those around us. Everyone in the entire school knows each other's name. It's striking to see this in an independent school with two nurseries – striking to comprehend that the sense of community and the value in community is so strong.

During our weekly Friday assembly, the senior team speaks to the whole school – the children, the staff and the parents at once. We unpack salient themes from the bible, values and our beliefs in humanity. We sing happy birthday, praise and commend our pupils for their successes. We are a Christian school and we unpack Christian beliefs in a modern world, and those parents and children who are not Christian still hold the same values – Love. Wisdom. Truth.

A parent once said to me "I know that my children will be successful in life, whatever they do or wherever they end up. I just want them to get there in one piece".

This phrase struck me at the time and continues to shape my approach to education to this day. We have a responsibility to instil values in children which not only stand the test of time, but are also applicable today to shape them into responsible citizens. Dolphin School children programme robots, they sing, write poetry, compete on the sports field (our girls are particularly feisty footballers) dance or solve equations – all that you expect them to do. They are subtly ambitious, thirsty for knowledge and yet humble with their friends and peers.

Dolphin School children do not need to compete with each other for their senior schools, to be the most popular or for their teacher's attention.

This school is not a plantation for academic success, but a natural ecosystem in which all children are nourished, given space and time to grow, and learn under the protection of our canopy. If a plant isn't thriving, you change its environment, not the plant itself – we are a greenhouse, not a hothouse. It is this reason that our pupils do get there in one piece and senior school head teachers often reflect that they know a Dolphin School pupil when they see one.

In the history of Dolphin School, never have these three words meant so much. Love. Wisdom. Truth.

For more information about Dolphin School, see page 48

The intrinsic and undeniable value of a child centred approach

Genevieve Mackenzie, Head of Early Years at Hampton Court House, on the benefits of a bespoke curriculum

"What is essential is that children learn independently, not in bunches; that they learn out of interest and curiosity, not to please appease the adults in power; and that they ought to be in control of their own learning, deciding for themselves what they want to learn and how they want to learn it"

John Holt

Early years pedagogy has always valued the unique and individual child. The Montessori Method asks teachers to "follow the child" (Maria Montessori). The Early Years Foundation Stage describes the "unique child" (EYFS, 2021). While the Reggio Emilia approach puts children in control of their own education. When we think about early years education from this perspective, it is simple to

acknowledge that an individualised approach should be used. But what does it mean to be truly child centred in your approach to early years education? So much of what teachers do today are driven and determined by assessments. Where their focus is on pushing children to conform, gaining the knowledge they need to meet certain criteria and planning lessons and activities to ensure they do. Whilst I understand and endorse necessary assessments that are required to protect children from falling behind and ensure they are making progress, assessment should be used to create each child's curriculum. I truly believe that providing a bespoke and truly child centred approach has the biggest impact and ensures children make the best progress.

Creating a bespoke curriculum for each individual

child is no easy task. "Child-centered teaching is placing the pupil at the centre of the learning process in classroom" (Gravoso, Pasa, Labra & Mori, 2008). "The teacher provides pupils with opportunities to learn independently and from one another and coaches them in the skills they need to do so effectively" (Collins & O'Brien, 2003). At Hampton Court House, we have managed to create this using a variety of pedagogues, including the EYFS and Forest School as well as Montessori and Reggio Emilia influences. It requires a dedicated team with exceptional teaching skills, differentiation and flexibility across the curriculum. In addition, consideration of every child's needs and the resources to support this tailored approach. We know that all children learn differently, they have different interests and different needs. When we assess children, we consider everything we need to create opportunities for learning.

"Being child-centred is about elevating the status of children's interests, rights, and views in the work of your organisation. It involves considering the impact of decisions and processes on children, and seeking their input when appropriate to inform your work." (Office of the Children's Commissioner website) Some examples of how we do this: For a child who is interested in writing, we help them to develop their fine motor coordination by introducing them to the Montessori 'practical life materials'. For a toddler who loves trains and starting to distinguish colours we provide them with different coloured trains. Our project work may stem from a question that a child asks – "where do animals live" creates a project around animal habitats. For a child who learn better outdoors, we use the forest school approach.

What makes this child-centred approach so important? Children learn by doing and through their experiences and play. When they are interested, they concentrate and when they choose, they feel valued and a sense of belonging. They intrinsically access a better variety of activities, which ensures a holistic education. They develop independence, learn to make decisions and problem solve. They develop self-respect and have a deeper understanding of themselves and the world they live in.

Someone asked me at an open morning: what sets Hampton Court House apart from all the other schools? I have to admit that I felt rather delighted to reply. But my reply was not solely about our very distinct location; for those of you who have not had the opportunity to visit us yet, Hampton Court House is a manor house with front steps that lead onto beautiful and majestic gardens,

and our back steps lead onto Bushy Park. This is a place where magic happens. I can't think of anywhere else in the world where a stag comes to the window and bows his head to ask for a piece of fruit – this happens daily and gives me goosebumps every time. But the second reason we are so distinctive is our wonderfully bespoke and child-centred ethos. That we take time to reflect on and consider every decision we make, placing the children at the centre. This ensures that every child is supported to have the freedom to create their own excellent programme that enables them to reach their own potential and to be their own person.

"Let the children be free; encourage them; let them run outside when it's raining; let them remove their shoes when they find a puddle of water; and, when the grass of the meadows is damp with dew, let them run on it and trample it with their bare feet; let them rest peacefully when a tree invites them to sleep beneath its shade; let them shout and laugh when the sun wakes them in the morning as it wakes every living creature that divides its day between waking and sleeping."

Maria Montessori

For more information about Hampton Court House, see page 91

Freedom from stereotyping

John Doy, Head of Sixth Form, Mayfield School, celebrates an inspiring environment

One of the main arguments for an all-girls' education is the freedom from the stereotyping that seems to creep in to any mixed environment. At A Level the statistics are quite startling. For example, a girl at a GSA school (Girls School Association, of which Mayfield is a member) is 75% more likely to take Maths at A Level, 70% more likely to take Chemistry, and two and a half times more likely to take Physics, all subjects traditionally considered as 'hard', male-oriented subjects. This is certainly something I have witnessed at Mayfield – Maths and the Sciences are far and away our most popular subjects at A Level (as an English graduate I concede this with a slightly heavy heart) and, if I look at our latest batch of university hopefuls, almost half of the cohort of 60 are going on

to study Maths or Science based courses: we have engineers, physicists, chemists, earth and planetary scientists, medics, vets all going on to develop their skills in higher education. It is genuinely exciting to see young women fired up about science and technology and my experience tells me it is because they have been given the space to develop these interests in an environment that by its very nature dispenses with any kind of concept of boys' or girls' subjects.

Engaging with these kind of statistics and thinking in this way, however, always seems, to me at least, to court a kind of counter-factual approach to the individual narratives of the students involved. The nature of time and space dictates that we can never know precisely which factors lead us to our ultimate destinations. It's for this reason I would prefer to focus on the individual narratives of some of the students in my care to illustrate how schools like Mayfield challenge stereotypes rather than rely too heavily on statistical data. I think it is more important to bring to life those points on the graph or figures in the performance table, because often it is the bits you can't measure that make all the difference.

Take for example one of our engineers, now studying Engineering at Cambridge, who was able to combine her interest in science with her artistic ability by producing an A Level Art project that evolved from scientific drawings of insects and flowers. Or how about another enterprising student who set up her own bespoke trainer designing business and got straight onto a Fine Art degree without needing to take a Foundation year and is still growing her online business at university? Or one of our students who is now studying Earth and Planetary Science at Imperial College but who also spent her break and lunch times supporting Year 7 and 8 students with their Maths homework.

These are just some examples from this year's cohort of Year 13s and I suppose what I'm trying to illustrate by briefly sketching their aspirations and achievements is where the freedom and breadth of an educational experience afforded by a school like Mayfield can lead. I can't tell you for sure if it's because the girls are in a single-sex environment; I can only report what I can see happening here, and it's dynamic, empowering and exciting to witness.

In this sense then, the higher uptake of STEM subjects I referred to at the start is, rather than being an end in itself, instead a wonderful by-product of an atmosphere that fosters independence of thought, confidence and a

can-do attitude that makes for outstanding students and ultimately fulfilled and happy adults.

For more information about Mayfield School, see page 97

It is genuinely exciting to see young women fired up about science and technology and my experience tells me it is because they have been given the space to develop these interests in an environment that by its very nature dispenses with any kind of concept of boys' or girls' subjects

Teaching children to know themselves

Lucas Motion, Head of Faraday Prep School, on meeting the challenges of post-lockdown education

Faraday is a small, nurturing school committed to academic excellence and children's wellbeing and emotional health. With a little more than 100 children in total and average class sizes of 15, every teacher knows every child and we tailor instruction to meet the needs of individual children.

We recognise that with the right support, children learn to articulate and manage their emotions, deal with conflict, solve problems and understand things from another person's perspective. Now more than ever, it is essential that we teach these social and emotional skills which are so effective in supporting learning and beneficial to outcomes in later life.

The world is faster, smarter and more demanding than ever before and children need language and high

quality interactions with adults throughout their daily lives to help them navigate it. With the pressure to cover the curriculum and succeed academically, it might feel as if there is little time for developing such skills. Given our size, we are able to prioritise these high quality social interactions with every child while maintaining high expectations and a love of learning that is so integral to their transition to secondary school and beyond.

In the wake of the pandemic, our youngest children have lived much of their lives under lockdowns, many with interrupted social paths. I am not alone in noticing that 4 and 5 year olds have taken longer to settle in. Some find it a real challenge to play together, to share and to regulate their emotions. Some children's communication and language skills are delayed and meaningful conversations are important for language development, enabling children to practise language and social skills and receive feedback from children and adults.

At Faraday children develop lifelong relationships with their teachers and friends in an environment where they are known and appreciated as a whole person. These strong relationships help our children to feel safe and included, to recognise similarities and celebrate our differences.

Our aim is to teach children to know themselves, to know others, to look after one another, to respect diversity, show empathy and be responsible. In order to do that we have built a cycle of values, chosen by children and staff, that reflects the vision, values and context of our school. These include friendship, independence, forgiveness, trust, perseverance and love. Values are introduced at the beginning of each month in a whole-school assembly and filter into lessons and activities in the classroom. This allows for the vocabulary of values to be shared and modelled so that it becomes intrinsic to the culture and ethos of the school. At the end of each month, each class chooses their 'values champions' who are recognised and rewarded in celebration assemblies.

Our children are happy, confident and articulate and, above all, they love coming to school. This means they are highly engaged and have a sense of personal responsibility for their learning and for the community. Pupils also have opportunities to participate in clubs, house events, sports and the arts, allowing them to mix with other year groups while developing meaningful hobbies and interests.

Faraday's unique riverside location provides a magical environment and access to a stimulating, creative community on Trinity Buoy Wharf, E14. We are proud to be part of this creative hub for arts and cultural activities. The area is also a base for the English National Ballet, The Big Draw and The Prince's Foundation to name a few significant neighbours, so our children have a strong sense of community, often visiting the Wharf and inviting its residents in for workshops and assemblies.

In the complex realities of twenty-first century life, society thrives or falls by the quality of our relationships. I believe that our sense of community, coupled with sensitive and stimulating interactions, will empower children to be the teachers and leaders of the future and give them the best possible start in life.

For more information about Faraday Prep School, see page 50

Choosing a school – what to consider

However much a school may appeal at first sight, you still need sound information to form your judgement

Schools attract pupils by their reputations, so most go to considerable lengths to ensure that parents are presented with an attractive image. Modern marketing techniques try to promote good points and play down (without totally obscuring) bad ones. But every Head knows that, however good the school prospectus is, it only serves to attract parents through the school gates. Thereafter the decision depends on what they see and hear. Research we have carried out over the years suggests that in many cases the most important factor in choosing a school is the impression given by the Head. As well as finding out what goes on in a school, parents need to be reassured by the aura of confidence that they expect from a Head. How they judge the latter may help them form their opinion of the former. In other words, how a Head answers questions is important in itself and, to get you started, we have drawn up a list of

points that you may like to consider. Some can be posed as questions and some are points you'll only want to check in your mind. They are not listed in any particular order and their significance will vary from family to family, but they should be useful in helping you to form an opinion.

Before visiting and asking questions, **check the facts** – such as which association the school belongs to, how big it is, how many staff *etc*. Is there any form of financial pie chart showing how the school's resources are used? The answers to questions like these should be in the promotional material you've been sent. If they aren't, you've already got a good question to ask!

Check the website. Is it up-to-date? Look at the school's social media feeds and videos. What type of tone do they set? That first impression is very important.

When you get to the school you will want to judge the

Leighton Park School – see editorial on page 12

overall atmosphere and decide whether it will suit you and your child. Are any other members of the family going to help to pay the fees? If so, their views are important and the school's attitude towards them may be instructive.

When you make it to the inner sanctum, **what do you make of the Head as a person?** Age? Family? Staying? Moving on? Retiring? Busted flush? Accessible to children, parents and staff? If you never get to see the Head, but deal with an admissions person of some sort, it may not mean you should rule the school out, but it certainly tells you something about the school's view of pupil recruitment.

Academic priorities – attitude towards league tables? This is a forked question. If the answer is 'We're most concerned with doing the best for the child', you pitch them a late-developer; if the answer is, 'Well, frankly, we have a very high entry threshold', then you say 'So we have to give you a foolproof academic winner, do we?'

Supplementary questions:

- What is the ratio of teachers to pupils?
- What are the professional qualifications of the teaching staff?
- What is the school's retention rate? In prep schools this means how many pupils do they lose at 11 when the school goes on to 13.
- How long is the school day – and week?
- What are the school's exam results?
- What are the criteria for presenting them?
- Were they consistent over the years?
- Is progress accelerated for the academically bright?
- How does the school cope with pupils who do not work?
- Where do pupils go when they leave?
- How important and well resourced are sports, extra-curricular and after school activities, music and drama?
- What cultural or other visits are arranged away from the school?

Other topics to cover:

- What is the school's mission?
- What is its attitude to religion?
- How well is the school integrated into the local community?
- How have they responded to the Charities Act initiatives?
- What are the responsibilities and obligations at weekends for parents, pupils and the school?
- Does the school keep a watching brief or reserve the option to get involved after a weekend incident?
- What is the school's attitude to discipline?
- Have there been problems with drugs, drink or sex? How have they been dealt with?
- What is the school's policy on bullying?
- How does the school cope with pupils' problems?
- What sort of academic and pastoral advice is available?
- What positive steps are taken to encourage good manners, behaviour and sportsmanship?
- What is the uniform?
- What steps are taken to ensure that pupils take pride in their personal appearance?
- How often does the school communicate with parents through reports, parent/teacher meetings or other visits?
- What level of parental involvement is encouraged both in terms of keeping in touch with staff about your own child and more generally, eg a Parents' Association?

And finally – and perhaps most importantly – what does your child make of the school, the adults met, the other children met, pupils at the school in other contexts, and the website?

Initial advice

Educational institutions often belong to organisations that encourage high standards. Here we give a brief guide to what some of the initials mean.

BSA

The Boarding Schools' Association

Since its foundation in 1966, the Boarding Schools' Association (BSA) has had the twin objectives of promoting boarding education and the development of quality boarding through high standards of pastoral care and boarding accommodation. Parents and prospective pupils choosing a boarding school can, therefore, be assured that more than 600 schools in nearly 40 countries worldwide that make up the membership of the BSA are committed to providing the best possible boarding environment for their pupils.

A UK boarding school can only be a full member of the BSA if it is also a member of one of the Independent Schools Council (ISC) constituent associations, or in membership of the State Boarding Forum (SBF). These two bodies require member schools to be regularly inspected by the Independent Schools' Inspectorate (ISI) or Ofsted. Other boarding schools who are not members of these organisations can apply to be affiliate members. Similar arrangements are in place for overseas members. Boarding inspection of ISC accredited independent schools has been conducted by ISI since September 2012. Ofsted retains responsibility for the inspection of boarding in state schools and non-association independent schools.

Boarding inspections must be conducted every three years. Boarding is judged against the National Minimum Standards for Boarding Schools which are due to be updated in the next few months.

Relationship with government

The BSA is in regular communication with the Department for Education (DfE) on all boarding matters. The Children Act (1989) and the Care Standards Act (2001) require boarding schools to conform to national legislation and the promotion of this legislation and the training required to carry it out are matters on which the DfE and BSA work together. BSA has worked especially closely with the DfE and other government departments during the coronavirus pandemic over the past 18 months, support the safety and continuity of education for its member schools' pupils and staff, both domestically and internationally.

Boarding training

BSA delivers the world's largest professional development programme for boarding staff. It offers:

- Two-year courses for graduate and non-graduate boarding staff– these involve eight study days and two assignments, each about 4,000 words long. This is the flagship training opportunity for staff seriously interested in boarding excellence

- A Diploma course for senior experienced boarding staff, involving three study days and two assignments spread between March and October

- A broad range of day seminars on topics of particular interest to boarding/pastoral staff – e.g. Essentials of Boarding, Leading the Boarding Team, Meeting the Needs of Overseas Boarders

- Specialists one or two-day conferences for Boarding Staff, Heads, Health & Wellbeing staff**, Marketing and Admissions staff* and State Boarding Schools staff and Safeguarding Leads**& Basic training online, for those very new to boarding.

* With Sacpa (Safeguarding and Child Protection Association), part of the BSA Group
**With Hieda (Heath in Education Association) part of the BSA Group
**With BAISIS (British Association of Independent Schools with International Students), part of the BSA Group

State Boarding Forum (SBF)

BSA issues information with regards to its state boarding school members and BSA should be contacted for details of these schools. In these schools, parents pay for boarding but not for education, so fees are

substantially lower than in an independent boarding school.

Chief Executive: Robin Fletcher
Chief Operating Officer: Aileen Kane

The Boarding Schools' Association
First Floor
27 Queen Anne's Gate
London, SW1H 9BU.
Tel: 020 7798 1580
Email: bsa@boarding.org.uk
Website: www.boarding.org.uk

GSA

The Girls' Schools Association, to which Heads of independent girls' schools belong

The Girls' Schools Association is the 'expert voice of girls' education', helping girls and their teachers to flourish. They represent the Heads of a diverse range of largely independent girls' schools, among which are some of the top-performing schools in the UK.

GSA schools are experts in educating girls. They encourage the highest standards of education, pastoral care and co-curricular activity, with a wealth of extra-curricular opportunity in art, music, drama, science, sport and more. A lack of gender stereotyping and high-quality teaching enable students to develop the resilience, skills and confidence to lead a healthy, fulfilling life, with their mental and physical well-being a top priority.

The innovative practice and academic rigour of GSA schools attract pupils from around the world. Students thrive in the humanities and do disproportionately well in 'difficult' modern languages and STEM (science, technology, engineering, maths) subjects. The overwhelming majority continue their studies at top universities in the UK, the US and elsewhere, and there is a growing interest in higher and degree apprenticeships.

GSA schools share experience, specialisms, events and facilities in a variety of inter-school partnerships, and some schools offer means-tested bursaries for families of limited means.

GSA highlights the benefits of being taught in a predominantly girls-only environment, helping to inform and influence the national education debate and enabling continual professional development through a wide range of collaborative conferences and courses.

They work closely with the Association of School and College Leaders, are a member of the Independent Schools Council, and join hands with organisations in the UK and internationally – such as the Association of State Girls' Schools (UK), the National Coalition of Girls' Schools (USA) and the Alliance of Girls' Schools Australasia – in the interests of girls' education worldwide.

Twenty first century girls' schools come in many different shapes and sizes. Some cater for 100% girls,

others provide a predominantly girls-only environment with boys in the nursery and/or sixth form. Some follow a diamond model, with equal numbers of boys but separate classrooms between the ages of 11 to 16. Educational provision across the Association offers a choice of day, boarding, weekly, and flexi-boarding education. Schools range in type from large urban schools to small rural schools. Many schools have junior and pre-prep departments and can offer a complete education from age 3/4 to 18. Some have religious affiliations. Heads of schools in the Girls' Day School Trust (GDST) are members of the GSA.

As the GSA is one of the constituent bodies that make up the Independent Schools' Council (ISC), schools whose Heads are full GSA members are required to undergo a regular cycle of inspections to ensure that rigorous standards are maintained.

The Association's secretariat is based in Leicester.

Suite 105, 108 New Walk, Leicester LE1 7EA
Tel: 0116 254 1619
Email: office@gsa.uk.com
Website: www.gsa.uk.com
Twitter: @GSAUK

President 2021/22: Samantha Price, Benenden School
President 2022/23: Heather Hanbury, Lady Eleanor Holles School
Chief Executive: Donna Stevens

HMC

The Headmasters' and Headmistresses' Conference, to which the Heads of leading independent schools belong

Founded in 1869 the HMC exists to enable members to discuss matters of common interest and to influence important developments in education. It looks after the professional interests of members, central to which is their wish to provide the best possible educational opportunities for their pupils.

The Heads of some 296 leading independent schools are members of The Headmasters' and Headmistresses' Conference, whose membership now includes Heads of boys', girls' and coeducational schools. International membership includes the Heads of around 56 schools throughout the world.

The great variety of these schools is one of the strengths of HMC but all must exhibit high quality in the education provided. While day schools are the largest group, about a quarter of HMC schools consist mainly of boarders and others have a smaller boarding element including weekly and flexible boarders.

All schools are noted for their academic excellence and achieve good results, including those with pupils from a broad ability band. Members believe that good education consists of more than academic results and schools provide pupils with a wide range of educational co-curricular activities and with strong pastoral support.

Only those schools that meet with the rigorous membership criteria are admitted and this helps ensure that HMC is synonymous with high quality in education. There is a set of membership requirements and a Code of Practice to which members must subscribe. Those who want the intimate atmosphere of a small school will find some with around 350 pupils. Others who want a wide range of facilities and specialisations will find these offered in large day or boarding schools. Many have over 1000 pupils. 32 schools are for boys only, others are coeducational throughout or only in the sixth form. The first girls-only schools joined HMC in 2006. There are now 39 girls-only schools.

Within HMC there are schools with continuous histories as long as any in the world and many others trace their origins to Tudor times, but HMC continues to admit to membership recently-founded schools that have achieved great success. The facilities in all HMC schools will be good but some have magnificent buildings and grounds that are the result of the generosity of benefactors over many years. Some have attractive rural settings, others are sited in the centres of cities.

Pupils come from all sorts of backgrounds. Bursaries and scholarships provided by the schools give about a third of the 240,000 pupils in HMC schools help with their fees. These average about £35,000 per annum for boarding schools and £15,000 for day schools. About 190,000 are day pupils and 45,000 boarders.

Entry into some schools is highly selective but others are well-suited to a wide ability range. Senior boarding schools usually admit pupils after the Common Entrance examination taken when they are 13.

Most day schools select their pupils by 11+ examination. Many HMC schools have junior schools, some with nursery and pre-prep departments. The growing number of boarders from overseas is evidence of the high reputation of the schools worldwide.

The independent sector has always been fortunate in attracting very good teachers. Higher salary scales, excellent conditions of employment, exciting educational opportunities and good pupil/teacher ratios bring rewards commensurate with the demanding expectations. Schools expect teachers to have a good education culminating in a good honours degree and a professional qualification, though some do not insist on the latter especially if relevant experience is offered. Willingness to participate in the whole life of the school is essential.

Parents expect the school to provide not only good teaching that helps their children achieve the best possible examination results, but also the dedicated pastoral care and valuable educational experiences outside the classroom in music, drama, games, outdoor pursuits and community service. Over 89% of pupils go on to higher education, many of them winning places on the most highly-subscribed university courses.

All members attend the Annual Conference, usually held in a large conference centre in September/October. There are ten divisions covering England, Wales, Scotland and Ireland where members meet once a term on a

Leading
Independent
Schools

regional basis, and a distinctive international division.

The chair and committee, with the advice of the general secretary and membership secretary, make decisions on matters referred by membership-led sub-committees, steering groups and working parties. Close links are maintained with other professional associations in membership of the Independent Schools Council and with the Association of School and College Leaders.

Membership Secretary: Dr Simon Hyde
Tel: 01858 469059

12 The Point, Rockingham Road
Market Harborough, Leicestershire LE16 7QU
Email: gensec@hmc.org.uk
Website: www.hmc.org.uk

IAPS

The Independent Association of Prep Schools (IAPS) is a membership association representing leading headteachers and their prep schools in the UK and overseas

With around 660 members, IAPS schools represent a multi-billion pound enterprise, educating more than 170,000 children and employing more than 15,000 staff. As the voice of independent prep school education, IAPS actively defends and promotes the interests of its members.

IAPS schools must reach a very high standard to be eligible for membership, with strict criteria on teaching a broad curriculum, maintain excellent standards of pastoral care and keeping staff members' professional development training up-to-date. The head must be suitably qualified and schools must be accredited through a satisfactory inspection. IAPS offers its members and their staff a comprehensive and up-to-date programme of professional development courses to ensure that these high professional standards are maintained.

Member schools offer an all-round, values-led broad education which produces confident, adaptable, motivated children with a passion for learning. The targets of the National Curriculum are regarded as a basic foundation which is greatly extended by the wider programmes of study offered. Specialist teaching begins at an early age and pupils are offered a range of cultural and sporting opportunities.

IAPS organises a successful sports programme where member schools compete against each other in a variety of sports. In 2019-20, over 17,000 competitors took part in 119 events across 7 sports.

Our schools are spread throughout cities, towns and the countryside and offer pupils the choice of day, boarding, weekly and flexible boarding, in both singe sex and co-educational schools. Most schools are charitable trusts, some are limited companies and a few are proprietary. There are also junior schools attached to senior schools, choir schools, those with a particular religious affiliation and those that offer specialist provision as well as some schools with an age range extending to age 16 or above.

Although each member school is independent and has its own ethos, they are all committed to delivering an excellent, well-rounded education to the pupils in their care, preparing them for their future.

IAPS
Bishop's House
Artemis Drive
Tachbrook Park
CV34 6UD
Tel: 01926 887833
Email: iaps@iaps.uk
Website: iaps.uk

ISA

The Independent Schools Association, with membership across all types of school

The Independent Schools Association (ISA), established in 1879, is one of the oldest of the Headteachers' associations of independent schools that make up the Independent Schools' Council (ISC). It began life as the Association of Principals of Private Schools, which was created to encourage high standards and foster friendliness and cooperation among Heads who had previously worked in isolation. In 1895 it was incorporated as The Private Schools Association and in 1927 the word 'private' was replaced by 'independent'. The recently published history of the association, *Pro Liberis*, demonstrates the strong links ISA has with proprietorial schools, which is still the case today, even though boards of governors now run the majority of schools.

Membership is open to any Head or Proprietor, provided they meet the necessary accreditation criteria, including inspection of their school by a government-approved inspectorate. ISA's Executive Council is elected by members and supports all developments of the Association through its committee structure and the strong regional network of co-ordinators and area committees. Each of ISA's seven areas in turn supports members through regular training events and meetings.

ISA celebrates a wide-ranging membership, not confined to any one type of school, but including all: nursery, pre-preparatory, junior and senior, all-through schools, coeducational, single-sex, boarding, day and performing arts and special schools.

Promoting best practice and fellowship remains at the core of the ISA, as it did when it began 140 years ago. The association is growing, and its 569 members and their schools enjoy high quality national conferences and courses that foster excellence in independent education. ISA's central office also supports members and provides advice, and represents the views of its membership at national and governmental levels. Pupils in ISA schools enjoy a wide variety of competitions, in particular the wealth of sporting, artistic and academic activities at area and national level.

President: Lord Lexden
Chief Executive: Rudolf Eliott Lockhart

ISA House, 5-7 Great Chesterford Court, Great Chesterford, Essex CB10 1PF
Tel: 01799 523619
Email: isa@isaschools.org.uk
Website: www.isaschools.org.uk

ISA celebrates a wide-ranging membership, not confined to any one type of school, but including all: nursery, pre-preparatory, junior and senior, all-through schools, coeducational, single-sex, boarding, day and performing arts and special schools

The Society of Heads

The Society of Heads represents the interests of independent secondary schools

The Society of Heads represents the interests of independent, secondary schools. Established in 1961, The Society has as its members 125 Heads of well-established secondary schools, many with a boarding element, meeting a wide range of educational needs. All member schools provide education up to 18, with sixth forms offering both A and AS levels and/or the International Baccalaureate. Also some offer vocational courses. Many have junior schools attached to their foundation. A number cater for pupils with special educational needs, whilst others offer places to gifted dancers and musicians. All the schools provide education appropriate to their pupils' individual requirements together with the best in pastoral care.

The average size of the schools is about 350, and all aim to provide small classes ensuring favourable pupil:teacher ratios. The majority are coeducational and offer facilities for both boarding and day pupils. Many of the schools are non-denominational, whilst others have specific religious foundations.

The Society believes that independent schools are an important part of Britain's national education system. Given their independence, the schools can either introduce new developments ahead of the maintained sector or offer certain courses specifically appropriate to the pupils in their schools. They are able to respond quickly to the needs of parents and pupils alike.

Schools are admitted to membership of the Society only after a strict inspection procedure carried out by the Independent Schools Inspectorate. Regular inspection visits thereafter ensure that standards are maintained.

The Society is a constituent member of the Independent Schools Council and every full member in the Society has been accredited to it. All the Society's Heads belong to the Association of School and College Leaders (ASCL) (or another recognised union for school leaders) and their schools are members of AGBIS.

The Society's policy is: to maintain high standards of education, acting as a guarantee of quality to parents who choose a Society school for their children; to ensure the genuine independence of member schools; to provide an opportunity for Heads to share ideas and common concerns for the benefit of the children in their care; to provide training opportunities for Heads and staff in order to keep them abreast of new educational initiatives; to promote links with higher and further education and the professions, so

> The average size of the schools is about 350, and all aim to provide small classes ensuring favourable pupil: teacher ratios. The majority are coeducational and offer facilities for both boarding and day pupils. Many of the schools are non-denominational, whilst others have specific religious foundations

that pupils leaving the Society's schools are given the best advice and opportunities for their future careers; and to help Heads strengthen relations with their local communities.

The Society of Heads Office,
12 The Point, Rockingham Road, Market Harborough,
Leicestershire LE16 7QU
Tel: 01858 433760
Email: info@thesocietyofheads.org.uk
Website: www.thesocietyofheads.org.uk

The Independent Schools Council

The Independent Schools Council (ISC) works with its members to promote and preserve the quality, diversity and excellence of UK independent education both at home and abroad

What is the ISC?

The ISC brings together seven associations of independent schools, their heads, bursars and governors. Through our member associations we represent more than 1,350 independent schools in the UK and overseas. These schools are among the best in the world and educate more than half a million children each year.

The ISC's work is carried out by a small team of dedicated professionals in an office in central London. We are assisted by contributions from expert advisory groups in specialist areas. Our priorities are set by the board of directors led by our chairman, Barnaby Lenon. We are tasked by our members to protect and promote the sector in everything we do.

ISC schools

Schools in UK membership of the ISC's constituent associations offer a high quality, rounded education. Whilst our schools are very academically successful, their strength also lies in the extra-curricular activities offered – helping to nurture pupils' soft skills and encourage them to be self-disciplined, ambitious and curious. There are independent schools to suit every need, whether you want a day or boarding school, single sex or co-education, a large or a small school, or schools offering specialisms, such as in the arts.

Our schools are very diverse: some are selective and highly academic, while others have very strong drama or music departments full of creative opportunities in plays, orchestras and choirs. For children with special needs such as dyslexia or autism there are many outstanding independent schools that offer some of the best provision in the country.

Academic results

Typically, the ISC publishes a sector-wide analysis of Year 11 and Year 13 exam results for independent schools every August. However, due to the coronavirus pandemic, there was no sector-wide publication of results in 2020 or 2021 because exams were temporarily replaced by different assessment processes that Ofqual had to create in response to the crisis. Schools provided students with their grades in August as they normally would in both 2020 and 2021.

Looking back at 2019, when exam results were last published, 45.7% of Year 13 exam entries at independent schools were graded A*/A, compared to the national average of 25.5%. That year also saw 95.6% of Year 11 exams at independent schools graded C/4 or higher, compared to the national average of 67.3%. Figures recorded in 2019 also demonstrated more students were following different pathways post-GCSE.

Fee assistance

Schools take issues around affordability very seriously and are acutely aware of the sacrifices families make when choosing an independent education. Schools work hard to remain competitive whilst facing pressures on salaries, pensions and maintenance and utility costs. They are strongly committed to widening access and have made strenuous efforts to increase the amount they can offer in bursaries. Despite the financial strain brought about by the pandemic, many schools have extended their bursary provision – this year, £455m was provided in means-tested fee assistance, an increase of £15m from last year. Almost 180,000 pupils currently benefit from reduced fees, representing over a third of pupils at our schools.

Our schools are very diverse: some are selective and highly academic, while others have very strong drama or music departments full of creative opportunities in plays, orchestras and choirs.

School partnerships

Independent and state schools have been engaged in partnership activity for many years, with the majority of ISC schools currently involved in important cross-sector initiatives. These collaborations involve the sharing of expertise, best practise and facilities, and unlock exciting new opportunities for all involved. To learn more about the partnership work taking place between state and independent schools, visit the Schools Together website: www.schoolstogether.org/

ISC Associations

There are seven member associations of the ISC, each with a distinctive ethos in their respective entrance criteria and quality assurance: Girls' Schools Association (GSA), Headmasters' and Headmistresses' Conference (HMC), Independent Association of Prep Schools (IAPS) Independent Schools Association (ISA), The Society of Heads, Association of Governing Bodies of Independent Schools (AGBIS), and the Independent Schools' Bursars Association (ISBA).

Further organisations who are affiliated to the ISC: Boarding Schools Association (BSA), Council of British International Schools (COBIS), Scottish Council of Independent Schools (SCIS) and Welsh Independent Schools Council (WISC).

The Independent Schools Council can be contacted at:
First Floor,
27 Queen Anne's Gate,
London,
SW1H 9BU
Telephone: 020 7766 7070
Website: www.isc.co.uk

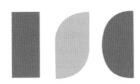

independent
schools
council

Help in finding the fees

Chris Procter, Managing Director of SFIA Wealth Management, outlines a planned approach to funding your child's school fees

Despite the challenges of the Covid-19 pandemic, the independent sector remains resilient, according to the latest Independent Schools Council (ISC) survey, conducted in January 2021. The number of pupils in ISC schools stood at 532,237, the third highest in history.

Average school fee increases were only 1.1% between the 2019/20 and 2020/21 school years, the lowest annual rise ever recorded in the ISC Census. The average day school fees were £5,064 per term, an increase of 0.9%. The average boarding school fees were £12,000 per term, an increase of 1.7%.

Fees charged by schools vary by region – for example, the average day school fees ranged from £8,969 per term in the North East to £13,884 per term in Greater London; the average day school fees ranged between £3,725 per term in the North West and £6,036 per term in Greater London.

Over £1.1bn of fee assistance was provided in the 2020/21 school year, of which £938m came from schools themselves. Over a third of pupils in ISC schools received at least one type of fee support.

£455m of means-tested fee assistance was provided, an increase of £15m on the previous year. The average means-tested bursary stood at over £10,200. Nearly half of all pupils on means-tested bursaries had more than half of their fees remitted.

The overall cost of school fees (including university fees) might seem daunting: the cost of educating one child privately could well be very similar to that of buying a house but, as with house buying, the school fees commitment for the majority of parents can be made possible by spreading it over a long period rather than funding it all from current resources.

It is vital that parents do their financial homework, plan ahead, start to save early and regularly.

Grandparents who have access to capital could help out; by contributing to school fees they could also help to reduce any potential future inheritance tax liability.

Parents would be well-advised to consult a specialist financial adviser as early as possible, since a long-term plan for the payment of fees – possibly university as well – can prove very advantageous from a financial point of view and offer greater peace of mind. Funding fees is neither science, nor magic, nor is there any panacea. It is quite simply a question of planning and using whatever resources are available, such as income, capital, or tax planning opportunities.

The fundamental point to recognise is that you, your circumstances and your wishes or ambitions, for your children, or grandchildren are unique. They might well appear similar to those of other people but they will still be uniquely different. There will be no single solution to your problem. In fact, after a review of all your circumstances, there might not be a problem at all.

So, what are the reasons for seeking advice about education expenses?

- To reduce the overall cost
- To get some tax benefit
- To reduce your cash outflow
- To invest capital to ensure that future fees are paid
- To set aside money now for future fees
- To provide protection for school fees
- Or just to make sure that, as well as educating your children, you can still have a life

Any, some, or all of the above – or others not listed – could be on your agenda, the important thing is to develop a strategy.

At this stage, it really does not help to get hung up on which financial 'product' is the most suitable. The composition of a school fees plan will differ for each family depending on a number of factors. That is why there is no one school fees plan on offer.

The simplest strategy but in most cases, the most expensive option, is to write out a cheque for the whole bill when it arrives and post it back to the school. Like most simple plans, that can work well, if you have the money. Even if you do have the money, is that really the best way of doing things? Do you know that to fund £1,000 of school fees as a higher rate taxpayer paying 40% income tax, you currently need to earn £1,667, this rises to £1,818 if you are an additional rate taxpayer where the rate is 45%.

How then do you start to develop your strategy? As with most things in life, if you can define your objective, then you will know what you are aiming at. Your objective in this case will be to determine how much money is needed and when.

You need to draw up a school fees schedule or what others may term a cash flow forecast. So, you need to identify:

- How many children?
- Which schools and therefore what are the fees? (or you could use an average school fee)
- When are they due?

- Any special educational needs?
- Inflation estimate?
- Include university costs?

With this basic information, the school fees schedule/cash flow forecast can be prepared and you will have defined what it is you are trying to achieve.

Remember though, that senior school fees are typically more than prep school fees – this needs to be factored in. Also, be aware that the cost of university is not restricted to the fees alone; there are a lot of maintenance and other costs involved: accommodation, books, food, to name a few. Don't forget to build in inflation, I refer you back to the data at the beginning of this article.

You now have one element of the equation, the relatively simple element. The other side is the resources you have available to achieve the objective. This also needs to be identified, but this is a much more difficult exercise. The reason that it is more difficult, of course, is that school fees are not the only drain on your resources. You probably have a mortgage, you want to have holidays, you need to buy food and clothes, you may be concerned that you should be funding a pension.

This is a key area of expertise, since your financial commitments are unique. A specialist in the area of school fees planning can help identify these commitments, to record them and help you to distribute your resources according to your priorities.

The options open to you as parents depend completely upon your adviser's knowledge of these complex personal financial issues. (Did I forget to mention your tax position, capital gains tax allowance, other tax allowances, including those of your children and a lower or zero rate tax paying spouse or partner? These could well be used to your advantage.)

A typical school fees plan can incorporate many elements to fund short, medium and long-term fees.

Each plan is designed according to individual circumstances and usually there is a special emphasis on what parents are looking to achieve, for example, to maximise overall savings and to minimise the outflow of cash.

Additionally, it is possible to protect the payment of the fees in the event of unforeseen circumstances that could lead to a significant or total loss of earnings.

Short-term fees

Short-term fees are typically the termly amounts needed within five years: these are usually funded from such things as guaranteed investments, liquid capital, loan plans (if no savings are available) or maturing insurance policies, investments etc. Alternatively, they can be funded from disposable income.

Medium-term fees

Once the short-term plan expires, the medium-term funding is invoked to fund the education costs for a further five to ten years. Monthly amounts can be invested in a low-risk, regular premium investment ranging from a building society account to a friendly society savings plan to equity ISAs. It is important to understand the pattern of the future fees and to be aware of the timing of withdrawals.

Long-term fees

Longer term funding can incorporate a higher element of risk (as long as this is acceptable to the investor), which will offer higher potential returns. Investing in UK and overseas equities could be considered. Solutions may be the same as those for medium-term fees, but will have the flexibility to utilise investments that may have an increased 'equity based' content.

Finally, it is important to remember that most investments, or financial products either mature with a single payment or provide for regular withdrawals; rarely do they provide timed termly payments.

Additionally, the overall risk profile of the portfolio should lean towards the side of caution (for obvious reasons).

There are any number of advisers in the country, but few who specialise in the area of planning to meet school and university fees. SFIA is the largest organisation specialising in school fees planning in the UK.

This article has been contributed by SFIA and edited by Chris Procter, Managing Director.
Chris can be contacted at: SFIA, 27 Moorbridge Road, Maidenhead, Berkshire, SL6 8LT
Tel: 01628 566777
Email: enquiries@sfia.co.uk
Web: www.sfia.co.uk

Profiles

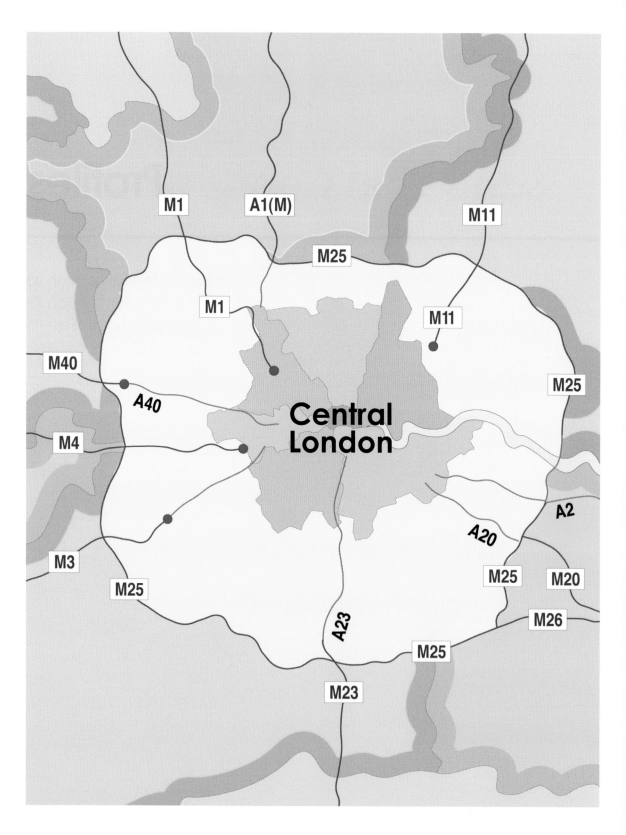

Schools in Central London

Broomwood Hall Lower School
Part of Northwood Schools

50 Nightingale Lane, London, SW12 8TE

Tel: 020 8682 8840

Email: admissions@northwoodschools.com

Website: www.northwoodschools.com

Head: Miss Jo Townsend

School type: Co-educational Pre-Prep

Religious Denomination: Church of England, all denominations welcome

Age range of pupils: 4–8 years

No. of pupils enrolled as at 01/01/2022: 320

Fees as at 01/01/2022:

Day: £5,820 per term

Average class size: Max 20

ABOUT US: Broomwood Hall Lower School is a co-educational pre-prep school for children aged 4-8 in Wandsworth, South West London offering an excellent and rounded education. We offer a broad, modern and innovative curriculum designed to provide mastery of the building blocks of education, delivered in an inclusive, exciting and enjoyable way, harnessing curiosity and creating a desire to learn. All children have specialist teaching in arts, sport, music and French. Maths mastery is a speciality.

MOTTO: 'To do your best, to be your best' exemplifies our ethos. We help each child develop to the best of their individual ability and believe that a supportive but focused environment, without undue stress or 'hot-housing', is the best way to enable them to fulfil their potential, both inside and outside the classroom.

GAMES & THE ARTS: All children take part in PE and Games for at least five periods per week and progress from learning basic skills to playing in competitive matches. Great emphasis on building confidence through art, drama and musical performance. A multitude of clubs from Year 1 onwards include karate, coding, art and cookery. We hold a prestigious Gold Artsmark Award.

PASTORAL CARE: The school is split between two buildings a short walk from each other. Each site is small enough, and intimate enough, for all children to be well known to all staff. We have a strong pastoral team which includes learning support, a full time school nurse and a qualified school counsellor.

ADMISSIONS: Entry into our Reception classes is by random ballot which is designed to ensure an equal mix of boys and girls and a good spread of birthdays. Entry at other ages is subject to a satisfactory school report and a baseline assessment. Children from the Lower School progress automatically to either Northcote Lodge, (boys) or Broomwood Hall Upper School (girls) at the age of 8 providing these are the right schools for them. We also offer a limited intake at age 7 for children wishing to move on to either of these prep schools.

HEAD TEACHER'S PHILOSOPHY: We embrace the best of tradition with the best of modern innovative teaching to deliver an outstanding education that excites, stimulates and nurtures the whole child. Our five learning powers: Curiosity, Communication, Creativity, Independence and Resilience plus our Mastery and Thematic learning approach, are the bedrock for all we do and designed to equip children with the problem solving and analytical skills they need to succeed in the workplaces of the future.

In September 2021 Northwood Schools joined the wider Dukes Education family. Together we're extraordinary.

Broomwood Hall Upper School
Part of Northwood Schools

68-74 Nightingale Lane, London, SW12 8NR

Tel: 020 8682 8810
Email: admissions@northwoodschools.com
Website: www.northwoodschools.com
Head: Mrs Louisa McCafferty
School type: Girls' Preparatory

Religious Denomination: Church of England, all denominations welcome
Age range of girls: 8–13 years
No. of pupils enrolled as at 01/01/2022: 250
Fees as at 01/01/2022:
Day: £7,140 per term
Average class size: Av 17

ABOUT US: Broomwood Hall Upper School is a girls' prep school in Wandsworth, SW London preparing for both 11+ & 13+ exits which offers an excellent and rounded education that nurtures and stretches in equal measure. Our winning combination of traditional values and innovative teaching coupled with an exciting enrichment programme challenges and stimulates both breadth and depth of learning. Broomwood girls are happy, confident, rounded individuals who are well prepared for future success.

THE CURRICULUM: A broad and stimulating mastery approach, with technology used at every level fosters a love of learning, bolsters self-confidence, creativity and critical thinking, helping girls to maximise their potential.

GAMES & THE ARTS: Sport and the arts are an important part of our curriculum and we offer a surprisingly wide variety. We place great value on creativity with exceptionally strong music, art and drama departments. New Art and DT block. Winners of prestigious Artsmark Gold Award. Leiths Cookery school on-site for Years 6 & 7.

PASTORAL CARE: We know that happy children thrive academically. With small class sizes, an excellent tutor system and mindfulness and wellbeing programmes built into the curriculum, we pride ourselves on nurturing the whole child and developing individual strengths so that when girls leave us at 11 or 13, they are confident, happy, well-rounded individuals with a strong sense of purpose.

ADMISSIONS & EXIT: Entry at ages 8 and 11 is automatic for girls coming from the Lower School. We take pride in the breadth of our curriculum and get wonderful results in all areas with girls regularly winning awards and scholarships at both 11 and 13, in all subjects, to some of the country's best schools, both day and boarding including Alleyn's, Benenden, Emanuel Marlborough, Bradfield, JAGS, Streatham & Clapham High, Woldingham, Wellington, Cranleigh and King's, Canterbury. On average, around 25 per cent of leavers win awards across all areas: academic, art, music, drama and sport.

HEAD'S PHILOSOPHY: We prepare for life, not just the next school. Our focus on the essential skills of creativity, critical thinking, resilience, independence and confidence, provides girls with the benefits of a holistic education where everything is important, and each girl is supported and enabled to be and do her best and is prepared for an exciting future.

In September 2021 Northwood Schools joined the wider Dukes Education family. Together we're extraordinary.

Dallington School

(Founded 1978)

8 Dallington Street, Islington,
London, EC1V 0BW
Tel: 020 7251 2284
Email: hercules@dallingtonschool.co.uk
Website: www.dallingtonschool.co.uk
Head: Linda Kiernan
Appointed: 2022

School type:
Co-educational Day and Nursery
Age range of pupils: 3–11 years
No. of pupils enrolled as at 01/01/2022: 81
Boys: 58 *Girls:* 23
Fees as at 01/01/2022:
Day: £11,490–£14,490
Teacher/pupil ratio: 1:10 (with full time TA)

A family-run, independent, co-educational day school for children aged 3 to 11, in the heart of London

Dallington is a school that holds a unique place in the constellation of outstanding London schools – a vibrant oasis of creativity; proudly and fiercely independent. Established and led for over 40 years by Mogg Hercules MBE, a Dallington education continues to celebrate and embody her vision and ethos.

Dallington offers a rich and ambitious curriculum, with excellence in core skills as the foundation. In addition, the creative and performing arts are embedded in the Dallington experience from the very beginning. The Dallington child is defined by the attitudes that ensure their future success in a fast changing world – Curiosity, Courage, Compassion, Creativity and Collaboration.

We actively encourage our children to be informed, to find their voice, to develop opinions and to explore their place in the world; to see themselves as global citizens from the earliest age and to understand that they are never too young to be heard or to make a difference.

Our children learn in bright and airy open-plan classrooms spread over five floors. First names are used and we do not have a school uniform.

Personal tours each day of the week. Non-selective entry policy. Early registration advised.

Devonshire House Preparatory School

(Founded 1989)

2 Arkwright Road, Hampstead,
London, NW3 6AE
Tel: 020 7435 1916
Email: enquiries@dhprep.co.uk
Website:
www.devonshirehouseschool.co.uk
Headmistress: Mrs S. Piper BA(Hons)
School type: Preparatory,
Pre-preparatory & Nursery Day School

Religious Denomination:
Non-denominational
Age range of boys: 2.5–13 years
Age range of girls: 2.5–11 years
No. of pupils enrolled as at 01/01/2022: 543
Boys: 317 **Girls:** 226
Fees as at 01/01/2022:
Day: £9,870–£20,475

Devonshire House, the co-educational preparatory and pre-preparatory school with its own nursery, is a place where families come together for their children's most formative years. The School's commitment is to outstanding care and education, to help discover, inspire and develop pupils' talents and to support them throughout their years at the School and in their move to their next schools.

The results for senior school entry are exceptionally good, with some forty scholarships and exhibitions to senior schools in the last three years. However, the School is perhaps proudest that this is achieved in such a creative and happy school with its broad curriculum and with so many extra-curricular activities.

"*Pupils leave the school as confident, resilient young people who have a strong self-esteem and a well-developed understanding of how to improve their own learning.*" ISI Inspection Report.

The School aims to create adaptable and creative minds, for a changing world.

The Head, Senior Leadership Team and Staff are committed to an open, trusting dialogue with parents about their children and to be available to advise and help throughout each child's school career.

Pupils learn how to work hard for their own achievements and to work with others with commitment, understanding and co-operation. They learn many things

– traditional and innovative – and above all they learn how to grow their talents and how they may want to apply them in their lives.

Devonshire House has fine buildings, with substantial grounds and games areas, in the heart of Hampstead.

The School seeks to inspire not only a love of learning, but a love of thinking for oneself and the strength and resilience to do so, to make the most of life and to help others along this journey.

"*A wonderful experience for my children. I am truly thankful for all the teachers and friends in DHS.*" Junior School Parent

Dolphin School
(incorporating Noah's Ark Nursery Schools)

(Founded 1986)

106 Northcote Road, London, SW11 6QW

Tel: 020 7924 3472

Email: admissions@dolphinschool.org.uk

Website: www.dolphinschool.org.uk

Head Teacher: Mr S Gosden

Appointed: September 2021

School type:

Co-educational Day and Nursery

Age range of pupils: 2–11 years

No. of pupils enrolled as at 01/01/2022: 162

Fees as at 01/01/2022:

Day: £12,885–£14,085

Average class size:

18 in school: 8 in Nursery

Teacher/pupil ratio: 1:8 Nursery,

1:9 (Lower School), 1:18 (Upper School)

Curriculum

Our small class sizes enable us to get to know your child extremely well so that we can not only set specific individualised academic targets, but also discover how he or she learns best. We give priority to English and maths as well as hands-on science, colourful geography, history (with outings to the real thing) and whole-school Spanish.

Games and the arts

We train pupils in the arts with fantastic specialist teaching and a plethora of performing and exhibiting opportunities. We also coach children in a wide range of sports through dynamic teaching and a superb fixture list.

Pastoral care

We are committed to giving both time and care to grow your child's character on his or her journey from Reception to Year 6. Our Christian ethos leads us to believe that personal growth ultimately matters more than anything. So while we are thrilled that our leavers win academic or sporting scholarships to a range of excellent secondary schools, we are even more excited about who they are – and pleased that they enjoyed the journey.

Entry requirements

Reception class: appointment with the Head Teacher. Years 1-6: assessment day and past school reports.

Head Teacher's philosophy

If we want children to be the best they can be, academically, artistically, in sport or as people, we must start by valuing them for who they are.

Outstanding characteristics

The combination of nurture and dynamism. The passionate commitment of the staff. A fantastic all-round education.

Examinations offered

11+ entry examinations.

Senior exit schools: Alleyns, Box Hill, Caterham, Christs Hospital, Dulwich College, Emanuel, Epsom College, Francis Holland, Frensham Heights, Hurstpierpoint, Ibstock Place, JAG's, Kew House, Kings College, Streatham & Clapham High, Reeds, Royal Russell, St John's Leatherhead, Sydenham High, Thames Christian School, Trinity, Tudor Hall, Whitgift, Woldingham, Worth.

Dolphin School Trust is a registered charity (No. 1145113) and exists to promote a high quality of education for all its children based upon Christian principles.

École Jeannine Manuel – London

ÉCOLE Jeannine Manuel
International understanding through a bilingual education

(Founded 2015)

43-45 Bedford Square, London, WC1B 3DN

Tel: 020 3829 5970

Email: admissions@jmanuel.uk.net

Website:
www.ecolejeanninemanuel.org.uk

Head of School: Pauline Prévot

School type: Co-educational Day

Age range of pupils: 3–18 years

No. of pupils enrolled as at 01/01/2022: 585

Fees as at 01/01/2022:

Day: £20,760

Average class size: 16

Teacher/pupil ratio: 1:8

École Jeannine Manuel in London is a French, bilingual, international school which opened its doors in September 2015 in Bloomsbury, steps away from the British Museum.

Our school welcomes pupils from all nationalities and cultural backgrounds, from Nursery to Year 13. Sixth Formers take either the French Baccalaureate (with an international option) or the International Baccalaureate. Both diplomas are recognised by the most prestigious universities across the globe.

École Jeannine Manuel is the young sister school of its Paris namesake, a UNESCO associated school founded in 1954 and one of France's most prestigious schools, ranked first among French high schools (public and independent) for overall academic performance for the past nine years. As is the case in France, École Jeannine Manuel London's mission is "to promote international understanding through the bilingual education of a multicultural community of students, the fostering of pedagogical innovation, and the constant exploration of best practices in the context of an ever-changing global environment."

A bilingual education

École Jeannine Manuel offers an enriched, bilingual adaptation of the French national curriculum, including English, Science and Chinese programmes developed by its sister school in Paris. In History, the French national curriculum is complemented to help pupils gain coherent knowledge and understanding of Britain's past and that of the wider world. Extra-curricular activities include sports – with outdoor facilities within walking distance of the school – as well as a broad range of artistic and tech-based clubs.

English and French are spoken equally in class. Our aim is to bring pupils to a native proficiency – orally and in writing – in both languages. We welcome non French-speaking students at all levels and help them adapt to the demands of a bilingual curriculum. With respect to English, the school accommodates beginners up to Year 7. Experience shows that studying in French and in English yields a strong and mutually reinforced command of both languages as well as a deep understanding of the cultures they express. A bilingual education enhances pupils' capacity for abstract, conceptual thinking and develops a sense of nuance, nurtured by exposure to multiple perspectives.

A multicultural community of students

Looking beyond French and bi-national families, the school welcomes pupils from all nationalities, cultural traditions and native languages. École Jeannine Manuel in London is positioned, as is the case in Paris, as a unique, truly bicultural institution with a multicultural student body representing more than 45 nationalities. We attract international and internationally minded families deeply invested in the education and well being of their children. Living within this cultural melting pot every day yields a special consciousness of one's place in the world, an appreciation for the broad landscape of culture and civilizations that we learn to understand and value together.

The fostering of pedagogical innovation

The key drivers of our school's pedagogy are coherence and innovation. Whether inspired by current research in the cognitive sciences, by best practices from around the world or home-grown, our teaching methods are constantly evolving. Our international teams of teachers stimulate new ideas that lead to a creative, pioneering education. Hands-on manipulations in math, inquiry- based learning in the sciences, and teamwork are among the practices that foster pupil engagement and growth. Our aim is to have pupils think, do and share. The school's pedagogical principles are founded on four pillars: the early mastery of core academic skills; the development of autonomy; the encouragement of collaborative work; and the nurturing of curiosity, creativity and a lifelong appetite for culture.

© Paul Riddle

Faraday Prep School

Old Gate House, 7 Trinity Buoy Wharf, London, E14 0JW

Tel: 020 8965 7374

Email: info@newmodelschool.co.uk

Website: www.faradayschool.co.uk

Head Teacher: Lucas Motion

School type: Co-educational Day

Age range of pupils: 4–11 years

No. of pupils enrolled as at 01/01/2022: 100

Fees as at 01/01/2022:

Day: £3,981 per term

Average class size: 14

Founded in 2009, Faraday Prep School offers inspirational learning in an inspirational setting. A happy, vibrant and diverse independent primary school in East London, the school's historic and artistic riverside location, provides a magical environment and access to a stimulating, creative community that offers exciting learning opportunities.

We give every child a first-class education rooted in a creative curriculum, with small classes, quality teaching and a personal approach in a caring and kind environment.

In these formative years our aim is to inspire a love of learning and that the desire to explore, grow and create will stay with our pupils for life. We place a strong focus on literacy and numeracy, with a targeted approach that enables each child to progress at their own level.

Our lessons stretch, challenge and engage pupils of all abilities and interests. We present children with the great literature, music and works of art to help them acquire an increased understanding of the world in which they live and build a thorough understanding of knowledge in each subject. As such, our curriculum is broad and stimulating, and includes specialist teaching in French, Music, Drama and Physical Education.

Children join our Reception class in their fifth year and leave for senior school at the age of eleven. The school day runs from 8.45 am until 3.30 pm, with our private buses running before and after school from a range of East London locations. We support busy parents by welcoming children from 8.15 am and by offering after-school care until 5.30 pm each day, with a wide range of extra-curricular activities on offer from gardening to robotics.

We were founded in 2009 and maintain strong links with our sister school, Maple Walk, in North West London. Our setting beside the River Thames, opposite the iconic O2 arena and beside the Trinity Lighthouse, gives our pupils an inspirational location in which to learn. We are fortunate enough to be surrounded by creative industries and we make the best of all that London has to offer, with regular trips to museums, historic attractions and galleries.

Entry into Reception is non-selective and based on the date the completed registration form is returned to our Registrar, with siblings given priority. Entry higher up the school is by interview and informal assessment in the classroom. We offer regular open days and welcome private tours.

Fulham School

Fulham SCHOOL

(Founded 1996)

1-3 Chesilton Road, London, SW6 5AA

Tel: 020 8154 6751

Email: senioradmin@fulham.school

Website: fulham.school

Pre-Prep & Nursery Head: Di Steven

Prep Head: Neill Lunnon

Senior & Sixth Form Head: Chris Cockerill

School type: Co-educational Day

Religious Denomination: Non-denominational

Age range of pupils: 3–18 years

No. of pupils enrolled as at 01/01/2022: 650

Fees as at 01/01/2022:

Day: £18,420–£21,567

Average class size: 18

About Fulham School

Fulham School is independent and co-educational, providing a rich and diverse curriculum to boys and girls from aged 3 to age 18. Situated in the heart of Fulham, the three school sites, Nursery & Pre-Prep, Prep and Senior, are ideally located to take advantage of London and the endless opportunities it offers to enhance education.

Founded in 1996, Fulham School believes in co-education in its broadest sense: not just girls and boys learning together but learners of all abilities understanding that they have much to offer each other, and teachers as keen to learn and evolve as their students.

Specialist teachers and support staff inspire pupils to work to the limits of their potential, so they are prepared for the next steps in life, while learning more about themselves and developing a broad range of interests.

Personalised Learning

Combining the best of tradition with innovative skills and methods Fulham School celebrates diverse abilities across academic, creative, and sporting pursuits. Teachers encourage the development of creative, problem-solving individuals who have tenacity, kindness, and self-worth. From the most academic to the most creative, the most driven to the most supportive, Fulham School wants each pupil to delight in what they do as they discover personal interests, gifts, and talents.

Support

Fulham School supports the highest of academic high-flyers to achieve the scholarships and university places that will challenge them most alongside pupils whose chief passions and interests are expressed in practice and rehearsal rooms or on the sports field. All pupils are encouraged to make contributions where their strengths lie and recognise the contributions of others.

"We seek to provide life skills, the ability to make connections between and beyond subjects, the ability to work together to achieve more than any individual can alone." Chris Cockerill, Head

L'Ecole de Battersea

(Founded 2005)
Trott Street, Battersea, London, SW11 3DS

Tel: 020 7371 8350
Email: admin@lecoledespetits.co.uk
Website: www.lecoledespetits.co.uk
Principal: Mrs F Brisset
Head: Mr L Balerdi
Founder: Mrs M Otten
School type: Independent Bilingual Pre-Primary and Primary (Partenaire AEFE)

Religious Denomination: All denominations welcome
Age range of pupils: 3–11 years
No. of pupils enrolled as at 01/01/2022: 250
Fees as at 01/01/2022:
Day: £4,745 per term
Average class size: 18 (max 21)

L'Ecole de Battersea opened in 2005 following on from the success of its sister school, L'Ecole des Petits. The school is unique in that it offers a **continuous bilingual education from age three through until age eleven** at the end of primary, where both the French and English educational systems operate together.

The teaching emphasis throughout the school is fundamentally based on the French system, into which aspects of the English curriculum and methodology are integrated. **The highly motivated bilingual team of teachers are qualified in both the English and French educational systems**.

This bilingual facility enables children and parents to choose to progress on to either the English private school system or on to the French Lycée system, and is also ideal for the increasingly popular International Baccalaureate.

The school welcomes bilingual pupils from a range of cultures, and so aims to generate a **truly international atmosphere. Partnership with the family** is paramount in the school's ethos, and the school successfully seeks **to develop confident and balanced children** with experience of a wide range of activities, an appreciation of artistic and cultural heritage and a thoughtful and considerate attitude towards others.

We have installed high performance air purification equipment in all classrooms, gyms and canteens. These remove PM2.5 pollution particles, viruses (Covid) and bacteria from the air, reducing risk of infection.

The school is only **a five-minute drive from Chelsea** and operates a twice daily school bus service between South Kensington and Battersea, as well as a link to its sister school in Fulham, ten minutes distance.

The school is inspected by both the French Inspectorate and Ofsted and achieves excellent academic results. **OFSTED 2018 report said the school was "Outstanding in all categories"** and it has been selected as one of the top 225 private schools in the country in The Tatler Education Guides 2009-2022.

L'Ecole des Petits

(Founded 1977)
2 Hazlebury Road, Fulham,
London, SW6 2NB

Tel: 020 7371 8350
Email: admin@lecoledespetits.co.uk
Website: www.lecoledespetits.co.uk
Principal: Mrs F Brisset
Head: Miss E Mesnage
Founder: Mrs M Otten
School type: Independent Bilingual
Pre-Primary (Partenaire AEFE)

Religious Denomination: All
denominations welcome
Age range of pupils: 3–6 years
No. of pupils enrolled as at 01/01/2022: 120
Fees as at 01/01/2022:
Day: £4,615 per term
Average class size: 14 (max 18)

L'Ecole des Petits is a flourishing pre-primary school situated in Fulham, just **ten minutes from Chelsea**, with easy access by public transport. The school also runs its own daily morning and afternoon **bus service between South Kensington and Fulham**, and between its sister school in Battersea.

The school was founded in 1977 to cater for English and French families who want their children to **grow up in a bilingual environment**. By combining the Early Years curriculum with the French National curriculum, the school provides all aspects of education in both French and English, and today has a wonderfully **international flavour with children from more than 20 different countries** attending.

Children are taught by qualified and highly-motivated bilingual teachers. The school aims to provide **an education that enhances early learning skills in the controlled environment of small classes**.

The school has a warm and friendly atmosphere, which encourages children to express themselves whilst following the structured bilingual curriculum. We consider **maintaining traditional family values** a very important aspect of our approach.

Our philosophy is to develop confident and happy children by providing **the best possible all-round education and care**, with an abundance of sports, drama, clubs, school outings and events as well as academic lessons.

We prepare our children to move onto both English and French schools, and many continue their primary education at our sister school, L'Ecole de Battersea.

According to one of our parents, "This is an exceptional school that provides a nurturing environment, as well as good discipline and a wonderful education, and my child could not be happier and more confident about going to school."

OFSTED March 2020 report: "Outstanding in all categories".

Lloyd Williamson School Foundation

LLOYD WILLIAMSON
——— S C H O O L S ———

12 Telford Road, London, W10 5SH

Tel: 020 8962 0345
Email: admin@lws.org.uk
Website: www.lloydwilliamson.co.uk
Co-Principals:
Ms Lucy Meyer & Mr Aaron Williams
Appointed: December 1999
School type: Co-educational Day

Age range of pupils: 4 months–16 years
Fees as at 01/01/2022:
Day: £17,550
Nursery: £92.50 per 10.5 hours
Average class size: 12-16
Teacher/pupil ratio: 1:12

Over the past twenty-two years, Lloyd Williamson Schools have built an excellent reputation for being schools with high academic standards, personalised learning for individual children and a friendly, happy environment in which to learn. All our GCSEs were at 9/A*in 2021. We foster initiative and a love for learning.

We are pleased to offer parents important extras:

- Breakfast and after-school club at no extra cost (the school and nurseries are open 7.30am – 6pm).
- Holiday clubs (we are open 50 weeks of the year).
- Small classes (max 16 to Year 6, max 18 in Secondary).
- Sensible fees.
- Home-cooked meals freshly prepared every day by our in-house chefs.

We boast excellent facilities, a homely atmosphere with school pets, and dedicated teachers who support the children to be focused, positive and enthusiastic.

"All staff are keen for pupils to be the best they can. The family ethos of the school promotes pupils' personal development very well. The working relationships pupils have with their teachers and other adults promote a harmonious environment." (Ofsted)

In the words of our children: *"I'm really happy here – the teachers really listen and if I get stuck they help!" "There is always someone who listens to me." "I like the way the big children look after the little children."* And the parents: *"You always know a Lloyd Williamson child – they're so polite!" "I think the school is, beyond doubt, the best I could wish for." "The best-kept secret in London!"*

To visit the school or nurseries, please contact the school admin team on 020 8962 0345 or admissions@lws.org.uk.

Lycée Français Charles de Gaulle de Londres

(Founded 1915)

35 Cromwell Road, London, SW7 2DG

Tel: 020 7584 6322

Email: inscription@lyceefrancais.org.uk

Website: www.lyceefrancais.org.uk

Headteacher: Didier Devilard

School type: Co-educational Day

Age range of pupils: 3–18 years

No. of pupils enrolled as at 01/01/2022: 3450

Fees as at 01/01/2022:

Day: £7,066–£14,782

The Lycée Français Charles de Gaulle de Londres is governed by the AEFE (Agence de l'Enseignement Français à l'Etranger, a vast network with over 500 French schools in about 140 countries). 3,450 pupils are taught, spread over the main site in South Kensington and the 3 locations of its primary schools: Ecole Marie d'Orliac (Fulham), Ecole de Wix (Clapham) and Ecole André Malraux (Ealing).

Since its inception in 1915, the school has evolved: more than forty nationalities now make up its community. One thing has not changed though: its ability to develop educational practices whilst never losing sight of its tradition of excellence. Whichever section it be, British, International, Bilingual, Multilingual or French – this balance of tradition with modernity provides our students with a unique experience in an exceptional environment.

Delivering first-class education, this centennial institution offers various curricula leading towards public examinations (French brevet and baccalauréat, GCSEs, A-Levels) with consistent outstanding results. Typical success rates are 100% for the Brevet with over 74% "Très bien" honours and over 99% for the Baccalauréat (over 64% "Très bien" honours); in the British section, 100% for A-levels (over 79% A*/A) and 100% for GCSEs with 79% 9-7 grades.

The school makes a simple and honest commitment: to offer each child the best conditions to realise their academic potential, to be able to develop and thrive in a peaceful environment and achieve the level of excellence required to access their desired course even at the most competitive universities and higher education institutions worldwide.

Headmaster Didier Devilard confirms: *"We nurture each individual with care and help them build self-confidence – this remains our pledge to our families as much today as it has been for over a century."*

Lyndhurst House Prep School

LYNDHURST HOUSE
PREPARATORY SCHOOL

(Founded 1952)

24 Lyndhurst Gardens, Hampstead,
London, NW3 5NW

Tel: 020 7435 4936
Email: jorrett@lyndhursthouse.co.uk
Website: www.lyndhursthouse.co.uk
Head of School:
Mr Andrew Reid MA (Oxon)
Appointed: September 2008
School type: Boys' Day Preparatory

Age range of boys: 4–13 years
No. of pupils enrolled as at 01/01/2022: 125
Fees as at 01/01/2022:
Day: £18,360–£20,790
Average class size: 15
Teacher/pupil ratio: 1:8

"A wonderful, nurturing and supportive environment. My son goes in every morning with a smile on his face." Year One Parent

Lyndhurst House has an outstanding history of achievement and exceptional pastoral care. The boys win places, by scholarship or at Common Entry, particularly to the major London independent day senior schools. The School takes boys from the ages of four to thirteen.

The School's approach helps boys build self-confidence, easy, happy friendships and the key skills to discover, innovate and achieve. The boys have self-respect, respect for others and a very strong sense of commitment.

Individual attention to support academic progress and personal development have always been at the forefront at Lyndhurst.

The School seeks to understand what matters most to each family and encourages parents to visit as early as possible to meet the Head. It is a privilege for any school to have the care and responsibility of a child's early education and at Lyndhurst House this is supported by the close open relationship with parents.

"Pupils are extremely considerate, caring and respectful of each other and all members of their school community. This is strongly encouraged by positive relationships with staff, firmly underpinned by strong values." ISI Inspection Report

The dynamic between exceptional academic education and the nurture and wider development of personality are complementary, and Lyndhurst House has a long record of success delivering this combination.

Lyndhurst is a warm, friendly place where boys discover and grow their talents and initiative. The School develops adaptable and innovative skills, but also helps the boys to understand that some things remain as important as ever: kindness and understanding others' perspectives; being able to be independent, but being kind to oneself; hard work. These all matter as much as ever, as does learning to find ways to relax.

In the coming years, much in society and the workplace generally will change radically, and the education at Lyndhurst emphasises adaptability, independent thought and the building of the skills and character, to be resilient at all stages of life.

"His confidence has grown and he has formed lovely friendships with his peers. We think the staff at Lyndhurst do an amazing job." Year One Parent

Maida Vale School

(Founded 2020)

18 Saltram Crescent, London, W9 3HR

Tel: 020 4511 6000

Email: admissions@maidavaleschool.com

Website: www.maidavaleschool.com

Headmaster: Steven Winter

School type: Co-educational

Age range of pupils: 11–18 years

No. of pupils enrolled as at 01/01/2022: 121

Fees as at 01/01/2022:

Day: £7,674 per term

Maida Vale School is a co-educational, independent school in London for 11-18 year olds. Founded in 2020, it is the fourth school opened by the Gardener Schools Group, a family founded company celebrating 30 years this year.

Maida Vale School welcomes pupils with varying academic profiles, encouraging the individual abilities of each child, placing emphasis on confidence, self-esteem and creativity. We believe this approach produces high levels of achievement for each pupil.

We operate a true 'Open Door' policy, welcoming parents and members of the wider community to become a part of school life. Our school seeks to cultivate the feeling of a family and social hub that offers emotional support and security for all students and employees.

With a broad curriculum, a vast enrichment programme and an extended school day, Maida Vale School has the variety and flexibility to enable pupils to develop their individual talents and fulfil their potential. Our small teaching and tutor groups, combined with the importance we place on communication between home and school, allow us to provide the highest level of pastoral care.

Maida Vale School takes a fresh approach to all areas of school life and is not bound by current conventions and practices which no longer seem useful. Whilst retaining the core traditional values established in our schools, we will continue to make decisions about the curriculum, timetabling and the length and shape of the school day and term which reflect this.

Maida Vale School is a beautiful Victorian building that was once a former college. The Victorians believed in light-filled classrooms with high ceilings and large windows, and we have built on this, taking the school into the 21st Century by fitting it with cutting edge facilities and equipment.

Mander Portman Woodward – MPW London

M|P|W

(Founded 1973)

90-92 Queen's Gate, London, SW7 5AB
Tel: 020 7835 1355
Email: london@mpw.ac.uk
Website: www.mpw.ac.uk
Principal: Mr John Southworth BSc MSc
Appointed: August 2016
School type: Co-educational Day

Age range of pupils: 14–19
No. of pupils enrolled as at 01/01/2022: 600
Fees as at 01/01/2022:
Day: £10,252 per term
Average class size: 6
Teacher/pupil ratio: 1:6

Tailored, not uniform: when it comes to a good education, one size does not necessarily fit all.

Founded in 1973, MPW London is one of the UK's leading Sixth Form colleges, offering a distinctive alternative to traditional schools. Situated in the heart of one of the capital's most exclusive and vibrant locations, the college offers a socially relaxed yet highly academically disciplined environment.

A bespoke approach

Our model is based around a strong focus on exam preparation and equipping students with the skills, attitude and confidence to succeed at the country's top universities.

Students choose their own unique paths with GCSEs and A levels offered in over 40 subjects and in any combination. Whichever combination they choose, each student has a Director of Studies, who provides them with tailored academic and pastoral support. The teaching method has been devised with a focus on individual attention too – teaching is in small Oxbridge-style tutorial groups, each with fewer than 10 students.

But it's not just in the academic realm where students can express themselves. Walk over the threshold of an MPW college and you will immediately sense the relaxed, yet focused atmosphere. Students are treated like the young adults that they are; there is no school uniform, they are on first-name terms with their tutors, they are not patronised by allowing low expectations of behaviour or attainment and they are encouraged to take responsibility for themselves.

Strong results and progression

Despite having a non-selective admissions policy and a wide variety of courses targeted at students of different academic abilities, our students achieve outstanding overall results year after year. In particular, our 'value-added' score (the progress students make from GCSE to A level) is exceptional.

In 2021, 62% of A level grades were A*/A. These results unlock the doors to some of the UK's best universities – in the last three years, two-thirds of our students progressed to top tier universities (Russell Group, University of London and specialist institutions).

Learning to secure those prestigious university places is also a key element of the MPW experience. Students are given unrivalled support in completing UCAS applications by the same experts who put together the renowned *Getting into* series of books, which offers invaluable advice and guidance on how to secure that coveted place at a first-choice university.

Stunning location

MPW London is located in South Kensington (Zone 1), one of the most exclusive and affluent parts of the capital. It is just a few minutes' walk from Hyde Park, Imperial College and many world-famous museums, including the Science Museum, the Natural History Museum and the Victoria & Albert Museum.

Rated Excellent by ISI

In our last Independent School Inspectorate (ISI) report, we received the highest rating of 'Excellent', prompting the inspectors to report, "The quality of the students' spiritual, moral, social and cultural development is excellent. In line with the aims of the college, students are encouraged to develop confidence, self-belief and self-discipline."

Maple Walk Prep School

MAPLE WALK
PREP SCHOOL

62A Crownhill Road, London, NW10 4EB
Tel: 020 8963 3890

Email: admin@maplewalkschool.co.uk
Website: www.maplewalkschool.co.uk
Head Teacher: Claire Murdoch
School type: Co-educational Day
Age range of pupils: 4–11 years

No. of pupils enrolled as at 01/01/2022: 190
Fees as at 01/01/2022:
Day: £3,866 per term
Average class size: 20

Maple Walk, judged excellent in all areas (ISI Inspection, March 2020), is a happy, vibrant, exceptional value prep school for boys and girls aged 4-11 in north west London, nurturing children's wellbeing and academic best through fun, kindness and respect for one another.

We provide a safe, supportive and stimulating environment with small class sizes for outstanding learning and personal development where children flourish, developing self-confidence, self-esteem and social awareness.

Cultivating a growth mindset, Maple Walk's innovative, creative curriculum underpinned by academic rigour instils a love of learning and resilience ensuring each child is well prepared for whatever the future holds. The numerous opportunities outside the classroom are fundamental to the school day. Through sporting activities, first class music, art and drama, we encourage every child to find their own particular strength with many gaining scholarships at top independent secondary schools. We are proud pupils receive secondary offers of their choice and often with multiple offers!

Our enriching selection of after school clubs allows pupils to explore a diverse range of activities beyond the school day including skateboarding, gymnastics, animation, robotics and plenty more.

Known as 'the small school with a big heart', we have a great school community and that strong community spirit goes beyond the school gates connecting and building relationships with the local community.

We are housed in purpose-built accommodation and comes with a host of eco credentials, including a ground source heat pump for our heating and hot water, solar PV panels for electricity and a growing sedum roof to attract local wildlife.

Entry into Reception is non-selective and based on the date the completed registration form is returned to our Registrar, with siblings given priority. Entry higher up the school is by interview and informal assessment in the classroom.

More House School

MORE
HOUSE
SCHOOL
KNIGHTSBRIDGE

(Founded 1952)

22-24 Pont Street, Knightsbridge,
London, SW1X 0AA
Tel: 020 7235 2855
Email: registrar@morehousemail.org.uk
Website: www.morehouse.org.uk
Head: Ms Faith Hagerty
Appointed: April 2021

School type: Independent Girls' Day
Age range of girls: 11–18 years
No. of pupils enrolled as at 01/01/2022: 140
Fees as at 01/01/2022:
Day: £7,250 per term
Average class size: 16
Teacher/pupil ratio: 1:5

More House is a small school that means big business. Having taught girls since 1952, we know how girls learn best. Our pupils skip up our steps as 11-year-old children and leave us at 18, as accomplished and emotionally intelligent young women, ready to go out and change the world.

As a school, we embrace a number of juxtapositions. Inside our historic building, we deliver a progressive Catholic education. Our lessons start in Knightsbridge but extend to the wider world. Our small class sizes engage our pupils in big thinking.

We are preparing our pupils for the juggling act of adulthood. Our core values of commitment, integrity and compassion are evident in the students academic and co-curricular achievements, their relationships with others and through initiatives such as our More Green sustainability group and Faith in Action programme. Our outstanding pastoral care enables our girls to flourish in a nurturing environment that recognises and cherishes the whole person.

More House is committed to the expression of the Catholic faith, both explicitly and – perhaps more importantly – in our daily life together. Girls are expected to be tolerant, thoughtful, and good stewards of the life they have been given and as global citizens, and to act with integrity, honesty, and a sense of justice. While we are a Catholic school, we warmly welcome children of all faiths or none.

Our central London location provides a launchpad for access to London's best sporting venues, galleries, museums and theatres.

As a school, we are innovative and encourage creativity right across the curriculum. What the world needs at this very moment is versatile and ethical leaders who are driven by more than the traditional measures of success.

It is the nurturing of the individual at More House that cultivates young women who are confident and creative enough to channel their strengths and be agents of change. We are proud to be a greenhouse, not a hothouse.

North Bridge House

North Bridge House

(Founded 1939)

65 Rosslyn Hill, London, NW3 5UD

Tel: 020 7428 1520

Email: admissionsenquiries@northbridgehouse.com

Website: www.northbridgehouse.com

Head of Nursery & Pre-Prep Schools: Mrs. Christine McLelland

Head of Prep School: Mr. James Stenning

Head of Senior Schools: Mr. Brendan Pavey

School type: Co-educational Day

Age range of pupils: 2–18 years

No. of pupils enrolled as at 01/01/2022: 1430

Fees as at 01/01/2022:

Nursery: £8,145 (half day) – £16,275 (full time)

Pre-Reception & Reception: £15,165–£18,960

Pre-Prep: £19,665

Prep School: £20,520

Senior School: £20,520

Sixth Form: £21,735

Average class size: 20

Founded in 1939, North Bridge House shares a warm, family atmosphere across six North London school sites, providing a unique and personalised education for pupils aged 2 to 18 years. Shaped by centuries-old heritage and boasting many modern facilities, our schools provide an inspiring learning environment at the heart of the Capital. Children benefit from educational partnerships with the likes of the Zoological Society of London and the Estorick Collection of Modern Italian Art, while specialist, individualised teaching prepares pupils for every milestone of their school career.

At North Bridge House, we are on a constant journey of getting to know and understand every learner as a unique and rounded individual, fostering academic excellence while cultivating character and promoting wellbeing. Happy children learn best and our pupils are notably high-achieving. Our Early Years and Key Stage 1 standards in English and maths exceed the national average by over 20%. The Prep School is renowned for first-class results in boys' and girls' senior school entrance examinations, with many pupils awarded highly competitive scholarship places. NBH Senior Schools also celebrate outstanding exam results, with Sixth Form students gaining places at top Russell Group and Oxbridge destinations. 2021 saw an impressive 67% 7-9 grades at GCSE and 65% A*-A grades at A-Level.

We are committed to giving our pupils more than simply an academic education. In our curricular design we have embedded timetabled enrichment opportunities, which together with our broad range of extra-curricular activities, are key to our character education programme. Forest School, residential and day trips, LAMDA, Duke of Edinburgh and our Inspiring Futures programme also enhance the whole school experience, while specialist pastoral care and the school's wellbeing charter further empower our children to find and realise their true personal potential. Furthermore, North Bridge House provides 1-2-1 devices for all pupils in Year 3 and above, facilitating their learning both in school and at home.

Pupils also enjoy a wide range of sports during weekly PE and Games sessions, which make the most of both on site facilities and the school's prime north London location. From our Regent's Park home ground to Allianz Park, Hampstead Heath, Highbury Fields, Lee Valley White Water Centre and local leisure centres, students frequent the best facilities for track and field, outdoor adventure and water sports, as well as yoga, martial arts and fitness classes.

At the heart of the school is a highly qualified team of specialist teachers, dedicated to setting every child on their own individual path to success – so that they fulfil their time at North Bridge House and beyond. From the fundamental foundations that are established in the early years of education to the expert UCAS and careers advice that is provided at A-Level, North Bridge House prepares confident and determined boys and girls for the challenges and rewards of real life.

Our schools

North Bridge House Nursery Hampstead
33 Fitzjohn's Avenue, London NW3 5JY

North Bridge House Pre-Prep Hampstead
8 Netherhall Gardens, London NW3 5RR

North Bridge Nursery & Pre-Prep West Hampstead
85-87 Fordwych Road, London NW2 3TL

North Bridge House Prep Regent's Park
1 Gloucester Avenue, London NW1 7AB

North Bridge House Senior Hampstead
65 Rosslyn Hill, London NW3 5UD

North Bridge House Senior Canonbury
6-9 Canonbury Place, London N1 2NQ

Northcote Lodge
Part of Northwood Schools

26 Bolingbroke Grove, London, SW11 6EL

Tel: 020 8682 8888
Email: admissions@northwoodschools.com
Website: www.northwoodschools.com
Head: Mr Clive Smith-Langridge
School type: Boys' Preparatory

Religious Denomination: Church of England, all denominations welcome
Age range of boys: 8–13 years
No. of pupils enrolled as at 01/01/2022: 260
Fees as at 01/01/2022:
Day: £7,140 per term
Average class size: Av 17

THE CURRICULUM: Boys thrive in our busy yet friendly school which provides outstanding teaching that stimulates, stretches, nurtures and develops individual strengths to prepare boys for entry to top secondary schools at 11 and 13 – both in and out of London.

GAMES & THE ARTS: Our sports team includes FA, RFU, and ECB qualified staff with a wealth of experience of playing sport to a high level who aim to inspire boys to enjoy and work hard in all sports, offering a high quality and wide varied sporting programme. All boys play matches in the major sports and teams are very competitive even against much bigger schools. A wide-ranging clubs programme includes karate, coding and spy-club. Thriving and vibrant music, drama and art departments with ambitious projects, multiple ensembles and exciting performances.

PASTORAL CARE: Our tutor system ensures that each boy has someone looking out for him over and above the care he receives from every staff member. The small and friendly community enables staff and boys to get to know each other well. Parent partnership is actively encouraged, and the Headmaster's door is always open.

ENTRANCE & EXIT: Automatic entry for boys from Broomwood Hall Lower School if it's the right school for them. Around 6-10 places a year for external candidate at 8 and some at 11 Exit to a broad mix of London day and out of town boarding at 11 & 13 including Bradfield, Dulwich, Harrow, Tonbridge, Marlborough, Wellington, Epsom, Emanuel, Trinity, Whitgift, Charterhouse, Sherborne, Cranleigh and Eton. Strong record in scholarships in all areas including academic, music, DT, drama and sport.

HEAD TEACHER'S PHILOSOPHY: 'The whole child is the whole point': academic rigour, a focus on traditional manners, outstanding extra-curricular opportunities, holistic pastoral care and most importantly, running a school that allows the boys to be happy so that they fulfil their academic potential.

OUTSTANDING CHARACTERISTICS: Northcote Lodge really understands how to get the very best out of boys, giving them an outstanding all-round education in a stimulating yet nurturing learning environment and preparing them for exciting futures.

In September 2021 Northwood Schools joined the wider Dukes Education family. Together we're extraordinary.

Northwood Senior
Part of Northwood Schools

3 Garrad's Road, London, SW16 1JZ

Tel: 020 8161 0301

Email: NWSsenior@northwoodschools.com

Website: www.northwoodschools.com

Head: Mrs Susan Brooks

School type: Co-educational Secondary

Religious Denomination: Church of England, all denominations welcome

Age range of pupils: 11–16 years

Fees as at 01/01/2022:

Day: £7,140 per term

Average class size: Av 15, Max 20

Northwood Senior opened in September 2020 as the fourth member of the Northwood Schools group. As a deliberately smaller school, it aims to offer an excellent secondary education in a more personal setting with an emphasis on equipping pupils with the skills and experiences they need to face their future with confidence. Alongside preparing for a wide range of GCCEs/IGCEs, we place great importance on well-being, community and social responsibility and in building and bolstering confidence within a friendly and supportive community.

THE CURRICULUM: Transformative teaching lies at the heart of our modern, stimulating curriculum which includes thematic studies, maths mastery and hands-on science, alongside well-being, community and life-skills. Our innovative approach leads to more active engagement in lessons, the development of higher-order thinking skills, strong teamwork, and motivated pupils who are better able to develop the real-world analytical and problem solving skills that pays dividends in examinations and stands them in good stead for the future.

GAMES & THE ARTS: As well as traditional sports such as football and netball, we are keen to explore alternative sports. We have our own sports court and located next to Tooting Common with the Lido and athletics track close by, and Streatham Leisure Centre and Ice Rink a short stroll away.

We strongly encourage creativity and have seen some great emerging talent in Art, DT, drama and film club.

PASTORAL CARE: We offer outstanding pastoral care to help each pupil develop the skills required for the challenges of modern life. Well-being is built into the weekly timetable and our tutorial system and thematic learning approach ensures that every pupil is well known, with all staff invested in the success and happiness of each pupil.

ENTRANCE AND EXIT: Main entrance in Year 7. Additional places in Year 9. Assessment via digital testing data and Head's interview. All-Rounder Scholarships worth up to 20% of fees available at both Year 7 and Year 9 entry.

Exit to study A Levels, IB or Btec at sixth form at another school or sixth form college.

HEAD TEACHER'S PHILOSOPHY: Education should be modern, relevant, and prepare children for the ever-changing world in which we live. In setting up a new school, I am in the fortunate position of being able to bring together the best, current practices in education with committed, innovative teachers who can transform the educational experience of our pupils so that they can move on to the next stage of their education with confidence.

In September 2021 Northwood Schools joined the wider Dukes Education family. Together we're extraordinary.

Ravenscourt Park Preparatory School

(Founded 1991)

16 Ravenscourt Avenue, London, W6 0SL

Tel: 020 8846 9153

Email: admissions@rpps.co.uk

Website: www.rpps.co.uk

Headmaster: Mr Carl Howes MA (Cantab), PGCE (Exeter)

Appointed: September 2015

School type: Co-educational

Age range of pupils: 4–11 years

No. of pupils enrolled as at 01/01/2022: 409

Fees as at 01/01/2022:

Day: £6,304 per term

Average class size: 20

Ravenscourt Park Preparatory School (RPPS) is a lively, co-educational, independent school for children aged 4 to 11 in West London. Owned by the Gardener Schools Group, a family founded company set up in 1991 and celebrating 30 years this year, RPPS was the first of four schools to open, followed by Kew Green Preparatory School, Kew House Senior School and Maida Vale School.

There is a palpable sense of community at RPPS, and visitors often comment on the warm and happy atmosphere, and the family feel that they notice around the school.

Our school is situated next to Ravenscourt Park, a twenty-acre park which provides the setting for the majority of PE and Games lessons. RPPS has specialist on-site facilities such as a multi-purpose Auditorium, Library, Music Suite, Art Studio and Science Laboratory. Additional facilities include a designated gymnasium, ICT suite and large outdoor playground space.

RPPS provides an education of the highest quality with an engaging curriculum that is varied, exciting and forward-looking, whilst also preparing pupils for transfer at the end of Year 6 to London Day Schools and 11+ boarding schools.

Our pupils engage in the excitement of learning and develop the confidence to question, analyse and express their opinions. We encourage children to develop a Growth Mindset so that they become resourceful, resilient, reflective and enthusiastic learners who are able to learn from their mistakes and build on their successes.

We form strong and trusting partnerships with our parents and we operate an 'Open Door' policy, where parents' comments, views, contributions and suggestions are valued.

The Independent Schools Inspectorate (ISI) visited RPPS in 2021 and we were delighted to have received the judgement of 'excellent' in both of the report's key outcomes.

Riverston School

63/69 Eltham Road, Lee, London, SE12 8UF
Tel: 020 8318 4327
Email: office@riverstonschool.co.uk
Website: riverstonschool.co.uk

Headmaster: Mr David A T Ward MA
School type: Co-educational Day
Age range of pupils: 9 months–19 years

Riverston School is a co-educational and non-selective school in South-East London that celebrated its 95th anniversary in 2021. Riverston has a Nursery and Early Years Department for children aged 9 months to 4 years and a Senior School for children aged 11-19. The School has become synonymous with its ability to support children with moderate learning needs in a caring environment and is part of the Chatsworth School family of schools.

The ethos of Riverston School is that of helping every child fulfil their potential, through a genuinely bespoke and child-centred, multi-disciplinary approach to learning. The school provides a warm, caring and stimulating environment where children learn new skills and excels at providing each child with the right

skills to prepare them for life in the wider world. Riverston is part of a community characterised by a profound respect for and encouragement of diversity, where important differences among children and adults are celebrated.

All pupils are encouraged to take an active role in the learning process through a lively mixture of discussion, reading and writing. In English, pupils have the opportunity to enter poetry and writing competitions and the dynamic way in which Maths is taught ensures an excitement and enthusiasm for the subject so that pupils share their teachers' passion. Science is taught in three science laboratories with access to a wide range of interactive and engaging software to enhance and support learning and in Art and Design, children are encouraged to

express their creative skills to the best of their ability.

Riverston has developed a Parallel Curriculum for children working slightly below age expected attainment levels. This curriculum is designed to allow children the space, time and content to ensure they are learning at the right time, right pace and crucially do not feel judged. Whilst children are grouped by ability for lessons, they re-join children their own age for food technology, drama and PE. Riverston believes that this is an important part of children feeling comfortable and happy at school and makes for a positive community outlook.

Riverston understands that every child has unique and sometimes very specific, learning needs which may become apparent at any point in that child's educational 'career'. Sometimes, this can be achieved simply through a more sensitive application of teaching strategies within the traditional school curriculum. For some children with greater or more complex needs, additional learning support will be required to ensure they can continue to participate fully in the life of the school, progress in their studies and continue to develop their knowledge, skills and abilities. Riverston provides outstanding expertise and support for these children and their families from the multi-disciplinary team offering in-depth assessment, diagnosis and therapy input as well as providing bespoke learning programmes. The team includes speech and language therapists, occupational therapists, a counsellor, specialist teachers and learning support assistants.

The PE and Games programme at Riverston is vital in ensuring that every child appreciates the importance of having a healthy lifestyle. The programme is specifically designed to help children develop their fitness levels, motor skills,

strength and love of sport. Sport for life is actively encouraged and boys and girls of all ages are given a variety of opportunities in which to explore their own strengths and weaknesses, likes and dislikes. Riverston has had many National Champions over the years in athletics, swimming, cross-country, football and most recently karate.

As the children progress throughout the school, Riverston College offers students of 16 years and above a selection of courses to help them develop a range of life skills to further their independence, confidence and self-belief. These programmes allow them to achieve success, realise their ambitions and progress further. More 'traditional' academic subject offerings are also offered and students are able to study these at GCSE, BTEC and A Level. The College offers students huge flexibility from the ability to offer these programmes over more than the usual 2-year programme.

The atmosphere and opportunities offered at Riverston enable all pupils to grow as individuals within the security of a close and supportive community.

Sarum Hall School

(Founded 1929)

15 Eton Avenue, London, NW3 3EL
Tel: 020 7794 2261
Email: admissions@sarumhallschool.co.uk
Website: www.sarumhallschool.co.uk
Headteacher: Victoria Savage
School type: Girls' Day

Age range of girls: 3–11 years
No. of pupils enrolled as at 01/01/2022: 184
Fees as at 01/01/2022:
£5,155 (Nursery) per term
£5,575 (Reception – Year 6) per term

Sarum Hall is a modern and successful school located in the heart of Belsize Park, in which pupils are motivated to learn, inspired to fulfil their potential, and encouraged to achieve excellence. Our motto of *spirit, happiness, success* underpins our philosophy of individuality, inclusivity and positivity. The Golden Values of kindness, courage, respect, honesty, fairness and resilience ensure that every girl develops as an individual with a strong sense of purpose and moral compass both in the school community and society beyond. We encourage children to engage with their future and understand their role in shaping the world in which they will live and work.

Our modern facilities were purpose built in 1995 and the girls benefit from spacious classrooms which promote creativity and curiosity in their learning. The girls have a wonderful variety of lessons with specialist teachers in which high standards are set and an emphasis on practical activities and the application of information is nurtured. We are proud of our outdoor space which boasts a floodlit netball court and 4 short tennis courts, garden, pond and our iconic treehouse and beach huts, which allow us to house a wealth of activities both in the curriculum and as part of our extensive clubs programme. In addition, our dedicated Science Lab, Art Room, Food Studio, Library, ICT suite and

separate Music and Drama classrooms provide cross-curricular learning opportunities and enable us to deliver a broad and engaging curriculum.

Our main entry point is at 3+ and we are non-selective as we advocate an individual approach to each child's educational journey; we feed to the most selective senior schools in the area and beyond. We believe in teaching the girls a set of transferrable skills, which they will use and apply in all aspects of life, establishing them as strong, confident and independent young women with a zest for life and a thirst for knowledge.

St John's Wood Pre-Preparatory School

(Founded 1982)
St Johns Hall, Lords Roundabout,
London, NW8 7NE
Tel: 020 7722 7149
Email: info@sjwpre-prep.org.uk
Website: www.sjwpre-prep.org.uk

Principal: Adrian Ellis
School type: Co-educational Day
Age range of pupils: 3–7
Average class size: 16
Teacher/pupil ratio: 1:8

Happiness is at the heart of the philosophy at St Johns' Wood Pre-Prep School, and it works. This small school, described by owner and Principal, Adrian Ellis, as feeling more like a private members' club, is a 7+ specialist school. The School is immensely proud of the 2020/2021 Year 2 pupils for their outstanding entrance results. Places have been accepted at: Belmont; City of London School for Girls; Highgate; Pembridge Hall, Queen's College

Prep, South Hampstead High School; St Paul's Juniors; UCS Junior School and Westminster Under School.

With a friendly and caring environment as its strength for three-to seven-year-old boys and girls, Mr Ellis believes that the excellent ratio of staff to pupils allows each child to reach their full potential. "*Of course, together with parents, we look to establish each child's unique qualities and particular talents and aim to develop*

them as fully as possible," said Mr Ellis.

Parents have high expectations of the school. Mr Ellis points out this is a two way street, "*Equally, we have high expectations of our parents. This combination is the recipe for success*".

Following this year's excellent results, St John's Wood Pre-Prep remains a recommended 'feeder' to many of London's top prep schools.

St Benedict's School

(Founded 1902)
54 Eaton Rise, Ealing, London, W5 2ES

Tel: 020 8862 2000
Email: admissions@stbenedicts.org.uk
Website: www.stbenedicts.org.uk
Headmaster: Mr A Johnson BA
Appointed: September 2016
School type: Co-educational Day
Age range of pupils: 3–18 years

No. of pupils enrolled as at 01/01/2022: 1073
Boys: 702 **Girls:** 371 **Sixth Form:** 203
Fees as at 01/01/2022:
Day: £13,995–£18,330
Average class size: Junior School: 17;
Senior School: 18; Sixth Form: 7
Teacher/pupil ratio: 1:10

St Benedict's is London's leading independent Catholic co-educational school, situated in Ealing. The School is a successful blend of the traditional and the innovative, providing a seamless education from Nursery to the Sixth Form.

St Benedict's has very strong academic standards. Inspirational teaching, tutorial guidance and exceptional pastoral care are at the heart of the education we offer, allowing children to develop their full potential.

The Junior School and Nursery provide a supportive and vibrant environment in which to learn. Sharing excellent facilities with the Senior School and a programme of cross-curricular activities help ease the transition at 11+ to the Senior School, which is on the same site.

At St Benedict's, there is a vital focus on personal development, and our outstanding co-curricular programme helps pupils to thrive by enabling them to find and develop their unique gifts and talents. St Benedict's has a distinguished sporting tradition, and Music and Drama are both excellent, with regular concerts and termly drama productions.

We encourage principled leadership, resilience and character in our pupils, and promote the Christian values of integrity, fairness and generosity to others. St Benedict's welcomes families of all faiths and of no faith.

Recent developments include a new Sixth Form Centre and Art Department. Our new Nursery and Pre-Prep Department provides our youngest pupils with a first-rate learning environment.

St Benedict's School is unique. Come and visit us and see what we have to offer.

St Mary's School Hampstead

ST MARY'S SCHOOL HAMPSTEAD

(Founded 1871)

47 Fitzjohn's Avenue, Hampstead,
London, NW3 6PG
Tel: 020 7435 1868
Email: office@stmh.co.uk
Website: www.stmh.co.uk
Head Teacher: Mrs Harriet Connor-Earl
Appointed: September 2016
School type: Girls' Day

Religious Denomination: CISC
Age range of girls:
2 years 9 months–11 years
No. of pupils enrolled as at 01/01/2022: 300
Fees as at 01/01/2022:
Day: £9,060–£16,740
Average class size: Max 20
Teacher/pupil ratio: 1:9.5

St Mary's School Hampstead provides an outstanding and inspirational Catholic education to girls from 3-11 years.

St Mary's School celebrates the uniqueness of every pupil and their achievements. The rigorous, challenging curriculum places a strong emphasis on high academic achievement within a culture of care and support.

The School aims to instil four key habits of learning in their pupils. The children are encouraged to be risk takers, not only in their play, but also in their learning. They are also taught to be resilient and not to fall at the first hurdle. Staff ask the children to make mistakes because in the process of challenging themselves, they make more academic progress. The girls at St Mary's School are respectful, not just of each other, but of themselves. Finally, pupils are encouraged to be reflective, of their behaviour and their academic work.

An extensive refurbishment programme has been completed to deliver the most enriching and stimulating learning environments. The Global Learning Centre is a cutting-edge space that includes an Engineering and Robotics Lab, Virtual Reality Launch Pad, Art and Design Studio as well as a Green Room. This technology is used to support and enhance all curriculum areas and learning every day from Nursery to Year 6.

The focus on technology is equally balanced with an emphasis on creative and physical development.

Music, drama, art and sports are an essential part of school life and involve everyone. St Mary's School is a leafy oasis in the heart of Hampstead. The extensive and self-contained outside space includes climbing equipment and the full-size netball court has been upgraded enabling football, rugby, cricket and tennis to be enjoyed.

Used together – the integrated technology and the broad curriculum – the girls at St Mary's are flourishing. They are adopting habits of learning and making independent choices that they can take forward into their secondary education.

Leavers achieve impressive results, gaining offers and Academic Scholarships from schools including City of London School for Girls, Francis Holland School, Highgate School, North London Collegiate, South Hampstead High School, St Mary's Ascot and St Paul's Girls' School.

St Mary's School Hampstead offers an outstanding and inspirational Catholic education for girls 3-11 years. Find out more about this remarkable school at: www.stmh.co.uk.

St Paul's Cathedral School

ST PAUL'S
CATHEDRAL
SCHOOL

(Founded 12th Century or earlier)
2 New Change, London, EC4M 9AD
Tel: 020 7248 5156

Email: admissions@spcs.london.sch.uk
Website: www.spcslondon.com
Headmaster:
Simon Larter-Evans BA (Hons), PGCE, FRSA
Appointed: September 2016
School type: Co-educational Pre-Prep,
Day Prep & Boarding Choir School
Religious Denomination: Church of
England, admits pupils of all faiths

Age range of pupils: 4–13 years
No. of pupils enrolled as at 01/01/2022: 258
Boys: 157 **Girls:** 101
No. of boarders: 31
Fees as at 01/01/2022:
Day: £15,174 – £16,338
Full Boarding: £9,178
Average class size: 15-20
Teacher/pupil ratio: 1:10

Curriculum

A broad curriculum, including the International Primary Curriculum, prepares all pupils for 11+, 13+, scholarship and Common Entrance examinations. There is a strong musical tradition and choristers' Cathedral choral training is outstanding. A wide variety of games and other activities is offered. At the latest ISI inspection in May 2017, the school was rated 'Excellent'.

Entry requirements

Entry at 4+, 7+ and 11+ years: Pre-prep and day pupils interview and short test; Choristers voice trials and tests held throughout the year for boys between 6-8 years. Scholarships available at 11+ years.

St Paul's Cathedral School is a registered charity (No. 312718), which exists to provide education for the choristers of St Paul's Cathedral and for children living in the local area.

St. Anthony's School for Boys

ST. ANTHONY'S SCHOOL FOR BOYS

(Founded 1952)

90 Fitzjohn's Avenue, Hampstead,
London, NW3 6NP
Tel: 020 7431 1066
Email: pahead@stanthonysprep.co.uk
Website: www.stanthonysprep.org.uk
Head of School:
Mr Richard Berlie MA (Cantab)
School type:
Boys' Day Prep with Co-educational Nursery

Religious Denomination:
Roman Catholic, all faiths welcome
Age range of boys: 2.5–13 years
Age range of girls: 2.5–4 years
No. of pupils enrolled as at 01/01/2022: 280
Fees as at 01/01/2022:
Co-Ed Nursery: £2,800–£4,800 per term
Boys Prep School: £6,750–£6,950 per term

St Anthony's School for Boys is an academic IAPS preparatory school for boys between the ages of 4 and 13 with a Co-Ed Nursery for children between the ages of 2.5-4. It is Roman Catholic but welcomes boys of other faiths. The school has a family atmosphere, relaxed and unstuffy, but with a rigorous approach to learning. It is not a 'hot house' and great care is taken to ensure that pupils feel happy and at ease in the school environment. The majority of boys transfer to leading independent school.

The school operates a two-form entry with approximately 20 boys in each class from Reception up to and including Year 6. About half the year group leave St Anthony's to join Year 7 senior schools including UCS, City of London and Highgate. The remaining pupils stay on to prepare for Common Entrance at the end of Year 8 before proceeding to leading boarding and day schools such as Harrow, Eton, St Paul's and Westminster.

The school is not super-selective and promotes a caring, nurturing environment

promoting the holistic education of each child. We speak of St Anthony's as a greenhouse rather than a hothouse! Pastoral and academic expectations are high amongst parents and staff. The school adds significant value to pupils' learning and there is great emphasis on regular communication between boys, staff and pupils.

St Anthony's achieved 'Excellent' in all categories of the ISI full-school inspection in November 2019 – the school is now pursuing an ambitious development plan incorporating digital literacy with outstanding academic, pastoral and co-curricular provision.

School Life

The school follows the EYFS programme for boys in Reception who will also start learning French (or another modern language) and Mandarin. The curriculum from Year 1 through to Year 6 is shaped by the National Curriculum Key Stages with greater academic content and rigour. In Years 7 and 8 boys are prepared to sit Common Entrance papers (in June of Year 8) before joining 13+ schools.

Lessons are planned around maximising pupil outcomes especially deepening knowledge and understanding of topics. The added dimension is encouraging the boys to enquire and think, to problem-solve and to respond individually as well as part of a group.

Sport, music and drama are all incorporated into the timetable. There is plenty of scope for boys to perform or play from elementary to the highest standard. In addition, there is a host of clubs and hobbies offered before and after school.

St. Anthony's School for Girls

ST. ANTHONY'S SCHOOL
FOR GIRLS

Ivy House, 94-96 North End Road,
London NW11 7SX
Tel: 020 3869 3070
Email: admissions@stanthonysgirls.co.uk
Website: www.stanthonysgirls.co.uk
Head of School: Mr Donal Brennan

School type: Girls' Day Preparatory
Religious Denomination: Catholic
Age range of girls: 2.5–11 years
No. of pupils enrolled as at 01/01/2022: 85
Fees as at 01/01/2022:
Day: £18,000

St Anthony's School for Girls and Nursery is a confident, nurturing, family school offering a high-quality education within an environment which delivers a happy, healthy academically challenging curriculum.

The school is located at Ivy House, adjacent to Golders Hill Park and is a short bus ride from its sister school St Anthony's Boys in Hampstead.

St Anthony's Girls achieves outstanding 11+ results, regularly receiving offers from a plethora of academic north London schools: Highgate to Channing, South Hampstead High to Haberdasher's School for Girls; Francis Holland Girls to City of London, North London Collegiate to Mill Hill and further afield to Queenswood, Wycombe Abbey, and St Swithun's.

The school owes its success to committed pupils, ambitious teachers and supportive parents who embrace the recipe for success which has been established at the school.

A touch of kindness never goes amiss at St Anthony's, where it is seen as a fundamental tenet to a happy school experience. Adults model and engage in mutually respectful exchanges which the children in turn will role-play as best practice in their relationships. Observing a year 6 girl taking time out from her friends at playtime to sit with a year 1 girl who needed some quiet solace is not an uncommon expression of kindness at St Anthony's.

The girls at St Anthony's are curious: encouraged to ask questions and Big Questions at our Talk Time Assembly leads to robust discussions on the eternal questions. "What does it mean to be thoughtful, why is it difficult to share, why do leaves fall off trees to why are the days shortening during September?" In this environment of curiosity, the girls grow in courage and confidence and can verbalise complex thoughts and feelings.

Respect is witnessed in many ways at St Anthony's. All adults feel valued as equals in the eyes of the girls, the sense of community is strengthened where children develop a confident respect for themselves as unique, valuable individuals. An appreciation for all those who care for them from their parents to their teachers to the bus drivers to the chef who prepares their lunch. Being respectful of their world and the need to be guardians for future generations ensure that the girls are quick to respond

to global and community causes. It is not uncommon for the child-led, charities committee to launch an appeal among their peers to host fundraising events for the koala bears, refugee women and local homeless children.

Being inspired to embrace new challenges is at the heart of the teaching at St Anthony's. From Forest School activities to specialist Music, Drama, Mandarin, French, Rhythmic Gymnastics, Ballet, Science and Sports interwoven into the girls' timetable allow for the girls to have their imagination enriched and developed. From a buffet of creative teaching comes a perfect blend of original and individualised responses. The school clubs schedule further embeds this with girls choosing from Netball, Cross-Country, Yoga, Maths, Environmental Club, Debating, Minnie-Vinnies, Rhythmic Gymnastics, Irish Dancing, Science and Musical Drama.

St Anthony's Girls take responsibility for their actions, accepting praise, being willing to give compliments to others and understanding that at times saying sorry is important. Sincerity and fairness matter hugely to the girls allowing for happy confident relationships to develop at the school.

The establishment of a co-ed nursery at St. Anthony's School for Girls in September

2021 has been a huge success. Families seeking a nurturing and kind learning environment founded upon the values of both the boys' and girls' schools, which is academically enriching at the same time, have been delighted with the experience to date.

The curriculum is informed by the EYFS (Early Years) programme and is designed to encourage curiosity, interaction, independence and most importantly, a love of learning.

The nursery programme aims to help prepare children for reception. Teachers ensure children develop key skills as well as knowledge and an understanding of the world around them, with regular 'learning in nature' lessons at Golders Hill Park.

Children will also be stronger communicators and self-assured as learners owing to the carefully planned timetable they follow. Drama, music, French, Mandarin, sport and dance have been interwoven into the nursery schedule allowing pupils to benefit from the rich specialist curriculum on offer across the school.

The nursery children enjoy talk time, singing and celebration assemblies, feel inspired by 'Whacky Wednesday' science focus, participate in all major school events, such as Harvest Food Appeal, STEAM week, remembrance service, the

Christmas show and the end of term disco.

The nursery children have enjoyed a very colourful and creative autumn term, finding treasure buried in the sandpit at Golders Hill Park, travelling to space in their own bespoke spaceship, welcoming their teddy bears to school on 'Hug a Bear Day' and discovering the fossilised remains of a dinosaur in the nursery sandpit.

We look forward to welcoming families for personalised tours with the headteacher.

The Roche School

The
Roche
School

(Founded 1988)

11 Frogmore, London, SW18 1HW
Tel: 020 8877 0823
Email: office@therocheschool.com
Website: www.therocheschool.com
Headmistress:
Mrs Vania Adams BA(Hons), PGCE, MA
Appointed: September 2010
School type: Co-educational Day

Religious Denomination:
Non-denominational
Age range of pupils: 2–11 years
No. of pupils enrolled as at 01/01/2022: 274
Boys: 134 **Girls:** 140
Fees as at 01/01/2022:
Day: £15,600–£16,290
Average class size: 18
Teacher/pupil ratio: 1:9

The Roche School is a vibrant, aspirational family-run school in South West London committed to developing pupils intellectually, creatively and in sporting terms, within the context of a warm, inclusive and friendly culture.

Core subjects are grouped according to focus so that pupils are challenged appropriately and everyone receives a high level of attention. The school seeks continually to build on its fine academic reputation which sees children placed at a wide range of London Day Schools after the 11+ examinations.

Parents favour local secondary schools. King's College Wimbledon, Wimbledon High, Dulwich College, Emanuel, Ibstock Place School and Whitgift feature prominently.

A new Year 6 Centre from September 2022 will ensure that pupils make the move to senior school in a position of academic, social and emotional strength.

The Roche School is also delighted to be offering an additional Spanish Bilingual Stream in Reception from September 2022, alongside the respected provision of their traditional Reception classes. Mornings in the Spanish Bilingual Stream will consist of the same high quality curriculum in English as the English Reception, and afternoons will involve National Curriculum-based lessons in Spanish, all delivered by a fully qualified teacher with in-depth Spanish fluency. The current host of specialist teachers in music and sport will still provide enrichment to the children's learning.

The school has a strong focus on personal happiness and respect for oneself and others. It is values-based, using The Roche Approach as a cohesive strategy in this respect. There is a commitment to diversity and a deep understanding of Equal Opportunities is embedded, with pupils accessing non-gender bias initiatives in sport, growth mindset programmes and Philosophy 4 Children. Expressive arts are strong and the emphasis on holistic development reaps dividends in terms of confidence and individuality.

Schools in Greater London

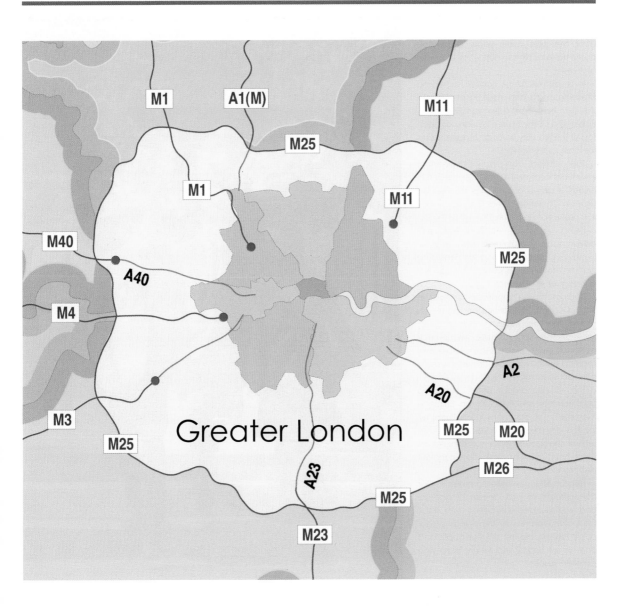

Babington House School

(Founded 1887)

Grange Drive, Chislehurst, Kent BR7 5ES

Tel: 020 8467 5537

Email: enquiries@babingtonhouse.com

Website: www.babingtonhouse.com

Headmaster: Mr Tim Lello MA, FRSA, NPQH

Appointed: 2013

School type: Co-educational Day

Age range of pupils: 3–18 years

No. of pupils enrolled as at 01/01/2022: 439

Fees as at 01/01/2022:

Nursery: £3,950 per term (inclusive of lunches) based on 12 week term

Preparatory (Reception to Year 6): £4,590 per term (inclusive of lunches)

Seniors & Sixth Form (11 to 18): £5,725 per term (inclusive of lunches)

Teacher/pupil ratio: 1:20

Inspiring Teachers, Inspiring Children

Over the past three years, Babington pupils have achieved 80% A* to B grades at A Level.

It is an excellent school achieving amazing results and inspiring pupils from the Sixth Form right down to the Nursery. Babington's Early Years provision has been top of the Bromley Borough league tables for three years running.

The school is an independent coeducational day school, situated in a beautiful group of buildings on Grange Drive in Chislehurst, near Bromley. It has 439 pupils from age 3 to 18.

Being a small school has BIG advantages. It has high standards of behaviour, dress and conduct, benefiting from no more than 20 pupils in a class and a strong sense of community.

Babington is an academic school. The School is committed to outstanding music, drama, sport and the arts in their broadest sense and offers a wealth of extracurricular opportunities. Our academic, social and sporting endeavours are underpinned by core Christian values.

The co-educational Senior School is academically selective with an Entrance Examination for Year 7 entry. In Sixth Form, the focus is very much on A-level study in small sets with the opportunity for work experience, which helps university applications stand out and provides great self-confidence.

Headmaster, Tim Lello comments *"Our commitment to provide an academic and well-rounded education with small class sizes, tailored to the needs of our pupils is really paying off, our pupils and parents are happy and we are achieving excellent results."*

Kew Green Preparatory School

(Founded 2004)

Layton House, Ferry Lane, Kew Green,
Richmond, Surrey TW9 3AF
Tel: 020 8948 5999
Email: admissions@kgps.co.uk
Website: www.kgps.co.uk
Headmistress: Mrs N Gibson
Appointed: September 2022

School type: Co-educational
Age range of pupils: 4–11 years
No. of pupils enrolled as at 01/01/2022: 273
Fees as at 01/01/2022:
Day: £6,304 per term
Average class size: 20
Teacher/pupil ratio: 1:6.4

Kew Green Preparatory School (KGPS) is a lively, co-educational, independent school for children aged 4 to 11 near Kew Gardens in Richmond. Owned by the Gardener Schools Group, a family founded company celebrating 30 years this year, KGPS is the sister school to Ravenscourt Park Preparatory School, Kew House Senior School and Maida Vale Senior School.

KGPS is housed in an attractive building, surrounded by mature trees and nestled in a peaceful corner of Kew Green. It is flanked by the Royal Botanical Gardens and the River Thames and we use these regularly along with the green itself.

We offer our children the opportunity to succeed, be recognised and be valued. Our pupils grow with the faculties required to tackle the many challenges that life may have to offer. We instil tolerance and respect for others and the capacity to celebrate diversity, embrace change and understand the importance of contributing to society. Above all, we believe that children need to be nurtured, guided, motivated and inspired to allow them to blossom.

We believe children thrive in an environment that is loving and supportive. Physically, socially, emotionally and intellectually – our pupils develop and

constantly achieve during their time with us. Our aim is that they leave as skilled and adaptable young citizens who will grow to meet the challenges of the 21st century. We believe in a broad and balanced curriculum, nurturing creativity and collaboration, resilience and determination whilst developing a strong self-esteem in each individual child. We enthusiastically share our pupil's education with their parents through our 'Open Door' policy.

KGPS is a thriving school community where laughter and enjoyment go hand-in-hand with the process of delivering a first-rate education.

Kew House School

Kew House, 6 Capital Interchange Way,
London, Middlesex TW8 0EX

Tel: 0208 742 2038
Email: admissions@kewhouseschool.com
Website: www.kewhouseschool.com
Headmaster: Mr Will Williams
School type: Co-educational

Age range of pupils: 11–18 years
No. of pupils enrolled as at 01/01/2022: 576
Fees as at 01/01/2022:
Day: £7,674 per term
Average class size: 22

Located in West London, Kew House School is a co-educational, independent senior school for pupils aged 11-18 years. Owned by the Gardener Schools Group, a family founded company set up in 1991 and celebrating 30 years this year, Kew House is the sister school to Ravenscourt Park Preparatory School, Kew Green Preparatory School and Maida Vale Senior School.

Kew House School takes a modern and pioneering approach to every aspect of school life. The school recognises and enhances the individual abilities of each child, welcoming pupils with varying academic profiles and placing emphasis on confidence, self-esteem and creativity.

By operating a true 'Open Door' policy that welcomes parents and members of the wider community to become a part of school life, Kew House has developed the feeling of a family and social hub that provides emotional support and security for all pupils and employees.

Sport is an important part of the curriculum and Kew House pupils achieve national and regional championship. Pupils benefit from using state of the art facilities at sporting locations just a stone's throw away from the school, including professional tennis courts and cricket grounds. Just a short walk from the River Thames, rowing is also part of the curriculum.

In September 2017, Kew House opened a brand new Sixth Form Centre which benefits from a beautifully designed independent learning centre on the ground floor. Facilities include a Sixth Form Cafe, library, roof terrace, audio-visual suite, recording studio and Sixth Form seminar rooms.

Following an inspection of the school in February 2018 by the Independent Schools Inspectorate (ISI), Kew House was particularly delighted to learn from the lead inspector that the results of the student and parent questionnaires were the most positive they had ever seen.

Marymount London

George Road, Kingston upon Thames, Surrey KT2 7PE

Tel: +44 (0)20 8949 0571
Email: admissions@marymountlondon.com
Website: www.marymountlondon.com
Headmistress: Mrs Margaret Giblin
School type: Girls' Day & Boarding
Age range of girls: 11–18 years

No. of pupils enrolled as at 01/01/2022: 258
Fees as at 01/01/2022:
Day: £27,250
Weekly Boarding: £44,180
Full Boarding: £46,130
Average class size: 12
Teacher/pupil ratio: 1:6

Marymount London is an independent, day and boarding school for girls which nurtures the limitless potential of curious, motivated students (ages 11 to 18) of diverse faiths and backgrounds. Founded in 1955 through the charism of the Religious of the Sacred Heart of Mary (RSHM), we proudly stand as the first all-girls' school in the United Kingdom to adopt the International Baccalaureate curriculum (IB MYP and Diploma), where girls are inspired to learn in a creative, collaborative, interdisciplinary, and exploratory environment.

Students are empowered to build their confidence, leadership skills, and sense of self on a seven-acre garden campus conveniently located just twelve miles from Central London. The campus offers outstanding facilities, including a STEAM Hub, sports hall, dance studio, modern dining hall, tennis courts and an All-Weather Pitch. The School's challenging academic program is based on the International Baccalaureate curricula:

- The Middle Years Programme (MYP), offered in Grades 6 to 10, encourages students to draw meaningful connections between eight broad and varied subject groups. With a central focus on the development of conceptual understanding and effective approaches to learning (ATL) skills, the MYP is a student-centered, inquiry-based programme rooted in interdisciplinary learning.
- The International Baccalaureate Diploma Programme (DP) for Grades 11 and 12 builds on the strong foundation of the MYP, leading to independent research opportunities as well as exceptional university placement within the UK and around the world.
- Our 2021 results are exceptional: 100% pass rate and an average of 38,2 points; the School provides a bespoke, student-centred college counselling programme which leads to successful placements in top universities in the UK and around the world.

Marymount's holistic approach to learning delivers a well-rounded education that encourages critical thinking, intercultural understanding, and participation in a wide array of interesting extracurricular offerings. Robust transport service from London/surrounding areas and boarding options (full, weekly, and flexi) are available.

Marymount offers year-round rolling admission as space allows. The admissions section of the website, featuring an online application portal, provides all of the information necessary to get started. Applicant families are encouraged to learn more about the School's strong tradition of excellence by exploring the website, making contact by phone/email, and scheduling a campus/virtual tour.

Schools in the South-East

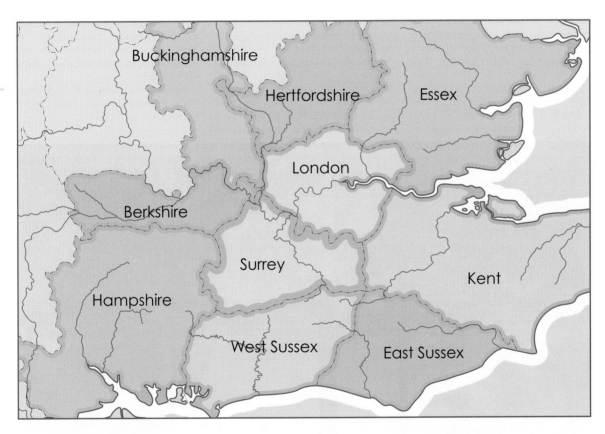

The following unitary authorities are also within the councils listed

Berkshire
Bracknell Forest, Reading, Slough, Windsor & Maidenhead and Wokingham

Brighton & Hove

Buckinghamshire

East Sussex

Essex

Hampshire

Kent

Medway

Milton Keynes

Peterborough

Portsmouth & Southampton

Thurrock and Southend-on-Sea

Aberdour School

Aberdour

floret qui laborat

(Founded 1928)

Brighton Road, Burgh Heath, Tadworth,
Surrey KT20 6AJ

Tel: +44 (0)1737 354119

Email: enquiries@aberdourschool.co.uk

Website: www.aberdourschool.co.uk

Headmaster: Mr S. D. Collins

School type:
Independent Co-educational Day

Age range of pupils: 2–11 years

No. of pupils enrolled as at 01/01/2022: 343

Fees as at 01/01/2022:

Day: £4,710–£16,272

Finding the brilliance in every child
Enquire now for September 2022
Independent day school for girls and boys aged 2-11 years

Every child has the potential to shine. At Aberdour, we aim to find the brilliance in every child, by providing an individual tailored education that identifies their potential and maximises their opportunities to learn, grow and succeed.

Founded in 1928 Aberdour is a thriving and extremely successful preparatory school for girls and boys aged 2-11 years. Set in 12 acres of beautiful Surrey parkland,

Aberdour is truly a hidden gem, providing a safe and happy haven for your child. With our many purpose-built facilities for learning, sport and play, your child can develop his or her talents and skills whilst experiencing an exceptional breadth of opportunity both inside and outside the classroom.

Aberdour developed Personalised Achievement Learning® in 2007, providing a truly personalised education with breadth and flexibility. We have supported P.A.L® with major investments in our staff, our systems, our buildings, our

IT and our resources, and the combination of a child-focused education. Through P.A.L®, we believe that every child will fulfil their individual potential if we nurture the talent that is within them, whatever that talent may be. Genuinely innovative teaching has made a real difference to the children's skills, achievements and enjoyment of life. We invite you to come see for yourself.

Please visit our website for information on our Admissions process and to contact our Registrar.

Belmont School

(Founded 1880)

Pasturewood Road, Holmbury St Mary,
Dorking, Surrey RH5 6LQ

Tel: 01306 730852

Email: admissions@belmont-school.org

Website: www.belmont-school.org

Headmistress:

Mrs Helen Skrine BA, PGCE, NPQH, FRSA

School type:

Co-educational Day & Weekly Boarding

Age range of pupils: 3–16 years

No. of pupils enrolled as at 01/01/2022: 200

Fees as at 01/01/2022:

Reception: £3,580 per term

Year 3: £5,550 per term

Year 7: £6,020 per term

Year 9: £6,420 per term

At Belmont School, we believe that the happiness and well-being of every pupil is of paramount importance and lies at the heart of a successful education.

Founded in 1880, Belmont School is nestled in the Surrey Hills on its own private estate in Holmbury St Mary and is an independent school for boys and girls from Early Years to GCSE. Pupils have 65 acres of wooded parkland to explore for activities such as Forest School, cross-country and mountain biking, including the School's own mountain biking academy and bespoke MTB bike trails.

From the age of three, pupils receive specialist teaching in Music, Performing Arts, French, Forest School, Art, IT and PE as well as the option to learn Ballet. Throughout their time at Belmont, pupils encounter a broad and challenging curriculum in small class sizes and each child is stretched or supported to reach their personal best.

Belmont's aim is for each pupil to leave as a well-rounded individual and so the academic curriculum is enriched by sport, performing arts, visual arts and other cultural and creative opportunities.

Alongside the facilities and academic provision at Belmont, every pupil is given excellent pastoral care and a family feel permeates throughout. The children's wellbeing is given equal priority alongside their achievements as encapsulated in the School's strapline, 'Achievement through Happiness'.

Belmont seeks to oil the wheels of family life and parents can drop children off for breakfast at 7.30am. In the evenings, pupils may stay for after school clubs or day board until 8pm. Pupils from as young as seven can board and many look forward to a night's flexi boarding enjoying activities like Nerf battles, swimming, film and pizza nights.

To find out more about Belmont School, please visit the website: www.belmont-school.org, where you can arrange to visit in person or take a virtual tour.

Berkhamsted School

BERKHAMSTED
— 1541 —

(Founded 1541)
Overton House, 131 High Street,
Berkhamsted, Hertfordshire HP4 2DJ

Tel: 01442 358001
Email: admissions@berkhamsted.com
Website: www.berkhamsted.com
Principal:
Mr Richard Backhouse MA(Cantab)
Appointed: January 2016
School type: Co-educational &
single-sex, day & boarding
Age range of pupils: 3–18 years

No. of pupils enrolled as at 01/01/2022: 2001
Sixth Form: 408
Pre-Prep/Prep: 527
Senior Boys: 719 **Senior Girls:** 579
Fees as at 01/01/2022:
Day: £10,830–£22,170
Weekly Boarding: £29,850
Full Boarding: £35,610
Average class size: 20

With a history dating back to 1541, an excellent reputation and an accessible location, Berkhamsted School offers much to make it worthy of consideration by parents across London and the South East. Our patron, who visited in 2016 to mark the School's 475th anniversary, is Her Majesty The Queen. Located in the historic market town of Berkhamsted, the School is a 30 minute train journey from Euston Station, and a short drive from Junction 20 of the M25. Full, weekly and flexi boarding, as well as term-time and holiday wraparound care for younger pupils, are on offer to support working parents. Berkhamsted is one of only a small number of schools in the country to offer a 'diamond' structure that combines both single-sex and co-educational teaching. Boys and girls are taught together until the age of 11, separately from 11-16, before coming back together again in a joint Sixth Form. In senior school, boys and girls are taught separately on different sites, but share in academic trips and visits and in some co-curricular activities, such as drama productions, orchestras, Duke of Edinburgh's Award and the Combined Cadet Force.

Academic results are consistently strong with around 80% A*- B grades at A Level over the last five years. In 2020, GCSE students achieved 75% of grades 7 and above. Berkhamsted offers all the key components of a traditional independent school education: small class sizes, specialist staff and excellent standards of teaching throughout the school. Alongside this, an outstanding cocurricular programme seeks to foster and develop a wide range of interests and hobbies – music, sport, drama, public speaking, and a vibrant outdoor education programme. The school timetable is structured to accommodate a wide selection of clubs and societies within core school hours. Berkhamsted also has a strong tradition of undertaking service within the local community from Year 9 (13+) onwards.

Pupils across the School enjoy the benefits of being part of a small, supportive community based in an environment appropriate to their specific educational needs, yet with access to the state-of-the art facilities of a large school; a 500-seat theatre, a six-lane 25m swimming pool and sports centre, 40 acres of playing fields, a High Ropes Course and a large art department.

The School prides itself on offering outstanding levels of pastoral care and, in an echo of its boarding roots, the House system is a key feature of Berkhamsted. Senior School pupils are allocated to Houses and the Head of House, supported by House Tutors, has the primary responsibility for the academic and pastoral progress of each student in their House. Over and above the close academic supervision and support, this structure provides an excellent social base for pupils, allowing them to mix and get to know others across the year groups. Berkhamsted offers scholarships – academic, art, drama, music and sport – and means-tested bursaries to talented pupils on entry to the school.

Cobham Hall School

(Founded 1962)
Brewers Road, Cobham, Kent DA12 3BL

Tel: 01474 823371
Email: enquiries@cobhamhall.com
Website: www.cobhamhall.com
Headteacher: Mrs Wendy Barrett
School type: Girls' Boarding & Day

Age range of girls: 11–18
No. of pupils enrolled as at 01/01/2022: 150
Fees as at 01/01/2022:
Day: £6,804–£8,246 per term
Full Boarding: £10,279–£12,831 per term

Dive into an education at Cobham Hall, where we aim for each student to discover there is more in her than she thought. Cobham Hall is an independent Round Square Boarding and Day School for girls, with approximately 150 students representing some 25 nationalities. Offering full, weekly and flexi-boarding, Cobham Hall provides ultimate flexibility for families.

Nestled in 150 acres of stunning historic parkland, the School is housed in a 16th Century Manor House; an idyllic rural setting, yet close to A2/M2, A20/M20 and M25 and Ebbsfleet International Station. For Day Girls and Weekly Boarders, local daily minibus transport is available, serving areas including Greenwich, Blackheath, Chislehurst and Sidcup.

At the heart of Cobham Hall lie our core values: Trust, Respect, Honesty, Kindness and Tolerance. These, alongside the Round Square IDEALS, provide the foundation for our Personal Discovery Framework, which encourages our students to explore and discover their talents, attributes and strengths.

We know brilliance lies within each of our students. We provide the academic knowledge for them to flourish and inspire each student to discover their future path. We encourage each student to develop the confidence to pursue goals and chase aspirations. A wide range of subject options are offered at GCSE and A Level, with small class sizes ensuring students have the attention they need academically. Cobham Hall encourages

students to achieve their fullest all-round potential, supplementing an integrated academic programme with a wide range of co-curricular activities. Furthermore, Wellbeing is at the core of all we do, with the knowledge that by looking after our students' emotional and physical wellbeing, they feel happier and will thrive. Alongside this strong academic and pastoral support, Cobham Hall actively promotes the development of Life Skills, ensuring all students leave the School capable of adapting to life's challenges.

Cobham Hall is part of the Mill Hill School Foundation. Currently a girls' school for ages 11 to 18, Cobham Hall is hoping to become co-educational in the Sixth Form from September 2022.

Davenies School

DAVENIES
Day Preparatory School for boys aged 4 to 13 years

(Founded 1940)
Station Road, Beaconsfield,
Buckinghamshire HP9 1AA

Tel: 01494 685400
Email: office@davenies.co.uk
Website: www.davenies.co.uk
Headmaster: Mr Carl Rycroft BEd (Hons)
Appointed: September 2015
School type: Boys' Day Preparatory

Age range of boys: 4–13 years
No. of pupils enrolled as at 01/01/2022: 337
Fees as at 01/01/2022:
Day: £12,105–£18,255
Average class size: Max 20

Davenies is a thriving IAPS day school for boys aged 4-13. Our ethos and philosophy enable the boys to make the most of their preparatory years, supported by high-quality pastoral care, a broad and stimulating curriculum and numerous extra-curricular opportunities.

Davenies has its own distinct character and from their earliest years children are encouraged to relish the learning experience.

We are committed to an education both in and out of the classroom, thereby enabling the academic, artistic, musical, creative and physical potential of each child to flourish. This school is a warm, caring and happy one, where self-esteem is nurtured and grown; we believe that by fostering a wide range of interests and passions we provide the boys with every opportunity to develop in confidence. Our high-quality teachers have an excellent track record of preparing children for life at the country's leading senior schools and beyond.

Enterprises such as the unique Davenies Award Scheme and the permeation of technology in our teaching and learning ensure we offer a truly independent educational experience.

At Davenies, our outstanding facilities support us in providing a positive learning experience with our own language of learning that nurtures each boy's understanding of how he learns. Davenies' boys are polite and friendly with their own individual characters, personalities, passions and interests.

The School is owned by Beaconsfield Educational Trust Limited, a company limited by guarantee, whose registered office is at 73 Station Road, Beaconsfield, Bucks HP9 1AA. Registration No. 717500 Registered Charity No. 313120.

Hampton Court House

Hampton Court House

(Founded 2000)

Hampton Court Road, East Molesey, Surrey KT8 9BS
Tel: +44 (0)20 8943 0889
Email: reception@hchnet.co.uk
Website: www.hamptoncourthouse.co.uk
Headteacher: Dr Adrian Rainbow
School type: Co-educational Day

Age range of pupils: 3 months–18 years
No. of pupils enrolled as at 01/01/2022: 300
Fees as at 01/01/2022:
Day: £14,637–£20,895
Average class size: Approx 20
Teacher/pupil ratio: 1:10

Hampton Court House is a leading independent co-educational day school. An "all-through school" (2 – 18), we educate children from pre-nursery to great success in their GCSEs and A Levels in Year 11 and Year 13, who then go on to some of the top universities and courses worldwide. A stone's throw away from the Palace, Hampton Court House is situated in its own private parkland nestled in Bushy Park, a 30 to 40 minute drive from central London or a 35 minute train journey from London Waterloo Station.

We believe that children need some (guided) freedom in order to develop their own style with taste and discretion. Pupils and staff have mutual respect for each other. The staff, including the Headmaster, are addressed by their first names. Whilst there is a dress code, there is no uniform.

Aside from outstanding academic results, Hampton Court House boasts a range of programmes to give your child a head start. These include our bilingual French programmes, for which we were awarded the Label FrancÉducation by the Institut Français in 2022, and our Pre-Nursery and Daycare programmes preparing pupils for Reception.

Our commitment to the highest quality bespoke pastoral care was recognised by Optimus Education who awarded us the Wellbeing Award for Schools in 2022.

Hampton Court House holds regular tours throughout the Academic Year and parents are encouraged to register online on our website.

King Edward's Witley

King Edward's
WITLEY

Petworth Road, Godalming, Surrey GU8 5SG
Tel: 01428 686735
Email: admissions@kesw.org
Website: www.kesw.org
Head: Mrs Joanna Wright
School type:
Co-educational Day & Boarding

Religious Denomination: Christian
Age range of pupils: 11–18 years
No. of pupils enrolled as at 01/01/2022: 420
Fees as at 01/01/2022:
£5,595–£11,665 per term
Average class size: 15

Pupils thrive at King Edward's. We encourage them to be the best versions of themselves because individual achievement and personal growth count for more than league tables. Our unique heritage and place among British co-educational independent schools means that we can provide the best preparation for adult life to a wider range of young people than almost any other institution.

King Edward's offers your son or daughter a school that can feel as warm and welcoming as home. A springboard to a lifelong love of learning which can nurture confidence, foster collaboration and prepare them for life in a multicultural world. Most of all it can help them discover who they are. This is a school shaped by generosity of spirit, not by background.

Academic focus
A King Edward's education is a rounded education. All academic staff are subject specialists, GCSE/IGCSE in Year 11 followed by a choice of A-level courses or the IB Diploma programme in the Sixth Form. Young people discover skills, talents and enthusiasms they never knew they had and are encouraged to set their sights high and be ambitious in their learning. Our rich co-curricular programme broadens their horizons.

Pastoral
All our pupils benefit from small class sizes and our House system with its supportive pastoral networks is at the heart of school life. Each House is committed to strong connections uniting and blending boarders and day pupils into a single team. Diversity has been a strength since our foundation in 1553 and while most of our 420 pupils are local, we attract international pupils from more than 30 countries. They help teach us what it means to be part of the wider human family.

Boarding
King Edward's is a thriving community with four senior boys and two senior girls Houses for day, weekly and flexi boarders. Lower School pupils in Years 7 and 8 reside in Queen Mary House, an impressive family-oriented building steeped in history. We will be unveiling our Upper Sixth Form House in 2022, which will become home to all Upper Sixth Form pupils, both boys and girls, in their final year at King Edward's. The new House will benefit from landscaped outdoor space, study and social areas and boarders will have their own study bedrooms with full en suite facilities. Our Upper Sixth Form House will provide the perfect stepping stone to university and independent living.

Hobbies and activities

On our leafy, 100-acre site amid the Surrey Hills we have space for all the sport, drama, music, hobbies, and intellectual pursuits a young mind can take. King Edward's is a wonderfully safe place for youthful adventure and curiosity.

The School creates a foundation for life both now and for the future. Our timeless education reaches far beyond the exciting and challenging academic curriculum and the broad range of opportunities in all areas of school life – sporting, artistic, social and cultural.

Pupils leave as independent free-thinkers – agile, motivated, and self-disciplined. The creative, entrepreneurial thinking they develop here gives the next generation of inventors, designers and problem-solvers the ability to grasp life with both hands.

Sport

Our ethos ensures there is ample choice for boys and girls to enjoy a wide variety of sports. Our sports programme is built on the latest research with activities that blend breadth with specific development, hence offering a vast array of Physical Education programmes.

Weekly sports matches are played on Saturdays and mid-week, and in recent years the School is proud to have achieved regional and national success in football, tennis, basketball, table tennis, fencing, climbing and athletics. If a pupil asks to participate in a particular sport, we will find an opportunity for them to do so. If a girl or boy has an aptitude for a sport, we support them in obtaining specialist and expert coaching, join programmes and local clubs to develop their skills and compete. We help plan the pursuit of coaching qualifications for our pupils.

Music

Music flourishes inside and outside the classroom with some twenty choirs, orchestras and specialist instrumental ensembles from chamber music to rock bands. A carefully structured programme enables pupils of all abilities and aspirations to perform from informal showcase concerts and workshops to masterclasses and large-scale concerts. Annual instrumental and vocal competitions are held for soloists and ensembles. Annual House Music competitions, 'Battle of the Bands' and 'Musician of the Year' all bring the school community together. The Music and Drama Departments regularly collaborate in school productions and, thanks to our strong link to the City of London, pupils often perform at events in the City.

We aim to inspire a love of independent learning, a wealth of lasting friendships, Christian values and hopeful vision. King Edward's is an extraordinary, distinctive, forward-thinking and global minded community. It is a wonderful place to be.

Leighton Park School

LEIGHTON PARK
FOUNDED 1890

Shinfield Road, Reading,
Berkshire RG2 7ED

Tel: 0118 987 9600
Email: admissions@leightonpark.com
Website: www.leightonpark.com
Head: Mr Matthew L S Judd BA, PGCE
Appointed: September 2018
School type:
Co-educational Day & Boarding

Religious Denomination: Quaker
Age range of pupils: 11–18 years
No. of pupils enrolled as at 01/01/2022: 520
Fees as at 01/01/2022:
£6,745–£13,485 per term
Average class size: 16
Teacher/pupil ratio: 1:7

Introduction

A vibrant learning community, our values-based education focuses on each individual – with impressive results.

At its core, a Leighton Park education offers achievement with values, character and community.

The success of our academic approach is demonstrated by the latest UK Government analysis, which recognised Leighton Park as the best performing school in Berkshire and in the top 14 boarding schools in the country for the academic progress of our leavers. Our A Level students achieved 72% A*/A last year. The Independent School Inspectorate (ISI) have awarded Leighton Park a 'double excellent' standard, the highest possible attainment for an independent school, in recognition of both the quality of pupils' personal development and the quality of their academic progress.

Academic focus

An IB World School, our emphasis on problem-solving, critical thinking and intercultural skills ensures that every student can succeed in an ever-changing, globalised world. Central to the school's approach, we have particular strengths in Science, Technology, Engineering and Maths (STEM) as well as the Creative Arts (Music, Drama, Art and Dance). Combining these strengths, our students benefit from an interdisciplinary approach, fusing analytical skills from STEM with creative and interpersonal soft skills. Leighton Park won the national Award for Excellence in STEAM Education in 2020.

Music is another particular strength of the School with a brand new Music and Media Centre providing students with exceptional facilities, including a Yamaha Live Lounge recording studio. Our Music department is accredited as a Flagship Yamaha Music Education Partner, the only school in Europe to hold this status, with 50% of students studying an instrument and 27 music teachers on staff.

In Sixth Form, students can choose between the International Baccalaureate Diploma Programme (IB) or A Levels, and are offered an extensive selection of subject options, including Psychology, Politics, Economics/Business Studies, Dance, a BTEC in Music Technology and a CTEC in Physical Education.

Pastoral

All our students benefit from small class sizes. The average is 16 students per class, going down to 7 students in Sixth Form. Our dedicated teachers are able to cater lessons to each student and ensure they are kept on track both inside and out of lessons. This allows an unparalleled level of support and also a relationship between students and teachers that allows students to feel that they can speak honestly and openly to teachers about any problems they may be facing.

Boarding

Leighton Park has a thriving boarding community, offering full, weekly and flexible options for students. The Lower School (Years 7 and 8) offers co-educational boarding in a House with separate wings for accommodation by gender. The single-sex accommodation is arranged for Senior students in School House for boys and Reckitt House for girls. Students represent 39 countries, with strong UK representation. The Houses mix boarding and day students, creating vibrant communities, with day students welcome to stay until 9pm to spend time with friends or have time and space to focus on their prep.

House parents create homely environments supported by tutors and matrons, ensuring each student feels relaxed and comfortable. With a dedicated staff and plenty of opportunity to socialise with other students, each House is very much its own community.

Hobbies and other activities

Our wrap-around provision, which welcomes day students from 7.15am to 9pm, offers all our pupils the time to discover and develop their greatest talents. Students can choose from 90 different co-curricular activities to extend their learning, increase confidence, try new things and make new friends.

Sports

Sport plays an important role in life at Leighton Park with many individual performers and teams reaching county and regional level in sports. The school's Advanced Performer Programme supports elite athletes. While the school does very well in traditional sports such as rugby, netball, boys' cricket and hockey it also has strong teams in football and girls' cricket. The school is very supportive of individual talents and interests from rowing to gymnastics.

Music

Music and creative media is a particular strength at Leighton Park, reflected by the school's status as a Yamaha Flagship Music Education Partner. Students have so many opportunities to play or perform at Leighton Park, with the Music Department being one of the busiest places in school, catering for all musical tastes from classical to jazz, indie to rock. Opportunities to perform include regular concerts and tours abroad.

Facilities

Leighton Park has the facilities you would expect of a leading independent school, including a new Music and Media Centre, an impressive library, swimming pool and a combination of high tech and historic buildings. The school's innovative use of the latest teaching and learning technologies is supported by continuous investment in technology, including Google Classroom, CleverTouch screens in classrooms and personal ChromeBook laptops for students.

School life

The quiet moments and the calm atmosphere of our 65 acre park, encourage students to collect their thoughts and reflect within a caring community, providing high academic standards, excellent pastoral care and a rich and diverse co-curricular programme of activities. All of this, and the focus on mutual respect, create a stable, unique and sustainable environment where children can live, learn and grow.

LVS Ascot

PATRON
HM THE QUEEN

(Founded 1803)
London Road, Ascot, Berkshire SL5 8DR

Tel: 01344 882770
Email: enquiries@lvs.ascot.sch.uk
Website: www.lvs.ascot.sch.uk
Principal: Mrs Christine Cunniffe BA
(Hons), MMus, MBA
Appointed: September 2010
School type:
Co-educational Day & Boarding

Religious Denomination:
Non-denominational
Age range of pupils: 4–18 years
No. of pupils enrolled as at 01/01/2022: 800
Fees as at 01/01/2022:
Day: £12,915–£19,335
Full Boarding: £27,585–£33,975
Average class size: 18

LVS Ascot is an award winning, all-ability, independent day and boarding school that inspires boys and girls from 4 to 18 to exceed their expectations and become independent adults, through a rounded education that delivers academic rigor alongside sporting, performing and creative opportunities.

The campus includes all Infant & Junior School, Senior School and Sixth Form Facilities as well as four Boarding Houses within a spacious 26 acre site. LVS Ascot facilities include: Infant & Junior School environmental garden, indoor swimming pool, fully equipped 250 seater theatre with state of the art light and sound, learning resource centre, astro pitch, fitness centre and wellbeing hub.

Proud of its excellent academic & pastoral care, staff across the school work together to ensure that every student's personal development is nurtured, believing that encouragement and support are essential to help young people become caring, confident citizens for the future.

Being one of three schools owned and managed by the Licensed Trade Charity, income generated by the School is re-invested in the site, to offer the highest standard of educational and co-curricular facilities and is also used to fund the work of the Charity.

Mayfield School

Mayfield

(Founded 1872)

The Old Palace, Mayfield,
East Sussex TN20 6PH
Tel: 01435 874642
Email: registrar@mayfieldgirls.org
Website: www.mayfieldgirls.org
Head: Ms Antonia Beary MA, MPhil
(Cantab), PGCE
School type: Girls' Boarding & Day

Religious Denomination: Catholic
(we accept all faiths and none)
Age range of girls: 11–18 years
No. of pupils enrolled as at 01/01/2022: 405
Fees as at 01/01/2022:
Day: £7,750 per term
Full Boarding: £12,250 per term
Flexi Boarding from: £80 per night
Average class size: 15-17

Mayfield is a leading independent boarding and day school for girls aged 11 to 18. Founded in 1872, a Mayfield education combines academic rigour, breadth of opportunity and a strong sense of community.

Set within the beautiful Sussex Countryside, conveniently located within an hour of central London and with easy access to Gatwick and Heathrow airports, the School has an excellent academic record, exceptional pastoral care and an extensive co-curricular programme. Every girl is encouraged and supported to find her strengths and develop them in an inspiring learning environment, which encourages independent critical thinking, determination and resilience. Mayfield

girls develop a lifelong love of learning, a range of transferable skills that will prepare them for their futures and friendships that will last a lifetime.

Mayfield's ethos reflects its Catholic foundation and encourages integrity, initiative, respect and a desire to be the best you can be within a vibrant and inclusive community. One of the School's greatest strengths is its proven ability to unlock and develop the unique potential and talent of each girl in an inspiring learning environment. Small classes, exemplary pastoral care, and a happy and vibrant community, ensure girls thrive and challenge themselves both inside and outside the classroom.

Mayfield's innovative curriculum

encourages questioning, reflection, creativity and the freedom to learn from mistakes. Pupils progress to prestigious universities, including Oxford and Cambridge, and increasingly to the US and Europe to study a wide range of subjects, with a regular stream of engineers, medics, vets, lawyers, economists, designers and architects.

For the past 150 years, Mayfield has nurtured generations of enterprising, purposeful young women with the skills and confidence to make a positive difference in the world. The skills, values, aspiration and resilience instilled in the girls prepares them to respond to the opportunities and challenges of the 21st century, whatever path they choose.

Queen Anne's School

Queen Anne's
CAVERSHAM

(Founded 1894)

**Henley Road, Caversham,
Berkshire RG4 6DX**
Tel: 0118 918 7300
Email: office@qas.org.uk
Website: www.qas.org.uk
Head: Ms Elaine Purves
School type: Girls' Day & Boarding

Age range of girls: 11–18 years
No. of pupils enrolled as at 01/01/2022: 450
Fees as at 01/01/2022:
Full Boarding: £13,590 per term
Flexi Boarding: £12,250 – £12,920 per term
Day: £8,370 per term
Average class size: 18–20

Queen Anne's is an inspirational day and boarding school for girls aged 11-18 set in 35 acres in the heart of Berkshire with easy access to London. Founded in 1894, the school is steeped in history and tradition and is known for its pioneering education that prepares girls for the challenges of the modern world. The school is part of the United Westminster Grey Coat Foundation that was founded in 1699 in Westminster as the Grey Coat Hospital.

From the Sixth Form centre that could be mistaken for Google offices, to the careful support of the wellbeing programme, this girls' day and boarding school is breaking down barriers and revolutionising the way that teenagers are taught, deploying the latest educational neuroscience research. Every girl is inspired to explore and enjoy her individuality, free from gender-stereotypes, in a safe environment that champions excellence and deep creativity.

A three-time recipient of the prestigious Microsoft Showcase Schools Award for its extensive digital teaching and learning, Queen Anne's is also known for its exceptional 'value added' scores with students achieving on average one full grade better than expected at GCSE.

Performing and creative arts
Offline, and the school is known for its performing and creative arts offering. It boasts a state-of-the-art music centre; outstanding art, design, animation, and ceramics provision; plus, a 250-seat theatre and a thriving dance department.

Sport
Throughout the extensive sports facilities, you will find an ethos of excellence and inclusion where physical activity is promoted as essential for well-being

and development. Lacrosse, netball, tennis, dance, trampolining, swimming, and athletics all feature highly both in academic PE and in the bursting extra-curricular programme, with football, badminton and cricket recent growing additions. Elite sportswomen are supported at county, regional and national level with representation across a vast array of sports.

Transport

London families welcome the flexi and weekly boarding options at Queen Anne's with a weekly London Service offering collection on Monday morning and drop-off on Friday afternoon across Brentford, Chiswick, Hammersmith, Fulham and Kensington. Further daily transport across Berkshire, Oxfordshire and into Buckinghamshire and Surrey accommodates pupils from the local area.

Curriculum

A rich and diverse curriculum sees students undertake studies that are engaging and relevant. Small class sizes means that teachers can accommodate individual student needs and students feel confident and able to make meaningful contributions in lessons. Students gain a wide knowledge base, and become passionate about their studies, often taking part in 'stretch and challenge' activities set by teachers. From September 2022 Criminology, Environmental Science, Film Studies, Media Studies, Music Technology and Sociology have been added to the A Level curriculum increasing the students' options to 29 subjects.

Co-Curricular

The curriculum is accompanied by a wide and varied co-curricular programme that enables students to build confidence, stretch their abilities, and find new passions. Whether they are interested in art, drama, music, chess, or debating, there is something for everyone. It's not uncommon for a student to be representing the school or even their country in sporting events, to be practising with one of the school's many ensembles or bands, ready for a concert, rehearsing for a school play or at one of the early morning swim sessions. Each year the school sees students selected for England Lacrosse, achieve music qualifications from Trinity College London and even receive awards from the Royal Society of Biology.

Boarding

The junior boarding house for students in Lower 4 to Upper 4 (Year 7 to 9) is located at the far end of the school field, offering younger boarders an idyllic, safe, and happy home-from-home. The house gardens offer girls the chance to spend time in nature and play together with their 'house family'. From bonfire nights and stargazing to cricket matches and swing-ball, there is always something fun happening in the junior house.

The three senior boarding houses for students in Lower 5 to Upper 6 (Year 10 to 13) are a hub of activity, located in the centre of the school's campus. Senior boarders are encouraged to explore their independence with increasing levels of responsibility, which aims to prepare them for life after Queen Anne's.

Each house has bedrooms that can accommodate one to three girls, a large 'sit' where girls meet for house meetings, movie nights or just to hang out with friends and a well-equipped kitchen where girls are able to cook meals or catch up with their friends over a hot chocolate.

Head of Queen Anne's

In January 2022 Ms Elaine Purves took on Headship at Queen Anne's, bringing a wealth of experience, a modern outlook and huge enthusiasm for outstanding education. Since starting as Head, Ms Purves has ensured she has got to know the school and what makes it such a special place to be, rarely missing a concert, show or weekend fixture.

Reddam House Berkshire

REDDAM HOUSE
BERKSHIRE

(Founded 2015)
Bearwood Road, Sindlesham,
Wokingham, Berkshire RG41 5BG

Tel: +44 (0)118 974 8300
Email: registrar@reddamhouse.org.uk
Website: www.reddamhouse.org.uk
Principal: Mr Rick Cross
School type:
Co-educational Day & Boarding
Religious Denomination:
Non-denominational

Age range of pupils: 3 months–18 years
No. of pupils enrolled as at 01/01/2022: 675
Fees as at 01/01/2022:
Day: £11,490–£18,420
Weekly Boarding: £27,981–£32,244
Full Boarding: £29,526–£33,789

Reddam House Berkshire is a co-educational, independent school that aspires to excellence in education for children from three months to 18 years old. This truly majestic school set in 125 acres of stunning woods and parkland is conveniently located near Wokingham in the English countryside of Berkshire, a vibrant hub with easy access to the M3, M4, Heathrow and London.

Reddam House Berkshire is renowned for its academic, cultural, and sporting excellence. It has a strong, recognisable culture that acknowledges a community of students who are nurtured as individuals, with their distinct attributes, traits and strengths celebrated.

The broad range of subjects creates a curriculum that accentuates independent inquiry. Students study up to 11 GCSEs with a free choice outside of the core subjects of Maths, English and Science. All students are encouraged to take on the Extended Project Qualification (EPQ), highly regarded by universities as demonstrating students' preparedness for undergraduate study.

Exam Results
Exam results in 2021 were outstanding with 62% of A level grades awarded being A*/A, and 63% of GCSE results being 9-7. The vast majority of students go on to higher education, with recent destinations including Cambridge, UCL and Manchester.

Boarding
Reddam House offers a range of flexible boarding options for students from the age of 8, including full and weekly boarding, extended days, and ad-hoc stays. Students who board at Reddam House can expect to be part of an inclusive, respectful, and international community where independence and self-confidence are developed and celebrated.

Beyond the Classroom
Academics is just one area in which students thrive, the extensive extracurricular activities programme provides plenty of opportunities for students to explore and develop their interests. Activities include performing and visual arts, music, photography, and computing. Regular sports fixtures include rugby, hockey, football, cricket, netball, swimming, tennis, basketball, golf, cross country, and judo.

Roedean School

ROEDEAN

(Founded 1885)
Roedean Way, Brighton,
East Sussex BN2 5RQ

Tel: 01273 667500
Email: info@roedean.co.uk
Website: www.roedean.co.uk
Headmaster:
Mr. Oliver Bond BA(Essex), PGCE, NPQH
School type: Girls' Day & Boarding
Age range of girls: 11–18 years
No. of pupils enrolled as at 01/01/2022: 675

Sixth Form: 155
Fees as at 01/01/2022:
Day: £5,670–£7,415 per term
Weekly Boarding:
£10,030–£11,185 per term
Full Boarding: £10,990–£13,305 per term
Average class size: 18
Teacher/pupil ratio: 1:7

A Roedean education is unique. The School's genuinely holistic ethos brings together excellent academic results, a wide range of activities, outstanding facilities, and the space for every girl to forge her own path. Academic results are consistently strong: in 2020, at A Level, nearly 80% of all grades were A*-A, and 40% were A* grades; at GCSE, the majority of all grades, 71%, were at Grade 9-8, and over one third, 43%, were awarded Grade 9.

Roedean is a wonderful school, now numbering 675 girls, up from 360 on roll in 2014. The School enjoys very strong interest, both from local families and from those in London and the South-East who often become weekly and flexi-boarders; they come to the school for its fantastic grounds and facilities, and also

for a school that focuses on developing academic strengths without losing the enjoyment and delight that must be part of an all-round education. The girls grow up at their own pace, not constrained by finite external expectations, and they have the freedom to develop their talents and passions.

Roedean's ethos is focused on the remarkable benefits of a holistic approach to education, in which academic pursuits are complemented by a wide range of co-curricular activities. With well over 100 activities on offer every week, the girls enjoy sea-swimming (we are entering the 2022 Cross-Channel relay race), international travel awards, pygmy goats on our Farm, House competitions, and our flood-lit all-weather pitch. Roedean girls excel in a range of sports, many musicians

play beyond Grade 8 level, and girls achieve at the very highest level in ballet. It is precisely this rounded education which produces independent and creative young women who will make their mark in the world.

Roedean is an extraordinary school – the girls play cricket and hockey with the sea's blue in front of them and the green of the South Downs behind them, the Maths and Humanities classrooms have perhaps the best views of any in the country, and which other boarding houses have been likened to a boutique hotel? But it is not just the location, but the strong academic focus with a genuine belief in the importance of creativity and an all-round education that makes Roedean unique.

St Edmund's School

ST EDMUND'S SCHOOL
CANTERBURY

(Founded 1749)
St Thomas Hill, Canterbury, Kent CT2 8HU

Tel: 01227 475601
Email: admissions@stedmunds.org.uk
Website: www.stedmunds.org.uk
Head: Mr Edward O'Connor MA (Cantab), MPhil (Oxon), MEd (Cantab)
School type:
Co-educational Day & Boarding
Age range of pupils: 2–18

No. of pupils enrolled as at 01/01/2022: 602
Fees per term as at 01/01/2021:
Pre-Prep from: £3,698
Junior from: £5,459 (day)–£9,782 (boarding)
Senior from: £7,400 (day)–£12,846 (boarding)
Average class size: 7-20
Teacher/pupil ratio: 1:7

St Edmund's School Canterbury is a dynamic co-educational 2-18 day and boarding school. Our pupils benefit from a caring and supportive environment, high-calibre teaching and a holistic educational approach that seeks to develop creativity, leadership qualities and original thinking. A broad academic curriculum and extraordinarily diverse co-curricular programme enable pupils to find their path and grow to 'be all they can be'. Our small class sizes enable the personalisation of learning so that pupils receive the attention and academic challenge they need to excel, and every pupil here is known and understood. The fact that we educate children from the age of 2 to 18 underpins the strong family atmosphere and sense of community that pervade the school.

Established in 1749, St Edmund's combines respect for tradition and history with a fresh, engaging and forward-thinking attitude to the education of young people. Our approach is focused on the unique abilities and needs of individual pupils. All our pupils are valued for their contribution to the school and we take great pride in their successes. Creativity flourishes here. Our Drama, Music and Art departments are renowned for their outstanding achievements. However, creativity is celebrated across the whole curriculum, as innovative teaching and small classes encourage pupils to think independently and express themselves with confidence and originality.

The school has a long-established reputation for outstanding pastoral care. This is our starting point. We believe if pupils feel happy, secure and supported at school they will naturally benefit from our outstanding educational opportunities and enjoy the wealth of stimulating extra-curricular activities on offer.

We also look to develop the whole person. Our dynamic sports provision, extensive activities programme and exciting range of outdoor education opportunities enable pupils to develop vital qualities such as leadership experience, inter-personal communication, the ability to work in teams and empathy for others. As a result, our school produces remarkable young people. Pupils leave St Edmund's as assured, articulate, thoughtful individuals who possess a strong social conscience.

Academic Ethos

St Edmund's is proud of its pupil-centred and ambitious academic ethos. We seek to foster original thinkers with the intellectual and personal skills to be leaders and decision makers in future.

We offer a variety of challenging and exciting I/GCSE and A-level courses which appeal to young people whatever their strengths and interests. Highly-qualified teachers and small class sizes mean that young people receive inspirational instruction, with vibrant debate and individual attention. Pupils develop learning skills through project work and research opportunities such as the Extended Project Qualification and the Durrell Essay. We encourage cross-curricular work to promote original ideas and multi-dimensional thinking.

Essentially, our pupils are encouraged and nurtured throughout their time at St Edmund's to aim for and achieve the very highest academic standards they possibly can.

Pastoral Care & Wellbeing

At St Edmund's, great emphasis is placed upon the importance of supporting young people and recognising the individual. We understand that our pupils come to us with different experiences and aspirations. This diversity makes our community stronger and richer. The pastoral team comprises the Deputy Head Pastoral, Director of Safeguarding, Chaplain, Director of Boarding, housemasters, deputy housemasters, tutors, resident boarding staff, Director of Wellbeing, matrons, Medical Centre staff and Counsellor. Each of them works closely with pupils and parents, and understands that they are trusted to offer good, salient advice. We are confident that our pupils feel able to approach these adults should they want to discuss anything of concern to them.

Choristerships

St Edmund's School is proud to educate and care for the choristers of Canterbury Cathedral. They are a very special part of our school and benefit from all the same teaching and resources as our other pupils. The opportunity to be a chorister is something truly unique, given the international profile and prestige of Canterbury Cathedral. Choristership is a life-changing experience that creates a great sense of pride and personal fulfilment. Some choristers go on to distinguished musical careers, and for all the leadership, team work and organisational skills they learn are extremely useful in their lives at the school, at university and beyond. The Canterbury Cathedral Girls' Choir was founded in 2014: girls in Year 8 can audition, and a number of St Edmund's girls are currently in the choir.

I hope that you will be able to visit St Edmund's in the near future and experience the wonderful community and stunning setting of our school.

St Hilda's School

St Hilda's School
HARPENDEN

Caring, Curious & Confident

28 Douglas Road, Harpenden,
Hertfordshire AL5 2ES
Tel: 01582 712307
Email: office@sthildasharpenden.co.uk
Website: www.sthildasharpenden.co.uk
Headmaster: Mr Dan Sayers

School type: Co-educational Nursery,
Girls' Day 4-11
Age range of girls: 2.5–11 years
No. of pupils enrolled as at 01/01/2022: 150
Fees as at 01/01/2022:
Day: £3,285–£4,260 per term

Prospective parents often ask us for a definition of the St Hilda's USP. This is summed up in our strapline 'Caring, Curious and Confident' which is quantified in our daily aim to ensure that our pupils can access as broad a range of learning experiences as possible whilst developing resilience for our fast-changing world is achieved within a safe, caring and family atmosphere where the needs of each and every pupil are attended to.

St Hilda's has been part of the Harpenden community for 130 years and our pupils receive a first-class education in a family atmosphere where every day provides rigour, breadth and fun. In a world where relentless pressure can cause huge anxiety for the rising generation of our society, our mission at St Hilda's is to ensure that our pupils can develop self-confidence and self-worth as paramount aims. This is summed up by these spontaneous comments of appreciation from parents whose pupils are at the beginning, middle and end of their St Hilda's careers:

'If the pursuit of happiness is a life ideal, one only has to witness the arrival of the children each morning to see that you have achieved that so brilliantly. You have opened the door to the world of education and have shown your pupils what an amazing and exciting place that can be.'

'Your amazing staff have encouraged and inspired our child into a confident spirited individual once more. I cannot thank you enough.'

Early Years, where pupils can start from two and a half, provides a fabulous learning environment – including specialist sport, music, phonics and French – and a terrific grounding, building confidence and inspiring our pupils to develop a 'can do' attitude, whilst giving them an academically stimulating experience that links seamlessly into the rest of the School.

At the other end of their St Hilda's journey, our girls advance to Senior School well-prepared for the next stage of their education and life beyond. This year all pupils have gained a place at their first choice of school and amassed a range of scholarships. Whether pursuing academic excellence or encouraging blossoming creativity inside and outside through the creative arts, aiming for your zenith in sporting endeavour or increasing your confidence amongst a caring, family atmosphere, St Hilda's has something for everyone.

Come and see for yourself what this outstanding School can give your child.

St John's Beaumont Preparatory School

ST JOHN'S BEAUMONT
(Founded 1888)

Priest Hill, Old Windsor, Berkshire SL4 2JN
Tel: 01784 494 053
Email: sjb.admissions@sjb.email
Website: www.sjbwindsor.uk
Headmaster:
Mr G E F Delaney BA(Hons), PGCE, MSc

School type:
Boys' Day & Boarding Preparatory
Age range of boys: 3–13 years
No. of pupils enrolled as at 01/01/2022: 240
Fees as at 01/01/2022:
Day: £3,540–£6,820 per term
Full Boarding: £10,415 per term

Introduction

St John's Beaumont is a Roman Catholic preparatory boarding and day school for boys aged 3-13 years. Set in a rural location, adjacent to Windsor Great Park, St John's was founded in 1888 and is the oldest purpose-built preparatory school in the country. We combine the rich traditions of Jesuit education with the very best that modern teaching techniques and technology can offer.

Facilities

The school is set within 70 acres of established woodland, playing fields and enjoys excellent sporting facilities. There is plenty of space for cross-country, rugby, football, cricket and more. A 25m indoor swimming pool, a rowing suite and a climbing wall are also highlights of our facilities. Of equal importance to Sport is Music, Drama and the Arts, with the majority of boys learning an instrument and outstanding LAMDA results as well as a much-acclaimed annual drama production in the outdoor theatre.

Philosophy

We pursue excellence in teaching and learning through the development and care of the whole child. At our core is the principle of cura personalis – care for each person, so that boys may flourish academically, emotionally, socially, physically and spiritually.

Leavers

Our boys leave St John's aged 13 and move to some of the country's finest schools, but more importantly do so as confident, aspirational and resilient young men, aware of their own potential and their ability to leave a positive impression on the lives of others.

Boarding

Our vibrant boarding community, comprising of tailored (2 or 3 nights/week), weekly and full boarders, enjoys a full evening & weekend program. The boys are making the most of the school's facilities as well as the proximity to Windsor and London for regular trips. Special activities for the boarders include a Diving (PADI) course, polo lessons and trips to Thorpe Park.

Tonbridge School

TONBRIDGE
SCHOOL

(Founded 1553)

High Street, Tonbridge, Kent TN9 1JP
Tel: 01732 304297
Email: admissions@tonbridge-school.org
Website: www.tonbridge-school.co.uk
Headmaster: Mr James Priory MA (Oxon)
Appointed: August 2018
School type: Boys' Boarding & Day

Age range of boys: 13–18 years
No. of pupils enrolled as at 01/01/2022: 798
Fees as at 01/01/2022:
Day: £33,636
Full Boarding: £44,835
Average class size: GCSE 18, A level 10
Teacher/pupil ratio: 1:8

Tonbridge is one of the leading boys' boarding and day schools in the UK and is highly respected, both here and internationally, for providing a world-class education.

The School occupies an extensive site of 150 acres in North Tonbridge, Kent – just a 40-minute train ride from London Charing Cross. There are some 800 boys in seven Boarding Houses and five Day Houses. One of the key strengths of Tonbridge is that it blends tradition and innovation very successfully, and that high achieving boys wear their gifts lightly.

Our pupils are encouraged to be creative and intellectually curious; to approach new opportunities with confidence; and to learn to think for themselves and develop leadership skills while being mindful of the needs and views of others.

'Only connect'
The question for any family considering a school like ours should be, 'What makes any one school different from another?' The easy answer is the readily visible – the manicured cricket square, the pristine swimming pool, the timeless chapel, the world-class Barton Science Centre.

But what really makes the difference between one school and another is the people. The pupils of all kinds, the staff of all kinds, the parents of all kinds.

For sure, at Tonbridge we have some of the finest, most beautiful facilities and grounds in the country, and yet it is our people who make us stand out. Our latest Good Schools Guide report states: 'Tonbridge is a brilliant school that somehow remains totally unsnobby. Boys make the most of world-class opportunities to learn and have fun, but that is not the best bit – Tonbridge's modern, proactive approach to social responsibility and bursary funding ensures that they stay firmly grounded whilst doing so.'

We encourage the boys to make connections of all kinds, from our traditions to our innovations, from ideas to realities, from high achievement to a strong moral compass.

Our ethos here is 'Only connect' – ultimately to connect a fine mind to a good heart.

Co-curricular

A Tonbridge education includes a vibrant programme of co-curricular breadth and depth. We offer more than 20 sports, and boys of all abilities are encouraged to take part and to enjoy themselves. Tonbridge manages to do 'sporting excellence' and 'mass participation' equally well.

Plays, musicals and drama workshops take place in the School's own EM Forster Theatre. Music also plays an important part in Tonbridge life: nearly half of boys learn an instrument, and about a third learn more than one. We have regular performances and concerts across all genres, as well as an outstanding choral tradition thanks to our School Chapel.

We offer a wide range of clubs, societies and activities, including Junior Science, CCF, Beekeeping, Rocketry, Debating, Robotics and Conservation. Bridge The Gap was started by boys at the School and is about diversity. Wide participation in co-curricular activities is encouraged at both House and School levels.

Social responsibility

Boys at Tonbridge develop a strong sense of belonging to, and serving, both local and wider communities. More than 24,000 hours of volunteering time are given by pupils and staff in a typical year. The annual 'Sleepout' by First Years, for example, has in recent years raised record sums in support of Porchlight, the homelessness charity. Child Action Lanka is Tonbridge's overseas partner charity: following fundraising activities, the School has been able to provide a new computer suite in the Child Action Lanka base in Kilinochchi, Sri Lanka.

Academic achievement

The School is renowned for its high-quality, innovative teaching and learning and for academic achievement. Exam results at GCSE and A-level are outstanding, and each year boys progress to leading universities in the UK and worldwide.

Tonbridge leavers attended more than 50 different institutions between 2018 and 2021, with the largest numbers (other than Oxford and Cambridge) going to high-tariff, leading universities including St Andrews, Durham, Bristol, Exeter, Imperial College, LSE, Manchester, Newcastle, University College London, Southampton, Warwick and York.

A proportion also choose to study abroad and progress to leading universities around the world, particularly in the USA. Destinations have included Berkeley, Columbia, New York University, the University of Toronto and Hong Kong University.

Pastoral care

Pastoral care at Tonbridge is based around an outstanding House system. Strong and positive relationships between boys, staff and parents are central to its success, and the School strives to ensure that each pupil, whether a boarder or a day boy, feels fully at home and well supported.

A culture of House dining supports the family ethos. Mindfulness in schools was first developed at Tonbridge. There is an on-site Medical Centre, Chaplaincy, dedicated school counsellor and welfare group.

St Swithun's School

St Swithun's
WINCHESTER

(Founded 1884)

Alresford Road, Winchester,
Hampshire SO21 1HA
Tel: 01962 835700
Email: office@stswithuns.com
Website: www.stswithuns.com
Head of School:
Jane Gandee MA(Cantab)
Appointed: 2010

School type: Girls' Boarding & Day
Age range of girls: 11–18 years
No. of pupils enrolled as at 01/01/2022: 510
No. of boarders: 220
Fees as at 01/01/2022:
Day: £21,918
Full Boarding: £36,339

St Swithun's School is a renowned independent day, weekly and full-boarding school for girls set in 45 acres overlooking the Hampshire Downs on the outskirts of Winchester, yet only 50 minutes by train from central London. It offers excellent teaching, sporting and recreational facilities.

The school has a long-standing reputation for academic rigour and success. Girls are prepared for public examinations and higher education in a stimulating environment in which they develop intellectual curiosity, independence of mind and the ability to take responsibility for their own learning. They achieve almost one grade higher at GCSE than their already significant baseline ability would suggest, and approximately half a grade higher at A level. St Swithun's offers a comprehensive careers and higher education support service throughout the school years. Its Oxbridge preparation is part of a whole-school academic enrichment programme providing additional challenge and stimulation.

Whilst achieving academic excellence, girls also have the opportunity to do 'something else'. There is an extensive co-curricular programme of over 100 weekly and 50 weekend activities to choose from.

As well as academic classrooms and science laboratories, there is a magnificent performing arts centre with a 600-seat auditorium, a music school, an art and technology block, a sports hall and a full-size indoor swimming pool. There is an impressive library and ICT facility. The grounds are spacious and encompass sports fields, tennis courts and gardens.

With kindness and tolerance at the heart of its community, St Swithun's provides a civilised and caring environment in which all girls are valued for their individual gifts. By the time a girl leaves she will be courageous, compassionate, committed and self-confident with a love of learning, a moral compass and a sense of humour.

Directory

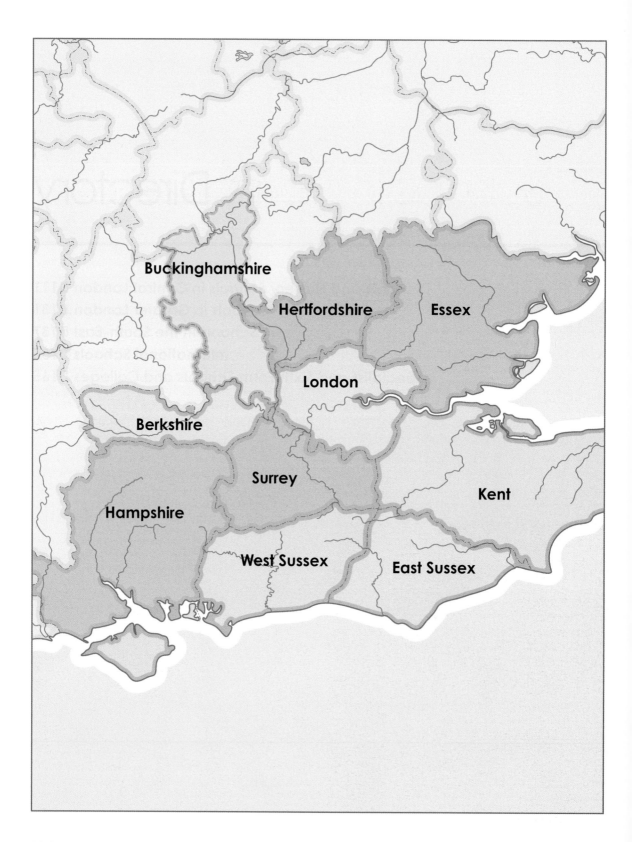

Schools and Nursery Schools in Central London

KEY TO SYMBOLS

- 🧍 *Boys' school*
- 🧍 *Girls' school*
- 🌐 *International school*
- 16 *Tutorial or sixth form college*
- Ⓐ *A levels*
- 🛏 *Boarding accommodation*
- £ *Bursaries*
- IB *International Baccalaureate*
- ✏ *Learning support*
- 16 *Entrance at 16+*
- 🎓 *Vocational qualifications*
- IAPS *Independent Association of Prep Schools*
- HMC *The Headmasters' & Headmistresses' Conference*
- ISA *Independent Schools Association*
- GSA *Girls' School Association*
- BSA *Boarding Schools' Association*
- S *Society of Heads*

Unless otherwise indicated, all schools are coeducational day schools. Single-sex and boarding schools will be indicated by the relevant icon.

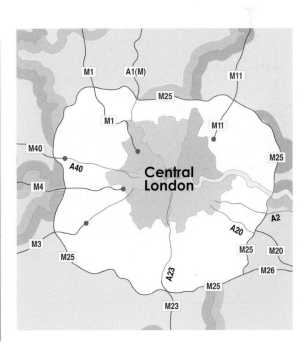

Central London

Accent London
12 Bedford Square,
London WC1B 3JA
Tel: 020 7813 7723
Head: Natasa Blecic

Broadgate Day Nursery
21 Curtain Road, Hackney,
London EC2A 3LW
Tel: 020 7247 3491
Principal: Jacky Roberts NNEB
Age range: 0–5
No. of pupils: 50

CATS London
43-45 Bloomsbury Square,
London WC1A 2RA
Tel: 02078 411580
Principal: Mario Di Clemente
Age range: 15–24

Cavendish College
35-37 Alfred Place,
London WC1E 7DP
Tel: 020 7580 6043
Principal: Dr J Sanders BSc, MBA,
PhD

Charterhouse Square School
40 Charterhouse Square,
London EC1M 6EA
Tel: 020 7600 3805
Head of School: Mrs Caroline Lloyd
BEd (Hons)
Age range: 3–11 years

City Lit Centre & Speech Therapy
Keeley House, Keeley Street,
London WC2B 4BA
Tel: 020 7492 2600
Principal: Mr G W Horgan

City of London School
Queen Victoria Street,
London EC4V 3AL
Tel: 020 3680 6300
Head: Mr A R Bird MSc
Age range: B10–18 years
No. of pupils: 950 VIth250
Fees: Day £19,995

City of London School for Girls
St Giles' Terrace, Barbican,
London EC2Y 8BB
Tel: 020 7847 5500
Headmistress: Mrs E Harrop
Age range: G7–18
No. of pupils: 725

DALLINGTON SCHOOL
For further details see p. 46
8 Dallington Street, Islington,
London EC1V 0BW
Tel: 020 7251 2284
Email: hercules@
dallingtonschool.co.uk
Website:
www.dallingtonschool.co.uk
Head: Linda Kiernan
Age range: 3–11 years
No. of pupils: 81
Fees: Day £11,490–£14,490

ÉCOLE JEANNINE MANUEL – LONDON
For further details see p. 49
43-45 Bedford Square,
London WC1B 3DN
Tel: 020 3829 5970
Email: admissions@
jmanuel.uk.net
Website: www.
ecolejeanninemanuel.org.uk
Head of School: Pauline Prévot
Age range: 3–18 years
No. of pupils: 585
Fees: Day £20,760

Guildhall School of Music & Drama
Barbican, London EC2Y 8DT
Tel: 020 7382 7192
Principal: Barry Ife CBE, FKC,
HonFRAM

Hansard Society
40-43 Chancery Lane,
London WC2A 1JA
Tel: 020 7438 1222
Head: Fiona Booth

Italia Conti Academy of Theatre Arts
Italia Conti House, 23 Goswell
Road, London EC1M 7AJ
Tel: 020 7608 0047
Director: Chris White
Age range: 10–21

Kensington College
23 Bloomsbury Square,
London WC1A 2PJ
Tel: 020 7580 1113

London College of English & Advanced Studies Ltd
178 Goswell Road,
London EC1V 7DT
Tel: 020 7250 0610
Fees: Day £0

London College of International Business Studies
Surrey Quays Road,
London SE16 2XU
Tel: 020 7242 1004
Heads: Mr Philip Moore & Ms Irene
Chong

Royal Academy of Dramatic Art
62-64 Gower Street,
London WC1E 6ED
Tel: 020 7636 7076
Principal: Nicholas Barter MA, FRSA

Smithfield House Children's Nursery
14 West Smithfield,
London EC1A 9HY
Tel: 020 7236 1000
Manager: Janet MacGregor
Age range: 0–5

ST PAUL'S CATHEDRAL SCHOOL
For further details see p. 73
2 New Change,
London EC4M 9AD
Tel: 020 7248 5156
Email: admissions@
spcs.london.sch.uk
Website: www.spcslondon.com
Headmaster: Simon Larter-Evans
BA (Hons), PGCE, FRSA
Age range: 4–13 years
No. of pupils: 258
Fees: Day £15,174–
£16,338 FB £9,178

The College of Central London
Tower Bridge Business Centre, 46-48
East Smithfield, London E1W 1AW
Tel: +44 (0) 20 3667 7607

The Courtauld Institute of Art
Somerset House, Strand,
London WC2R 0RN
Tel: 020 7848 2777
Director: Dr Deborah Swallow

The London Film School
24 Shelton Street,
London WC2H 9UB
Tel: 020 7836 9642
Director: Ben Gibson
Fees: Day £0

The Lyceum School
65 Worship Street,
London EC2A 2DU
Tel: +44 (0)20 7247 1588
Headmistress: Mrs Hilary Wyatt
Age range: 3–11 years

The Method Studio London
Conway Hall, 25 Red Lion
Square, London WC1R 4RL
Tel: 020 7831 7335

Urdang Academy
The Old Finsbury Town
Hall, Rosebery Avenue,
London EC1R 4RP
Tel: +44 (0)20 7713 7710
Age range: 16+

Williams College
Thavies Inn House, 5 Holborn
Circus, London EC1N 2HB
Tel: 020 7583 9222
Head: Mr Mujeeb Pathamanathan

East London

Al-Falah Primary School
48 Kenninghall Road,
Hackney, London E5 8BY
Tel: 020 8985 1059
Headteacher: Mr M A Hussain
Age range: 5–11

Al-Mizan School
46 Whitechapel Road,
London E1 1JX
Tel: 020 7650 3070
Head: Mr Askor Ali
Age range: B7–11

Alphabet House Day (Montessori) Nursery
Methodist Church, Windmill
Lane, Stratford, London E15 1PG
Tel: 020 8519 2023
Principal: Ms Kemi Balogun

Alphabet House Nursery School
23 Harold Road, Upton
Park, London E13 0SQ
Tel: 020 8548 9466
Principal: Ms Kemi Balogun

Ann Tayler Children's Centre
1-13 Triangle Road (off Westgate
Street), Hackney, London E8 3RP
Tel: 020 7275 6022
Fees: Day £10

Azhar Academy
235A Romford Road, Forest
Gate, London E7 9HL
Tel: 020 8534 5959
Headteacher: Mrs R Rehman
Age range: G11–16
No. of pupils: 189

Beis Trana Girls' School
186 Upper Clapton Road,
London E5 9DH
Tel: 020 8815 8000
Head of School: Mrs M Shmaya
Age range: G3–16

Bethnal Green Montessori School
68 Warner Place, Bethnal Green, London E2 7DA
Tel: 020 7739 4343
Head: Sidonie Winter
Age range: 2–6

Building Crafts College
Kennard Road, Stratford, London E15 1AH
Tel: 020 8522 1705
Principal: Mr John Taylor
16+ ✿

Busy Bees at Chingford
2 Larkswood Leisure Park, 175 New Road, Chingford, London E4 9EY
Tel: 020 8524 7063
Nursery Manager: Natalie Keyes
Age range: 3 months–5 years

Busy Bees in London ExCel
5 Western Gateway, Royal Victoria Docks, London E16 1XL
Tel: 020 7474 7487
Nursery Manager: Rebecca Davy
Age range: 0–5

Chingford House School
22 Marlborough Road, Waltham Forest, London E4 9AL
Tel: 020 8527 2902; 07749 899 498
Head teacher: Helen McNulty
Age range: 0–5
✐

City of London College
71 Whitechapel High Street, London E1 7PL
Tel: 020 7247 2166
Head: Mr David Nixon
16+

East End Computing & Business College
149 Commercial Road, London E1 1PX
Tel: 020 7247 8447
Head: Anthony Wilkinson
16+

Forest School
College Place, Snaresbrook, London E17 3PY
Tel: 020 8520 1744
Warden: Mr Cliff Hodges
Age range: 4–18
No. of pupils: 1355 VIth260
Fees: Day £13,095–£18,681
A £ ✐ 16+

Gatehouse School
Sewardstone Road, Victoria Park, London E2 9JG
Tel: 020 8980 2978
Head of School: Mrs Sevda Corby
Age range: 3–11 years
No. of pupils: 489
Fees: Day £4,130–£4,353
✐

Grangewood Independent School
Chester Road, Forest Gate, London E7 8QT
Tel: 020 8472 3552
Headteacher: Mrs B A Roberts B.Ed (Hons); PG Cert (SEN)
Age range: 2–11
No. of pupils: 71
Fees: Day £5,157–£6,751
✐

Happy Faces at Wisdom Kids Nursery
524 High Street, London E12 6QN
Tel: 020 8478 2805

Hyland House School
Holcombe Road, Tottenham, London N17 9AD
Tel: 0208 520 4186
Head Teacher: Mrs Gina Abbequaye
Age range: 3–11
Fees: Day £2,520

Independent Place Nursery
26/27 Independent Place, Shacklewell Lane, Hackney, London E8 2HD
Tel: 020 7275 7755
Head: Ms Dawn Pennington
Age range: 0–5
No. of pupils: 43
✐

Kaye Rowe Nursery School
Osborne Road, London E7 0PH
Tel: 020 8534 4403

Kids Inc Day Nursery – Chingford
3 Friday Hill West, Chingford Hatch, London E4 6UP
Tel: 020 8524 6745

Kids Inc Day Nursery – South Woodford
71 Cleveland Road, South Woodford, London E18 2AE
Tel: 020 8518 8855

Lanterns Nursery and Pre-school
Unit D, Great Eastern Enterprise Centre, 3 Millharbour, London E14 9XP
Tel: 020 7363 0951

Little Green Man Nursery
15 Lemna Road, Waltham Forest, London E11 1HX
Tel: 020 8539 7228
Age range: 0–5
No. of pupils: 46

London East Academy
46 Whitechapel Road, London E1 1JX
Tel: 020 7650 3070
Headteacher: Askor Ali
Age range: B11–18
✝ Ⓐ

London School of Commerce & IT
128 Commercial Road, London E1 1NL
Tel: 020 7702 2509
Head: Dr Abul Kalam
16+

Low Hall Nursery
Low Hall Lane, London E17 8BE
Tel: 020 8520 1689

Lubavitch House School (Junior Boys)
135 Clapton Common, London E5 9AE
Tel: 020 8800 1044
Head: Mr R Leach
Age range: B5–11
No. of pupils: 101
✝

Madani Girls School
Myrdle Street, London E1 1HL
Tel: 020 7377 1992
Headteacher: Muhammad S. Rahman
Age range: G11–18 years
✝

Magic Roundabout Nursery – Docklands
Jack Dash House, 2 Lawn House Close, Marsh Wall, London E14 9YQ
Tel: 020 7364 6028

Magic Roundabout Nursery – Walthamstow
161 Wadham Road, Centre Way, Walthamstow, London E17 4HU
Tel: 020 8523 5551

Market Nursery
Wilde Close, Off Pownall Road, Hackney, London E8 4JS
Tel: 020 7241 0978
Head: Ms Hazel Babb
No. of pupils: 24
✐

Noah's Ark Nursery
within Mildmay Hospital, Hackney Road, London E2 7NA
Tel: 020 7613 6346

Normanhurst School
68-74 Station Road, Chingford, London E4 7BA
Tel: 020 8529 4307
Headmistress: Mrs Claire Osborn
Age range: 2–16
No. of pupils: 250
Fees: Day £10,350–£13,050
✐

Oliver Thomas Nursery School
Mathews Avenue, East Ham, London E6 6BU
Tel: 020 8552 1177
Head Teacher: Dianne Walls
Age range: 3–5
✐

Pillar Box Montessori Nursery & Pre-Prep School
107 Bow Road, London E3 2AN
Tel: 020 8980 0700
Director: Lorraine Redknapp
Age range: 2–5
Fees: Day £12,000

Quwwat-ul Islam Girls School
16 Chaucer Road, Forest Gate, London E7 9NB
Tel: 020 8548 4736
Headteacher: Ms Shazia Member
Age range: G4–11
✝

River House Montessori School
3-4 Shadwell Pierhead, Glamis Road, London E1W 3TD
Tel: 020 7538 9886
Headmistress: Miss S Greenwood
Age range: 3–16
Fees: Day £3,410–£3,625
✐

Snaresbrook Preparatory School
75 Woodford Road, South Woodford, London E18 2EA
Tel: 020 8989 2394
Head of School: Mr Ralph Dalton
Age range: 3–11
Fees: Day £8,922–£11,934
✐

Talmud Torah Machzikei Hadass School
1 Belz Terrace, Clapton, London E5 9SN
Tel: 020 8800 6599
Headteacher: Rabbi C Silbiger
Age range: B3–16
✝

The Grove Montessori Nursery
Grosvenor Road, Wanstead, London E11 2EW
Tel: 0203 404 4380
Age range: 3 months–5 years

The Happy Nest Nursery Ltd
Fellows Court Family Centre, Weymouth Terrace, Hackney, London E2 8LR
Tel: 020 7739 3193

The Music School
59a High Street, Wanstead, London E11 2AE
Tel: 020 8502 0932
16+

Tom Thumb Nursery
1-7 Beulah Road, London E17 9LG
Tel: 020 8520 1329
Age range: 2–5
No. of pupils: 32

Treehouse Nursery Schools – Cambridge Park
25 Cambridge Park,
Wanstead, London E11 2PU
Tel: 020 853 22535
Age range: 3 months–5 years

Treehouse Nursery Schools – Woodbine Place
35 Woodbine Place,
London E11 2RH
Tel: 020 8532 2535
Age range: 3 months–5 years

Whitechapel College
67 Maryland Square,
Stratford, London E15 1HF
Tel: 020 8555 3355
Principal: Luke Julias Maughan-Pawsey
16+

Winston House Preparatory School
140 High Road, London E18 2QS
Tel: 020 8505 6565
Head Teacher: Mrs Marian Kemp
Age range: 3–11

North London

5 E College of London
Selby Centre, Selby Road,
London N17 8JL
Tel: 020 8885 3456/5454
Head: Mr Raj Doshi
16+

Annemount School
18 Holne Chase, Hampstead
Garden Suburb, London N2 0QN
Tel: 020 8455 2132
Principal: Mrs G Maidment
BA(Hons), MontDip
Age range: 2–7 years

Asquith Nursery – Crouch Hill
33 Crouch Hill, London N4 4AP
Tel: 020 7561 1533

Avenue Pre-Prep & Nursery School
2 Highgate Avenue,
Highgate, London N6 5RX
Tel: 020 8348 6815
Principal: Mrs. Mary Fysh
Age range: 2–8

Beis Chinuch Lebonos Girls School
Woodberry Down Centre,
Woodberry Down, London N4 2SH
Tel: 020 88097 737
Age range: G2–16

Beis Malka Girls School
93 Alkham Road, London N16 6XD
Tel: 020 8806 2070
Age range: G2–16

Beis Rochel D'Satmar Girls School
51-57 Amhurst Park, London N16 5DL
Tel: 020 8800 9060
Headmistress: Mrs E Katz
Age range: G2–18

Bnois Jerusalem School
79-81 Amhurst Park,
London N16 5DL
Tel: 020 8211 7136
Age range: G3–16

Bobov Primary School
87-90 Egerton Road,
London N16 6UE
Tel: 020 8809 1025
Headmaster: Mr Chaim Weissman
Age range: B3–13

Busy Bees at Enfield Highlands Village
2 Florey Square, Highlands
Village, London N21 1UJ
Tel: 020 8360 6610
Nursery Manager: Simone Prince
Age range: 3 months–5 years

Busy Bees Nursery
c/o David Lloyd Leisure Club,
Leisure Way, High Road,
Finchley, London N12 0QZ
Tel: 020 8343 8500
Manager: Toni Difonzo
Age range: 3months–5
No. of pupils: 18

Channing School
The Bank, Highgate, London N6 5HF
Tel: 020 8340 2328
Head: Mrs B M Elliott
Age range: G4–18
No. of pupils: 746 VIth108
Fees: Day £17,610–£19,410

City of London Business College
Ebenezer House, 726-728 Seven
Sisters Road, London N15 5NH
Tel: 020 8800 6621
Head: Mr Kwateng
16+

Coconut Nursery
133 Stoke Newington Church
Street, London N16 0UH
Tel: 020 7923 0720

Court Theatre Training Co
55 East Road, London N1 6AH
Tel: 020 7739 6868
Artistic Director: June Abbott
16+

Dwight School London
6 Friern Barnet Lane,
London N11 3LX
Tel: 020 8920 0600
Head: Chris Beddows
Age range: 2–18 years

Finchley & Acton Yochien School
6 Hendon Avenue, Finchley,
London N3 1UE
Tel: 020 8343 2191
Headteacher: J Tanabe
Age range: 2–6
No. of pupils: 145

Finsbury Park Day Nursery & Preschool
Dulas Street, Finsbury Park,
Islington, London N4 3AF
Tel: 0330 127 2279

Floral Place Day Nursery
2 Floral Place, Northampton
Grove, London N1 2PL
Tel: 020 7354 9945

Grange Park Preparatory School
13 The Chine, Grange Park,
Winchmore Hill, London N21 2EA
Tel: 020 8360 1469
Headteacher: Miss F Rizzo
Age range: G4–11
No. of pupils: 90
Fees: Day £10,300–£10,378

Greek Secondary School of London
22 Trinity Road, London N22 8LB
Tel: +44 (0)20 8881 9320
Headteacher: Nikos Kazantzakis
Age range: 13–18
(A) 16+

Hackney Care For Kids
61 Evering Road, Hackney,
London N16 7PR
Tel: 020 7923 3471

Highgate
North Road, Highgate,
London N6 4AY
Tel: 020 8340 1524
Head Master: Mr A S Pettitt MA
Age range: 3–18
No. of pupils: 1541 VIth312
Fees: Day £18,165–£20,970
(A) (£) 16+

Highgate Junior School
Cholmeley House, 3 Bishopswood
Road, London N6 4PL
Tel: 020 8340 9193
Principal: Mr S M James BA
Age range: 7–11
Fees: Day £19,230

Highgate Pre-Preparatory School
7 Bishopswood Road,
London N6 4PH
Tel: 020 8340 9196
Principal: Mrs Diane Hecht
Age range: 3–7
No. of pupils: 150
Fees: Day £18,165

Impact Factory
Suite 121, Business Design Centre,
52 Upper Street, London N1 0QH
Tel: 020 7226 1877
Founding Partners: Robin Chandler & Jo Ellen Grzyb
16+

Keble Prep
Wades Hill, Winchmore
Hill, London N21 1BG
Tel: 020 8360 3359
Headmaster: Mr P Gill BA (Hons)
Age range: B4–13 years

Kerem House
18 Kingsley Way, London N2 0ER
Tel: 020 8455 7524
Headmistress: Mrs D Rose
Age range: 2–5
No. of pupils: 96
Fees: Day £2,025–£5,160

Kerem School
Norrice Lea, London N2 0RE
Tel: 020 8455 0909
Head Teacher: Miss Alyson Burns
Age range: 3–11
Fees: Day £9,435

Laurel Way Playgroup
Nansen Village, 21 Woodside
Avenue, London N12 8AQ
Tel: 020 8445 7514
Head: Mrs Susan Farber
Age range: 3–5

London Studio Centre
42-50 York Way, Kings
Cross, London N1 9AB
Tel: 020 7837 7741
Director & CEO: Mr Nic Espinosa
Age range: 18+
16+

Lubavitch House School (Senior Girls)
107-115 Stamford Hill,
Hackney, London N16 5RP
Tel: 020 8800 0022
Headmaster: Rabbi Shmuel Lew
FRSA
Age range: G11–18
No. of pupils: 102
Fees: Day £3,900
(A)

Lubavitch Orthodox Jewish Nursery – North London
107-115 Stamford Hill,
Hackney, London N16 5RP
Tel: 020 8800 0022
Head: Mrs F Sudak

MARS Montessori Islington Green Nursery
4 Collins Yard, Islington Green, London N1 2XU
Tel: 020 7704 2805
Head: Angela Euesden
Age range: 2–5
No. of pupils: 24

New Park Montessori School
67 Highbury New Park, Islington, London N5 2EU
Tel: 020 7226 1109

New Southgate Day and Nursery School
60 Beaconsfield Road, New Southgate, London N11 3AE
Tel: 0333 920 4841
Nursery Manager: Ms Katerina Barotsaki
Age range: 3 months–5 years

Norfolk House School
10 Muswell Avenue, Muswell Hill, London N10 2EG
Tel: 020 8883 4584
Headteacher: Mr Paul Jowett
Age range: 2–11
No. of pupils: 220
Fees: Day £4,143

North London Grammar School
110 Colindeep Lane, Hendon, London NW9 6HB
Tel: 0208 205 0052
Headteacher: Mr Fatih Adak
Age range: 7–18 years

North London Rudolf Steiner School
1-3 The Campsbourne, London N8 7PN
Tel: 020 8341 3770
Age range: 0–7
No. of pupils: 40

One-Tech (UK) Ltd
1st Floor, 12 Cheapside, High Road, London N22 6HH
Tel: 020 8889 0707
Head: Mr Len Sutherland

Palmers Green High School
Hoppers Road, Winchmore Hill, London N21 3LJ
Tel: 020 8886 1135
Headmistress: Mrs Wendy Kempster
Age range: G3–16
No. of pupils: 300
Fees: Day £5,880–£15,930

Pardes House Primary School
Hendon Lane, Finchley, London N3 1SA
Tel: 020 8343 3568
Headteacher: Rabbi J Sager MA, B.Ed, NPQH, FCCT
Age range: B4–11 years

Pentland Day Nursery
224 Squires Lane, Finchley, London N3 2QL
Tel: 020 8970 2441
Principal: Rachele Parker

Phoenix Academy
85 Bounces Road, Edmonton, London N9 8LD
Tel: 020 8887 6888
Headteacher: Mr Paul Kelly
Age range: 5–18
No. of pupils: 19

Phoenix Montessori Nursery
27 Stamford Hill, London N16 5TN
Tel: 020 8880 2550
Manageress: Kelly Murphy
Age range: 0–5 years

Rainbow Nursery
Yorkshire Grove Estate, 22-26 Nevill Road, London N16 8SP
Tel: 020 7254 7930
Age range: 3 months–5 years

Rosemary Works Independent School
1 Branch Place, London N1 5PH
Tel: 020 7739 3950
Head: Rob Dell
Age range: 3–11
No. of pupils: 104
Fees: Day £14,097

Salcombe Day Nursery & Preschool
33 The Green, Southgate, London N14 6EN
Tel: 0371 705 3478

Salcombe Preparatory School
224-226 Chase Side, Southgate, London N14 4PL
Tel: 020 8441 5356
Headmistress: Mrs Sarah-Jane Davies BA(Hons) QTS MEd
Age range: 3–11
No. of pupils: 250
Fees: Day £11,673

Salcombe Pre-School
Green Road, Southgate, London N14 4AD
Tel: 020 8441 5356
Headmistress: Mrs Sarah-Jane Davies BA(Hons) QTS MEd

Shakhsiyah School, London
1st Floor, 277 St Ann's Road, London N15 5RG
Tel: 020 8802 8651
Head Teacher: Mrs Foziya Reddy
Age range: 3–14 years

St Andrew's Montessori
St Andrew's Church, Thornhill Square, London N1 1BQ
Tel: 020 7700 2961
Principal: Samantha Rawson MontDip
Age range: 2–6
No. of pupils: 40
Fees: Day £4,200–£6,525

St Paul's Steiner School
1 St Paul's Road, Islington, London N1 2QH
Tel: 020 7226 4454
College of Teachers: College of Teachers
Age range: 2–14
No. of pupils: 136

Sunrise Nursery, Stoke Newington
1 Cazenove Road, Stoke Newington, Hackney, London N16 6PA
Tel: 020 8806 6279
Principal: Didi Ananda Manika

Sunrise Primary School
55 Coniston Road, Tottenham, London N17 0EX
Tel: 020 8806 6279 (Office); 020 8885 3354 (School)
Head: Mrs Mary-Anne Lovage MontDipEd, BA
Age range: 2–11
No. of pupils: 30
Fees: Day £5,550

Talmud Torah Chaim Meirim School
26 Lampard Grove, London N16 6XB
Tel: 020 8806 0898
Principal: Rabbi S Hoffman
Age range: B4–13

Talmud Torah Yetev Lev School
111-115 Cazenove Road, London N16 6AX
Tel: 020 8806 3834
Age range: B2–11 years

Tawhid Boys School
21 Cazenove Road, London N16 6PA
Tel: 020 8806 2999
Headteacher: Mr Usman Mapara
Age range: B10–15
No. of pupils: 115

Tayyibah Girls School
88 Filey Avenue, Hackney, London N16 6JJ
Tel: 020 8880 0085
Headmistress: Mrs N B Qureishi MSc
Age range: G5–18

The Children's House School Nursery
77 Elmore Street, London N1 3AQ
Tel: 020 7354 2113
Head of School: Salima Keshavjee
Age range: 2–4 years
Fees: Day £3,060–£5,020

The Children's House Upper School
King Henry's Walk, London N1 4PB
Tel: 020 7249 6273
Head of School: Kate Orange
Age range: 4–7 years
Fees: Day £5,310

The City College
University House, 55 East Road, London N1 6AH
Tel: 020 7253 1133
Principal: A Andrews MCMI
Age range: 18–40

The Dance Studio
2 Farm Road,, Winchmore Hill, London N21 3JA
Tel: 020 8360 5700

The Gower School Montessori Nursery
18 North Road, Islington, London N7 9EY
Tel: 020 7700 2445
Principal: Miss Emma Gowers
Age range: 3 months–5 years
No. of pupils: 237

The Gower School Montessori Primary
10 Cynthia Street, Barnsbury, London N1 9JF
Tel: 020 7278 2020
Principal: Miss Emma Gowers
Age range: 4–11
No. of pupils: 237
Fees: Day £15,576

The Grove Nursery
Shepperton House, 83-93 Shepperton Road, Islington, London N1 3DF
Tel: 020 7226 4037
Owners: Ms Rebecca Browne & Ms Elaine Catchpole
Age range: 0–5

The Highgate Activity Nurseries
1 Church Road, Highgate, London N6 4QH
Tel: 020 8348 9248
Head: Helena Prior
Age range: 2–5
Fees: Day £5,460–£9,620

The Sam Morris Nursery
Sam Morris Centre, Parkside Crescent, London N7 7JG
Tel: 020 7609 1735

TTTYY School
14 Heathland Road,
London N16 5NH
Tel: 020 8802 1348
Head of School: Rabbi A Friesel
Age range: B2–13

Twinkle Stars Day Nursery
416 Seven Sisters Road,
Hackney, London N4 2LX
Tel: 020 8802 0550
Admin Officer: Noori Mohamed
Age range: 1–5

Vita et Pax School
Priory Close, Southgate,
London N14 4AT
Tel: 020 8449 8336
Headteacher: Miss Gillian
Chumbley
Age range: 3–11
Fees: Day £9,360

Woodberry Day Nursery
63 Church Hill, Winchmore
Hill, London N21 1LE
Tel: 020 8882 6917
Manager: Michelle Miller
Age range: 6 weeks–5
No. of pupils: 62

**Yesodey Hatorah
Senior Girls' School**
Egerton Road, London N16 6UB
Tel: 020 8826 5500
Acting Head Teacher: Mrs C
Neuberger
Age range: 3–16
No. of pupils: 920

North-West London

Abbey Nursery School
Cricklewood Baptist Church,
Sneyd Road, Cricklewood,
London NW2 6AN
Tel: 020 8208 2202
Head: Mrs Ruby Azam

Al-Sadiq & Al-Zahra Schools
134 Salusbury Road,
London NW6 6PF
Tel: 020 7372 7706
Headteacher: Dr M Movahedi
Age range: 4–16

Arnold House School
1 Loudoun Road, St John's
Wood, London NW8 0LH
Tel: 020 7266 4840
Headmaster: Mr Giles F Tollit
Age range: B3–13 years

Barnet Hill Academy
10A Montagu Road, Hendon,
London NW4 3ES
Tel: 02034112660
Principal: Mr Alim Shaikh MA,
PGCE, MPhil, NPQH
Age range: 3–11 G11–16
Fees: Day £3,000

**Beehive On Queens
Park Montessori School**
147 Chevening Rd,
London NW6 6DZ
Tel: 020 8969 2235
Headmistress: Ms Lucilla Baj
Age range: 2–5
Fees: Day £2,550

Beis Soroh Schneirer
Arbiter House, Wilberforce
Road, London NW9 6AX
Tel: 020 8201 7771
Head of School: Mrs Sonia
Mossberg
Age range: G2–11

**Belmont, Mill Hill
Preparatory School**
The Ridgeway, London NW7 4ED
Tel: 020 8906 7270
Headmaster: Mr Leon Roberts MA
Age range: 7–13 years
No. of pupils: 550
Fees: Day £19,560

**Beth Jacob Grammar
School for Girls**
Stratford Road, Hendon,
London NW4 2AT
Tel: 020 8203 4322
Headteacher: Mrs M Gluck
Age range: G11–17

Bluebells Nursery
Our Lady Help of Christians
Church Hall, Lady Margaret
Road, London NW5 2NE
Tel: 020 7284 3952
Principal: Ms Anita Pearson
Age range: 2–5
No. of pupils: 20

Brampton College
Lodge House, Lodge Road,
Hendon, London NW4 4DQ
Tel: 020 8203 5025
Principal: B Canetti BA(Hons), MSc
Age range: 15–20
Fees: Day £19,935

**Bright Horizons
Bush Hill Park**
2 Queen Anne's Place, Bush Hill
Park, Enfield, London EN1 2PX
Tel: 0333 242 6851

**British American
Drama Academy**
14 Gloucester Gate,
London NW1 4HG
Tel: 020 7487 0730
Head: Paul Costello

Broadhurst School
19 Greencroft Gardens,
London NW6 3LP
Tel: 020 7328 4280
Headmistress: Mrs Zoe Sylvester
Age range: 2–5
No. of pupils: 145
Fees: Day £6,480–£10,950

**Brondesbury
College for Boys**
8 Brondesbury Park,
London NW6 7BT
Tel: 020 8830 4522
Headteacher: Mr Amzad Ali
Age range: B11–16
No. of pupils: 93

Busy Bees at Mill Hill
30 Mill Way, Mill Hill,
London NW7 3RB
Tel: 0208 906 9123
Nursery Manager: Danielle Baker
Age range: 0–5

**Camden Community
Nurseries**
16 Acol Road, London NW6 3AG
Tel: 020 7624 2937

**Chaston Nursery & Pre-
preparatory School**
Chaston Place, Off Grafton
Terrace, London NW5 4JH
Tel: 020 7482 0701
Head: Mrs Sandra Witten DipEd,
DMS
Age range: 0–5
No. of pupils: 69
Fees: Day £7,020–£12,732

City Mission Nursery
2 Scrub Lane, London NW10 6RB
Tel: 020 8960 0838
Age range: 6 months–5 years

**Collège Français
Bilingue de Londres**
87 Holmes Road, Kentish
Town, London NW5 3AX
Tel: 020 7993 7400
**Head of School (from September
2021):** Mr David Gassian
Age range: 3–15 years
No. of pupils: 700

**Francis Holland School,
Regent's Park, NW1**
Clarence Gate, Ivor Place,
Regent's Park, London NW1 6XR
Tel: 020 7723 0176
Head: Mr C B Fillingham MA (King's
College London)
Age range: G11–18
No. of pupils: 495 VIth120
Fees: Day £19,260

**Golders Green Day
Nursery & Preschool**
212 Golders Green Road, Golders
Green, London NW11 9AT
Tel: 0371 454 3885

Golders Hill School
666 Finchley Road,
London NW11 7NT
Tel: 020 8455 2589
Headmistress: Mrs A T Eglash
BA(Hons)
Age range: 2–7
No. of pupils: 180
Fees: Day £1,575–£13,827

Goodwyn School
Hammers Lane, Mill Hill,
London NW7 4DB
Tel: 020 8959 3756
Principal: Struan Robertson
Age range: 3–11
No. of pupils: 193
Fees: Day £5,436–£11,943

**Grimsdell, Mill Hill Pre-
Preparatory School**
Winterstoke House, Wills Grove,
Mill Hill, London NW7 1QR
Tel: 020 8959 6884
Head: Mrs Kate Simon BA, PGCE
Age range: 3–7 years
No. of pupils: 188
Fees: Day £15,095

**Hampstead Fine
Arts College**
Centre Studios, 41-43 England's
Lane, London NW3 4YD
Tel: +44 (0)207 586 0312
Principal: Ms Candida Cave
Age range: 13–19 years

**Hampstead Hill Pre-
Prep & Nursery School**
St Stephen's Hall, Pond Street,
Hampstead, London NW3 2PP
Tel: 020 7435 6262
Principal: Mrs Andrea Taylor
Age range: B2–7+ G2–7+
Fees: Day £10,175–£16,830

Happy Child Day Nursery
St Anne's & St Andrew's Church
Hall, 125 Salusbury Road, Queens
Park, London NW6 6RG
Tel: 020 7625 1966
Age range: 2–5

Heathside School Hampstead
84a Heath Street, Hampstead,
London NW3 1DN
Tel: +44 (0)20 3058 4011
Headteacher: Katherine Vintiner
Age range: 2–13 years
No. of pupils: 230
Fees: Day £16,800–£19,400

Hendon Day Nursery & Preschool
46 Allington Road, Hendon,
London NW4 3DE
Tel: 0330 127 7304

Hendon Prep School
20 Tenterden Grove, Hendon,
London NW4 1TD
Tel: 020 8203 7727
Head of School: Mrs Tushi Gorasia
Age range: 2–11 years
No. of pupils: 165
Fees: Day £6,975–£15,600

Hereward House School
14 Strathray Gardens,
Hampstead, London NW3 4NY
Tel: 020 7794 4820
Headmaster: Mr P Evans
Age range: B4–13 years
Fees: Day £15,615–£16,065

Highgate Day Nursery and Preschool
Highgate Studios, 53-79 Highgate
Road, London NW5 1TL
Tel: 020 7485 5252
Principal: Lorraine Thompson

ICS London
7B Wyndham Place,
London W1H 1PN
Tel: +44 (0)20 729 88800
Head of School: David Laird
Age range: 3–19 years
No. of pupils: 175
Fees: Day £19,650–£28,770

IRIS School
100 Carlton Vale, London NW6 5HE
Tel: 020 7372 8051
Headteacher: Mr Seyed Abbas Hosseini
Age range: 6–16 years

Islamia Girls' High School
129 Salusbury Road,
London NW6 6PE
Tel: 020 7372 3472
Headteacher: Mrs Fawziah Islam
Age range: G11–16 years
Fees: Day £6,900

Joel Nursery
214 Colindeep Lane, Colindale,
London NW9 6DF
Tel: 020 820 00189
Age range: 3 months–5 years

Kentish Town Day Nursery
37 Ryland Road, London NW5 3EH
Tel: 020 7284 3600
Manager: Carol Kewley
Age range: 3 months–5 years
No. of pupils: 55

Lakefield Catering & Educational Centre
Maresfield Gardens,
Hampstead, London NW3 5RY
Tel: 020 7794 5669
Course Director: Mrs Maria Brown
Age range: G16–24
No. of pupils: 16
Fees: FB £1,160

London Academy of Dressmaking and Design
18 Dobree Avenue, Willesden,
London NW10 2AE
Tel: 020 8451 7174
Principal: Mrs P A Parkinson MA
Age range: 13+
Fees: Day £2,650

LYNDHURST HOUSE PREP SCHOOL
For further details see p. 56
24 Lyndhurst Gardens,
Hampstead, London NW3 5NW
Tel: 020 7435 4936
Email: jorrett@
lyndhursthouse.co.uk
Website:
www.lyndhursthouse.co.uk
Head of School: Mr Andrew Reid
MA (Oxon)
Age range: B4–13 years
No. of pupils: 125
Fees: Day £18,360–£20,790

MAPLE WALK PREP SCHOOL
For further details see p. 60
62A Crownhill Road,
London NW10 4EB
Tel: 020 8963 3890
Email: admin@
maplewalkschool.co.uk
Website:
www.maplewalkschool.co.uk
Head Teacher: Claire Murdoch
Age range: 4–11 years
No. of pupils: 190
Fees: Day £3,866

Maria Montessori Children's House – West Hampstead
St Mary's Community Hall, 134a
Abbey Road, London NW6 4SN
Tel: 020 7624 5917

Maria Montessori Institute
26 Lyndhurst Gardens,
Hampstead, London NW3 5NW
Tel: 020 7435 3646
Director of Training & School: Mrs
Lynne Lawrence BA, Mont Int
Dip(AMI)
Age range: 2–12
No. of pupils: 50
Fees: Day £5,580–£13,560

Maria Montessori School – Hampstead
26 Lyndhurst Gardens,
Hampstead, London NW3 5NW
Tel: +44 (0)20 7435 3646
Director of School: Miss L Kingston
Age range: 2–12
No. of pupils: 100
Fees: Day £6,270–£13,560

Mill Hill School
The Ridgeway, Mill Hill
Village, London NW7 1QS
Tel: 020 8959 1176
Head: Mrs Jane Sanchez BSc (Hons)
PGCE
Age range: 13–18 years
No. of pupils: 876 VIth312
Fees: Day £21,987 WB
£31,140 FB £36,900

Naima Jewish Preparatory School
21 Andover Place, London NW6 5ED
Tel: 020 7328 2802
Headmaster: Mr Bill Pratt
Age range: 3–11

Nancy Reuben Primary School
Finchley Lane, Hendon,
London NW4 1DJ
Tel: 020 82025646
Head: Anthony Wolfson
Age range: 3–11
No. of pupils: 207

NORTH BRIDGE HOUSE NURSERY AND PRE-PREP HAMPSTEAD
8 Netherhall Gardens,
London NW3 5RR
Tel: 020 7428 1520
Head of School: Mrs
Christine McLelland
Age range: 2–7 years
No. of pupils: 190

NORTH BRIDGE HOUSE NURSERY AND PRE-PREP WEST HAMPSTEAD
85-87 Fordwych Rd,
London NW2 3TL
Tel: 020 7428 1520
Head of School: Mrs
Christine McLelland
Age range: 2–7 years

NORTH BRIDGE HOUSE PREP SCHOOL REGENT'S PARK
1 Gloucester Avenue,
London NW1 7AB
Tel: 020 7428 1520
Head of School: Mr
James Stenning
Age range: 7–13 years
No. of pupils: 385
Fees: Day £18,960–£20,520

NORTH BRIDGE HOUSE SENIOR CANONBURY
6-9 Canonbury Place,
Islington, London N1 2NQ
Tel: 020 7428 1520
Head of School: Mr
Brendan Pavey
Age range: 11–18 years
No. of pupils: 220
Fees: Day £19,230–£21,735

NORTH BRIDGE HOUSE SENIOR HAMPSTEAD
For further details see p. 62
65 Rosslyn Hill, London NW3 5UD
Tel: 020 7428 1520
Email: admissionsenquiries@
northbridgehouse.com
Website:
www.northbridgehouse.com
Head of Nursery & Pre-Prep Schools: Mrs. Christine
McLelland
Age range: 2–18 years
No. of pupils: 1430

NW5 Theatre School
14 Fortess Road, London NW5 2EU
Tel: 020 8340 1498
Age range: 16–30

Rainbow Montessori School
13 Woodchurch Road,
Hampstead, London NW6 3PL
Tel: 020 7328 8986
Head Mistress: Maggy Miller
MontDip
Age range: 2–5
Fees: Day £12,240–£12,417

Ready Steady Go – Camden
123 St Pancras Way,
London NW1 0SY
Tel: 020 7586 5862
Age range: 2–4

Ready Steady Go – Fitzroy Road
Primrose Hill Community Centre,
29 Hopkinson's Place, Fitzroy
Road, London NW1 8TN
Tel: 020 7586 5862
Age range: 2–3

Ready Steady Go – Primrose Hill
12a King Henry's Road, London NW3 3RP
Tel: 020 7586 5862
Age range: 3–5

Ready Steady Go – St John's Wood
21 Alexandra Road, London NW8 0DP
Tel: 020 7586 5862
Age range: 2–5

Saint Christina's School
25 St Edmunds Terrace, Regent's Park, London NW8 7PY
Tel: 020 7722 8784
Headteacher: Miss J Finlayson
Age range: 3–11
No. of pupils: 224
Fees: Day £13,500
£ ✐

SARUM HALL SCHOOL
For further details see p. 68
15 Eton Avenue, London NW3 3EL
Tel: 020 7794 2261
Email: admissions@sarumhallschool.co.uk
Website: www.sarumhallschool.co.uk
Headteacher: Victoria Savage
Age range: G3–11 years
No. of pupils: 184
☗ £

South Hampstead High School GDST
3 Maresfield Gardens, London NW3 5SS
Tel: 020 7435 2899
Head of School: Mrs V Bingham
Age range: G4–18
No. of pupils: 900
Fees: Day £15,327–£18,654
☗ A £ ✐ 16+

Southbank International School – Hampstead
16 Netherhall Gardens, London NW3 5TH
Tel: 020 7243 3803
Principal: Shirley Harwood
Age range: 3–11 years
No. of pupils: 210
🌐 IB ✐

St Christopher's School
32 Belsize Lane, Hampstead, London NW3 5AE
Tel: 020 7435 1521
Head: Emma Crawford-Nash
Age range: G4–11
No. of pupils: 235
Fees: Day £14,700
☗ £ ✐

ST JOHN'S WOOD PRE-PREPARATORY SCHOOL
For further details see p. 69
St Johns Hall, Lords Roundabout, London NW8 7NE
Tel: 020 7722 7149
Email: info@sjwpre-prep.org.uk
Website: www.sjwpre-prep.org.uk
Principal: Adrian Ellis
Age range: 3–7

St Margaret's School
18 Kidderpore Gardens, Hampstead, London NW3 7SR
Tel: 020 7435 2439
Principal: Mr M Webster BSc, PGCE
Age range: G4–16
No. of pupils: 156
Fees: Day £12,591–£14,589
☗ £

St Marks Square Nursery School
St Mark's Church, St Mark's Square, Regents Park Road, London NW1 7TN
Tel: +44 (0)20 7586 8383
Head: Dr Sheema Parsons B.Ed OBE
Age range: 2–6

St Martin's School
22 Goodwyn Avenue, Mill Hill, London NW7 3RG
Tel: 020 8959 1965
Head Teacher: Mrs Samantha Mbah
Age range: 3–11
No. of pupils: 90
Fees: Day £7,800
£ ✐

ST MARY'S SCHOOL HAMPSTEAD
For further details see p. 72
47 Fitzjohn's Avenue, Hampstead, London NW3 6PG
Tel: 020 7435 1868
Email: office@stmh.co.uk
Website: www.stmh.co.uk
Head Teacher: Mrs Harriet Connor-Earl
Age range: G2 years 9 months–11 years
No. of pupils: 300
Fees: Day £9,060–£16,740
☗ £

St Nicholas School
22 Salmon Street, London NW9 8PN
Tel: 020 8205 7153
Headmaster: Mr Matt Donaldson BA (Hons), PGCE, PGDip (Surv)
Age range: 3 months–11
No. of pupils: 80
Fees: Day £8,550–£8,850

ST. ANTHONY'S SCHOOL FOR BOYS
For further details see p. 74
90 Fitzjohn's Avenue, Hampstead, London NW3 6NP
Tel: 020 7431 1066
Email: pahead@stanthonysprep.co.uk
Website: www.stanthonysprep.org.uk
Head of School: Mr Richard Berlie MA (Cantab)
Age range: B2.5–13 years G2.5–4 years
No. of pupils: 280
☗ ✐

ST. ANTHONY'S SCHOOL FOR GIRLS
For further details see p. 76
Ivy House, 94-96 North End Road, London NW11 7SX
Tel: 020 3869 3070
Email: admissions@stanthonysgirls.co.uk
Website: www.stanthonysgirls.co.uk
Head of School: Mr Donal Brennan
Age range: G2.5–11 years
No. of pupils: 85
Fees: Day £18,000
☗

The Academy School
3 Pilgrims Place, Rosslyn Hill, Hampstead, London NW3 1NG
Tel: 020 7435 6621
Headteacher: Mr Garth Evans BA (Lond)

The American School in London
One Waverley Place, London NW8 0NP
Tel: 020 7449 1221
Head: Robin Appleby
Age range: 4–18
No. of pupils: 1350
Fees: Day £27,050–£31,200
🌐 16+

The Beehive Montessori on Queen's Park
147 Chevening Road, London NW6 6DZ
Tel: 020 8969 2235
Age range: 2–5

The Cavendish School
31 Inverness Street, Camden Town, London NW1 7HB
Tel: 020 7485 1958
Headmistress: Miss Jane Rogers
Age range: G3–11
No. of pupils: 260
Fees: Day £15,300
☗ £ ✐

The Hall School
23 Crossfield Road, Hampstead, London NW3 4NU
Tel: 020 7722 1700
Headmaster: Mr Chris Godwin
Age range: B4–13 years
☗

The Interior Design School
22 Lonsdale Road, Queens Park, London NW6 6RD
Tel: 020 7372 2811
Principal: Ms Iris Dunbar
16+

The Islamia Schools' Trust
129 Salusbury Road, London NW6 6PE
Tel: 020 7372 3472

The King Alfred School
Manor Wood, North End Road, London NW11 7HY
Tel: 020 8457 5200
Head: Robert Lobatto MA (Oxon)
Age range: 4–18
No. of pupils: 650 VIth100
Fees: Day £15,531–£18,723
A £ ✐ 16+

The Mount, Mill Hill International
Milespit Hill, London NW7 2RX
Tel: +44 (0)20 3826 33
Head of School: Ms Sarah Bellotti
Age range: 13–17 years
No. of pupils: 80
Fees: Day £27,000 WB £37,500 FB £44,250
🌐 ⚑

The Mulberry House School
7 Minster Road, West Hampstead, London NW2 3SD
Tel: 020 8452 7340
Headteacher: Ms Victoria Playford BA Hons, QTS
Age range: 2–7 years
No. of pupils: 223

The Oak Tree Nursery
2 Arkwright Road, Hampstead, London NW3 6AD
Tel: 020 7435 1916
Head: Mrs S Alexander
Age range: 2–3
Fees: Day £4,650

The Village Prep School
2 Parkhill Road, Belsize Park, London NW3 2YN
Tel: 020 7485 4673
Head of School: Ms Morven MacDonald
Age range: G2.5–11 years
☗ £ ✐

Theatretrain
69 Great North Way, London NW4 1HS
Tel: 020 8202 2006
Director: Kevin Dowsett CertEd, AdvDip(Drama in Education)
Age range: 6–18
16+

Toddlers Inn Nursery School
Cicely Davies Hall, Cochrane Street, London NW8 7NX
Tel: 020 7586 0520
Principal: Ms Laura McCole

Torah Vodaas
Brent Park Road, West Hendon
Broadway, London NW9 7AJ
Tel: 020 3670 4670
Head of School: Rabbi Y Feldman
Age range: B2–11

Trevor-Roberts School
55-57 Eton Avenue,
London NW3 3ET
Tel: 020 7586 1444
Headmaster: Simon Trevor-Roberts
BA
Age range: 5–13
Fees: Day £14,700–£16,200

**University College School
Hampstead (UCS) Junior**
11 Holly Hill, Hampstead,
London NW3 6QN
Tel: 020 7435 3068
Headmaster: Mr Lewis Hayward
Age range: B7–11 years

**University College School
Hampstead (UCS) Pre-Prep**
36 College Crescent,
Hampstead, London NW3 5LF
Tel: 020 7722 4433
Headmistress: Ms Zoe Dunn
Age range: B4–7 years

**University College School
Hampstead (UCS) Senior**
Frognal, Hampstead,
London NW3 6XH
Tel: 020 7435 2215
Headteacher: Mr Mark J Beard
Age range: B11–18 years
G16–18 years

Wentworth College
6-10 Brentmead Place,
London NW11 9LH
Tel: 020 8458 8524/5
Principal: Manuel Guimaraes
Age range: 14–19
No. of pupils: 115

**West Hampstead Day
Nursery & Preschool**
11 Woodchurch Road, West
Hampstead, London NW6 3PL
Tel: 0371 454 3596

York Rise Nursery
St Mary Brookfield Hall, York
Rise, London NW5 1SB
Tel: 020 7485 7962
Headmistress: Miss Becca Coles
Age range: 2–5

South-East London

Alleyn's School
Townley Road, Dulwich,
London SE22 8SU
Tel: 020 8557 1500
Head of School: Jane Lunnon
Age range: 4–18 years

**Anerley Montessori
Nursery**
45 Anerley Park, London SE20 8NQ
Tel: 020 8778 2810
Headmistress: Mrs P Bhatia
Age range: 3 months–5
Fees: Day £2,750–£4,600

Bellenden Day Nursery
Faith Chapel, 198 Bellenden
Road, London SE15 4BW
Tel: 020 7639 4896
Manager: Jason Cranston

Bellerbys College London
Bounty House, Stowage,
Greenwich, London SE8 3DE
Tel: +44 (0)208 694 7000
Age range: 14–19 years

Blackheath Day Nursery
The Rectory Field, Charlton,
London SE3 8SR
Tel: 020 8305 2526
Headmistress: Mrs Shipley
Age range: 0–5
No. of pupils: 61

**Blackheath High
School GDST**
Vanbrugh Park, Blackheath,
London SE3 7AG
Tel: 020 8853 2929
Head: Mrs Carol Chandler-
Thompson BA (Hons) Exeter, PGCE
Exeter
Age range: G3–18
No. of pupils: 780

**Blackheath
Montessori Centre**
Independents Road,
Blackheath, London SE3 9LF
Tel: 020 8852 6765
Headmistress: Mrs Jane Skillen
MontDip
Age range: 3–5
No. of pupils: 36

Blackheath Prep
4 St Germans Place,
Blackheath, London SE3 0NJ
Tel: 020 8858 0692
Head: Alex Matthews
Age range: 3–11 years
No. of pupils: 385

**Bright Horizons at
Tabard Square**
10-12 Empire Square, Tabard
Street, London SE1 4NA
Tel: 020 7407 2068

Broadfields Day Nursery
96 Broadfields Road, Catford,
London SE6 1NG
Tel: 020 8697 1488
Head: Elainne Dalton
Age range: 4 months–5

Clive Hall Day Nursery
rear of 54 Clive Road,
London SE21 8BY
Tel: 020 8761 9000

Colfe's Junior School
Horn Park Lane, Lee,
London SE12 8AW
Tel: 020 8463 8240
Head: Ms C Macleod
Age range: 3–11
No. of pupils: 355
Fees: Day £13,230–£13,995

Colfe's School
Horn Park Lane, Lee,
London SE12 8AW
Tel: 020 8852 2283
Head: Mr R F Russell MA(Cantab)
Age range: 3–18
No. of pupils: 1120

DLD College London
199 Westminster Bridge
Road, London SE1 7FX
Tel: +44 (0)20 7935 8411
Principal: Irfan H Latif BSc (Hons)
PGCE FRSA FRSC
No. of pupils: 426
Fees: Day £23,500–£29,950
FB £18,000–£28,000

Dulwich College
Dulwich Common,
London SE21 7LD
Tel: 020 8693 3601
Master: Dr J A F Spence
Age range: B0–18 years
Fees: Day £21,672 WB
£42,408 FB £45,234

**Dulwich College
Kindergarten &
Infants School**
Eller Bank, 87 College
Road, London SE21 7HH
Tel: 020 8693 1538
Head: Mrs Miranda Norris
Age range: 3 months–7 years
No. of pupils: 251

Dulwich Nursery
adj Sainsbury's Dulwich Store, 80
Dog Kennel Hill, London SE22 8DB
Tel: 020 7738 4007
Principal: Amanda Shead

Dulwich Prep London
42 Alleyn Park, Dulwich,
London SE21 7AA
Tel: 020 8766 5500
Head Master: Miss Louise Davidson
Age range: B3–13 years G3–5 years

**East Greenwich Day
Nursery and Preschool**
Chavening Road, Greenwich,
London SE10 0LB
Tel: 0203 7803053
Nursery Manager: Ms Loraine
Thorpe
Age range: 3 months–5 years

Eltham College
Grove Park Road, Mottingham,
London SE9 4QF
Tel: 0208 857 1455
Headmaster: Guy Sanderson
Age range: 7–18
No. of pupils: 911 VIth199

**Eltham Elizabeth Terrace
Day Nursery & Preschool**
18-22 Elizabeth Terrace,
Eltham, London SE9 5DR
Tel: 0370 218 4543

Eltham Green Day Nursery
5 Lionel Road, Eltham,
London SE9 6DQ
Tel: 0800 085 4074
Age range: 3months–5
No. of pupils: 30

**First Steps Montessori Day
Nursery & Pre School**
254 Upland Road, East
Dulwich, London SE22 0DN
Tel: 020 8299 6897
Principal: Karime Dinkha
Age range: 2–5
No. of pupils: 43

**Five Steps Community
Nursery**
31-32 Alpine Road, London SE16 2RE
Tel: 020 7237 2376

Greenwich Steiner School
Woodlands, 90 Mycenae Road,
Blackheath, London SE3 7SE
Tel: 020 8858 4404
Head of School: Mr Adrian Dow
Age range: 3–14
No. of pupils: 180
Fees: Day £7,310–£8,100

GSM London
Meridian House, Royal Hill,
Greenwich, London SE10 8RD
Tel: 0203 544 3171
Head: Dr W G Hunt

**Half Moon Montessori
Nursery**
Methodist Church Hall, 155 Half
Moon Lane, London SE24 9HU
Tel: 020 7326 5300
Age range: 2–5

Happy Faces Nursery
161 Sumner Road, Peckham,
London SE15 6JL
Tel: 020 7701 3320

Heath House Preparatory School
37 Wemyss Road, Blackheath,
London SE3 0TG
Tel: 020 8297 1900
Head Teacher: Mrs Sophia Laslett
CertEd PGDE
Age range: 3–11
No. of pupils: 125
Fees: Day £13,485–£14,985
£ 🌱

Herne Hill School
The Old Vicarage, 127 Herne
Hill, London SE24 9LY
Tel: 020 7274 6336
Headteacher: Mrs Ngaire Telford
Age range: 2–7
No. of pupils: 296
Fees: Day £6,225–£14,955

Hillyfields Day Nursery
41 Harcourt Road, Brockley,
London SE4 2AJ
Tel: 020 8694 1069
Head: Ms Lisa Reeves

James Allen's Girls' School
144 East Dulwich Grove,
Dulwich, London SE22 8TE
Tel: 020 8693 1181
Head of School: Mrs Sally-Anne
Huang MA, MSc
Age range: G4–18
No. of pupils: 1075
🧍 A £ 🌱 16

Kings Kids Christian School
100 Woodpecker Road,
Newcross, London SE14 6EU
Tel: 020 8691 5813
Headteacher: Mrs M Okenwa
Age range: 5–11

Little Cherubs Day Nursery
2a Bell Green Lane,
London SE26 5TB
Tel: 020 8778 3232

Lollipops Child Care Ltd
88 Southwood Road,
London SE9 3QT
Tel: 020 8859 5832
Principal: Miss L Thompson

London Bridge Business Academy
7-13 Melior Street, London SE1 3QP
Tel: 020 7378 1000
Head: Shmina Mandal
16

London Christian School
40 Tabard Street, London SE1 4JU
Tel: 020 3130 6430
Headmistress: Miss N Collett-White
Age range: 3–11
No. of pupils: 105
Fees: Day £9,390
£

London College of Engineering & Management
18-36 Wellington Street,
London SE18 6PF
Tel: 020 8854 6158
Head: Mr Shakhar Sharman
16

Magic Roundabout Nursery – Kennington
35 Sutherland House, Sutherland
Square, London SE17 3EE
Tel: 020 7277 3643

Marathon Science School
1-9 Evelyn Street, Surrey
Quays, London SE8 5RQ
Tel: +44 (0)20 7231 3232
Headteacher: Mr Uzeyir Onur
Age range: B11–16
No. of pupils: 67
🧍 🏛

McAlpine Dance Studio
Longfield Hall, 50 Knatchbull
Road, London SE5 9QY
Tel: 020 8673 4992
16

Mother Goose Nursery
248 Upland Road, East
Dulwich, London SE22 0NU
Tel: 020 8693 9429
Age range: 1–5

Mother Goose Nursery
34 Waveney Avenue,
Nunhead, London SE15 3UE
Tel: 020 7277 5951
Age range: 1–5

Mother Goose Nursery
The Pavilion, 65 Greendale Fields,
off Wanley Road, London SE5 8JZ
Tel: 020 7738 7700
Age range: 0–5

Mother Goose Nursery (Head Office)
133 Brookbank Road,
Lewisham, London SE13 7DA
Tel: 020 8694 8700
Age range: 1–5

Nell Gwynn Nursery
Meeting House Lane,
London SE15 2TT
Tel: 020 7252 8265
Executive Head Teacher: Lynne
Cooper

New Eltham Day Nursery & Preschool
699 Sidcup Road, New
Eltham, London SE9 3AQ
Tel: 0370 218 4271

Oakfield Preparatory School
125-128 Thurlow Park Road, West
Dulwich, London SE21 8HP
Tel: 020 8670 4206
Head of School: Mrs Moyra
Thompson
Age range: 2–11 years
No. of pupils: 310
Fees: Day £12,324

Octavia House School, Kennington
214b Kennington Road,
London SE11 6AU
Tel: 020 3651 4396 (option 3)
Executive Headteacher: Mr P Foster

Octavia House School, Vauxhall
Vauxhall Primary School, Vauxhall
Street, London SE11 5LG
Tel: 020 3651 4396 (option 1)
Executive Headteacher: Mr P Foster
Age range: 5–14

Octavia House School, Walworth
Larcom House, Larcom
Street, London SE17 1RT
Tel: 020 3651 4396 (option 2)
Executive Headteacher: Mr P Foster

Peckham Rye Day Nursery & Preschool
24 Waveney Avenue, Peckham
Rye, London SE15 3UE
Tel: 0372 291 2937

RIVERSTON SCHOOL
For further details see p. 66
63/69 Eltham Road, Lee,
London SE12 8UF
Tel: 020 8318 4327
Email: office@
riverstonschool.co.uk
Website: riverstonschool.co.uk
Headmaster: Mr David A T
Ward MA
Age range: 9 months–19 years

Rosemead Preparatory School & Nursery, Dulwich
70 Thurlow Park Road,
London SE21 8HZ
Tel: 020 8670 5865
Headmaster: Mr Phil Soutar
Age range: 2–11
No. of pupils: 366
Fees: Day £10,272–£11,286
£ 🌱

School of Technology & Management
Kingshead House, Kingshead
Yard, London SE1 1NA
Tel: 020 7378 0052
16

Skallywags Nursery
St Crispin Hall, Southwark
Park Road, Rotherhithe,
London SE16 2HU
Tel: 020 7252 3225
Headmistress: Miss Allison
Armstrong NVQ
Age range: 3 months–5 years

St Dunstan's College
Stanstead Road, London SE6 4TY
Tel: 020 8516 7200
Headmaster: Mr Nicholas Hewlett
Age range: 3–18
No. of pupils: 870
🌐 A £ 16

St Olave's Preparatory School
106 Southwood Road, New
Eltham, London SE9 3QS
Tel: 020 8294 8930
Headteacher: Miss Claire Holloway
BEd, QTS
Age range: 3–11
No. of pupils: 220
Fees: Day £10,848–£12,300
🌱

St. Patrick's Montessori Day Nursery
91 Cornwall Road, London SE1 8TH
Tel: 020 7928 5557

Sydenham High School GDST
15 & 19 Westwood Hill,
London SE26 6BL
Tel: 020 8557 7004
Headmistress: Mrs Katharine
Woodcock
Age range: G4–18
No. of pupils: 665
🧍 A £ 🌱 16

The British School of Osteopathy
275 Borough High Street,
London SE1 1JE
Tel: 020 7407 0222
Principal & Chief Executive: Martin
Collins BSc(Hons), PhD, MSc, Cbiol,
MIBiol, FRSH, DO, ILTM
Fees: Day £0
16

The Pavilion Nursery
Catford Cricket Club Pavilion,
Penerley Road, London SE6 2LQ
Tel: 020 8698 0878
Head: Mrs Karen Weller
Age range: 2–5
🌱

The Pointer School
19 Stratheden Road,
Blackheath, London SE3 7TH
Tel: 020 8293 1331
Headmaster: Mr Adam M
Greenwood BSc (Hons), PGCE,
GCGI, MBA
Age range: 3–11 years

The Villa School & Nursery
54 Lyndhurst Grove, Peckham,
London SE15 5AH
Tel: 020 7703 6216
Head Teacher: Louise Maughan
Age range: 2–7

The Village Montessori
Kingswood Hall, Kingswood
Place, London SE13 5BU
Tel: 020 8318 6720

The Village Nursery
St Mary's Centre, 180 Ladywell
Road, Lewisham, London SE13 7HU
Tel: 020 8690 6766
Principal: Frances Rogers

**Toad Hall Montessori
Nursery School**
37 St Mary's Gardens,
Kennington, London SE11 4UF
Tel: 020 7735 5087
Principal: Mrs V K Rees NNEB,
MontDip
Age range: 2–5
No. of pupils: 40
Fees: Day £6,300

Trinity Child Care
Holy Trinity Church Hall, Bryan
Road, London SE16 5HF
Tel: 020 7231 5842
Manager: Sharron Williams
Age range: 2–5
No. of pupils: 60
Fees: Day £6,240

Waterloo Day Nursery
The Chandlery, 50 Westminster
Bridge Road, London SE1 7QY
Tel: 020 7721 7432
Principal: Julie Ellis

**West Dulwich Day
Nursery & Preschool**
Old Church, 226c Gipsy Road,
West Dulwich, London SE27 9RB
Tel: 0330 127 2141

**West Dulwich Day
Nursery and Pre-School**
Old Church, 226c Gipsy
Road, London SE27 9RB
Tel: 0333 122 1189
Nursery Manager: Ms Nazmin
Uddin
Age range: 3 months–5 years

Willow Park
19 Glenlyon Road, Eltham,
London SE9 1AL
Tel: 020 8850 8753
Principal: Mrs McMahon

South-West
London

345 Nursery School
Fitzhugh Community Clubroom,
Fitzhugh Grove, Trinity Road,
London SW18 3SA
Tel: 020 8870 8441
Principal: Mrs Annabel Dixon
Age range: 3–5
No. of pupils: 42
Fees: Day £3,555

**ABACUS Early Learning
Nursery School –
Balham Day Nursery**
135 Laitwood Road, Balham,
London SW12 9QH
Tel: 020 8675 8093

**ABACUS Early Learning
Nursery School –
Stretham Day Nursery**
7 Drewstead Road, Streatham
Hill, London SW16 1LY
Tel: 020 8677 9117
Principals: Mrs M Taylor BEd & Ms S
Petgrave
Age range: 12 mths–5 years
No. of pupils: 40

**Academy of Live &
Recorded Arts**
Studio1, Royal Victoria
Patriotic Building, John Archer
Way, London SW18 3SX
Tel: 020 8870 6475
Principal: Anthony Castro
Age range: 18+
No. of pupils: 108
Fees: Day £3,000–£9,888
16+ £ 🏊

Alphabet Nursery School
Chatham Hall, Northcote Road,
Battersea, London SW11 6DY
Tel: 020 8871 7473
Principal: Mrs A McKenzie-Lewis
No. of pupils: 40
Fees: Day £1,500–£1,800

Al-Risalah Nursery
10A Gatton Road, Tooting,
London SW17 0EE
Tel: 020 8767 0716
Head of School: Nasir Qurashi

**Al-Risalah Secondary
School**
145 Upper Tooting Road,
London SW17 7TJ
Tel: 020 8767 6057
Executive Principal: Suhayl Lee
Age range: 11–16 years

**Balham Day Nursery
& Preschool**
36 Radbourne Road, Balham,
London SW12 0EF
Tel: 0345 527 4956

**Battersea Day Nursery
& Preschool**
18 Latchemere Road,
Battersea, London SW11 2DX
Tel: 0203 906 6546

**Battersea Pre-
School & Nursery**
Riverlight, Nine Elms Lane, Kirtling
Street, Battersea, London SW8 5BP
Tel: 020 7720 9336

**Beechwood
Nursery School**
55 Leigham Court Road,
Streatham, London SW16 2NJ
Tel: 020 8677 8778
Age range: 0–5

Beehive Nursery School
St Margarets Church Hall, Putney
Park Lane, London SW15 5HU
Tel: 020 8780 5333
Headmistress: Lindsay Deans
Age range: 2–5
No. of pupils: 16
Fees: Day £1,140

Bees Knees Nursery School
within Brookside Community Hall,
12 Priory Lane, London SW15 5JL
Tel: 020 8876 8252
Headmistress: Jo Wood
Age range: 2–5

Bertrum House Nursery
290 Balham High Road,
London SW17 7AL
Tel: 020 8767 4051
Age range: 2–5
🏊

Bobby's Playhouse
16 Lettice Street, London SW6 4EH
Tel: 020 7384 1190
Principal: Mrs Emma Hannay
Age range: 3 months–5 years
Fees: Day £11,000

**BROOMWOOD HALL
LOWER SCHOOL**
For further details see p. 44
50 Nightingale Lane,
London SW12 8TE
Tel: 020 8682 8840
Email: admissions@
northwoodschools.com
Website:
www.northwoodschools.com
Head: Miss Jo Townsend
Age range: 4–8 years
No. of pupils: 320
Fees: Day £5,820

**BROOMWOOD HALL
UPPER SCHOOL**
For further details see p. 45
68-74 Nightingale Lane,
London SW12 8NR
Tel: 020 8682 8810
Email: admissions@
northwoodschools.com
Website:
www.northwoodschools.com
Head: Mrs Louisa McCafferty
Age range: G8–13 years
No. of pupils: 250
Fees: Day £7,140
🏃 🏊

Busy Bee Nursery School
19 Lytton Grove, Putney,
London SW15 2EZ
Tel: 020 8789 0132
Headmistress: Dr Sally Corbett
Age range: 2–5

Cameron Vale School
4 The Vale, Chelsea,
London SW3 6AH
Tel: 020 7352 4040
Headmistress: Mrs Bridget Saul
Age range: 4–11
Fees: Day £19,305
£ 🏊

**Carmena Christian
Day Nurseries**
47 Thrale Road, Streatham,
London SW16 1NT
Tel: 020 8677 8231
Head: Mrs S Allen

Centre Academy London
92 St John's Hill, Battersea,
London SW11 1SH
Tel: 020 7738 2344
Headteacher: Rachel Maddison
Age range: 9–19
🌐 £ 🏊 16+

Chelsea Kindergarten
St Andrews Church, Park Walk,
Chelsea, London SW10 0AU
Tel: 020 7352 4856
Headmistress: Miss Lulu Tindall
MontDip
Age range: 2–5
Fees: Day £3,900–£6,120
🏊

Clapham Day Nursery
3 Peardon Street, London SW8 3BW
Tel: 020 7498 3165
Manager: Nicolette Warnes NNEB,
NVQ4
Age range: 3 months–5
No. of pupils: 72

Clapham Montessori
St Paul's Community Centre,
St Paul's Church, Rectory
Grove, London SW4 0DX
Tel: 020 7498 8324
Head: Mrs R Bowles BSc, IntMontDip
Age range: 2–5

Clapham Park Montessori
St James' Church House, 10 West
Road, Clapham, London SW4 7DN
Tel: 020 7627 0352
Head: Mrs R Bowles BSc, IntMontDip
Age range: 2–5

Collingham College
23 Collingham Gardens,
London SW5 0HL
Tel: +44 (0)20 7244 7414
Principal: Sally Powell
Age range: 14–19
No. of pupils: VIth200
Fees: Day £4,260–£22,560
16+ A £ 🏊

Crown Kindergartens
Coronation House, Ashcombe
Road, Wimbledon,
London SW19 8JP
Tel: 020 8540 8820
Principal: Mrs Acres
Age range: 1–5
No. of pupils: 28
🏊

**Dawmouse Montessori
Nursery School**
34 Haldane Road, Fulham,
London SW6 7EU
Tel: 020 7381 9385
Principal: Mrs Emma V Woodcock
NNEB, MontDip
Age range: 2–5
No. of pupils: 72

DOLPHIN SCHOOL
For further details see p. 48
106 Northcote Road,
London SW11 6QW
Tel: 020 7924 3472
Email: admissions@
dolphinschool.org.uk
Website:
www.dolphinschool.org.uk
Head Teacher: Mr S Gosden
Age range: 2–11 years
No. of pupils: 162
Fees: Day £12,885–£14,085

Donhead Preparatory School
33 Edge Hill, Wimbledon,
London SW19 4NP
Tel: 020 8946 7000
Headmaster: Mr P J J Barr
Age range: B4–11 years

Eaton House Belgravia
3-5 Eaton Gate, London SW1W 9BA
Tel: 020 7924 6000
Head of School: Mr Huw May
Age range: B3–11 years

Eaton House The Manor
58 Clapham Common
Northside, London SW4 9RU
Tel: 020 7924 6000
Head of School: Mr Oliver Snowball
Age range: G3–11 years

Eaton House The Manor Pre Prep and Nursery
58 Clapham Common
Northside, London SW4 9RU
Tel: 020 7924 6000
Head of School: Mr David Wingfield
Age range: B3–8 years

Eaton House The Manor Prep School
58 Clapham Common
Northside, London SW4 9RU
Tel: 020 7924 6000
Head of School: Mrs Sarah Segrave
Age range: B8–13 years

Eaton Square Nursery School, Belgravia
28 & 30 Eccleston Street,
London SW1W 9PY
Tel: +44 (0)20 7823 6217
Age range: 2–4 years

Eaton Square Nursery School, Pimlico
32A Lupus Street, London SW1V 3DZ
Tel: +44 (0)20 7976 6511
Age range: 2–4 years

Eaton Square Prep School
55-57 Eccleston Square,
London SW1V 1PP
Tel: +44 (0)20 7931 9469
Head of School: Ms Trish Watt
Age range: 4–11 years

Ecole Charles De Gaulle – Wix
Clapham Common North
Side, London SW4 0AJ
Tel: +44 20 7738 0287
Headteacher: Mr Blanchard
Age range: 5–11
No. of pupils: 100

École Primaire Marie D'Orliac
60 Clancarty Road,
London SW6 3AA
Tel: +44 (0)20 7736 5863
Director: Mr Blaise Fenart
Age range: 4–11

Elm Park Nursery School
90 Clarence Avenue,
Clapham, London SW4 8JR
Tel: 020 8678 1990
Head: Ms Jacqueline Brooks
No. of pupils: 113

Emanuel School
Battersea Rise, London SW11 1HS
Tel: 020 8870 4171
Headmaster: Mr Robert Milne
Age range: 10–18 years
No. of pupils: 1050
Fees: Day £20,145

Eveline Day & Nursery Schools
14 Trinity Crescent, Upper
Tooting, London SW17 7AE
Tel: 020 8672 4673
Headmistress: Ms Eveline Drut
Age range: 3 months–11 years
No. of pupils: 80
Fees: Day £13,859

Falcons School for Girls
11 Woodborough Road,
Putney, London SW15 6PY
Tel: 020 8992 5189
Headmistress: Ms Sara Williams-Ryan
Age range: G4–11
Fees: Day £7,800–£15,705

Falkner House
19 Brechin Place, South
Kensington, London SW7 4QB
Tel: 020 7373 4501
Headteacher: Mrs Anita Griggs
BA(Hons), PGCE
Age range: B3–11 G3–11

Finton House School
171 Trinity Road, London SW17 7HL
Tel: 020 8682 0921
Head of School: Mr Ben Freeman
Age range: 4–11
No. of pupils: 300
Fees: Day £15,378–£15,588

First Steps School of Dance & Drama
234 Lillie Road, London SW6 7QA
Tel: 020 7381 5224
Age range: 3–17
Fees: Day £2,700

Francis Holland School, Sloane Square, SW1
39 Graham Terrace,
London SW1W 8JF
Tel: 020 7730 2971
Head: Mrs Lucy Elphinstone
MA(Cantab)
Age range: G4–18
No. of pupils: 520 VIth70
Fees: Day £17,760–£20,085

Garden House School
Boys' School & Girls' School,
Turk's Row, London SW3 4TW
Tel: 020 7730 1652
Boys' Head: Mr Christian Warland
BA(Hons), LLB.
Age range: 3–11
No. of pupils: 490
Fees: Day £17,700–£22,800

Gateway House Nursery School
St Judes Church Hall, Heslop
Road, London SW12 8EG
Tel: 020 8675 8258
Principal: Miss Elizabeth Marshall
Age range: 2–4
No. of pupils: 30
Fees: Day £1,010–£1,060

Glendower School
86/87 Queen's Gate,
London SW7 5JX
Tel: 020 7370 1927
Headmistress: Mrs Sarah Knollys
BA, PGCE
Age range: G4–11+
No. of pupils: 206
Fees: Day £19,200

Hall School Wimbledon
17, The Downs, Wimbledon,
London SW20 8HF
Tel: 020 8879 9200
Headmaster: Mr. A Hammond
Age range: 5–18 years
No. of pupils: 160
Fees: Day £4,570–£6,140

Hall School Wimbledon Junior School
17, The Downs, Wimbledon,
London SW20 8HF
Tel: 020 8879 9200
Headmaster: Mr. A Hammond
Age range: 5–11 years

Happy Nursery Days
Valens House, 132a Uppertulse
Hill, London SW2 2RX
Tel: 020 8674 7804
Age range: 3 months–5

Harrodian
Lonsdale Road, London SW13 9QN
Tel: 020 8748 6117
Headmaster: Mr James R Hooke
Age range: 4–18 years
No. of pupils: 1023
Fees: Day £5,000–£8,000

Hill House
17 Hans Place, Chelsea,
London SW1X 0EP
Tel: 020 7584 1331
Headmaster: Mr Richard Townend
Age range: 4–13
No. of pupils: 600
Fees: Day £15,000–£18,600

Hornsby House School
Hearnville Road, Balham,
London SW12 8RS
Tel: 020 8673 7573
Headmaster: Mr Edward Rees
Age range: 4–11
Fees: Day £14,280–£15,345

Hurlingham Nursery School
The Old Methodist Hall, Gwendolen
Avenue, London SW15 6EH
Tel: 020 8103 0807
Headmaster: Mr Simon Gould
Age range: 2–4 years

Hurlingham School
122 Putney Bridge Road,
Putney, London SW15 2NQ
Tel: 020 8103 1083
Headmaster: Mr Simon Gould
Age range: 4–11

Ibstock Place School
Clarence Lane, London SW15 5PY
Tel: 020 8876 9991
Head of School: Mr Christopher Wolsey
Age range: 4–18 years
No. of pupils: 990
Fees: Day £5,870–£7,450

Inchbald School of Design
Interior Design Faculty, 7 Eaton
Gate, London SW1W 9BA
Tel: 020 7730 5508
Principal: Mrs Jacqueline Duncan
FIIDA, FIDDA
Age range: 18–50
No. of pupils: 120

JJAADA Interior Design Academy
28 Abbeville Mews, 88 Clapham
Park Road, London SW4 7BX
Tel: 020 7494 3363

Judith Blacklock Flower School
4/5 Kinnerton Place South,
London SW1X 8EH
Tel: 020 7235 6235
Head: Judith Blacklock

Kensington Prep School
596 Fulham Road, London SW6 5PA
Tel: 0207 731 9300
Head of School: Mrs Caroline
Hulme-McKibbin
Age range: G4–11
No. of pupils: 289
Fees: Day £17,193

Kids Inc Day Nursery – East Sheen
459b Upper Richmond Road West,
East Sheen, London SW14 7PR
Tel: 020 8876 8144

King's College School
Southside, Wimbledon
Common, London SW19 4TT
Tel: 020 8255 5300
Acting Head: Ms Jude Lowson MA
Age range: B7–18 years
G16–18 years
No. of pupils: 1477 VIth419

Knightsbridge School
67 Pont Street, Knightsbridge,
London SW1X 0BD
Tel: +44 (0)20 7590 9000
Head of School: Ms Shona Colaço
Age range: 3–16 years

Ladybird Nursery School
9 Knowle Close, London SW9 0TQ
Tel: 020 7924 9505

L'ECOLE DE BATTERSEA
For further details see p. 52
Trott Street, Battersea,
London SW11 3DS
Tel: 020 7371 8350
Email: admin@
lecoledespetits.co.uk
Website:
www.lecoledespetits.co.uk
Principal: Mrs F Brisset
Age range: 3–11 years
No. of pupils: 250
Fees: Day £4,745

L'ECOLE DES PETITS
For further details see p. 53
2 Hazlebury Road, Fulham,
London SW6 2NB
Tel: 020 7371 8350
Email: admin@
lecoledespetits.co.uk
Website:
www.lecoledespetits.co.uk
Principal: Mrs F Brisset
Age range: 3–6 years
No. of pupils: 120
Fees: Day £4,615

L'Ecole du Parc
12 Rodenhurst Road,
London SW4 8AR
Tel: 020 8671 5287
Headteacher: Mrs E Sicking-Bressler
Age range: 1–5
No. of pupils: 55
Fees: Day £4,000–£7,500

Little People of Fulham
250a Lillie Road, Fulham,
London SW6 7PX
Tel: 020 7386 0006
Owner: Miss Jane Gleasure
Age range: 4 months–5

Little Red Hen Nursery School
Christchurch Hall, Cabul
Road, London SW11 2PN
Tel: 020 7738 0321
Age range: 2–5
Fees: Day £1,470–£1,740

London Film Academy
The Old Church, 52a Walham
Grove, London SW6 1QR
Tel: 020 7386 7711
Founders & Joint Principals: Daisy
Gili & Anna Macdonald

London Steiner School
9 Weir Road, Balham,
London SW12 0LT
Tel: 0208 772 3504
Age range: 3–14

LYCÉE FRANÇAIS CHARLES DE GAULLE DE LONDRES
For further details see p. 55
35 Cromwell Road,
London SW7 2DG
Tel: 020 7584 6322
Email: inscription@
lyceefrancais.org.uk
Website:
www.lyceefrancais.org.uk
Headteacher: Didier Devilard
Age range: 3–18 years
No. of pupils: 3450
Fees: Day £7,066–£14,782

Magic Roundabout Nursery – Stockwell
Surrey Hall, Binfield Road,
Stockwell, London SW4 6TB
Tel: 020 7498 1194

MANDER PORTMAN WOODWARD – MPW LONDON
For further details see p. 58
90-92 Queen's Gate,
London SW7 5AB
Tel: 020 7835 1355
Email: london@mpw.ac.uk
Website: www.mpw.ac.uk
Principal: Mr John Southworth
BSc MSc
Age range: 14–19
No. of pupils: 600
Fees: Day £10,252

Melrose House Nursery School – SW18
39 Melrose Road, Southfields,
London SW18 1LX
Tel: 020 8874 7769
Head of School: Ruth Oates
Age range: 2–5

Melrose House Nursery School – SW6
55 Finlay Street, Fulham,
London SW6 6HF
Tel: 020 7736 9296
Head of School: Caroline
O'Gorman
Age range: 2–5

Miss Daisy's Nursery School
Fountain Court Club Room, Ebury
Square, London SW1W 9SU
Tel: 020 7730 5797
Head: Daisy Harrison
Age range: 2–5
No. of pupils: 30
Fees: Day £1,050–£5,550

Montessori School
St Paul's Community Centre,
Rectory Grove, Clapham,
London SW4 0DX
Tel: 020 7498 8324
Age range: 6 months–6

MORE HOUSE SCHOOL
For further details see p. 61
22-24 Pont Street, Knightsbridge,
London SW1X 0AA
Tel: 020 7235 2855
Email: registrar@
morehousemail.org.uk
Website:
www.morehouse.org.uk
Head: Ms Faith Hagerty
Age range: G11–18 years
No. of pupils: 140
Fees: Day £7,250

Newton Prep
149 Battersea Park Road,
London SW8 4BX
Tel: 020 7720 4091
Headmistress: Mrs Alison Fleming
BA, MA Ed, PGCE
Age range: 3–13 years
No. of pupils: 628
Fees: Day £9,975–£21,135

Nightingale Montessori Nursery
St Lukes Community Hall, 194
Ramsden Road, London SW12 8RQ
Tel: 020 8675 8070
Principal: Mrs Tejas Earp
Age range: 2–5

Noah's Ark Nursery Schools (Dolphin School Trust)
St Michael's Church Hall, Cobham
Close, London SW11 6SP
Tel: 020 7924 3472 opt 2
Head: Miss Annette Miller
Age range: 2–5
No. of pupils: 40
Fees: Day £4,725

Noah's Ark Nursery Schools (Dolphin School Trust)
Endlesham Church Hall, 48
Endlesham Road, London SW12 8JL
Tel: 020 924 3472 opt 2
Head: Miss Annette Miller
Age range: 2–5
No. of pupils: 32
Fees: Day £4,725

Noddy's Nursery School
Trinity Church Hall, Beaumont Road,
Wimbledon, London SW19 6SP
Tel: 020 8785 9191
Principal: Mrs Sarah Edwards NNEB,
Mont Dip
Age range: 2–5

NORTHCOTE LODGE
For further details see p. 63
26 Bolingbroke Grove,
London SW11 6EL
Tel: 020 8682 8888
Email: admissions@
northwoodschools.com
Website:
www.northwoodschools.com
Head: Mr Clive Smith-Langridge
Age range: B8–13 years
No. of pupils: 260
Fees: Day £7,140

NORTHWOOD SENIOR
For further details see p. 64
3 Garrad's Road,
London SW16 1JZ
Tel: 020 8161 0301
Email: NWSsenior@
northwoodschools.com
Website:
www.northwoodschools.com
Head: Mrs Susan Brooks
Age range: 11–16 years
Fees: Day £7,140

Oliver House Preparatory School
7 Nightingale Lane,
London SW4 9AH
Tel: 020 8772 1911
Headteacher: Mr Rob Farrell
Age range: 3–11
No. of pupils: 144
Fees: Day £6,600–£15,090

Paint Pots Montessori School – The Boltons
St Mary The Boltons Church Hall,
The Boltons, London SW10 9TB
Tel: 07794 678 537
Head Teacher: Georgie Scully
Age range: 2 years 6
months–5 years

Parkgate House School
80 Clapham Common North
Side, London SW4 9SD
Tel: +44 (0)20 7350 2461
Principal: Miss Catherine Shanley
Age range: 2.5–11 years
No. of pupils: 220
Fees: Day £5,940–£15,600

Parsons Green Prep School
1 Fulham Park Road,
Fulham, London SW6 4LJ
Tel: 020 7371 9009
Headmaster: Tim Cannell
Age range: 4–11
No. of pupils: 200
Fees: Day £16,857–£18,201

Peques Anglo-Spanish School
St John's Church, North End
Road, Fulham, London SW6 1PB
Tel: 020 7385 0055
Managing Director: Margarita
Morro Beltran
Age range: 3 months–5

Playdays Nursery School Wimbledon
58 Queens Road, Wimbledon,
London SW19 8LR
Tel: 020 8946 8139
Nursery Manager: Charline Baker

Pooh Corner Kindergarten
St Stephen's Church Hall, 48
Emperor Gate, London SW7 4HJ
Tel: 020 7373 6111
Headmistress: Sarah Crowther

Prince's Gardens Preparatory School
10–13 Prince's Gardens,
London SW7 1ND
Tel: 0207 591 4622
Headmistress: Mrs Alison Melrose
Age range: 3–11 years

Prospect House School
75 Putney Hill, London SW15 3NT
Tel: 020 8246 4897
Headmaster: Mr Michael Hodge
BPED(Rhodes) QTS
Age range: 3–11 years
No. of pupils: 316
Fees: Day £9,480–£19,755

Putney Day Nursery & Preschool
107-109 Norroy Road, Putney,
London SW15 1PH
Tel: 0330 134 7587

Putney High School GDST
35 Putney Hill, London SW15 6BH
Tel: 020 8788 4886
Headmistress: Mrs Suzie Longstaff
BA, MA, PGCE
Age range: G4–18 years
No. of pupils: 976 VIth150

Queen's Gate School
133 Queen's Gate, London SW7 5LE
Tel: 020 7589 3587
Principal: Mrs R M Kamaryc BA,
MSc, PGCE
Age range: G4–18 years
No. of pupils: 500 VIth81

Raynes Park Bushey Road Day Nursery & Preschool
c/o David Lloyd Leisure
Club, Bushey Road, Raynes
Park, London SW20 8DE
Tel: 0371 454 3482

Raynes Park Nursery and PreSchool
3 Spencer Road, Raynes Park,
Wimbledon, London SW20 0QN
Tel: 0333 920 1909
Nursery Manager: Ms Leanne
Eustace
Age range: 3 months–5 years

Redcliffe School Trust Ltd
47 Redcliffe Gardens,
Chelsea, London SW10 9JH
Tel: 020 7352 9247
Head: Sarah Lemmon
Age range: 3–11
Fees: Day £6,660–£17,730

Ringrose Kindergarten Chelsea
St Lukes Church Hall, St Lukes
Street, London SW3 3RP
Tel: 020 7352 8784
Age range: 2–5 years

Royal Academy of Dance
36 Battersea Square,
London SW11 3RA
Tel: 020 7326 8000
Chief Executive: Luke Rittner

Royal College of Art
Kensington Gore, London SW7 2EU
Tel: 020 7590 4444
Rector & Vice-Provost: Professor
Christopher Frayling

Sinclair House Preparatory School
59 Fulham High Street,
Fulham, London SW6 3JJ
Tel: 0207 736 9182
Principal: Mrs Carlotta T M
O'Sullivan
Age range: 2–11
No. of pupils: 120
Fees: Day £5,280–£17,025

Southfields Day Nursery and Pre-School
Duntshill Mill, 21 Riverdale
Drive, London SW18 4UR
Tel: 0330 057 6434
Nursery Manager: Ms Lydia
Howards
Age range: 3 months–5 years

Square One Nursery School
Lady North Hall, 12 Ravenna
Road, Putney, London SW15 6AW
Tel: 020 8788 1546
Principal: Mrs King

St Mary Magdalen Montessori Nursery School
61 North Worple Way,
London SW14 8PR
Tel: 020 8878 0756
Head: Liz Maitland NNEB, RSH,
MontDip
Age range: 2–5

St Mary's Summerstown Montessori
46 Wimbledon Road, Tooting,
London SW17 0UQ
Tel: 020 8947 7359
Head: Liz Maitland NNEB, RSH,
MontDip
Age range: 18 months–5 years
No. of pupils: 30
Fees: Day £1,300

St Michael's Montessori Nursery School
St Michael's Church, Elm Bank
Gardens, Barnes, London SW13 0NX
Tel: 020 8878 0116
Head Teacher: Debbie Goldberg
Age range: 2 1/2–5

St Paul's Juniors
St Paul's School, Lonsdale
Road, London SW13 9JT
Tel: 020 8748 3461
Head of School: Maxine Shaw
Age range: B7–13 years

St Paul's School
Lonsdale Road, Barnes,
London SW13 9JT
Tel: 020 8748 9162
High Master: Ms Sally-Anne Huang
Age range: B13–18 years

St Philip's School
6 Wetherby Place, London SW7 4NE
Tel: 020 7373 3944
Headmaster: Mr Wulffen-Thomas
Age range: B7–13 years

Streatham & Clapham High School GDST
42 Abbotswood Road,
London SW16 1AW
Tel: 020 8677 8400
Headmaster: Dr Millan Sachania
Age range: G3–18
No. of pupils: 603 VIth70
Fees: Day £10,431–£19,743

Streatham Day Nursery and Preschool
113 Blegborough Road,
Streatham, London SW16 6DL
Tel: 0330 057 6267
Nursery Manager: Ms Nadia Kiani
Age range: 3 months–5 years

Streatham Montessori Nursery & Day Care
66 Blairderry Road, Streatham
Hill, London SW2 4SB
Tel: 020 8674 2208
Nursery Manager: Mrs Fehmida
Gangji
Age range: 1–5

Sussex House School
68 Cadogan Square,
London SW1X 0EA
Tel: 020 7584 1741
Headmaster: Mr N P Kaye
MA(Cantab), ACP, FRSA, FRGS
Age range: B8–13 years

Swedish School
82 Lonsdale Road, London SW13 9JS
Tel: 020 8741 1751
Head of School: Ms. Jenny
Abrahamsson
Age range: 3–18
No. of pupils: 300 VIth145
Fees: Day £8,600–£9,100

Thames Christian College
Wye Street, Battersea,
London SW11 2HB
Tel: 020 7228 3933
Executive Head: Stephen Holsgrove
PhD
Age range: 11–16
No. of pupils: 120
Fees: Day £15,780

The Boltons Nursery School
262b Fulham Road, Chelsea,
London SW10 9EL
Tel: 020 7351 6993
Age range: 2–5
No. of pupils: 60
Fees: Day £2,370–£4,200

The Bumble Bee Nursery School
Church of Ascension, Pountney
Road, London SW11 5TU
Headmistress: Deepti Bansal

The Castle Kindergarten
20 Henfield Road,
London SW19 3HU
Tel: 020 8544 0089
Principal: Ms Beverley Davis DipEd
Age range: 2–5

The Crescent I Kindergarten
Flat 1, No 10 Trinity Crescent,
London SW17 7AE
Tel: 020 8767 5882
Principal: Philip Evelegh

The Crescent II Kindergarten
Holy Trinity Church Hall, Trinity
Road, London SW17 7SQ
Tel: 020 8682 3020

The Eveline Day Nursery Schools, Furzedown
Seeley Hall, Chillerton Road,
Furzedown, London SW17 9BE
Tel: 020 8672 0501

The Eveline Day Nursery Schools, Tooting
30 Ritherdon Road, Upper Tooting, London SW17 8QD
Tel: 020 8672 7549
Principal: Mrs T Larche

The Eveline Day Nursery Schools, Wandsworth
East Hill United Reformed Church Hall, Geraldine Road, Wandsworth, London SW18 2NR
Tel: 020 8870 0966

The Eveline Day Nursery Schools, Wimbledon
89a Quicks Road, Wimbledon, London SW19 1EX
Tel: 020 8545 0699

The Hampshire School, Chelsea
15 Manresa Road, Chelsea, London SW3 6NB
Tel: 020 7352 7077
Head of School: Dr P Edmonds BEd (Hons) MEd EdD
Age range: 3–13
No. of pupils: 300
Fees: Day £16,965–£17,955
£ ✏

The Knightsbridge Kindergarten
St. Peter's Church, 119 Eaton Square, London SW1W 9AL
Tel: 020 7371 2306
Age range: 2–5

The Laurels School
126 Atkins Road, Clapham, London SW12 0AN
Tel: 020 8674 7229
Headmistress: Linda Sanders BA Hons (Bristol), MA (Madrid)
Age range: G11–18
🚶

The Maria Montessori Children's House
St John's Ambulance Hall, 122-124 Kingston Road, London SW19 1LY
Tel: 020 8543 6353
Age range: 2–5

The Marmalade Bear Nursery School
St. Magdalene Church Hall, Trinity Road, Tooting, London SW17 7HP
Tel: 0208 265 5224
Principal: Ms Rozzy Hyslop
Age range: 2–5
Fees: Day £3,270–£3,450
✏

The Merlin School
4 Carlton Drive, London SW15 2BZ
Tel: 020 8788 2769
Principal: Mrs Kate Prest
Age range: 4–8
No. of pupils: 130
Fees: Day £5,241

The Moat School
Bishops Avenue, Fulham, London SW6 6EG
Tel: 020 7610 9018
Headteacher: Mr K Claeys
Age range: 9–18
No. of pupils: 140
✏

The Montessori Childrens House Ltd
St John's Church, 1 Spencer Hill, London SW19 4NZ
Tel: 020 8971 9135
Age range: 2–5

The Montessori Pavilion – The Kindergarten School
Vine Road, Barnes, London SW13 0NE
Tel: 07554 277 746
Headmistress: Ms Georgina Dashwood
Age range: 3–8
No. of pupils: 50
✏

The Mouse House Nursery School
27 Mallinson Road, London SW11 1BW
Tel: 020 7924 1893
Headmistress: Amanda White-Spunner
Age range: 2–5
Fees: Day £1,650–£4,125
✏

The Norwegian School
28 Arterberry Road, Wimbledon, London SW20 8AH
Tel: 020 8947 6617
Head: Mr Ivar Chavannes
Age range: 3–16

The Oval Montessori Nursery School
within Vauxhall Park, Fentiman Road, London SW8 1LA
Tel: 020 7735 4816
Head: Ms Louise Norwood
Age range: 2–5
Fees: Day £3,000

The Park Kindergarten
St Saviours Church Hall, 351 Battersea Park Road, London SW11 4LH
Tel: 020 7627 5125
Principal: Miss Lisa Neilsen MontDip
Age range: 2–5
Fees: Day £2,370
✏

The Rainbow Playgroup
St Luke's Church Hall, St Luke's Street, London SW3 3RR
Tel: 020 7352 8156
Age range: 2–5

THE ROCHE SCHOOL
For further details see p. 78
11 Frogmore, London SW18 1HW
Tel: 020 8877 0823
Email: office@therocheschool.com
Website: www.therocheschool.com
Headmistress: Mrs Vania Adams BA(Hons), PGCE, MA
Age range: 2–11 years
No. of pupils: 274
Fees: Day £15,600–£16,290
£ ✏

The Rowans School
19 Drax Avenue, Wimbledon, London SW20 0EG
Tel: 020 8946 8220
Head Teacher: Mrs. Joanna Hubbard MA BA (Hons) PGCE QTS PGDipSEN
Age range: 3–8
Fees: Day £7,905–£13,170

The Study Preparatory School
Wilberforce House, Camp Road, Wimbledon Common, London SW19 4UN
Tel: 020 8947 6969
Head of School: Miss Vicky Ellis BSc (Hons), QTS, MA
Age range: G4–11
No. of pupils: 320
Fees: Day £4,925
🚶 £ ✏

The White House Preparatory School & Woodentops Kindergarten
24 Thornton Road, London SW12 0LF
Tel: 020 8674 9514
Principal: Mrs. Mary McCahery
Age range: 2–11
Fees: Day £4,436–£4,740
£

The Willow Nursery School
55 Grafton Square, Clapham Old Town, London SW4 0DE
Tel: 020 7498 0319
Head: Mrs Harriet Baring MontDip
Age range: 2–5
Fees: Day £3,000–£3,100
✏

The Zebedee Nursery School
4 Parsons Green, London SW6 4TN
Tel: 020 7371 9224
Headmistress: Miss Su Gahan NNEB, RSH
Age range: 2–5
No. of pupils: 32
Fees: Day £3,900
✏

Thomas's Kindergarten – Battersea
St Mary's Church, Battersea Church Road, London SW11 3NA
Tel: 020 7738 0400
Headmistress: Miss Iona Jennings
Age range: 2–5
Fees: Day £1,365–£2,100

Thomas's Kindergarten – Pimlico
14 Ranelagh Grove, London SW1W 8PD
Tel: 020 7730 3596
Headmistress: Miss Tamara Spierenburg HBO

Thomas's Preparatory School – Battersea
28-40 Battersea High Street, London SW11 3JB
Tel: 020 7978 0900
Head: Simon O'Malley
Age range: 4–13
No. of pupils: 547
Fees: Day £18,747–£20,868
✏

Thomas's Preparatory School – Clapham
Broomwood Road, London SW11 6JZ
Tel: 020 7326 9300
Headmaster: Mr Philip Ward BEd(Hons)
Age range: 4–13
No. of pupils: 647
Fees: Day £17,262–£19,518
£ ✏

Thomas's Preparatory School – Fulham
Hugon Road, London SW6 3ES
Tel: 020 7751 8200
Head: Miss Annette Dobson BEd(Hons), PGCertDys
Age range: 4–11
Fees: Day £17,880–£20,016

Tiggers Nursery School
87 Putney Bridge Road, London SW15 2PA
Tel: 020 8874 4668
Headmistress: Natasha Green MontDip
Age range: 2–5
Fees: Day £1,425–£1,725

Toots Day Nursery
214 Totterdown Street, Tooting, London SW17 8TD
Tel: 020 8767 7017
Principal: Angela Duffell
Age range: 1–5

Tower House School
188 Sheen Lane, London SW14 8LF
Tel: 020 8876 3323
Head: Mr Gregory Evans
Age range: B4–13 years
🚶 ✏

Twice Times Nursery School
The Cricket Pavilion in South Park, Clancarty Road, London SW6 3AF
Tel: 020 7731 4929
Heads: Mrs A Welch MontDip & Mrs S Henderson MontDip
Age range: 2–5
No. of pupils: 50

Ursuline Preparatory School
18 The Downs, Wimbledon, London SW20 8HR
Tel: 020 8947 0859
Head Teacher: Mrs Caroline Molina BA (Hons)
Age range: B3–4 years G3–11 years
No. of pupils: 169

Wandsworth Nursery & Pre-School Academy
Dolphin House, Riverside West, Smugglers Way, Wandsworth, London SW18 1DE
Tel: 020 8877 1135
Nursery Manager: Evelyn Herrera
Age range: 0–5

Wandsworth Preparatory School
The Old Library, 2 Allfarthing Lane, London SW18 2PQ
Tel: 0208 870 4133
Headteacher: Ms Jo Fife
Age range: 4–11
No. of pupils: 100
Fees: Day £4,710

Westminster Abbey Choir School
Dean's Yard, London SW1P 3NY
Tel: 0207 654 4918
Headmaster: Mr Peter Roberts
Age range: B7–10 years

Westminster Cathedral Choir School
Ambrosden Avenue, London SW1P 1QH
Tel: 020 7798 9081
Headmaster: Mr Neil McLaughlan
Age range: B4–13
No. of pupils: 150
Fees: Day £16,350–£19,233 FB £10,086

Westminster School
Little Dean's Yard, Westminster, London SW1P 3PB
Tel: 020 7963 1000
Head Master: Dr Gary Savage
Age range: B13–18 years G16–18 years

Westminster Tutors
86 Old Brompton Road, South Kensington, London SW7 3LQ
Tel: 020 7584 1288
Principal: Joe Mattei
Age range: 14–mature
No. of pupils: VIth40
Fees: Day £4,000–£25,000

Westminster Under School
27 Vincent Square, London SW1P 2NN
Tel: 020 7821 5788
Master: Mrs C J Jefferson
Age range: B7–13 years

Willington Prep
Worcester Road, Wimbledon, London SW19 7QQ
Tel: 020 8944 7020
Head of School: Mr Keith Brown
Age range: 3–11
No. of pupils: 220

Wimbledon Common Preparatory
113 Ridgway, Wimbledon, London SW19 4TA
Tel: 020 8946 1001
Head Teacher: Mrs Tracey Buck
Age range: B4–8
No. of pupils: 160
Fees: Day £13,185

Wimbledon High School GDST
Mansel Road, Wimbledon, London SW19 4AB
Tel: 020 8971 0900
Headmistress: Mrs Jane Lunnon
Age range: G4–18
No. of pupils: 900 VIth155
Fees: Day £14,622–£18,810

Wimbledon Park Montessori School
206 Heythorp Street, Southfields, London SW18 5BU
Tel: 020 8944 8584
Head: Ms Clare Collins
Age range: 2–5
Fees: Day £830–£950

Wimbledon School of Art
Merton Hall Road, London SW19 3QA
Tel: 020 8408 5000
Principal: Professor Roderick Bugg

Young England Kindergarten
St Saviour's Hall, St George's Square, London SW1V 3QW
Tel: 020 7834 3171
Principal: Mrs Kay C King MontDip
Age range: 2.5–5
Fees: Day £3,300–£4,950

West London

Abercorn School
38 Portland Place, London W1B 1LS
Tel: 020 7100 4335
Headmaster: Mr Christopher Hammond
Age range: 2–13 years

ABI College – London Campus
3 The Mount, Acton, London W3 9NW
Tel: 020 8993 4500

Acorn Nursery School
2 Lansdowne Crescent, London W11 2NH
Tel: 020 7727 2122
Principal: Mrs Jane Cameron BEd(Hons)
Age range: 2–5
Fees: Day £2,400

Acton Yochien Nursery School
The Pavilion, Queens Drive Playing Fields, Acton, London W3 0HT
Tel: 020 8343 2192

Alan D Hairdressing Education
4 West Smithfield, London EC1A 9JX
Tel: 020 7580 1030
Director of Education: Alan Hemmings
Fees: Day £200 FB £12,400

Albemarle Independent College
18 Dunraven Street, London W1K 7FE
Tel: 020 7409 7273
Co-Principals: Beverley Mellon & James Eytle
Age range: 16–19
No. of pupils: 160
Fees: Day £7,000–£24,000

ArtsEd Day School & Sixth Form
14 Bath Road, Chiswick, London W4 1LY
Tel: 020 8987 6666
Headteacher: Mr Adrian Blake
Age range: 11–18 years

Ashbourne Independent Sixth Form College
17 Old Court Place, Kensington, London W8 4PL
Tel: 020 7937 3858
Principal: Mr Michael Kirby MSc, BApSc, MInstD
Age range: 13–19 years

Avenue House School
70 The Avenue, Ealing, London W13 8LS
Tel: 020 8998 9981
Headteacher: Mr J Sheppard
Age range: 3–11
No. of pupils: 135
Fees: Day £11,250

Bales College
742 Harrow Road, Kensal Town, London W10 4AA
Tel: 020 8960 5899
Principal: William Moore
Age range: 11–19
No. of pupils: 90
Fees: Day £11,550–£12,750

Bassett House School
60 Bassett Road, Notting Hill, London W10 6JP
Tel: 020 8969 0313
Headmistress: Mrs Kelly Gray
Age range: 3–11 years
No. of pupils: 120
Fees: Day £5,499–£19,200

Blake College
162 New Cavendish Street, London W1W 6YS
Tel: 020 7636 0658
Course Director: D A J Cluckie BA, BSc
Fees: Day £4,720–£5,310

BPP University
Aldine Place, 142-144 Uxbridge Road, London W12 8AA
Tel: (+44) 03331 226478
Head: Martin Taylor

Busy Bees at Hammersmith
30-40 Dalling Road, Hammersmith, London W6 0JD
Tel: 020 8741 5382
Nursery Manager: Becky
Age range: 3 months–5 years

Bute House Preparatory School for Girls
Bute House, Luxumburg Gardens, London W6 7EA
Tel: 020 7603 7381
Head of School: Ms Sian Bradshaw
Age range: G4–11 years

Buttercups Day Nursery
38 Grange Road, Chiswick, London W4 4DD
Tel: 020 8995 6750

Buttercups Day Nursery
9 Florence Road, Ealing, London W5 3TU
Tel: 020 8840 4838

Buttercups Day Nursery
9 Florence Road, Ealing, London W5 3TU
Tel: 020 8840 4838

Buttons Day Nursery School
99 Oaklands Road, London W7 2DT
Tel: 020 8840 3355
Head: Julie Parhar BSc, NVQ3
Age range: 3 months–5
No. of pupils: 62

Campbell Harris Tutors
185 Kensington High Street, London W8 6SH
Tel: 020 7937 0032
Principals: Mr Mark Harris & Ms Claire Campbell
Age range: 13+
Fees: Day £4,000–£9,000

Caterpillar Montessori Nursery School
St Albans Church Hall, South Parade, Chiswick, London W4 3HY
Tel: 020 8747 8531
Head: Mrs Alison Scott
Age range: 2–5
Fees: Day £2,700

Chepstow House School
108a Lancaster Road, London W11 1QS
Tel: 0207 243 0243
Headteacher: Angela Barr
Age range: 2.5–12 years

Chiswick & Bedford Park Prep School
Priory House, Priory Avenue, London W4 1TX
Tel: 020 8994 1804
Head of School: Ms Henrietta Adams
Age range: B3–7+ years G3–11 years

Chiswick Nursery and Pre-School
4 Marlborough Road, Chiswick, London W4 4ET
Tel: 020 8742 0011
Nursery Manager: Roxane Lovell
Age range: 0–5

Chiswick Park Nursery and Pre-School
Evershed Walk, London W4 5BW
Tel: 0333 920 0404
Nursery Manager: Ms Rebecca Fergus
Age range: 3 months–5 years

Christie's Education
42 Portland Place, Marylebone, London W1W 5BD
Tel: 0207 389 2004
Academic Director: Jon Waldon

Clifton Lodge School
8 Mattock Lane, Ealing, London W5 5BG
Tel: 020 8579 3662
Head of School: Mrs Beth Friel
Age range: 3–13 years
No. of pupils: 130
Fees: Day £13,065–£15,600

College of Naturopathic & Complementary Medicine Ltd
41 Riding House Street, London W1W 7BE
Tel: 01342 410 505
Head: Hermann Keppler

Connaught House School
47 Connaught Square, London W2 2HL
Tel: 020 7262 8830
Principal: Mrs V Hampton
Age range: 4–11
No. of pupils: 75
Fees: Day £16,650–£18,300

David Game College
31 Jewry Street, London EC3N 2ET
Tel: 020 7221 6665
Principal: D T P Game MA, MPhil
Age range: 14–19
No. of pupils: 200 VIth150
Fees: Day £3,680–£30,630

Devonshire Day Nursery
The Vicarage, Bennet Street, Chiswick, London W4 2AH
Tel: 020 8995 9538
Manager: Dawn Freeman
Age range: 6 weeks–5
No. of pupils: 70

Durston House
12-14 Castlebar Road, Ealing, London W5 2DR
Tel: 020 8991 6530
Headmaster: Mr Giles Entwisle
Age range: B4–13 years
No. of pupils: 380
Fees: Day £4,490–£5,420

Ealing Independent College
83 New Broadway, Ealing, London W5 5AL
Tel: 020 8579 6668
Principal: Dr Ian Moores
Age range: 13–19
No. of pupils: 100 VIth70
Fees: Day £2,910–£18,120

Eaton Square Senior School
106 Piccadilly, Mayfair, London W1J 7NL
Tel: +44 (0)20 7491 7393
Head of School: Ms Caroline Townshend
Age range: 11–18 years

Ecole Francaise Jacques Prevert
59 Brook Green, London W6 7BE
Tel: 020 7602 6871
Headteacher: Delphine Gentil
Age range: 4–11

Elmwood Montessori School
St Michaels Centre, Elmwood Road, London W4 3DY
Tel: 020 8994 8177/995 2621
Headmistress: Mrs S Herbert BA
Age range: 2–5
Fees: Day £3,480–£4,440

FULHAM SCHOOL
For further details see p. 51
1-3 Chesilton Road, London SW6 5AA
Tel: 020 8154 6751
Email: senioradmin@fulham.school
Website: fulham.school
Pre-Prep & Nursery Head: Di Steven
Age range: 3–18 years
No. of pupils: 650
Fees: Day £18,420–£21,567

Godolphin and Latymer School
Iffley Road, Hammersmith, London W6 0PG
Tel: +44 (0)20 8741 1936
Head Mistress: Dr Frances Ramsey
Age range: G11–18 years
No. of pupils: 800
Fees: Day £23,085

Great Beginnings Montessori Nursery
39 Brendon Street, London W1H 5JE
Tel: 020 7258 1066
Head: Mrs Wendy Innes
Age range: 2–6

Greek Primary School of London
3 Pierrepoint Road, Acton, London W3 9JR
Tel: 020 899 26156
Primary School Head Teacher: Mrs Despoina Kyriakidou BA, MA, QTS
Age range: 1–11

Halcyon London International School
33 Seymour Place, London W1H 5AU
Tel: +44 (0)20 7258 1169
Headteacher: Mr Barry Mansfield
Age range: 11–18
No. of pupils: 195

Hammersmith Day Nursery & Pre-School
50 Richford Gate, 61-69 Richford Street, London W6 7HZ
Tel: 0207 622 0484
Manager: Marion Bones NVQ
Age range: 3 months–5 years
No. of pupils: 70

Happy Child Day Nursery
283-287 Windmill Road, Ealing, London W5 4DP
Tel: 020 8567 2244
Age range: 3 months–5

Happy Child Training Centre
109 Uxbridge Road, Ealing, London W5 5TL
Tel: 020 8579 3955

Harvington School
20 Castlebar Road, Ealing, London W5 2DS
Tel: 020 8997 1583
Headmistress: Mrs Anna Evans
Age range: B3–4 G3–11
No. of pupils: 140
Fees: Day £6,525–£12,615

Hawkesdown House School Kensington
27 Edge Street, Kensington, London W8 7PN
Tel: 020 7727 9090
Headmistress: Mrs S Gillam BEd (Cantab)
Age range: 2–8 years
No. of pupils: 100
Fees: Day £4,725–£21,120

Heathfield House School
Heathfield Gardens, Chiswick, London W4 4JU
Tel: 020 8994 3385
Headteacher: Mrs Goodsman
Age range: 4–11
No. of pupils: 197
Fees: Day £2,471–£3,676

Holland Park Day Nursery and Pre-School
34 Ladbroke Grove, Notting Hil, London W11 3BQ
Tel: 0333 363 4009
Age range: 3 months–5
Fees: Day £3,900

Holland Park Pre Prep School and Day Nursery
5, Holland Road, Kensington, London W14 8HJ
Tel: 020 7602 9066/020 7602 9266
Head Mistress: Mrs Kitty Mason
Age range: 3 months–8 years
No. of pupils: 39
Fees: Day £9,180–£18,120

Instituto Español Vicente Cañada Blanch
317 Portobello Road, London W10 5SZ
Tel: +44 (0) 20 8969 2664
Principal: Carmen Pinilla Padilla
Age range: 4–19
No. of pupils: 405

International School of London (ISL)
139 Gunnersbury Avenue, London W3 8LG
Tel: +44 (0)20 8992 5823
Principal: Mr Richard Parker
Age range: 3–18 years
No. of pupils: 500
Fees: Day £19,000–£26,300

James Lee Nursery School
Gliddon Road, London W14 9BH
Tel: 020 8741 8877

King Fahad Academy
Bromyard Avenue, Acton,
London W3 7HD
Tel: 020 8743 0131
Director General: Dr Tahani Aljafari
Age range: 3–19

La Petite Ecole Francaise
73 Saint Charles Square,
London W10 6EJ
Tel: +44 208 960 1278
Principal: Mme Marjorie
Lacassagne
Age range: 3–11

Ladbroke Square Montessori School
43 Ladbroke Square,
London W11 3ND
Tel: 020 7229 0125
Head Teacher: Lucy Morley
Age range: 3–5
Fees: Day £850–£1,350

Latymer Prep School
36 Upper Mall, Hammersmith,
London W6 9TA
Tel: 020 7993 0061
Principal: Ms Andrea Rutterford
B.Ed (Hons)
Age range: 7–11
No. of pupils: 165
Fees: Day £18,330

Latymer Upper School
King Street, Hammersmith,
London W6 9LR
Tel: 020862 92024
Head: Mr D Goodhew MA(Oxon)
Age range: 11–18
No. of pupils: 1400
Fees: Day £6,945

Le Herisson
River Court Methodist
Church, Rover Court Road,
Hammersmith, London W6 9JT
Tel: 020 8563 7664
Director: Maria Frost
Age range: 2–6
Fees: Day £8,730–£8,970

L'Ecole Bilingue
St David's Welsh Church, St
Mary's Terrace, London W2 1SJ
Tel: 020 7224 8427
Headteacher: Ms Veronique
Ferreira
Age range: 3–11
No. of pupils: 68
Fees: Day £9,960–£10,770

Leiths School of Food & Wine
16-20 Wendell Road, Shepherd's
Bush, London W12 9RT
Tel: 020 8749 6400
Managing Director: Camilla
Schneideman
Age range: 17–99
No. of pupils: 96

Little Cherubs Nursery School
The Carmelite Priory, Pitt Street,
Kensington, London W8 4JH
Tel: 020 7376 4460/07810
712241
Principal: Mrs M Colvin MontDip
Age range: 2–5
No. of pupils: 42

Little People of Willow Vale
9 Willow Vale, London W12 0PA
Tel: 020 8749 2877
Head: Miss Jane Gleasure
Age range: 4 months–5

Little Sweethearts Montessori
St Saviours Church Hall, Warwick
Avenue, London W9 2PT
Tel: 020 7266 1616

LLOYD WILLIAMSON SCHOOL FOUNDATION
For further details see p. 54
12 Telford Road, London W10 5SH
Tel: 020 8962 0345
Email: admin@lws.org.uk
Website:
www.lloydwilliamson.co.uk
Co-Principals: Ms Lucy Meyer &
Mr Aaron Williams
Age range: 4 months–16 years
Fees: Day £17,550

London Academy of Music & Dramatic Art
155 Talgarth Road,
London W14 9DA
Tel: 020 8834 0500
Head of Examinations: Dawn
Postans
Age range: 17+

London College
1st Floor, 23-25 Eastcastle
Street, London W1W 8DF
Tel: 020 7580 7552
Head: Mr David Kohn

London Welsh School Ysgol Gymraeg Llundain
Hanwell Community Centre,
Westcott Crescent, London W7 1PD
Tel: 020 8575 0237
Lead Teacher: Mrs Rachel King
Age range: 3–11

MAIDA VALE SCHOOL
For further details see p. 57
18 Saltram Crescent,
London W9 3HR
Tel: 020 4511 6000
Email: admissions@
maidavaleschool.com
Website:
www.maidavaleschool.com
Headmaster: Steven Winter
Age range: 11–18 years
No. of pupils: 121
Fees: Day £7,674

Maria Montessori Children's House – Notting Hill
28 Powis Gardens, London W11 1JG
Tel: 020 7221 4141
Head: Mrs L Lawrence
Age range: 2–6
No. of pupils: 20
Fees: Day £4,500

Maria Montessori Nursery School
Church of the Ascension
Hall, Beaufort Road,
Ealing, London W5 3EB
Tel: 07717 050761

Maria Montessori School – Bayswater
St Matthew's Church, St
Petersburgh Place, London W2 4LA
Tel: +44 (0)20 7435 3646

Melrose Nursery School – Acton
St Gabriel's Church Hall, Noel
Road, Acton, London W3 0JE
Tel: 020 8992 0855

Norland Place School
162-166 Holland Park Avenue,
London W11 4UH
Tel: 020 7603 9103
Headmaster: Mr Patrick Mattar MA
Age range: B4–8 years G4–11 years
Fees: Day £16,107–£18,072

Notting Hill & Ealing High School GDST
2 Cleveland Road, West
Ealing, London W13 8AX
Tel: (020) 8799 8400
Headmaster: Mr Matthew Shoults
Age range: G4–18
No. of pupils: 903 VIth150
Fees: Day £14,313–£18,561

Notting Hill Preparatory School
95 Lancaster Road,
London W11 1QQ
Tel: 020 7221 0727
Head of School: Mrs Sarah Knollys
Age range: 4–13
No. of pupils: 370
Fees: Day £7,130

One World Montessori Nursery
Church Court, London W6 0EU
Tel: 020 7603 6065
Age range: 1–4

Orchard House School
16 Newton Grove, Bedford
Park, London W4 1LB
Tel: 020 8742 8544
Headmaster: Mr Kit Thompson
Age range: 3–11 years
No. of pupils: 262
Fees: Day £9,480–£19,755

Oxford House College – London
24 Great Chapel Street,
London W1F 8FS
Tel: +44 (0) 20 7580 9785
Principal: Ms Muberra Orme

Paint Pots Montessori School – Bayswater
St Stephens Church, Westbourne
Park Road, London W2 5QT
Tel: 07527 100534
Head Teacher: Vinni Lewis
Age range: 2 years 6
months–5 years

Pembridge Hall School
18 Pembridge Square,
London W2 4EH
Tel: 020 7229 0121
Headmaster: Mr Henry Keighley-
Elstub
Age range: G4–11 years

Playhouse Day Nursery
Leighton Hall, Elthorne Park
Road, London W7 2JJ
Tel: 020 8840 2851
Head of School: Mrs Priti Patel

Portland Place School
56-58 Portland Place,
London W1B 1NJ
Tel: 0207 307 8700
Headmaster: Mr David Bradbury
Age range: 10–16 years

Queen's College
43-49 Harley Street,
London W1G 8BT
Tel: 020 7291 7000
Principal: Mr Richard Tillet
Age range: G11–18
No. of pupils: 360 VIth90

Queen's College Preparatory School
61 Portland Place, London W1B 1QP
Tel: 020 7291 0660
Headmistress: Mrs Emma Webb
Age range: G4–11

RAVENSCOURT PARK PREPARATORY SCHOOL
For further details see p. 65
16 Ravenscourt Avenue,
London W6 0SL
Tel: 020 8846 9153
Email: admissions@rpps.co.uk
Website: www.rpps.co.uk
Headmaster: Mr Carl Howes MA
(Cantab), PGCE (Exeter)
Age range: 4–11 years
No. of pupils: 409
Fees: Day £6,304

Ray Cochrane Beauty School
118 Baker Street, London W1U 6TT
Tel: 02033224738
Principal: Miss Baljeet Suri
Age range: 16–50
No. of pupils: 30
Fees: Day £650–£8,495

Rolfe's Nursery School
34A Oxford Gardens,
London W10 5UG
Tel: 020 7727 8300
Headteacher: Mrs Victoria O'Brien
Age range: 2–5
Fees: Day £4,950–£8,595

Sassoon Academy
58 Buckingham Gate,,
Westminster, London SW1E 6AJ
Tel: 020 7399 6902
Education Manager: Peter Crossfield
Age range: 16–45
Fees: Day £13,500

Southbank International School – Kensington
36-38 Kensington Park
Road, London W11 3BU
Tel: +44 (0)20 7243 3803
Principal: Siobhan McGrath
Age range: 3–18 years

Southbank International School – Westminster
63-65 Portland Place,
London W1B 1QR
Tel: 020 7243 3803
Principal: Dr Paul Wood
Age range: 11–19

St Augustine's Priory
Hillcrest Road, Ealing,
London W5 2JL
Tel: 020 8997 2022
Headteacher: Mrs Sarah Raffray M.A., N.P.Q.H
Age range: B3–4 G3–18
No. of pupils: 485
Fees: Day £11,529–£16,398

ST BENEDICT'S SCHOOL
For further details see p. 70
54 Eaton Rise, Ealing,
London W5 2ES
Tel: 020 8862 2000
Email: admissions@
stbenedicts.org.uk
Website:
www.stbenedicts.org.uk
Headmaster: Mr A Johnson BA
Age range: 3–18 years
No. of pupils: 1073 VIth203
Fees: Day £13,995–£18,330

St James Preparatory School
Earsby Street, London W14 8SH
Tel: 020 7348 1777
Headmistress: Mrs Catherine Thomlinson BA(Hons)
Age range: 3–11
Fees: Day £16,425–£17,910

St James Senior Girls' School
Earsby Street, London W14 8SH
Tel: 020 7348 1777
Headmistress: Mrs Sarah Labram BA
Age range: G11–18
No. of pupils: 295 VIth67
Fees: Day £20,100

St Matthews Montessori School
St Matthews Church Hall, North Common Road, London W5 2QA
Tel: 07495 898 760
Head Teacher: Mrs Farah Virani M.A, B.A., PGCE – Primary, Mont. Dip.Adv.
Age range: 2–5

St Patrick's International College
London Sceptre Court Campus,
40 Tower Hill, London EC3N 4DX
Tel: 020 7287 6664
Principal: Mr Girish Chandra

St Paul's Girls' School
Brook Green, London W6 7BS
Tel: 020 7603 2288
High Mistress: Mrs Sarah Fletcher
Age range: G11–18 years
No. of pupils: 778
Fees: Day £25,887–£27,831

St Peter's Nursery
59a Portobello Road,
London W11 3DB
Tel: 020 7243 2617
Head of Nursery: Tracey Lloyd

Sylvia Young Theatre School
1 Nutford Place, London W1H 5YZ
Tel: 020 7258 2330
Principal: Sylvia Young OBE
Age range: 10–16

Tabernacle School
32 St Anns Villas, Holland Park, London W11 4RS
Tel: 020 7602 6232
Headteacher: Mrs P Wilson
Age range: 3–16
Fees: Day £6,500–£9,500

The Falcons Pre-Preparatory School for Boys
2 Burnaby Gardens,
Chiswick, London W4 3DT
Tel: 020 8747 8393
Head of School: Ms Liz McLaughlin
Age range: B2–7 years G2–4 years
Fees: Day £7,500–£15,705

The Japanese School
87 Creffield Road, Acton,
London W3 9PU
Tel: 020 8993 7145
Age range: 6–16

The Jordans Montessori Nursery School
Holy Innocents Church,
Paddenswick Road,
London W6 0UB
Tel: 0208 741 3230
Principal: Ms Sara Green
Age range: 2–5
Fees: Day £1,356–£3,270

The Meadows Montessori School
Dukes Meadows Community Centre, Alexandra Gardens,
London W4 2TD
Tel: 020 8742 1327/8995 2621
Headmistress: Mrs S Herbert BA
Age range: 2–5
Fees: Day £3,030–£3,870

The Minors Nursery School
10 Pembridge Square,
London W2 4ED
Tel: 020 7727 7253
Headteacher: Ms Jane Ritchie
Age range: 2–5

The Square Montessori School
18 Holland Park Avenue,
London W11 3QU
Tel: 020 7221 6004
Principal: Mrs V Lawson-Tancred
No. of pupils: 20
Fees: Day £2,220

Thomas's Preparatory School – Kensington
17-19 Cottesmore Gardens,
London W8 5PR
Tel: 020 7361 6500
Headmistress: Miss Joanna Ebner MA, BEd(Hons)(Cantab), NPQH
Age range: 4–11
Fees: Day £20,526–£21,789

Treetops Ealing Common
Woodgrange Avenue, Ealing Common, London W5 3NY
Tel: 020 8992 0209
Age range: 3 months–5

Treetops West Ealing
Green Man Passage,
Ealing, London W13 0TG
Tel: 020 8566 5515
Age range: 3 months–5

West London College
Gliddon Road, Hammersmith,
London W14 9BL
Tel: 020 8741 1688
Principal: Paul S Smith BA(Hons), FRSA

Wetherby Preparatory School
Bryanston Square, London W1H 2EA
Tel: 020 7535 3520
Headmaster: Mr Nick Baker
Age range: B8–13 years

Wetherby Pre-Preparatory School
11 Pembridge Square,
London W2 4ED
Tel: 020 7727 9581
Headmaster: Mr Mark Snell
Age range: B2 1/2–8 years

Wetherby Senior School
100 Marylebone Lane,
London W1U 2QU
Tel: 020 7535 3530
Headmaster: Mr David Lawrence
Age range: B11–18 years
Fees: Day £22,995

Windmill Montessori Nursery School
62 Shirland Road, London W9 2EH
Tel: 020 7289 3410
Principal: Miss M H Leoni & Miss J Davidson
No. of pupils: 48
Fees: Day £3,600

World of Children
Log Cabin Childrens Centre, 259 Northfield Avenue, London W5 4UA
Tel: 020 8840 3400

Young Dancers Academy
25 Bulwer Street, London W12 8AR
Tel: 020 8743 3856
Head: Mrs K Williams
Age range: 11–16
Fees: Day £12,237–£12,690

Schools in Greater London

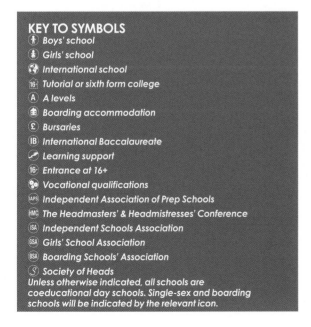

KEY TO SYMBOLS
- 🕆 *Boys' school*
- 🕈 *Girls' school*
- 🌐 *International school*
- 16↓ *Tutorial or sixth form college*
- Ⓐ *A levels*
- ♨ *Boarding accommodation*
- £ *Bursaries*
- ⒾⒷ *International Baccalaureate*
- ✐ *Learning support*
- 16↓ *Entrance at 16+*
- 🎓 *Vocational qualifications*
- (ᴵᴬᴾˢ) *Independent Association of Prep Schools*
- (ᴴᴹᶜ) *The Headmasters' & Headmistresses' Conference*
- (ᴵˢᴬ) *Independent Schools Association*
- (ᴳˢᴬ) *Girls' School Association*
- (ᴮˢᴬ) *Boarding Schools' Association*
- ⓢ *Society of Heads*

Unless otherwise indicated, all schools are coeducational day schools. Single-sex and boarding schools will be indicated by the relevant icon.

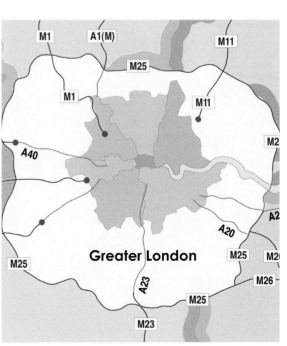

Greater London

Essex

Al-Noor Primary School
619-629 Green Lane, Goodmayes,
Ilford, Essex IG3 9RP
Tel: 020 8597 7576
Headteacher: Mrs Someera Butt
Age range: 4–10

Avon House Preparatory School
490 High Road, Woodford
Green, Essex IG8 0PN
Tel: 020 8504 1749
Headteacher: Mrs Amanda
Campbell
Age range: 3–11
No. of pupils: 268
Fees: Day £3,530–£3,950

Bancroft's School
High Road, Woodford
Green, Essex IG8 0RF
Tel: 020 8505 4821
Head: Mr Simon Marshall MA, PGCE
(Cantab), MA, MPhil (Oxon)
Age range: 7–18
No. of pupils: 1120 VIth247

Beehive Preparatory School
233 Beehive Lane, Redbridge,
Ilford, Essex IG4 5ED
Tel: 020 8550 3224
Head Teacher: Mr Jamie Gurr
Age range: 4–11

Braeside School
130 High Road, Buckhurst
Hill, Essex IG9 5SD
Tel: 020 8504 1133
Headmistress: Ms Chloe Moon
Age range: G3–16
Fees: Day £3,200–£4,400

Chigwell School
High Road, Chigwell, Essex IG7 6QF
Tel: 020 8501 5700
Headmaster: Mr M E Punt M.A.
M.Sc. P.G.C.E.
Age range: 4–18
Fees: Day £4,250–£6,295 FB £10,995

Daiglen School
68 Palmerston Road, Buckhurst
Hill, Essex IG9 5LG
Tel: 020 8504 7108
Headteacher: Mrs P Dear
Age range: 3–11 years
Fees: Day £3,375–£3,425

Eastcourt Independent School
1-5 Eastwood Road, Goodmayes,
Ilford, Essex IG3 8UW
Tel: 020 8590 5472
Headmistress: Mrs Christine
Redgrave BSc(Hons), DipEd, MEd
Age range: 4–11 years
No. of pupils: 220
Fees: Day £2,600

Gidea Park Preparatory School & Nursery
2 Balgores Lane, Gidea Park,
Romford, Essex RM2 5JR
Tel: 01708 740381
Head of School: Mr Callum Douglas
Age range: 2–11 years
No. of pupils: 100
Fees: Day £10,775

Guru Gobind Singh Khalsa College
Roding Lane, Chigwell,
Essex IG7 6BQ
Tel: 020 8559 9160
Principal: Mr Amarjit Singh Toor
BSc(Hons), BSc, BT
Age range: 3–19
Fees: Day £5,892–£6,720

Immanuel School
Havering Grange, Havering
Road, Romford, Essex RM1 4HR
Tel: 01708 764449
Head of School: Mr Simon Reeves
Age range: 3–16

Kids Inc Day Nursery – Beehive Lane, Ilford
229-231 Beehive Lane,
Ilford, Essex IG4 5EB
Tel: 020 8550 7400

Kids Inc Day Nursery – Clarence Avenue, Ilford
41 Clarence Avenue, Gants
Hill, Ilford, Essex IG2 6JH
Tel: 020 8518 4486

Kids Inc Day Nursery – Loughton
29 Old Station Road,
Loughton, Essex IG10 4PE
Tel: 020 8502 4488

Kids Inc Day Nursery – York Road, Ilford
81-85 York Road, Ilford,
Essex IG1 3AF
Tel: 020 8478 6510

Loyola Preparatory School
103 Palmerston Road,
Buckhurst Hill, Essex IG9 5NH
Tel: 020 8504 7372
Headmistress: Mrs K R Anthony
Age range: B3–11 years
No. of pupils: 200
Fees: Day £11,085

Maytime Montessori Nursery – Cranbrook Road
341 Cranbrook Road,
Ilford, Essex IG1 4UF
Tel: 020 8554 3079

Maytime Montessori Nursery – Eastwood Road
2 Eastwood Road,
Goodmayes, Essex IG3 8XB
Tel: 020 8599 3744

Maytime Montessori Nursery – Wanstead Road
293 Wanstead Park Rd,
Ilford, Essex IG1 3TR
Tel: 020 8554 6344
Age range: 0–6

Oakfields Preparatory School
Harwood Hall, Harwood Hall
Lane, Upminster, Essex RM14 2YG
Tel: 01708 220117
Headmistress: Katrina Carroll
Age range: 2–11 years
No. of pupils: 202
Fees: Day £10,296–£11,121

Oaklands School
8 Albion Hill, Loughton,
Essex IG10 4RA
Tel: 020 8508 3517
Group Managing Principal: Mr M
Hagger
Age range: 2–16
No. of pupils: 243
Fees: Day £10,350–£10,575

Park School for Girls
20-22 Park Avenue,
Ilford, Essex IG1 4RS
Tel: 020 8554 2466
Head Teacher: Mrs Androulla
Nicholas BSc Hons (Econ) PGCE
Age range: G4–16
No. of pupils: 160
Fees: Day £2,375–£3,580

St Aubyn's School
Bunces Lane, Woodford
Green, Essex IG8 9DU
Tel: 020 8504 1577
Headmaster: Mr Leonard Blom
BEd(Hons) BA NPQH
Age range: 3–13 years

St Mary's Hare Park School & Nursery
South Drive, Gidea Park,
Romford, Essex RM2 6HH
Tel: 01708 761220
Headteacher: Mr Ludovic Bernard
Age range: 2–11
No. of pupils: 180
Fees: Day £8,775

Stratford College of Management
1-7 Hainault Street,
Ilford, Essex IG1 4EL
Tel: 020 8553 0205
Head: Dr Raza

The Ursuline Preparatory School Ilford
2-8 Coventry Road,
Ilford, Essex IG1 4QR
Tel: 020 8518 4050
Headteacher: Mrs Victoria
McNaughton
Age range: G3–11
No. of pupils: 159
Fees: Day £7,320–£9,828

Woodford Green Preparatory School
Glengall Road, Woodford
Green, Essex IG8 0BZ
Tel: 020 8504 5045
Headmaster: Mr J P Wadge
Age range: 3–11 years
No. of pupils: 385
Fees: Day £3,725

Hertfordshire

Lyonsdown School
3 Richmond Road, New Barnet,
Barnet, Hertfordshire EN5 1SA
Tel: 020 8449 0225
Acting Co-Heads: Rittu Hall & Julia
Windsor
Age range: G3–11 years
No. of pupils: 180
Fees: Day £3,681–£11,766
(符号)

Mount House School
Camlet Way, Hadley Wood,
Barnet, Hertfordshire EN4 0NJ
Tel: 020 8449 6889
Principal: Sarah Richardson
Age range: 11–18
No. of pupils: 230
Fees: Day £16,560
(符号)

Susi Earnshaw
Theatre School
68 High Street, Barnet,
Hertfordshire EN5 5SJ
Tel: 020 8441 5010
Head of School: Julia VanEllis-
Hammond BA Hons
Age range: 9–16
No. of pupils: 60
Fees: Day £9,000–£12,000
(符号)

The Royal Masonic
School for Girls
Rickmansworth Park,
Rickmansworth,
Hertfordshire WD3 4HF
Tel: 01923 773168
Headmaster: Mr Kevin Carson
M.Phil (Cambridge)
Age range: G4–18
No. of pupils: 930 Vlth165
Fees: Day £11,475–£17,475 WB
£20,115–£27,495 FB £21,225–£29,835
(符号)

Kent

Ashgrove School
116 Widmore Road,
Bromley, Kent BR1 3BE
Tel: 020 8460 4143
Principal: Dr Patricia Ash CertEd,
BSc(Hons), PhD, CMath, FIMA
Age range: 3–11 years
(符号)

BABINGTON HOUSE
SCHOOL
For further details see p. 80
Grange Drive, Chislehurst,
Kent BR7 5ES
Tel: 020 8467 5537
Email: enquiries@
babingtonhouse.com
Website:
www.babingtonhouse.com
Headmaster: Mr Tim Lello MA,
FRSA, NPQH
Age range: 3–18 years
No. of pupils: 439
(符号)

Beckenham College
The Clockhouse Business Centre,
Unit 2, Thayers Farm Road,
Beckenham, Kent BR3 4LZ
Tel: 020 8650 3321
Principal: Mrs E Wakeling
Age range: 16+
Fees: Day £100–£3,500
(符号)

Benedict House
Preparatory School
1-5 Victoria Road, Sidcup,
Kent DA15 7HD
Tel: 020 8300 7206
Headteacher: Mr Craig Wardle
Age range: 3–11 years
(符号)

Bickley Park School
24 Page Heath Lane, Bickley,
Bromley, Kent BR1 2DS
Tel: 020 8467 2195
Headmaster: Mr Patrick Wenham
Age range: B2 1/2–13
years G2 1/2–4 years
(符号)

Bird College
The Centre, 27 Station Road,
Sidcup, Kent DA15 7EB
Tel: 020 8300 6004/3031
Principal & Chief Executive: Ms
Shirley Coen BA(Hons), FSRA
(符号)

Bishop Challoner School
228 Bromley Road, Shortlands,
Bromley, Kent BR2 0BS
Tel: 020 8460 3546
Headteacher: Mrs Paula Anderson
Age range: 3–18
No. of pupils: 340
Fees: Day £3,150–£4,500
(符号)

Breaside Preparatory
School
41-43 Orchard Road,
Bromley, Kent BR1 2PR
Tel: 020 8460 0916
Executive Principal: Mrs Karen A
Nicholson B.Ed, NPQH, Dip EYs
Age range: 2 1/2–11 years
No. of pupils: 376
Fees: Day £11,580–£13,494

Bromley High School GDST
Blackbrook Lane, Bickley,
Bromley, Kent BR1 2TW
Tel: 020 8781 7000/1
Head: Mrs A M Drew BA(Hons), MBA
(Dunelm)
Age range: G4–18
(符号)

Darul Uloom London
Foxbury Avenue, Perry Street,
Chislehurst, Kent BR7 6SD
Tel: 020 8295 0637
Principal: Mufti Mustafa
Age range: B11–18
No. of pupils: 160
Fees: FB £2,400
(符号)

Farringtons School
Perry Street, Chislehurst,
Kent BR7 6LR
Tel: 020 8467 0256
Head: Mr David Jackson
Age range: 3–18 years
No. of pupils: 700 Vlth100
Fees: Day £16,260 WB
£27,120 FB £34,050
(符号)

Merton Court
Preparatory School
38 Knoll Road, Sidcup,
Kent DA14 4QU
Tel: 020 8300 2112
Headmaster: Mr Dominic Price
BEd, MBA
Age range: 3–11 years
No. of pupils: 320
Fees: Day £3,095–£4,675
(符号)

St Christopher's
The Hall School
49 Bromley Road,
Beckenham, Kent BR3 5PA
Tel: 020 8650 2200
Headmaster: Mr A Velasco MEd,
BH(Hons), PGCE
Age range: 3–11
No. of pupils: 305
Fees: Day £3,750–£9,165

St. David's Prep
Justin Hall,, Beckenham Road,
West Wickham, Kent BR4 0QS
Tel: 020 8777 5852
Principal: Mrs J Foulger
Age range: 4–11
No. of pupils: 155
Fees: Day £5,850–£8,550
(符号)

West Lodge School
36 Station Road, Sidcup,
Kent DA15 7DU
Tel: 020 8300 2489
Head Teacher: Mr Robert Francis
Age range: 3–11
No. of pupils: 163
Fees: Day £5,475–£9,150
(符号)

Wickham Court School
Schiller International,
Layhams Road, West
Wickham, Kent BR4 9HW
Tel: 020 8777 2942
Principal: Ms Lisa Harries
Age range: 2–16
No. of pupils: 121
Fees: Day £6,983.40–£12,344.55

Middlesex

ACS Hillingdon International School
Hillingdon Court, 108 Vine Lane, Hillingdon, Uxbridge, Middlesex UB10 0BE
Tel: +44 (0) 1895 259 771
Head of School: Mr Martin Hall
Age range: 4–18

Alpha Preparatory School
21 Hindes Road, Harrow, Middlesex HA1 1SH
Tel: 020 8427 1471
Head: Mr P Fahy
Age range: 3–11 years

Ashton House School
50-52 Eversley Crescent, Isleworth, Middlesex TW7 4LW
Tel: 020 8560 3902
Headteacher: Mrs Angela Stewart
Age range: 3–11 years

Buckingham Preparatory School
458 Rayners Lane, Pinner, Harrow, Middlesex HA5 5DT
Tel: 020 8866 2737
Head of School: Mrs Sarah Hollis
Age range: B3–11 years G3–4 years

Buxlow Preparatory School
5/6 Castleton Gardens, Wembley, Middlesex HA9 7QJ
Tel: 020 8904 3615
Headteacher: Mr Ralf Furse
Age range: 2–11
Fees: Day £8,970–£9,330

Edgware Jewish Girls – Beis Chinuch
296 Hale Lane, Edgware, Middlesex HA8 8NP
Tel: 020 8905 4376
Headteacher: Mr M Cohen
Age range: G3–11

Halliford School
Russell Road, Shepperton, Middlesex TW17 9HX
Tel: 01932 223593
Head: Mr James Davies BMus (Hons) LGSM FASC ACertCM PGCE
Age range: B11–18 years G16–18 years
No. of pupils: 445
Fees: Day £17,985

Hampton Prep and Pre-Prep School
Gloucester Road, Hampton, Middlesex TW12 2UQ
Tel: 020 8979 1844
Headteacher: Mr Tim Smith
Age range: 3–11 years

Hampton School
Hanworth Road, Hampton, Middlesex TW12 3HD
Tel: 020 8979 9273
Headmaster: Mr Kevin Knibbs MA (Oxon)
Age range: B11–18
No. of pupils: 1200
Fees: Day £6,390

Harrow School
5 High Street, Harrow on the Hill, Middlesex HA1 3HT
Tel: 020 8872 8000
Head Master: Mr Alastair Land
Age range: B13–18
No. of pupils: 830 VIth320
Fees: FB £40,050

Holland House School
1 Broadhurst Avenue, Edgware, Middlesex HA8 8TP
Tel: 020 8958 6979
Headteacher: Mrs Emily Brown
Age range: 4–11
No. of pupils: 147

Jack and Jill School
30 Nightingale Road, Hampton, Middlesex TW12 3HX
Tel: 020 8979 3195
Principal: Miss K Papirnik BEd(Hons)
Age range: B2–5 G2–7
No. of pupils: 155
Fees: Day £4,608–£13,143

KEW HOUSE SCHOOL
For further details see p. 82
Kew House, 6 Capital Interchange Way, London, Middlesex TW8 0EX
Tel: 0208 742 2038
Email: admissions@kewhouseschool.com
Website: www.kewhouseschool.com
Headmaster: Mr Will Williams
Age range: 11–18 years
No. of pupils: 576
Fees: Day £7,674

Kids Inc Day Nursery – Enfield
8 Glyn Road, Southbury, Enfield, Middlesex EN3 4JL
Tel: 020 8805 1144

Lady Eleanor Holles
Hanworth Road, Hampton, Middlesex TW12 3HF
Tel: 020 8979 1601
Head of School: Mrs Heather Hanbury
Age range: G7–18
No. of pupils: 970
Fees: Day £21,738

Lady Nafisa Independent Secondary School for Girls
83A Sunbury Road, Feltham, Middlesex TW13 4PH
Tel: 020 8751 5610
Headteacher: Ms Fouzia Butt
Age range: G11–16

Melrose Nursery School – Wembley
St Michael's Church Hall, St Michael's Avenue, Tokyngton, Wembley, Middlesex HA9 6SL
Tel: 020 8795 1144

Menorah Grammar School
Abbots Road, Edgware, Middlesex HA8 0QS
Tel: 020 8906 9756
Head of School: Mr David Vincent
Age range: B11–21

Merchant Taylors' School
Sandy Lodge, Northwood, Middlesex HA6 2HT
Tel: 01923 820644
Head: Mr S J Everson MA (Cantab)
Age range: B11–18
No. of pupils: 865 VIth282
Fees: Day £19,998

Newland House School
Waldegrave Park, Twickenham, Middlesex TW1 4TQ
Tel: 020 8865 1234
Headmaster: Mr D A Alexander
Age range: B3–13 G3–11
No. of pupils: 425
Fees: Day £3,848–£4,306

North London Collegiate School
Canons, Canons Drive, Edgware, Middlesex HA8 7RJ
Tel: +44 (0)20 8952 0912
Headmistress: Mrs Sarah Clark
Age range: G4–18 years
No. of pupils: 1080
Fees: Day £5,956–£7,049

Northwood College for Girls GDST
Maxwell Road, Northwood, Middlesex HA6 2YE
Tel: 01923 825446
Head of School: Mrs Rebecca Brown
Age range: G3–18 years
No. of pupils: 844

Oak Heights
3 Red Lion Court, Alexandra Road, Hounslow, Middlesex TW3 1JS
Tel: 020 8577 1827
Head: Mr S Dhillon
Age range: 11–16
No. of pupils: 48
Fees: Day £6,000

Orley Farm School
South Hill Avenue, Harrow, Middlesex HA1 3NU
Tel: 020 8869 7600
Headmaster: Mr Tim Calvey
Age range: 4–13 years

Quainton Hall School & Nursery
91 Hindes Road, Harrow, Middlesex HA1 1RX
Tel: 020 8861 8861
Headmaster: S Ford BEd (Hons), UWE Bristol
Age range: B2–13 G2–11
Fees: Day £11,850–£13,050

Radnor House
Pope's Villa, Cross Deep, Twickenham, Middlesex TW1 4QG
Tel: +44 (0)20 8891 6264
Head: Mr Darryl Wideman MA Oxon, PGCE
Age range: 9–18 years

Rambert School of Ballet & Contemporary Dance
Clifton Lodge, St Margaret's Drive, Twickenham, Middlesex TW1 1QN
Tel: 020 8892 9960
Principal: R McKim
Age range: 16+

Reddiford School
36-38 Cecil Park, Pinner, Middlesex HA5 5HH
Tel: 020 8866 0660
Headteacher: Mrs J Batt CertEd, NPQH
Age range: 3–11
No. of pupils: 320
Fees: Day £4,860–£11,565

Regent College London
Regent House, 167 Imperial Drive, Harrow, Middlesex HA2 7HD
Tel: +44 (0)20 3870 6666
Co-Principals: Dr Selva Pankaj & Mrs Tharshiny Pankaj
Age range: 14–24 years

Roxeth Mead School
Buckholt House, 25 Middle Road, Harrow, Middlesex HA2 0HW
Tel: 020 8422 2092
Headmistress: Mrs A Isaacs
Age range: 3–7
No. of pupils: 54
Fees: Day £4,800–£10,665

St Catherine's Prep
Cross Deep, Twickenham, Middlesex TW1 4QJ
Tel: 020 8891 2898
Headmistress: Mrs Johneen McPherson MA
Age range: G4–11 years
No. of pupils: 102
Fees: Day £12,480–£13,470

St Christopher's School
71 Wembley Park Drive,
Wembley, Middlesex HA9 8HE
Tel: 020 8902 5069
Headteacher: Mr G. P. Musetti
Age range: 4–11
Fees: Day £9,006–£9,906

St Helen's College
Parkway, Hillingdon, Uxbridge,
Middlesex UB10 9JX
Tel: 01895 234371
Head: Mrs. Shirley Drummond BA,
PGCert, MLDP, FCCT
Age range: 2–11 years
No. of pupils: 380
Fees: Day £10,200–£12,600
⊘

St Helen's School
Eastbury Road, Northwood,
Middlesex HA6 3AS
Tel: +44 (0)1923 843210
Headmistress: Dr Mary Short BA,
PhD
Age range: G3–18
No. of pupils: VIth165
🚹 🚹 Ⓐ £ 16ᐩ

St John's School
Potter Street Hill, Northwood,
Middlesex HA6 3QY
Tel: 020 8866 0067
Headmaster: Mr Sean Robinson
Age range: B3–13 years
🚹

St Martin's School
40 Moor Park Road, Northwood,
Middlesex HA6 2DJ
Tel: 01923 825740
Headmaster: Mr S Dunn BEd (Hons)
Age range: B3–13 years
🚹 ⊘

St. Catherine's School
Cross Deep, Twickenham,
Middlesex TW1 4QJ
Tel: 020 8891 2898
Headmistress: Mrs Johneen
McPherson MA
Age range: G4–18 years
No. of pupils: 449
Fees: Day £12,480–£16,125
🚹 Ⓐ £ ⊘ 16ᐩ

St. John's Senior School
North Lodge, The Ridgeway,
Enfield, Middlesex EN2 8BE
Tel: +44 (0)20 8366 0035
Head Teacher: Mr A Tardios
Age range: 11–18 years
Ⓐ 16ᐩ

Tashbar of Edgware
Mowbray Road, Edgware,
Middlesex HA8 8JL
Age range: B3–11
🚹

**The Hall Pre-Preparatory
School & Nursery**
The Grange Country House,
Rickmansworth Road,
Northwood, Middlesex HA6 2RB
Tel: 01923 822807
Headmistress: Mrs S M Goodwin
Age range: 1–7
Fees: Day £4,650–£9,900
£ ⊘

The John Lyon School
Middle Road, Harrow on the
Hill, Middlesex HA2 0HN
Tel: 020 8515 9443
Head: Mrs Katherine Haynes BA,
MEd, NPQH
Age range: B11–18 years
No. of pupils: 600
Ⓐ £ ⊘ 16ᐩ

The Mall School
185 Hampton Road, Twickenham,
Middlesex TW2 5NQ
Tel: 0208 977 2523
Headmaster: Mr D C Price BSc, MA
Age range: B4–11 years
🚹 ⊘

**The St Michael
Steiner School**
Park Road, Hanworth Park,
London, Middlesex TW13 6PN
Tel: 0208 893 1299
Age range: 3–16 (17 from Jul 2014)
No. of pupils: 101
Fees: Day £3,850–£9,500
£ ⊘

**Twickenham
Preparatory School**
Beveree, 43 High Street,
Hampton, Middlesex TW12 2SA
Tel: 020 8979 6216
Headmaster: Mr Oliver Barrett
Age range: B4–13 years G4–11 years
⊘

Surrey

Al-Khair School
109-117 Cherry Orchard Road,
Croydon, Surrey CR0 6BE
Tel: 020 8662 8664
Headteacher: Mrs Aisha Chaudhry
Age range: 5–16 years

Broomfield House School
Broomfield Road, Kew Gardens,
Richmond, Surrey TW9 3HS
Tel: 020 8940 3884
Head of School: Ms Susie Byers
Age range: 3–11 years
⊘

Cambridge Tutors College
Water Tower Hill, Croydon,
Surrey CR0 5SX
Tel: 020 8688 5284/7363
Principal: Dr Chris Drew
Age range: 15–19
No. of pupils: 215 VIth200
Fees: Day £10,400–£22,995
16ᐩ Ⓐ 🛏 £ 16ᐩ

Canbury School
Kingston Hill, Kingston upon
Thames, Surrey KT2 7LN
Tel: 020 8549 8622
Headmistress: Ms Louise Clancy
Age range: 11–18
No. of pupils: 58
Fees: Day £16,401
£ ⊘

Collingwood School
3 Springfield Road, Wallington,
Surrey SM6 0BD
Tel: 020 8647 4607
Headmaster: Mr Leigh Hardie
Age range: 3–11 years
⊘

Croydon High School GDST
Old Farleigh Road, Selsdon,
South Croydon, Surrey CR2 8YB
Tel: 020 8260 7500
Headmistress: Mrs Emma Pattison
Age range: G3–18
No. of pupils: 580 VIth75
🚹 Ⓐ £ ⊘ 16ᐩ

**Cumnor House
Kindergarten & PreSchool,
South Croydon**
91 Pampisford Road, South
Croydon, Surrey CR2 6DH
Tel: 020 8660 4480
Head of School: Miss Emma
Edwards
Age range: 2–4 years

**Cumnor House
School for Boys**
168 Pampisford Road, South
Croydon, Surrey CR2 6DA
Tel: 020 8645 2614
Headmaster: Mr Daniel Cummings
Age range: B2–13 years
No. of pupils: 423
Fees: Day £3,880–£4,655
🚹 ⊘

**Cumnor House
School for Girls**
1 Woodcote Lane, Purley,
Surrey CR8 3HB
Tel: 020 8668 0050
Headmistress: Mrs Amanda
McShane
Age range: G4–11 years
🚹

Educare Small School
12 Cowleaze Road, Kingston
upon Thames, Surrey KT2 6DZ
Tel: 020 8547 0144
Head Teacher: Mrs E Steinthal
Age range: 3–11
No. of pupils: 46
Fees: Day £6,240
⊘

Elmhurst School
44-48 South Park Hill Rd, South
Croydon, Surrey CR2 7DW
Tel: 020 8688 0661
Head Teacher: Mr Tony Padfield
Age range: B3–11 years
🚹

Falcons Prep Richmond
41 Kew Foot Road, Richmond,
Surrey TW9 2SS
Tel: 020 8948 9490
Headmistress: Ms Olivia Buchanan
Age range: B7–13
Fees: Day £14,250–£17,835
🚹 ⊘

**Holy Cross Preparatory
School**
George Road, Kingston upon
Thames, Surrey KT2 7NU
Tel: 020 8942 0729
Headteacher: Mrs S Hair BEd(Hons)
Age range: G3–11 years
🚹 £ ⊘

**Homefield Preparatory
School**
Western Road, Sutton,
Surrey SM1 2TE
Tel: 0208 642 0965
Headmaster: Mr John Towers
Age range: B4–13 years
No. of pupils: 350
Fees: Day £6,345–£13,650
🚹 ⊘

Kew College
24-26 Cumberland Road,
Kew, Surrey TW9 3HQ
Tel: 020 8940 2039
Head: Mrs Jane Bond BSc, MA(Ed),
PGCE
Age range: 3–11 years
No. of pupils: 296
£ ⊘

KEW GREEN PREPARATORY SCHOOL
For further details see p. 81
Layton House, Ferry Lane,
Kew Green, Richmond,
Surrey TW9 3AF
Tel: 020 8948 5999
Email: admissions@kgps.co.uk
Website: www.kgps.co.uk
Headmistress: Mrs N Gibson
Age range: 4–11 years
No. of pupils: 273
Fees: Day £6,304

King's House School
68 King's Road, Richmond,
Surrey TW10 6ES
Tel: 020 8940 1878
Head: Mr Mark Turner BA, PGCE,
NPQH
Age range: B3–13 years G3–4 years
No. of pupils: 460
Fees: Day £1,860–£6,190

Kingston Grammar School
70 London Rd, Kingston upon
Thames, Surrey KT2 6PY
Tel: 020 8546 5875
Head: Mr Stephen Lehec
Age range: 11–18

Laleham Lea School
29 Peaks Hill, Purley, Surrey CR8 3JJ
Tel: 020 8660 3351
Headteacher: Ms K Barry
Age range: 3–11 years
No. of pupils: 131
Fees: Day £9,207

MARYMOUNT LONDON
For further details see p. 83
George Road, Kingston upon
Thames, Surrey KT2 7PE
Tel: +44 (0)20 8949 0571
Email: admissions@
marymountlondon.com
Website:
www.marymountlondon.com
Headmistress: Mrs Margaret
Giblin
Age range: G11–18 years
No. of pupils: 258
Fees: Day £27,250 WB
£44,180 FB £46,130

Oakwood Independent School
Godstone Road, Purley,
Surrey CR8 2AN
Tel: 020 8668 8080
Headmaster: Mr Ciro Candia
BA(Hons), PGCE
Age range: 3–11
No. of pupils: 176
Fees: Day £9,030–£9,840

Old Palace of John Whitgift School
Old Palace Road, Croydon,
Surrey CR0 1AX
Tel: 020 8688 2027
Head: Mrs. C Jewell
Age range: G3–18 years
No. of pupils: 650
Fees: Day £3,300–£5,536

Old Vicarage School
46-48 Richmond Hill,
Richmond, Surrey TW10 6QX
Tel: 020 8940 0922
Headmistress: Mrs G D Linthwaite
Age range: G3–11 years
No. of pupils: 200
Fees: Day £5,200

Park Hill School
8 Queens Road, Kingston upon
Thames, Surrey KT2 7SH
Tel: 020 8546 5496
Headmaster: Mr Alistair Bond
Age range: 2–11
No. of pupils: 100
Fees: Day £10,440

Rokeby School
George Road, Kingston upon
Thames, Surrey KT2 7PB
Tel: 020 8942 2247
Head: Mr J R Peck
Age range: B4–13 years

Royal Botanic Gardens
School of Horticulture, Kew,
Richmond, Surrey TW9 3AB
Tel: 020 8332 5545
Principal: Emma Fox BEd(Hons),
DipHort(Kew)(Hons)
Fees: Day £0

Royal Russell Junior School
Coombe Lane, Croydon,
Surrey CR9 5BX
Tel: 020 8651 5884
Junior School Headmaster: Mr
James C Thompson
Age range: 3–11
No. of pupils: 300
Fees: Day £11,160–£14,220

Royal Russell School
Coombe Lane, Croydon,
Surrey CR9 5BX
Tel: 020 8657 3669
Headmaster: Christopher
Hutchinson
Age range: 11–18
No. of pupils: 590 VIth180
Fees: Day £18,480 FB £36,525

Seaton House School
67 Banstead Road South,
Sutton, Surrey SM2 5LH
Tel: 020 8642 2332
Headmistress: Mrs Debbie Morrison
Higher Diploma in Education (RSA)
Age range: B3–5 G3–11
No. of pupils: 164
Fees: Day £10,188

Shrewsbury House School
107 Ditton Road, Surbiton,
Surrey KT6 6RL
Tel: 020 8399 3066
Executive Head: Ms Joanna
Hubbard MA BA(Hons) PGCE
PGDipSEN
Age range: B7–13 years

St David's School
23/25 Woodcote Valley Road,
Purley, Surrey CR8 3AL
Tel: 020 8660 0723
Headmistress: Cressida Mardell
Age range: 3–11
No. of pupils: 167
Fees: Day £6,375–£10,650

St James Senior Boys School
Church Road, Ashford,
Surrey TW15 3DZ
Tel: 01784 266930
Headmaster: Mr David Brazier
Age range: B11–18
No. of pupils: 403 VIth65
Fees: Day £18,930

Staines Preparatory School
3 Gresham Road, Staines-upon-
Thames, Surrey TW18 2BT
Tel: 01784 450909
Head of School: Ms Samantha
Sawyer B.Ed (Hons), M.Ed, NPQH
Age range: 3–11 years
No. of pupils: 307
Fees: Day £10,560–£12,660

Surbiton High School
13-15 Surbiton Crescent, Kingston
upon Thames, Surrey KT1 2JT
Tel: 020 8546 5245
Principal: Mrs Rebecca Glover
Age range: B4–11 G4–18
No. of pupils: 1210 VIth186
Fees: Day £10,857–£17,142

Sutton High School GDST
55 Cheam Road, Sutton,
Surrey SM1 2AX
Tel: 020 8642 0594
Headmistress: Mrs Katharine
Crouch
Age range: G3–18
No. of pupils: 600 VIth60
Fees: Day £10,095–£17,043

The Cedars School
Coombe Road, Lloyd Park,
Croydon, Surrey CR0 5RD
Tel: 020 8185 7770
Headmaster: Robert Teague Bsc
(Hons)
Age range: B11–18

The Royal Ballet School
White Lodge, Richmond,
Surrey TW10 5HR
Tel: 020 8392 8440
Artistic Director: Christopher
Powney
Age range: 11–19 years

The Secretary College
123 South End, Croydon,
Surrey CR0 1BJ
Tel: 0208 688 4440
Principal: Mr J E K Safo

The Study School
57 Thetford Road, New
Malden, Surrey KT3 5DP
Tel: 020 8942 0754
Head of School: Mrs Donna
Brackstone-Drake
Age range: 3–11
No. of pupils: 134
Fees: Day £4,860–£11,388

Trinity School
Shirley Park, Croydon,
Surrey CR9 7AT
Tel: 020 8656 9541
Head: Alasdair Kennedy MA
(Cantab)
Age range: B10–18 G16–18
No. of pupils: 1007
Fees: Day £16,656

Unicorn School
238 Kew Road, Richmond,
Surrey TW9 3JX
Tel: 020 8948 3926
Headmaster: Mr Kit Thompson
Age range: 3–11
Fees: Day £7,170–£13,170

Westbury House
80 Westbury Road, New
Malden, Surrey KT3 5AS
Tel: 020 8942 5885
Head of School: Matthew Burke
Age range: 3–11
Fees: Day £4,860–£11,115

Whitgift School
Haling Park, South Croydon,
Surrey CR2 6YT
Tel: +44 20 8633 9935
Headmaster: Mr Christopher
Ramsey
Age range: B10–18 years
No. of pupils: 1550
Fees: Day £21,240 WB
£34,260 FB £41,550

Schools in the South-East

KEY TO SYMBOLS

- ⚲ *Boys' school*
- ⚲ *Girls' school*
- 🌐 *International school*
- 16 *Tutorial or sixth form college*
- Ⓐ *A levels*
- 🏫 *Boarding accommodation*
- £ *Bursaries*
- IB *International Baccalaureate*
- ✐ *Learning support*
- 16 *Entrance at 16+*
- ❧ *Vocational qualifications*
- (APS) *Independent Association of Prep Schools*
- (HMC) *The Headmasters' & Headmistresses' Conference*
- (ISA) *Independent Schools Association*
- (GSA) *Girls' School Association*
- (BSA) *Boarding Schools' Association*
- ⑤ *Society of Heads*

Unless otherwise indicated, all schools are coeducational day schools. Single-sex and boarding schools will be indicated by the relevant icon.

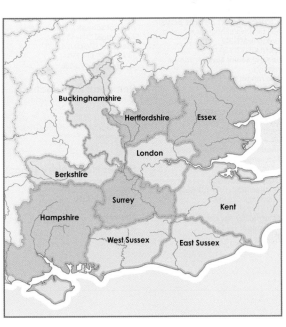

Berkshire

Alder Bridge Steiner-Waldorf School
Bridge House, Mill Lane, Padworth, Reading, Berkshire RG7 4JU
Tel: 0118 971 4471
Head of School: Lucia Dimarco
Age range: 3–14 years

Bradfield College
Bradfield, Berkshire RG7 6AU
Tel: 0118 964 4516
Headmaster: Dr Christopher Stevens
Age range: 13–18 years
No. of pupils: 820
Fees: Day £32,280 FB £40,350
🐾Ⓐ🏫£ⒾⒷ✏16▸

Caversham Preparatory School
16 Peppard Road, Caversham, Reading, Berkshire RG4 8JZ
Tel: 0118 478 684
Head of School: Mrs Naomi Williams
Age range: 3–11 years

Claires Court Junior Boys
Ridgeway, The Thicket, Maidenhead, Berkshire SL6 3QE
Tel: 01628 327400
Head of Juniors: Ms Leanne Kirby
Age range: B4–11 years
🐾✏

Claires Court Nursery, Girls and Sixth Form
1 College Avenue, Maidenhead, Berkshire SL6 6AW
Tel: 01628 327500
Head of Juniors: Ms Leanne Kirby
Age range: B16–18 years G4–18 years
🐾Ⓐ£✏16▸

Claires Court Senior Boys
Ray Mill Road East, Maidenhead, Berkshire SL6 8TE
Tel: 01628 327600
Head of Senior Boys: Mr James Wilding
Age range: B11–16 years
🐾Ⓐ£✏16▸

Crosfields School
Shinfield Road, Reading, Berkshire RG2 9BL
Tel: 0118 987 1810
Headmaster: Mr Craig Watson
Age range: 3–16 years

Dolphin School
Waltham Road, Hurst, Reading, Berkshire RG10 0FR
Tel: 0118 934 1277
Headmaster: Mr Adam Hurst
Age range: 3–13 years
£✏

Eagle House School
Sandhurst, Berkshire GU47 8PH
Tel: 01344 772134
Headmaster: Mr A P N Barnard BA(Hons), PGCE
Age range: 3–13 years
No. of pupils: 394
Fees: Day £18,615 FB £25,905
🏫£✏

Elstree School
Woolhampton Hill, Woolhampton, Reading, Berkshire RG7 5TD
Tel: 01189 713302
Headmaster: Mr Sid Inglis B.A. (Hons), P.G.C.E.
Age range: 3–13 years
No. of pupils: 270
🏫£✏

Eton College
Windsor, Berkshire SL4 6DW
Tel: +44 (0)1753 370 611
Head Master: Mr Simon Henderson MA
Age range: B13–18 years
No. of pupils: 1342
Fees: FB £44,094
🐾🌐Ⓐ🏫£✏16▸

Eton End School
35 Eton Road, Datchet, Slough, Berkshire SL3 9AX
Tel: 01753 541075
Head of School: Mrs Sophie Banks MEd
Age range: 3–11 years
No. of pupils: 244
Fees: Day £10,266–£13,119
£✏

Heathfield School
London Road, Ascot, Berkshire SL5 8BQ
Tel: 01344 898343
Head of School: Ms Sarah Wilson
Age range: G11–18 years
Fees: Day £7,840–£8,000 FB £12,650–£12,950
🐾Ⓐ🏫£✏16▸

Hemdean House School
Hemdean Road, Caversham, Reading, Berkshire RG4 7SD
Tel: 0118 947 2590
Head Teacher: Mrs Helen Chalmers
Age range: 2–11 years
£✏

Herries Preparatory School
Dean Lane, Cookham Dean, Berkshire SL6 9BD
Tel: 01628 483350
Headteacher: Mr Robert Grosse
Age range: 3–11 years
✏

Highfield Preparatory School
2 West Road, Maidenhead, Berkshire SL6 1PD
Tel: 01628 624918
Headteacher: Mrs Joanna Leach
Age range: B2–7 years G2–11 years
🐾£✏

Holme Grange School
Heathlands Road, Wokingham, Berkshire RG40 3AL
Tel: 0118 978 1566
Headteacher: Mrs Claire Robinson BA (Open) PGCE NPQH
Age range: 3–16 years
No. of pupils: 660
Fees: Day £10,665–£16,140
£✏

Kids Inc Day Nursery – Crowthorne
59-61 Dukes Ride, Crowthorne, Berkshire RG45 6NS
Tel: 01344 780670

Lambrook School
Winkfield Row, Nr Ascot, Berkshire RG42 6LU
Tel: 01344 882717
Headmaster: Mr Jonathan Perry
Age range: 3–13 years
No. of pupils: 600
🏫✏

LEIGHTON PARK SCHOOL
For further details see p. 94
Shinfield Road, Reading, Berkshire RG2 7ED
Tel: 0118 987 9600
Email: admissions@leightonpark.com
Website: www.leightonpark.com
Head: Mr Matthew L S Judd BA, PGCE
Age range: 11–18 years
No. of pupils: 520
🐾Ⓐ🏫£ⒾⒷ✏16▸

Long Close School
Upton Court Road, Upton, Slough, Berkshire SL3 7LU
Tel: 01753 520095
Headteacher: Miss K Nijjar BA (Hons), Med, MA
Age range: 2–16 years
No. of pupils: 329
£✏

Luckley House School
Luckley Road, Wokingham, Berkshire RG40 3EU
Tel: 0118 978 4175
Head: Mrs Areti Bizior
Age range: 11–18 years
🌐Ⓐ🏫£✏16▸

Ludgrove
Wokingham, Berkshire RG40 3AB
Tel: 0118 978 9881
Head of School: Mr Simon Barber
Age range: B8–13 years
🐾🏫£✏

LVS ASCOT
For further details see p. 96
London Road, Ascot, Berkshire SL5 8DR
Tel: 01344 882770
Email: enquiries@lvs.ascot.sch.uk
Website: www.lvs.ascot.sch.uk
Principal: Mrs Christine Cunniffe BA (Hons), MMus. MBA
Age range: 4–18 years
No. of pupils: 800
Fees: Day £12,915–£19,335 FB £27,585–£33,975
🐾Ⓐ🏫£✏16▸

Meadowbrook Montessori School
Malt Hill, Warfield, Berkshire RG42 6JQ
Tel: 01344 890869
Director of Education: Ms Serena Gunn
Age range: 4–11 years

Newbold School
Popeswood Road, Binfield, Bracknell, Berkshire RG42 4AH
Tel: 01344 421088
Headteacher: Mrs Jaki Crissey MA, BA, PGCE Primary
Age range: 3–11 years

OneSchool Global UK Reading Campus (Primary)
401 Old Whitley Wood Lane, Reading, Berkshire RG2 8QA
Tel: 0118 931 2938
Age range: 7–11 years

OneSchool Global UK Reading Campus (Senior)
The Quad, 14 Arkwright Road, Reading, Berkshire RG2 0LU
Tel: 03000 700421
Age range: 11–18 years

Our Lady's Preparatory School
The Avenue, Crowthorne, Wokingham, Berkshire RG45 6PB
Tel: 01344 773394
Headmaster: Mr Michael Stone
Age range: 3 months–11 years
✏

Padworth College
Sopers Lane, Reading, Berkshire RG7 4NR
Tel: 0118 983 2644
Principal: Lorraine Atkins
Age range: 14–19 years
🌐Ⓐ🏫£16▸

Pangbourne College
Pangbourne, Reading,
Berkshire RG8 8LA
Tel: 0118 984 2101
Headmaster: Thomas J C Garnier
Age range: 11–18 years
No. of pupils: 458
Fees: Day £6,300–£8,540 WB
£8,210–£11,510 FB £9,050–£12,680

Papplewick School
Windsor Road, Ascot,
Berkshire SL5 7LH
Tel: 01344 621488
Headmaster: Mr Tom Bunbury
Age range: B6–13 years

QUEEN ANNE'S SCHOOL
For further details see p. 98
6 Henley Road, Caversham,
Reading, Berkshire RG4 6DX
Tel: 0118 918 7300
Email: office@qas.org.uk
Website: www.qas.org.uk
Head: Ms Elaine Purves
Age range: G11–18 years
No. of pupils: G450
Fees: Day £8,370 FB £13,590

Reading Blue Coat School
Holme Park, Sonning Lane, Sonning,
Reading, Berkshire RG4 6SU
Tel: 0118 944 1005
Headmaster: Mr Peter Thomas
Age range: B11–18 years
G16–18 years

**REDDAM HOUSE
BERKSHIRE**
For further details see p. 100
Bearwood Road, Sindlesham,
Wokingham, Berkshire RG41 5BG
Tel: +44 (0)118 974 8300
Email: registrar@
reddamhouse.org.uk
Website:
www.reddamhouse.org.uk
Principal: Mr Rick Cross
Age range: 3 months–18 years
No. of pupils: 675
Fees: Day £11,490–£18,420
WB £27,981–£32,244 FB
£29,526–£33,789

Shakhsiyah School, Slough
Cippenham Lodge, Cippenham
Lane, Slough, Berkshire SL1 5AN
Tel: 01753 518 000
Head Teacher: Mrs Tahreem Sabir
Age range: 3–11 years

St Andrew's School
Buckhold, Pangbourne,
Reading, Berkshire RG8 8QA
Tel: 0118 974 4276
Head Master: Ed Graham
Age range: 3–13 years
Fees: Day £3,890–£6,525

**St Bernard's
Preparatory School**
Hawtrey Close, Slough,
Berkshire SL1 1TB
Tel: 01753 521821
Headteacher: Mrs A Verma
Age range: 2.5–11 years

St Edward's Prep
64 Tilehurst Road, Reading,
Berkshire RG30 2JH
Tel: 0118 957 4342
Head Master: Mr Jonathan Parsons
Age range: B3–11 years G3–5 years

St George's Ascot
Wells Lane, Ascot, Berkshire SL5 7DZ
Tel: 01344 629900
Headmistress: Mrs Liz Hewer MA
(Hons) (Cantab) PGCE
Age range: G11–18 years

**St George's School
Windsor Castle**
Windsor Castle, Windsor,
Berkshire SL4 1QF
Tel: 01753 865553
Head Master: Mr W Goldsmith BA
(Hons), FRSA, FCCT
Age range: 3–13 years

**ST JOHN'S BEAUMONT
PREPARATORY SCHOOL**
For further details see p. 105
Priest Hill, Old Windsor,
Berkshire SL4 2JN
Tel: 01784 494 053
Email: sjb.admissions@sjb.email
Website: www.sjbwindsor.uk
Headmaster: Mr G E F Delaney
BA(Hons), PGCE, MSc
Age range: B3–13 years
No. of pupils: 240
Fees: Day £3,540–
£6,820 FB £10,415

St Joseph's College
Upper Redlands Road,
Reading, Berkshire RG1 5JT
Tel: 0118 966 1000
Head of School: Mrs Laura
Stotesbury
Age range: 3–18 years

St Mary's School Ascot
St Mary's Road, Ascot,
Berkshire SL5 9JF
Tel: 01344 296614
Headmistress: Mrs Danuta Staunton
Age range: G11–18 years

St Piran's School
Gringer Hill, Maidenhead,
Berkshire SL6 7LZ
Tel: 01628 594300
Headmaster: Mr Sebastian Sales
Age range: 2–11 years

Sunningdale School
Dry Arch Road, Sunningdale,
Berkshire SL5 9PY
Tel: 01344 620159
Headmaster: Tom Dawson MA,
PGCE
Age range: B7–13 years

The Abbey School
Kendrick Road, Reading,
Berkshire RG1 5DZ
Tel: 0118 987 2256
Head: Mr Will le Fleming
Age range: G3–18 years
No. of pupils: 1000
Fees: Day £11,025–£18,885

**The King's House
School, Windsor**
King's House, 77A Frances Road,
Windsor, Berkshire SL4 3AQ
Tel: 01753 834850
Headteacher: Mrs Lyndsey Harding
Age range: 3–11 years

**The Marist Preparatory
School**
King's Road, Sunninghill,
Ascot, Berkshire SL5 7PS
Tel: 01344 624291
Vice Principal Prep Phase: Mrs
Jane Gow
Age range: G2–11 years

The Marist School
King's Road, Sunninghill,
Ascot, Berkshire SL5 7PS
Tel: 01344 624291
Principal: Ms Jo Smith
Age range: G2–18 years

**The Oratory
Preparatory School**
Great Oaks, Goring Heath,
Reading, Berkshire RG8 7SF
Tel: 0118 984 4511
Headmaster: Mr Rob Stewart
Age range: 2–13 years

The Oratory School
Woodcote, Reading,
Berkshire RG8 0PJ
Tel: 01491 683500
Head Master: Mr Joe Smith
BA(Hons), MEd, PGCE
Age range: 11–18 years

The Vine Christian School
Three Mile Cross Church,
Basingstoke Road, Three Mile
Cross, Reading, Berkshire RG7 1HF
Tel: 0118 988 6464
Head of School: Mrs René
Esterhuizen
Age range: 3–18 years

Trinity Christian School
11 Glebe Road, Reading,
Berkshire RG2 7AG
Tel: 0118 336 0477
Head of School: Mr Nigel Steele
Age range: 4–11 years

Upton House School
115 St Leonard's Road,
Windsor, Berkshire SL4 3DF
Tel: 01753 862610
Head: Mrs Rhian Thornton BA (Hons)
NPQH LLE PGCE
Age range: 2–11 years
No. of pupils: 287
Fees: Day £3,230–£5,400

**Waverley Preparatory
School & Day Nursery**
Waverley Way, Finchampstead,
Wokingham, Berkshire RG40 4YD
Tel: 0118 973 1121
Principal: Mr Guy Shore
Age range: 3 months–11 years

Wellington College
Duke's Ride, Crowthorne,
Berkshire RG45 7PU
Tel: +44 (0)1344 444000
Master: Mr James Dahl
Age range: 13–18 years
No. of pupils: 1090 VIth475
Fees: Day £31,140–£35,760
FB £42,630

Buckinghamshire

Ashfold School
Dorton House, Dorton, Aylesbury,
Buckinghamshire HP18 9NG
Tel: 01844 238237
Headmaster: Mr Colin MacIntosh
Age range: 3–13 years
(符)

Broughton Manor
Preparatory School
Newport Road, Broughton, Milton
Keynes, Buckinghamshire MK10 9AA
Tel: 01908 665234
Heads: Mr J Smith & Mrs R Smith
Age range: 2 months–11 years
(£)

Caldicott
Crown Lane, Farnham Royal,
Buckinghamshire SL2 3SL
Tel: 01753 649300
Headmaster: Mr Jeremy Banks BA
(Hons) QTS, MEd
Age range: B7–13 years
(符)(符)(符)

Chesham Preparatory
School
Two Dells Lane, Chesham,
Buckinghamshire HP5 3QF
Tel: 01494 782619
Headmaster: Mr Jonathan Beale
Age range: 3–13 years
(符)

Child First Aylesbury
Pre-School
35 Rickfords Hill, Aylesbury,
Buckinghamshire HP20 2RT
Tel: 01296 433224
Age range: 3–5 years

Crown House
Preparatory School
Bassetsbury Manor, Bassetsbury
Lane, High Wycombe,
Buckinghamshire HP11 1QX
Tel: 01494 529927
Headteacher: Mrs Sarah Hobby
Age range: 3–11 years
(符)

Dair House School
Bishops Blake, Beaconsfield
Road, Farnham Royal,
Buckinghamshire SL2 3BY
Tel: 01753 643964
Headmaster: Mr Terry Wintle
BEd(Hons)
Age range: 3–11 years
(£)(符)

DAVENIES SCHOOL
For further details see p. 90
Station Road, Beaconsfield,
Buckinghamshire HP9 1AA
Tel: 01494 685400
Email: office@davenies.co.uk
Website: www.davenies.co.uk
Headmaster: Mr Carl Rycroft
BEd (Hons)
Age range: B4–13 years
No. of pupils: 337
Fees: Day £12,105–£18,255
(符)(£)(符)

Gateway School
1 High Street, Great Missenden,
Buckinghamshire HP16 9AA
Tel: 01494 862407
Head of School: Mrs Cath Bufton-
Green
Age range: 2–11 years
(符)

Gayhurst School
Bull Lane, Gerrards Cross,
Buckinghamshire SL9 8RJ
Tel: 01753 969538
Headmaster: Gareth R A Davies
Age range: 3–11 years
(符)

Godstowe Preparatory
School
Shrubbery Road, High Wycombe,
Buckinghamshire HP13 6PR
Tel: 01494 529273
Headmistress: Ms Sophie Green
Age range: B3–7 years G3–13 years
(符)(符)(符)(£)(符)

Griffin House
Preparatory School
Little Kimble, Aylesbury,
Buckinghamshire HP17 0XP
Tel: 01844 346154
Headmaster: Mr Tim Walford
Age range: 3–11 years
(符)

Heatherton School
10 Copperkins Lane, Amersham,
Buckinghamshire HP6 5QB
Tel: 01494 726433
Headteacher: Mrs Nicola Nicoll
Age range: B3–4 years G3–11 years
No. of pupils: 148
Fees: Day £1,140–£13,335
(符)(符)

High March
23 Ledborough Lane, Beaconsfield,
Buckinghamshire HP9 2PZ
Tel: 01494 675186
Head of School: Mrs Kate Gater
Age range: B3–4 years G3–11 years
No. of pupils: 280
Fees: Day £5,850–£16,185
(符)(£)(符)

International School of
Creative Arts (ISCA)
Framewood Road, Wexham,
Buckinghamshire SL2 4QS
Tel: +44 (0)1753 208820
Head of School: Mr Robert Hunter
Age range: 15–19 years
(符)(符)

Kids Inc Day Nursery
– Aylesbury
The Pavilion, Watermead,
Aylesbury, Buckinghamshire
HP19 0FY
Tel: 01296 397407

Maltman's Green School
Maltmans Lane, Gerrards Cross,
Buckinghamshire SL9 8RR
Tel: 01753 883022
Headmistress: Mrs Jill Walker BSc
(Hons), MA Ed, PGCE
Age range: G2–11 years
No. of pupils: 320
Fees: Day £2,075–£5,370
(符)(£)(符)

Milton Keynes
Preparatory School
Tattenhoe Lane, Milton Keynes,
Buckinghamshire MK3 7EG
Tel: 01908 642111
Head of School: Mr Simon Driver
Age range: 2 months–11 years
(£)

Pipers Corner School
Pipers Lane, Great
Kingshill, High Wycombe,
Buckinghamshire HP15 6LP
Tel: 01494 718 255
Headmistress: Mrs H J Ness-Gifford
BA(Hons), PGCE
Age range: G4–18 years
(符)(A)(£)(符)(16+)(符)

St Mary's School
94 Packhorse Road, Gerrards
Cross, Buckinghamshire SL9 8JQ
Tel: 01753 883370
Head of School: Mrs Patricia Adams
Age range: G3–18 years
(符)(A)(£)(符)(16+)

Stowe School
Buckingham, Buckinghamshire
MK18 5EH
Tel: 01280 818000
Headmaster: Dr Anthony
Wallersteiner
Age range: 13–18 years
(符)(A)(符)(符)(16+)

Swanbourne House School
Swanbourne, Milton Keynes,
Buckinghamshire MK17 0HZ
Tel: 01296 720264
Head of School: Mrs Jane Thorpe
Age range: 4–13 years
(符)(£)(符)

Teikyo School UK
Framewood Road, Wexham,
Buckinghamshire SL2 4QS
Tel: 01753 663711
Age range: 15–18 years
(符)(符)

The Beacon School
15 Amersham Road,
Chesham Bois, Amersham,
Buckinghamshire HP6 5PF
Tel: 01494 433654
Headmaster: Mr William Phelps
Age range: B3–13 years
(符)(符)

The Grove Independent
School
Redland Drive, Loughton, Milton
Keynes, Buckinghamshire MK5 8HD
Tel: 01908 690590
Principal: Mrs Deborah Berkin
Age range: 3 months–13 years

The Webber
Independent School
Soskin Drive, Stantonbury
Fields, Milton Keynes,
Buckinghamshire MK14 6DP
Tel: 01908 574740
Principal: Mrs Hilary Marsden
Age range: 6 months–16 years
(A)(符)

Thornton College
College Lane, Thornton, Milton
Keynes, Buckinghamshire MK17 0HJ
Tel: 01280 812610
Headteacher: Mrs Val Holmes
Age range: G3–18 years
(Boarding from age 7)
No. of pupils: 402
Fees: Day £10,545–£16,815 WB
£18,525–£23,445 FB £23,040–£28,575
(符)(符)(A)(符)(符)

Thorpe House School
Oval Way, Gerrards Cross,
Buckinghamshire SL9 8QA
Tel: 01753 882474
Headmaster: Mr Nicholas Pietrek
Age range: B4–16 years
(符)(符)

Wycombe Abbey
Frances Dove Way, High Wycombe,
Buckinghamshire HP11 1PE
Tel: +44 (0)1494 520381
Headmistress: Mrs Jo Duncan MA
(St Andrews), PGCE (Cantab)
Age range: G11–18 years
No. of pupils: 663
Fees: Day £30,945 FB £41,250
(符)(符)(A)(符)(£)(符)(16+)

East Sussex

Bartholomews Tutorial College
22-23 Prince Albert Street, Brighton, East Sussex BN1 1HF
Tel: 01273 205965/205141
Head of School: Will Duncombe
Age range: 14+
No. of pupils: 40
Fees: Day £22,000

Battle Abbey School
Battle, East Sussex TN33 0AD
Tel: 01424 772385
Headmaster: Mr D Clark BA(Hons)
Age range: 2–18
No. of pupils: 286 VIth48
Fees: Day £6,939–£16,914
FB £26,649–£31,932

Bede's School
The Dicker, Upper Dicker, Hailsham, East Sussex BN27 3QH
Tel: +44 (0)1323843252
Head: Mr Peter Goodyer
Age range: 3 months–18
No. of pupils: 800 VIth295
Fees: Day £10,230–£17,400
FB £22,290–£25,650

Bellerbys College Brighton
1 Billinton Way, Brighton, East Sussex BN1 4LF
Tel: +44 (0)1273 339333
Age range: 14–19 years

Brighton & Hove Montessori School
67 Stanford Avenue, Brighton, East Sussex BN1 6FB
Tel: 01273 702485
Headteacher: Mrs Daisy Cockburn AMI, MontDip
Age range: 2–11

Brighton College
Eastern Road, Brighton, East Sussex BN2 0AL
Tel: 01273 704200
Head Master: Richard Cairns MA
Age range: 3–18
No. of pupils: 950
Fees: Day £10,050–£24,540 WB £33,390–£34,410 FB £37,470–£45,210

Brighton Girls GDST
Montpelier Road, Brighton, East Sussex BN1 3AT
Tel: 01273 280280
Head: Jennifer Smith
Age range: G3–18
No. of pupils: 680 VIth70
Fees: Day £7,191–£14,421

Brighton Steiner School
John Howard House, Roedean Road, Brighton, East Sussex BN2 5RA
Tel: 01273 386300
Chair of the College of Teachers: Carrie Rawle
Age range: 3–16
Fees: Day £7,800–£8,100

Buckswood School
Broomham Hall, Rye Road, Guestling, Hastings, East Sussex TN35 4LT
Tel: 01424 813 813
School Director: Mr Giles Sutton
Age range: 10–19
No. of pupils: 420

Charters Ancaster
Woodsgate Place, Gunters Lane, Bexhill-on-Sea, East Sussex TN39 4EB
Tel: 01424 216670
Nursery Manager: Susannah Crump
Age range: 6 months–5
No. of pupils: 125

Claremont Preparatory & Nursery School
Ebdens Hill, Baldslow, St Leonards-on-Sea, East Sussex TN37 7PW
Tel: 01424 751555
Headmistress: Abra Stoakley
Age range: 1–13
Fees: Day £6,900–£12,600

Claremont Senior & Sixth Form School
Bodiam, Nr Robertsbridge, East Sussex TN32 5UJ
Tel: 01580 830396
Headmaster: Mr. Giles Perrin
Age range: 14–18
Fees: Day £17,400

Darvell School
Darvell, Brightling Road, Robertsbridge, East Sussex TN32 5DR
Tel: 01580 883300
Head of School: Mr Timothy Maas
Age range: 4–16

Deepdene School
195 New Church Road, Hove, East Sussex BN3 4ED
Tel: 01273 418984
Heads: Mrs Nicola Gane & Miss Elizabeth Brown
Age range: 6 months–11 years
Fees: Day £8,349

Eastbourne College
Old Wish Road, Eastbourne, East Sussex BN21 4JX
Tel: 01323 452323 (Admissions)
Headmaster: Mr Tom Lawson MA (Oxon)
Age range: 13–18
No. of pupils: 650 VIth312
Fees: Day £23,895–£24,375
FB £36,420–£36,975

European School of Animal Osteopathy
25 Old Steine, Brighton, East Sussex BN1 1EL
Tel: 01273 673332
Head: Jean-Yves Girard

Greenfields Independent Day & Boarding School
Priory Road, Forest Row, East Sussex RH18 5JD
Tel: +44 (0)1342 822189
Executive Head: Mr. Jeff Smith
Age range: 2–19

Hove College
48 Cromwell Road, Hove, East Sussex BN3 3ER
Tel: 01273 772577
Director: Mr John Veale

JeMs Nursery
15 The Upper Drive, Hove, East Sussex BN3 6GR
Tel: 01273 328 675
Head of School: Ms. Penina Efune
Age range: 1–4

Lancing Prep Hove
The Droveway, Hove, East Sussex BN3 6LU
Tel: 01273 503452
Headmistress: Mrs Kirsty Keep BEd
Age range: 3–13 years

Lewes Old Grammar School
High Street, Lewes, East Sussex BN7 1XS
Tel: 01273 472634
Headmaster: Mr Robert Blewitt
Age range: 3–18
No. of pupils: 463 VIth50
Fees: Day £8,760–£14,625

MAYFIELD SCHOOL
For further details see p. 97
The Old Palace, Mayfield, East Sussex TN20 6PH
Tel: 01435 874642
Email: registrar@mayfieldgirls.org
Website: www.mayfieldgirls.org
Head: Ms Antonia Beary MA, MPhil (Cantab), PGCE
Age range: G11–18 years
No. of pupils: 405
Fees: Day £7,750 FB £12,250

Michael Hall School
Kidbrooke Park, Priory Road, Forest Row, East Sussex RH18 5JA
Tel: 01342 822275
Age range: 0 years–18 years
No. of pupils: VIth102
Fees: Day £9,245–£12,670

Roedean Moira House
Upper Carlisle Road, Eastbourne, East Sussex BN20 7TE
Tel: 01323 644144
Headmaster: Mr Andrew Wood
Age range: G0–18
No. of pupils: 289

ROEDEAN SCHOOL
For further details see p. 101
Roedean Way, Brighton, East Sussex BN2 5RQ
Tel: 01273 667500
Email: info@roedean.co.uk
Website: www.roedean.co.uk
Headmaster: Mr. Oliver Bond BA(Essex), PGCE, NPQH
Age range: G11–18 years
No. of pupils: 630 VIth155
Fees: Day £5,670–£7,415 WB £10,030–£11,185 FB £10,990–£13,305

Sacred Heart School
Mayfield Lane, Durgates, Wadhurst, East Sussex TN5 6DQ
Tel: 01892 783414
Headteacher: Mrs H Blake BA(Hons), PGCE
Age range: 2–11
No. of pupils: 121
Fees: Day £8,355

Skippers Hill Manor Preparatory School
Five Ashes, Mayfield, East Sussex TN20 6HR
Tel: 01825 830234
Headmaster: Mr Phillip Makhouli
Age range: 2–13
Fees: Day £2,660–£4,615

St Andrew's Prep
Meads Street, Eastbourne,
East Sussex BN20 7RP
Tel: 01323 733203
Headmaster: Tom Gregory
BA(Hons), PGCE
Age range: 9 months–13 years
No. of pupils: 374

St Bede's Preparatory School
Duke's Drive, Eastbourne,
East Sussex BN20 7XL
Tel: +44 (0)1323 734222
Age range: 3 months–13 years

St Christopher's School
33 New Church Road, Hove,
East Sussex BN3 4AD
Tel: 01273 735404
Head of School: Ms Elizabeth Lyle
Age range: 4–13 years

St George's Business & Language College
28-29 Grand Parade, Hastings,
East Sussex TN37 6DN
Tel: 01424 813696
Principal: Mr Richard Lawless

The Academy of Creative Training
8-10 Rock Place, Brighton,
East Sussex BN2 1PF
Tel: 01273 818266

The Drive Prep School
101 The Drive, Hove, East
Sussex BN3 6GE
Tel: 01273 738444
Head Teacher: Mrs S Parkinson
CertEd, CertPerfArts
Age range: 7–16 years

Vinehall
Robertsbridge, East Sussex TN32 5JL
Tel: 01580 880413
Headmaster: Joff Powis
Age range: 2–13 years
No. of pupils: 220
Fees: Day £10,350–£19,290 WB
£22,575–£23,100 FB £24,525–£25,125

Windlesham School
190 Dyke Road, Brighton,
East Sussex BN1 5AA
Tel: 01273 553645
Headmaster: Mr John Ingrassia
Age range: 3–11
No. of pupils: 195
Fees: Day £6,015–£8,955

Essex

Alleyn Court School
Wakering Road, Southend-
on-Sea, Essex SS3 0PW
Tel: 01702 582553
Headmaster: Mr Rupert W.J. Snow
B.Ed, NPQH
Age range: 2.5–11 years

Brentwood Preparatory School
Shenfield Road, Brentwood,
Essex CM15 8BD
Tel: +44 (0)1277 243300
Headmaster: Mr Jason Whiskerd
Age range: 3–11 years
No. of pupils: 591

Brentwood School
Middleton Hall Lane,
Brentwood, Essex CM15 8EE
Tel: 01277 243243
Headmaster: Mr Michael Bond
Age range: 3–18 years
No. of pupils: 1850
Fees: Day £20,598 FB £40,365

Colchester High School
Wellesley Road, Colchester,
Essex CO3 3HD
Tel: 01206 573389
Headteacher: Ms Karen Gracie-
Langrick
Age range: 2–16 years
No. of pupils: 320
Fees: Day £9,465–£13,620

Coopersale Hall School
Flux's Lane, off Stewards Green
Road, Epping, Essex CM16 7PE
Tel: 01992 577133
Headmistress: Miss Kaye Lovejoy
Age range: 2–11
No. of pupils: 275
Fees: Day £10,350–£10,575

Elm Green Preparatory School
Parsonage Lane, Little Baddow,
Chelmsford, Essex CM3 4SU
Tel: 01245 225230
Principal: Ms Ann Milner
Age range: 4–11
No. of pupils: 220
Fees: Day £8,844

Empire College London
Forest House, 16-20 Clements
Road, Ilford, Essex IG1 1BA
Tel: 020 8553 2683
Head: Ms Aaiesha Tak

Felsted Preparatory School
Felsted, Great Dunmow,
Essex CM6 3JL
Tel: 01371 822610
Age range: 4–13 years

Felsted School
Felsted, Great Dunmow,
Essex CM6 3LL
Tel: +44 (0)1371 822600
Headmaster: Mr Chris Townsend
Age range: 4–18 years

Gosfield School
Cut Hedge Park, Halstead Road,
Gosfield, Halstead, Essex CO9 1PF
Tel: 01787 474040
Headteacher: Mr Guy Martyn
Age range: 4–18
No. of pupils: VIth21
Fees: Day £6,690–£15,525

Heathcote School
Eves Corner, Danbury,
Chelmsford, Essex CM3 4QB
Tel: 01245 223131
Head of School: Mrs Samantha
Scott
Age range: 2–11 years
No. of pupils: 105
Fees: Day £9,450

Herington House School
1 Mount Avenue, Hutton,
Brentwood, Essex CM13 2NS
Tel: 01277 211595
Principal: Mr R. Dudley-Cooke
Age range: 3–11
No. of pupils: 130
Fees: Day £1,955–£3,865

Holmwood House Preparatory School
Chitts Hill, Lexden, Colchester,
Essex CO3 9ST
Tel: 01206 574305
Headmaster: Alexander Mitchell
Age range: 4–13
No. of pupils: 302
Fees: Day £10,140–£17,895 FB £35

Littlegarth School
Horkesley Park, Nayland,
Colchester, Essex CO6 4JR
Tel: 01206 262332
Headmaster: Mr Peter H Jones
Age range: 2–11 years
No. of pupils: 318
Fees: Day £3,205–£3,723

London Academy of Management Sciences
9th Floor Wentworth House,
350 Eastern Avenue,
Ilford, Essex IG2 6NN
Tel: 020 8554 9169
Head: Mr Asif Siddiqui

Maldon Court Preparatory School
Silver Street, Maldon,
Essex CM9 4QE
Tel: 01621 853529
Headteacher: Elaine Mason
Age range: 3–11
Fees: Day £8,236

New Hall School
The Avenue, Boreham,
Chelmsford, Essex CM3 3HS
Tel: 01245 467588
Principal: Mrs Katherine Jeffrey MA,
BA, PGCE, MA(Ed Mg), NPQH
Age range: 1–18 years
No. of pupils: 1400
Fees: Day £9,621–£20,502 WB
£18,234–£28,026 FB £21,177–£32,472

Oxford House School
2-4 Lexden Road, Colchester,
Essex CO3 3NE
Tel: 01206 576686
Head Teacher: Mrs Sarah Leyshon
Age range: 2–11
No. of pupils: 158

Saint Nicholas School
Hillingdon House, Hobbs Cross
Road, Harlow, Essex CM17 0NJ
Tel: 01279 429910
Headmaster: Mr D Bown
Age range: 4–16
No. of pupils: 400
Fees: Day £9,960–£12,660

Saint Pierre School
16 Leigh Road, Leigh-on-Sea,
Southend-on-Sea, Essex SS9 1LE
Tel: 01702 474164
Headmaster: Mr Peter Spencer-
Lane
Age range: 2 1/2–11 years

St Cedd's School
178a New London Road,
Chelmsford, Essex CM2 0AR
Tel: 01245 392810
Head: Mr Matthew Clarke
Age range: 3–11 years
No. of pupils: 400
Fees: Day £9,240–£11,820

St John's School
Stock Road, Billericay,
Essex CM12 0AR
Tel: 01277 623070
Head Teacher: Mrs F Armour
BEd(Hons)
Age range: 2–16 years
No. of pupils: 392
Fees: Day £5,328–£13,500

**St Margaret's
Preparatory School**
Hall Drive, Gosfield,
Halstead, Essex CO9 1SE
Tel: 01787 472134
Headteacher: Mrs Carolyn Moss
Age range: 2–11 years
Fees: Day £3,240–£4,055

St Mary's School
Lexden Road, Colchester,
Essex CO3 3RB
Tel: 01206 572544   **Admissions:**
01206 216420
Principal: Mrs H K Vipond MEd,
BSc(Hons), NPQH
Age range: B3–4 G3–16
No. of pupils: 430
Fees: Day £6,855–£14,985

**St Michael's
Church Of England
Preparatory School**
198 Hadleigh Road, Leigh-on-Sea,
Southend-on-Sea, Essex SS9 2LP
Tel: 01702 478719
Head: Steve Tompkins BSc(Hons),
PGCE, MA, NPQH
Age range: 3–11
No. of pupils: 271
Fees: Day £4,104–£9,600

**St Philomena's
Catholic School**
Hadleigh Road, Frinton-on-
Sea, Essex CO13 9HQ
Tel: 01255 674492
Head of School: Mrs P Mathews
ACIS, BA Hons, PGCE, MA, NPQH
Age range: 4–11
Fees: Day £6,240–£7,500

**St. Anne's Preparatory
School**
154 New London Road,
Chelmsford, Essex CM2 0AW
Tel: 01245 353488
Head of School: Valerie Eveleigh
Age range: 3–11 years

**Stephen Perse
Junior School, Dame
Bradbury's School**
Ashdon Road, Saffron
Walden, Essex CB10 2AL
Tel: 01223 454700 (Ext: 4000)
Age range: 1–11 years

**The Christian School
(Takeley)**
Dunmow Road, Brewers End,
Takeley, Bishop's Stortford,
Essex CM22 6QH
Tel: 01279 871182
Headmaster: M E Humphries
Age range: 3–16
Fees: Day £6,012–£8,436

Thorpe Hall School
Wakering Road, Southend-
on-Sea, Essex SS1 3RD
Tel: 01702 582340
Headmaster: Mr Andrew Hampton
Age range: 2–16 years
No. of pupils: 359
Fees: Day £9,000–£12,600

**Ursuline Preparatory
School**
Old Great Ropers, Great
Ropers Lane, Warley,
Brentwood, Essex CM13 3HR
Tel: 01277 227152
Headmistress: Mrs Pauline Wilson
MSc
Age range: 3–11
Fees: Day £6,450–£12,015

**Widford Lodge
Preparatory School**
Widford Road, Chelmsford,
Essex CM2 9AN
Tel: 01245 352581
Headteacher: Miss Michelle Cole
A.C.I.B. – P.G.C.E.
Age range: 2 1/2–11 years

**Woodlands School,
Great Warley**
Warley Street, Great Warley,
Brentwood, Essex CM13 3LA
Tel: 01277 233288
Head: Mr David Bell
Age range: 3 months–11 years

**Woodlands School,
Hutton Manor**
428 Rayleigh Road, Hutton,
Brentwood, Essex CM13 1SD
Tel: 01277 245585
Head: Paula Hobbs
Age range: 3 months–11 years

Hampshire

Alton School
Anstey Lane, Alton,
Hampshire GU34 2NG
Tel: 01420 82070
Head: Karl Guest
Age range: 0–18 years
No. of pupils: 400

Ballard School
Fernhill Lane, New Milton,
Hampshire BH25 5SU
Tel: 01425 626900
Headmaster: Mr Andrew McCleave
Age range: 2–16 years
No. of pupils: 451
Fees: Day £3,015–£5,550

**Bedales Prep
School, Dunhurst**
Petersfield, Hampshire GU32 2DP
Tel: 01730 300200
Head of School: Colin Baty
Age range: 8–13
No. of pupils: 200
Fees: Day £16,920–£18,765
FB £22,215–£24,930

Bedales School
Church Road, Steep, Petersfield,
Hampshire GU32 2DG
Tel: 01730 711733
Head of School: Magnus Bashaarat
Age range: 13–18
No. of pupils: 463
Fees: Day £28,515 FB £36,285

Boundary Oak School
Roche Court, Wickham Road,
Fareham, Hampshire PO17 5BL
Tel: 01329 280955
Executive Headmaster: Mr James
Polansky MA (Cantab) PGCE
Age range: 2–16 years
No. of pupils: 348
Fees: Day £9,195–£14,886 WB
£16,155–£21,078 FB £18,144–£23,067

**Brockwood Park &
Inwoods School**
Brockwood Park, Bramdean,
Hampshire SO24 0LQ
Tel: +44 (0)1962 771744
Principal: Mr Antonio Autor
Age range: 14–19
No. of pupils: 112 VIth39
Fees: Day £5,630–£6,400 FB £21,400

Churcher's College
Petersfield, Hampshire GU31 4AS
Tel: 01730 263033
Headmaster: Mr Simon Williams ,
MA, BSc
Age range: 3–18 years
Fees: Day £10,830–£16,440

Daneshill School
Stratfield Turgis, Basingstoke,
Hampshire RG27 0AR
Tel: 01256 882707
Head of School: Jim Massey
Age range: 3–13 years
No. of pupils: 303
Fees: Day £11,550–£15,615

Ditcham Park School
Ditcham Park, Petersfield,
Hampshire GU31 5RN
Tel: 01730 825659
Headmaster: Mr Graham
Spawforth MA, MEd
Age range: 2.5–16
No. of pupils: 379
Fees: Day £2,835–£4,753

Durlston Court
Becton Lane, Barton-on-Sea, New
Milton, Hampshire BH25 7AQ
Tel: 01425 610010
Head of School: Mr Richard May
Age range: 2–13 years
No. of pupils: 260

Embley
Embley Park, Romsey,
Hampshire SO51 6ZE
Tel: 01794 512206
Headteacher: Mr Cliff Canning
Age range: 2–18
No. of pupils: 500
Fees: Day £8,754–£31,338

Farleigh School
Red Rice, Andover,
Hampshire SP11 7PW
Tel: 01264 710766
Headmaster: Fr Simon Everson
Age range: 3–13 years
No. of pupils: 460

Farnborough Hill
Farnborough Road, Farnborough,
Hampshire GU14 8AT
Tel: 01252 545197
Head: Mrs A Neil BA, MEd, PGCE
Age range: G11–18
No. of pupils: 550 VIth90
Fees: Day £14,796

Forres Sandle Manor
Fordingbridge, Hampshire SP6 1NS
Tel: 01425 653181
Head of School: Mr Robert Tasker
Age range: 2–13 years
No. of pupils: 145

Glenhurst School
16 Beechworth Road, Havant,
Hampshire PO9 1AX
Tel: 023 9248 4054
Principal: Mrs E M Haines
Age range: 3 months–5 years

Highfield and Brookham Schools
Highfield Lane, Liphook,
Hampshire GU30 7LQ
Tel: 01428 728000
Headteachers: Mr Phillip Evitt MA
(Hons), PGCE & Mrs Sophie Baber
BA (Hons), PGCE, PG Cert
Age range: 2–13 years
No. of pupils: 448

King Edward VI School
Wilton Road, Southampton,
Hampshire SO15 5UQ
Tel: 023 8070 4561
Head Master: Mr N T Parker
Age range: 11–18 years
No. of pupils: 965
Fees: Day £17,631

Kingscourt School
182 Five Heads Road,
Catherington, Hampshire PO8 9NJ
Tel: 023 9259 3251
Head of School: Amanda
Bembridge
Age range: 3–11 years
No. of pupils: 158
Fees: Day £2,856

Lord Wandsworth College
Long Sutton, Hook,
Hampshire RG29 1TB
Tel: 01256 862201
Head of School: Mr Adam Williams
Age range: 11–18 years
No. of pupils: 615
Fees: Day £21,240–£24,390
WB £29,400–£33,000 FB
£30,345–£34,650

Mayville High School
35/37 St Simon's Road, Southsea,
Portsmouth, Hampshire PO5 2PE
Tel: 023 9273 4847
Headteacher: Mrs Rebecca Parkyn
Age range: 6 months–16 years
No. of pupils: 479
Fees: Day £7,635–£11,235

Meoncross School
Burnt House Lane, Stubbington,
Fareham, Hampshire PO14 2EF
Tel: 01329 662182
Headmaster: Mr Mark Cripps
Age range: 2–16 years
No. of pupils: 405
Fees: Day £8,736–£12,576

Moyles Court School
Moyles Court, Ringwood,
Hampshire BH24 3NF
Tel: 01425 472856
Headmaster: Mr Richard Milner-
Smith
Age range: 3–16
No. of pupils: 195
Fees: Day £6,885–£14,655
FB £21,246–£26,805

Portsmouth High School GDST
Kent Road, Southsea, Portsmouth,
Hampshire PO5 3EQ
Tel: 023 9282 6714
Headmistress: Mrs Jane Prescott
BSc NPQH
Age range: G3–18 years
No. of pupils: 500
Fees: Day £2,574–£4,800

Prince's Mead School
Worthy Park House, Kings Worthy,
Winchester, Hampshire SO21 1AN
Tel: 01962 888000
Headmaster: Peter Thacker
Age range: 4–11

Ringwood Waldorf School
Folly Farm Lane, Ashley,
Ringwood, Hampshire BH24 2NN
Tel: 01425 472664
Age range: 3–18
No. of pupils: 235
Fees: Day £6,240–£9,000

Rookwood School
Weyhill Road, Andover,
Hampshire SP10 3AL
Tel: 01264 325900
Headmaster: Mr A Kirk-Burgess BSc,
PGCE, MSc (Oxon)
Age range: 2–16
Fees: Day £9,360–£15,600
FB £23,250–£27,465

Salesian College
Reading Road, Farnborough,
Hampshire GU14 6PA
Tel: 01252 893000
Headmaster: Mr Gerard Owens
Age range: B11–18 G16–18
No. of pupils: 650 VIth140
Fees: Day £11,961

Sherborne House School
Lakewood Road, Chandlers Ford,
Eastleigh, Hampshire SO53 1EU
Tel: 023 8025 2440
Head Teacher: Mr Mark Beach
Age range: 3–11
No. of pupils: 293
Fees: Day £8,295–£9,675

Sherfield School
South Drive, Sherfield-on-Loddon,
Hook, Hampshire RG27 0HU
Tel: 01256 884800
Headmaster: Mr Nick Brain
BA(Hons), PGCE, MA, NPQH
Age range: 3 months–18 years
No. of pupils: 450
Fees: Day £10,320–£17,085 WB
£18,960–£26,130 FB £22,125–£30,495

St John's College
Grove Road South, Southsea,
Portsmouth, Hampshire PO5 3QW
Tel: 023 9281 5118
Head of School: Mrs Mary Maguire
Age range: 4–18
No. of pupils: 560 VIth86
Fees: Day £9,975–£13,125
FB £28,500–£32,250

St Neot's School
St Neot's Road, Eversley,
Hampshire RG27 0PN
Tel: 0118 9739650
Headmaster: Mr Jonathan Slot
Age range: 2–13 years
No. of pupils: 248
Fees: Day £3,931–£5,624

St Nicholas' School
Redfields House, Redfields
Lane, Church Crookham,
Fleet, Hampshire GU52 0RF
Tel: 01252 850121
Headmistress: Dr O Wright PhD, MA,
BA Hons, PGCE
Age range: B3–7 G3–16
No. of pupils: 325

St Swithun's Prep
Alresford Road, Winchester,
Hampshire SO21 1HA
Tel: 01962 835750
Head of School: Mr Jonathan
Brough
Age range: B3–4 years G3–11 years
No. of pupils: 186

Stockton House School
Stockton Avenue, Fleet,
Hampshire GU51 4NS
Tel: 01252 616323
Early Years Manager: Mrs Jenny
Bounds BA EYPS
Age range: 2–5

Stroud School, King Edward VI Preparatory School
Highwood House, Highwood Lane,
Romsey, Hampshire SO51 9ZH
Tel: 01794 513231
Headmistress: Mrs Rebecca Smith
Age range: 3–13 years
Fees: Day £3,838–£6,159

The Gregg Prep School
17-19 Winn Road, Southampton,
Hampshire SO17 1EJ
Tel: 023 8055 7352
Head Teacher: Mrs J Caddy
Age range: 3–11
Fees: Day £8,295

The Gregg School
Townhill Park House, Cutbush Lane,
Southampton, Hampshire SO18 2GF
Tel: 023 8047 2133
Headteacher: Mrs S Sellers PGDip,
MSc, BSc(Hons), NPQH, PGCE
Age range: 11–16
No. of pupils: 300
Fees: Day £12,825

The King's School
Lakesmere House, Allington Lane,
Fair Oak, Eastleigh, Southampton,
Hampshire SO50 7DB
Tel: 023 8060 0986
Headteacher: Mrs Heather Bowden
Age range: 4–16 years

The New Forest Small School
1 Southampton Road, Lyndhurst,
Hampshire SO43 7BU
Tel: 02380 284415
Headteacher: Maz Wilberforce
Age range: 3–16 years

The Pilgrims' School
3 The Close, Winchester,
Hampshire SO23 9LT
Tel: 01962 854189
Head: Dr Sarah Essex
Age range: B4–13 years

The Portsmouth Grammar School
High Street, Portsmouth,
Hampshire PO1 2LN
Tel: +44 (0)23 9236 0036
Headmistress: Dr Anne Cotton
Age range: 2–18
No. of pupils: 1556 VIth336
Fees: Day £10,233–£15,951

Thorngrove School
The Mount, Highclere, Newbury,
Hampshire RG20 9PS
Tel: 01635 253172
Headmaster: Mr Adam King
Age range: 2–13
Fees: Day £14,070–£17,595

£

Twyford School
Twyford, Winchester,
Hampshire SO21 1NW
Tel: 01962 712269
Headmaster: Mr Andrew Harvey
Age range: 3–13 years

Walhampton
Walhampton, Lymington,
Hampshire SO41 5ZG
Tel: 01590 613 300
Headmaster: Mr Titus Mills
Age range: 2–13
No. of pupils: 353
Fees: Day £9,000–£17,625
FB £20,250–£24,750

West Hill Park Preparatory School
Titchfield, Fareham,
Hampshire PO14 4BS
Tel: 01329 842356
Headmaster: A P Ramsay
BEd(Hons), MSc
Age range: 2–13
No. of pupils: 288
Fees: Day £10,800–£18,300
FB £19,500–£22,650

Winchester College
College Street, Winchester,
Hampshire SO23 9NA
Tel: 01962 621247
Headmaster: Dr. T R Hands
Age range: B13–18
No. of pupils: 690 Vlth280
Fees: FB £39,912

Yateley Manor School
51 Reading Road, Yateley,
Hampshire GU46 7UQ
Tel: 01252 405500
Headmaster: Mr Robert Upton
Age range: 3–13
No. of pupils: 453
Fees: Day £11,160–£15,300

Hertfordshire

Abbot's Hill School
Bunkers Lane, Hemel Hempstead,
Hertfordshire HP3 8RP
Tel: 01442 240333
Headmistress: Mrs K Gorman BA,
MEd (Cantab)
Age range: G4–16 years
No. of pupils: 482

Aldenham School
Elstree, Hertfordshire WD6 3AJ
Tel: 01923 858122
Head of School: Mr Andrew
Williams
Age range: 3–18

Aldwickbury School
Wheathampstead Road,
Harpenden, Hertfordshire AL5 1AD
Tel: 01582 713022
Headmaster: Mr V W Hales
Age range: B4–13 years

Beechwood Park School
Markyate, St Albans,
Hertfordshire AL3 8AW
Tel: 01582 840333
Headmaster: Mr E Balfour BA
(Hons), PGCE
Age range: 3–13 years

BERKHAMSTED SCHOOL
For further details see p. 88
Overton House, 131 High
Street, Berkhamsted,
Hertfordshire HP4 2DJ
Tel: 01442 358001
Email: admissions@
berkhamsted.com
Website:
www.berkhamsted.com
Principal: Mr Richard Backhouse
MA(Cantab)
Age range: 3–18 years
No. of pupils: 2001 Vlth408
Fees: Day £10,830–£22,170
WB £29,850 FB £35,610

Bishop's Stortford College
10 Maze Green Road, Bishop's
Stortford, Hertfordshire CM23 2PJ
Tel: 01279 838575
Headmaster: Mr Jeremy Gladwin
Age range: 13–18
No. of pupils: Vlth249
Fees: Day £20,349–£20,532 WB
£31,569–£31,917 FB £33,402–£33,930

Bishop's Stortford College Prep School
Maze Green Road, Bishop's
Stortford, Hertfordshire CM23 2PQ
Tel: 01279 838583
Head of the Prep School: Mr Bill
Toleman
Age range: 4–13 years

Champneys International College of Health & Beauty
Chesham Road, Wigginton,
Tring, Hertfordshire HP23 6HY
Tel: 01442 291333
College Principal: Ms Pam Clegg
Age range: 16+
No. of pupils: 61
Fees: Day £3,000–£9,050

Charlotte House Preparatory School
88 The Drive, Rickmansworth,
Hertfordshire WD3 4DU
Tel: 01923 772101
Head: Miss P Woodcock
Age range: G3–11
No. of pupils: 140
Fees: Day £3,432–£12,102

Duncombe School
4 Warren Park Road, Bengeo,
Hertford, Hertfordshire SG14 3JA
Tel: 01992 414100
Headmaster: Mr Jeremy Phelan
M.A. (Ed)
Age range: 2–11 years
No. of pupils: 301
Fees: Day £10,380–£14,565

Edge Grove School
Aldenham Village,
Hertfordshire WD25 8NL
Tel: 01923 855724
Head of School: Miss Lisa
McDonald
Age range: 3–13 years
No. of pupils: 501

Egerton Rothesay School
Durrants Lane, Berkhamsted,
Hertfordshire HP4 3UJ
Tel: 01442 865275
Headteacher: Mr Colin Parker
BSc(Hons), Dip.Ed (Oxon), PGCE,
C.Math MIMA
Age range: 6–19

Gurukula – The Hare Krishna Primary School
Hartspring Cottage, Elton Way,
Watford, Hertfordshire WD25 8HB
Tel: 01923 851 005
Head of School: Ms Gunacuda Dasi
(Gwyneth Milan)
Age range: 4–12 years

Haberdashers' Aske's School for Girls
Aldenham Road,
Elstree, Borehamwood,
Hertfordshire WD6 3BT
Tel: 020 8266 2300
Head of School: Ms Rose Hardy
Age range: G4–18
No. of pupils: 1190
Fees: Day £17,826–£19,311

Haileybury
Haileybury, Hertford,
Hertfordshire SG13 7NU
Tel: +44 (0)1992 706353
The Master: Mr Martin Collier MA
BA PGCE
Age range: 11–18 years
No. of pupils: 915 Vlth364
Fees: Day £18,240–£27,435
FB £23,610–£37,215

Heath Mount School
Woodhall Park, Watton-at-Stone,
Hertford, Hertfordshire SG14 3NG
Tel: 01920 830230
Headmaster: Mr Chris Gillam
BEd(Hons)
Age range: 3–13 years
No. of pupils: 492 B270 G222
Fees: Day £12,435–£19,185

High Elms Manor School
High Elms Lane, Watford,
Hertfordshire WD25 0JX
Tel: 01923 681 103
Headmistress: Ms Liadain O'Neill BA
(Hons), AMI 0-3, AMI 3-6, Early Years
FdA Dist.+
Age range: 2–12
No. of pupils: 100
Fees: Day £10,500–£12,675

Howe Green House School
Great Hallingbury, Bishop's
Stortford, Hertfordshire CM22 7UF
Tel: 01279 657706
Headmistress: Ms Deborah Mills BA
(Hons) Q.T.S
Age range: 2–11 years
No. of pupils: 177
Fees: Day £433–£4,313

Immanuel College
87/91 Elstree Road, Bushey,
Hertfordshire WD23 4EB
Tel: 020 8950 0604
Headmaster: Mr Gary Griffin
Age range: 4–18
No. of pupils: 520 Vlth127
Fees: Day £10,995

Kingshott
Stevenage Road, St Ippolyts,
Hitchin, Hertfordshire SG4 7JX
Tel: 01462 432009
Headmaster: Mr David Weston
Age range: 3–13 years
No. of pupils: 400
Fees: Day £6,555–£14,115

Little Acorns Montessori School
Lincolnsfield Centre,
Bushey Hall Drive, Bushey,
Hertfordshire WD23 2ER
Tel: 01923 230705
Head of School: Lola Davies BPA,
AMIDip
Age range: 12 months–6
No. of pupils: 28
Fees: Day £2,120

Lochinver House School
Heath Road, Little Heath, Potters
Bar, Hertfordshire EN6 1LW
Tel: 01707 653064
Headmaster: Mr Ben Walker
BA(Hons)
Age range: B4–13 years
No. of pupils: 345
Fees: Day £12,060–£15,840

Lockers Park
Lockers Park Lane, Hemel
Hempstead, Hertfordshire HP1 1TL
Tel: 01442 251712
Headmaster: Mr Gavin Taylor
Age range: B4–13 years
No. of pupils: 171
Fees: Day £11,505–£18,225
WB £26,325

Longwood School
Bushey Hall Drive, Bushey,
Hertfordshire WD23 2QG
Tel: 01923 253715
Head Teacher: Claire May
Age range: 3 months–11
Fees: Day £3,705–£7,800

Manor Lodge School
Rectory Lane, Ridge Hill, Shenley,
Hertfordshire WD7 9BG
Tel: 01707 642424
Head of School: Mrs A Lobo
BEd(Hons)
Age range: 3–11
No. of pupils: 427
Fees: Day £11,100–£12,300

Merchant Taylors' Prep
Moor Farm, Sandy Lodge
Road, Rickmansworth,
Hertfordshire WD3 1LW
Tel: 01923 825648
Headmaster: Dr Karen McNerney
BSc (Hons), PGCE, MSc, EdD
Age range: B3–13 years

Queenswood
Shepherd's Way, Brookmans Park,
Hatfield, Hertfordshire AL9 6NS
Tel: 01707 602500
Principal: Mrs Jo Cameron
Age range: G11–18
No. of pupils: 418
Fees: Day £7,115–£8,440 WB
7,325–10,615 FB £8,395–£11,810

Radlett Preparatory School
Kendal Hall, Watling Street,
Radlett, Hertfordshire WD7 7LY
Tel: 01923 856812
Principal: Mr M Pipe BA Hons, QTS
Age range: 4–11

Sherrardswood School
Lockleys, Welwyn,
Hertfordshire AL6 0BJ
Tel: 01438 714282
Headmistress: Mrs Anna Wright
Age range: 2–18
No. of pupils: 357
Fees: Day £10,383–£16,113

St Albans High School for Girls
Townsend Avenue, St Albans,
Hertfordshire AL1 3SJ
Tel: 01727 853800
Headmistress: Amber Waite
Age range: G4–18
No. of pupils: 940 VIth170

St Albans Independent College
69 London Road, St Albans,
Hertfordshire AL1 1LN
Tel: 01727 842348
Principals: Mr. A N Jemal & Mr Elvis
Cotena
Age range: 15+
Fees: Day £2,700–£5,900

St Albans School
Abbey Gateway, St Albans,
Hertfordshire AL3 4HB
Tel: 01727 855521
Headmaster: Mr JWJ Gillespie
MA(Cantab), FRSA
Age range: B11–18 G16–18
No. of pupils: 870
Fees: Day £18,600

St Christopher School
Barrington Road, Letchworth,
Hertfordshire SG6 3JZ
Tel: 01462 650 850
Head: Richard Palmer
Age range: 3–18
No. of pupils: 511 VIth78
Fees: Day £4,590–£18,075 WB
£19,950–£24,675 FB £31,650

St Columba's College
King Harry Lane, St Albans,
Hertfordshire AL3 4AW
Tel: 01727 892040
Head: Mr David Buxton
Age range: 4–18 years
No. of pupils: 780

St Edmund's College & Prep School
Old Hall Green, Nr Ware,
Hertfordshire SG11 1DS
Tel: 01920 824247
Headmaster: Mr Matthew Mostyn
BA (Hons) MA (Ed)
Age range: 3–18
No. of pupils: 852
Fees: Day £9,882–£18,345 WB
£24,165–£27,630 FB £28,302–£32,460

St Edmund's Prep
Old Hall Green, Ware,
Hertfordshire SG11 1DS
Tel: 01920 824239
Head: Mr Steven Cartwright BSc
(Surrey)
Age range: 3–11
No. of pupils: 185
Fees: Day £10,650–£13,365

St Francis' College
Broadway, Letchworth Garden
City, Hertfordshire SG6 3PJ
Tel: 01462 670511
Headmistress: Mrs B Goulding
Age range: G3–18
No. of pupils: 460 VIth75
Fees: Day £9,990–£16,980 WB
£22,350–£26,475 FB £27,990–£31,995

St Hilda's
High Street, Bushey,
Hertfordshire WD23 3DA
Tel: 020 8950 1751
Headmistress: Miss Sarah-Jane
Styles MA
Age range: B2–4 G2–11
Fees: Day £12,012–£12,843

ST HILDA'S SCHOOL
For further details see p. 104
28 Douglas Road, Harpenden,
Hertfordshire AL5 2ES
Tel: 01582 712307
Email: office@
sthildasharpenden.co.uk
Website:
www.sthildasharpenden.co.uk
Headmaster: Mr Dan Sayers
Age range: G2.5–11 years
No. of pupils: 150
Fees: Day £3,285–£4,260

St Joseph's In The Park
St Mary's Lane, Hertingfordbury,
Hertford, Hertfordshire SG14 2LX
Tel: 01992 513810
Head of School: Mr Douglas Brown
Age range: 3–11
No. of pupils: 150
Fees: Day £5,718–£16,899

St Margaret's School, Bushey
Merry Hill Road, Bushey,
Hertfordshire WD23 1DT
Tel: +44 (0)20 8416 4400
Headteacher: Lara Péchard
Age range: 2–18 years
No. of pupils: 530

St. John's Prep. School
The Ridgeway, Potters Bar,
Hertfordshire EN6 5QT
Tel: +44 (0)1707 657294
Head Teacher: Mrs C Tardios
Age range: 4–11

Stanborough School
Stanborough Park, Garston,
Watford, Hertfordshire WD25 9JT
Tel: 01923 673268
Acting Head Teacher: Ms Eileen
Hussey
Age range: 3–17
No. of pupils: 300
Fees: Day £6,630–£10,224
WB £10,350–£13,995

Stormont
The Causeway, Potters Bar,
Hertfordshire EN6 5HA
Tel: 01707 654037
Head Teacher: Miss Louise Martin
Age range: G4–11
Fees: Day £12,300–£13,050

The Haberdashers' Aske's Boys' School
Butterfly Lane, Elstree,
Borehamwood,
Hertfordshire WD6 3AF
Tel: 020 8266 1700
Headmaster: Gus Lock MA (Oxon)
Age range: B5–18 years
No. of pupils: 1428
Fees: Day £15,339–£20,346

The King's School
Elmfield, Ambrose Lane,
Harpenden, Hertfordshire AL5 4DU
Tel: 01582 767566
Principal: Mr Clive John Case BA,
HDE
Age range: 4–16
Fees: Day £7,680

The Purcell School, London
Aldenham Road, Bushey,
Hertfordshire WD23 2TS
Tel: 01923 331100
Headteacher: Dr Bernard Trafford
Age range: 10–18
No. of pupils: 180
Fees: Day £25,707 FB £32,826

Tring Park School for the Performing Arts
Mansion Drive, Tring, Hertfordshire HP23 5LX
Tel: 01442 824255
Principal: Mr Stefan Anderson MA, ARCM, ARCT
Age range: 8–19 years
No. of pupils: 370 VIth171
Fees: Day £15,405–£24,885
FB £26,190–£37,605

Westbrook Hay Prep School
London Road, Hemel Hempstead, Hertfordshire HP1 2RF
Tel: 01442 256143
Headmaster: Mark Brain
Age range: 3–13 years
No. of pupils: 340
Fees: Day £10,905–£15,690

York House School
Sarratt Road, Croxley Green, Rickmansworth, Hertfordshire WD3 4LW
Tel: 01923 772395
Headmaster: Mr Jon Gray BA(Ed)
Age range: 3–13 years
No. of pupils: 395
Fees: Day £3,876–£5,164

Kent

Ashford School
East Hill, Ashford, Kent TN24 8PB
Tel: 01233 739030
Head: Mr Michael Hall
Age range: 3 months–18 years
No. of pupils: 916 VIth127
Fees: Day £10,815–£18,294
WB £26,775 FB £38,778

Beech Grove School
Forest Drive, Nonington, Dover, Kent CT15 4FB
Tel: 01304 842980
Head of School: Mr Timothy Maas
Age range: 4–19

Beechwood Sacred Heart
12 Pembury Road, Tunbridge Wells, Kent TN2 3QD
Tel: 01892 532747
Acting Head: Mrs Helen Rowe
Age range: 3–18
No. of pupils: 400 VIth70
Fees: Day £8,685–£17,385
WB £26,850 FB £29,850

Benenden School
Cranbrook, Kent TN17 4AA
Tel: 01580 240592
Headmistress: Mrs S Price
Age range: G11–18
No. of pupils: 550
Fees: FB £12,650

Bethany School
Curtisden Green, Goudhurst, Cranbrook, Kent TN17 1LB
Tel: 01580 211273
Headmaster: Mr Francie Healy BSc, HDipEd, NPQH
Age range: 11–18 years
No. of pupils: 356 VIth73
Fees: Day £17,910–£19,785 WB £27,810–£30,705 FB £29,985–£33,750

Bronte School
Mayfield, 7 Pelham Road, Gravesend, Kent DA11 0HN
Tel: 01474 533805
Headmistress: Ms Emma Wood
Age range: 3–11
No. of pupils: 120
Fees: Day £9,330

Bryony School
Marshall Road, Rainham, Gillingham, Kent ME8 0AJ
Tel: 01634 231511
Head of School: Mrs N Gee
Age range: 2–11 years

CATS Canterbury
68 New Dover Road, Canterbury, Kent CT1 3LQ
Tel: +44 (0)1227866540
Principal: Severine Collins
Age range: 14–21 years
No. of pupils: 450
Fees: Day £17,370–£27,990
FB £13,230–£19,140

Chartfield School
45 Minster Road, Westgate on Sea, Kent CT8 8DA
Tel: 01843 831716
Head & Proprietor: Miss L P Shipley
Age range: 4–11

COBHAM HALL SCHOOL
For further details see p. 89
Brewers Road, Cobham, Kent DA12 3BL
Tel: 01474 823371
Email: enquiries@cobhamhall.com
Website: www.cobhamhall.com
Headteacher: Mrs Wendy Barrett
Age range: G11–18
No. of pupils: 150
Fees: Day £6,804–£8,246
FB £10,279–£12,831

Dover College
Effingham Crescent, Dover, Kent CT17 9RH
Tel: 01304 205969
Headmaster: Mr Gareth Doodes MA (Hons)
Age range: 3–18
No. of pupils: 301
Fees: Day £7,725–£16,050 WB £21,000–£25,500 FB £24,750–£31,500

Dulwich Prep Cranbrook
Coursehorn, Cranbrook, Kent TN17 3NP
Tel: 01580 712179
Headmaster: Mr Paul David BEd(Hons)
Age range: 3–13
No. of pupils: 535
Fees: Day £5,970–£18,390

Earlscliffe
29 Shorncliffe Road, Folkestone, Kent CT20 2NB
Tel: +44 (0)1303 253951
Director: Mr Tim Fish
Age range: 15–19 years

Elliott Park School
18-20 Marina Drive, Minster, Sheerness, Kent ME12 2DP
Tel: 01795 873372
Head: Ms Colleen Hiller
Age range: 3–11

European School of Osteopathy
Boxley House, The Street, Boxley, Maidstone, Kent ME14 3DZ
Tel: 01622 671 558
Principal: Mr Renzo Molinari DO

Fosse Bank School
Mountains, Noble Tree Road, Hildenborough, Tonbridge, Kent TN11 8ND
Tel: 01732 834212
Headmistress: Miss Alison Cordingley
Age range: 2–11
No. of pupils: 124
Fees: Day £10,605–£13,185

Gad's Hill School
Higham, Rochester, Medway, Kent ME3 7PA
Tel: 01474 822366
Headmaster: Mr Paul Savage
Age range: 3–16
No. of pupils: 370
Fees: Day £8,988–£12,504

Haddon Dene School
57 Gladstone Road, Broadstairs, Kent CT10 2HY
Tel: 01843 861176
Head: Miss Alison Hatch
Age range: 3–11
No. of pupils: 200
Fees: Day £5,700–£7,230

Hilden Grange School
62 Dry Hill Park Road, Tonbridge, Kent TN10 3BX
Tel: 01732 352706
Headmaster: Mr J Withers BA(Hons)
Age range: 3–13
No. of pupils: 311

Hilden Oaks Preparatory School & Nursery
38 Dry Hill Park Road, Tonbridge, Kent TN10 3BU
Tel: 01732 353941
Head of School: Mrs. K Joiner
Age range: 3 months–11 years

Holmewood House School
Barrow Lane, Langton Green, Tunbridge Wells, Kent TN3 0EA
Tel: 01892 860000
Headmaster: Mr Scott Carnochan
Age range: 3–13 years
No. of pupils: 450

Kent College Junior School
Harbledown, Canterbury, Kent CT2 9AQ
Tel: 01227 762436
Head: Mr Simon James
Age range: 0–11 years
No. of pupils: 200
Fees: Day £10,587–£16,473 FB £26,901

Kent College Pembury
Old Church Road, Pembury, Tunbridge Wells, Kent TN2 4AX
Tel: +44 (0)1892 822006
Head of School: Miss Katrina Handford
Age range: G3–18 years
No. of pupils: 500
Fees: Day £22,575 WB £28,200 FB £35,700

Kent College, Canterbury
Whitstable Road, Canterbury,
Kent CT2 9DT
Tel: +44 (0)1227 763 231
Head: Mr Mark Turnbull
Age range: 0–18 years
(Boarding from 8)
No. of pupils: 800
Fees: Day £5,797–£6,665
FB £8,967–£12,339
🌐 Ⓐ 🏫 £ ⒾⒷ 🖉 ⒃

Kids Inc Day Nursery – Bluewater
West Village, Bluewater,
Greenhithe, Kent DA9 9SE
Tel: 01322 386624

King's Preparatory School, Rochester
King Edward Road, Rochester,
Medway, Kent ME1 1UB
Tel: 01634 888577
Headmaster: Mr Tom Morgan
Age range: 8–13 years
🏫 🖉

King's Rochester
Satis House, Boley Hill,
Rochester, Kent ME1 1TE
Tel: 01634 888555
Principal: Mr B Charles
Age range: 13–18 years
No. of pupils: 600 VIth95
Fees: Day £20,700 FB £33,840
🌐 Ⓐ 🏫 £ 🖉 ⒃

Lorenden Preparatory School
Painter's Forstal, Faversham,
Kent ME13 0EN
Tel: 01795 590030
Head of School: Mr Richard McIntosh
Age range: 3–11 years
No. of pupils: 122
Fees: Day £3,085–£4,485
£ 🖉

Marlborough House School
High Street, Hawkhurst,
Kent TN18 4PY
Tel: 01580 753555
Head: Mr Eddy Newton
Age range: 2.5–13 years
No. of pupils: 250
Fees: Day £9,165–£18,690
🏫 £ 🖉

Northbourne Park School
Betteshanger, Deal, Kent CT14 0NW
Tel: 01304 611215/218
Headmaster: Mr Sebastian Rees BA(Hons), PGCE, NPQH
Age range: 2–13 years
No. of pupils: 195
Fees: Day £9,105–£17,346
WB £21,834 FB £25,281
🏫 £ 🖉

OneSchool Global UK Maidstone Campus
Heath Road, Maidstone,
Kent ME17 4HT
Tel: 03000 700 507
Age range: 7–18 years

Radnor House, Sevenoaks
Combe Bank Drive,
Sevenoaks, Kent TN14 6AE
Tel: 01959 563720
Head: Mr David Paton BComm (Hons) PGCE MA
Age range: 2.5–18
No. of pupils: 250
Ⓐ £ 🖉 ⒃ 🌼

Rochester Independent College
254 St Margaret's Banks,
Rochester, Kent ME1 1HY
Tel: +44 (0)163 482 8115
Head of School: Mr Alistair Brownlow
Age range: 11–18 years
🌐 ⒃ 🏫

Rose Hill School
Coniston Avenue, Tunbridge
Wells, Kent TN4 9SY
Tel: 01892 525591
Head: Emma Neville
Age range: 3–13
Fees: Day £11,325–£15,225
£ 🖉

Russell House School
Station Road, Otford,
Sevenoaks, Kent TN14 5QU
Tel: 01959 522352
Headmaster: Mr Craig McCarthy
Age range: 2–11

Sackville School
Tonbridge Rd, Hildenborough,
Tonbridge, Kent TN11 9HN
Tel: 01732 838888
Headmaster: Mr Justin Foster-Gandey BSc (hons)
Age range: 11–18
No. of pupils: 160 VIth29
Fees: Day £15,750
Ⓐ £ 🖉 ⒃ 🌼

Saint Ronan's School
Water Lane, Hawkhurst,
Kent TN18 5DJ
Tel: 01580 752271
Headmaster: William Trelawny-Vernon BSc(Hons)
Age range: 3–13 years
🏫 £ 🖉

Sevenoaks Preparatory School
Godden Green, Sevenoaks,
Kent TN15 0JU
Tel: 01732 762336
Headmaster: Mr Luke Harrison
Age range: 2–13 years
🖉

Sevenoaks School
High Street, Sevenoaks,
Kent TN13 1HU
Tel: +44 (0)1732 455133
Head of School: Mr Jesse R Elzinga AB MSt FCCT
Age range: 11–18 years
No. of pupils: 1172
Fees: Day £25,020–£28,413
FB £39,790–£42,084
🌐 🏫 £ ⒾⒷ 🖉 ⒃

Shernold School
Hill Place, Queens Avenue,
Maidstone, Kent ME16 0ER
Tel: 01622 752868
Head Teacher: Ms. Sandra Dinsmore BA Hons. PGCE
Age range: 3–11
No. of pupils: 142
Fees: Day £7,245–£8,190
£

Solefield School
Solefields Road, Sevenoaks,
Kent TN13 1PH
Tel: 01732 452142
Headmistress: Ms Helen McClure
Age range: B4–13 years
🏫 🖉

Somerhill
Tonbridge, Kent TN11 0NJ
Tel: 01732 352124
Principal: Mr Duncan Sinclair
Age range: 2–13 years

Spring Grove School
Harville Road, Wye, Kent TN25 5EZ
Tel: 01233 812337
Head of School: Mrs Thérésa Jaggard
Age range: 2–11 years
No. of pupils: 226
Fees: Day £9,459–£13,290
£ 🖉

St Andrew's School
24-28 Watts Avenue, Rochester,
Medway, Kent ME1 1SA
Tel: 01634 843479
Principal: Mrs E Steinmann-Gilbert
Age range: 2–11
No. of pupils: 367
Fees: Day £7,725–£8,178
🖉

St Edmund's Junior School
St Thomas Hill, Canterbury,
Kent CT2 8HU
Tel: 01227 475600
Head: Edward O'Connor
Age range: 3–13
No. of pupils: 230
Fees: Day £9,696–£16,101
WB £25,455 FB £27,933
🏫 🖉

St Faith's at Ash School
5 The Street, Ash, Canterbury,
Kent CT3 2HH
Tel: 01304 813409
Headmaster: Mr Lawrence Groves
Age range: 2–11
No. of pupils: 225
Fees: Day £5,415–£9,885
£ 🖉

St Lawrence College
Ramsgate, Kent CT11 7AE
Tel: 01843 572931
Head of College: Mr Barney Durrant
Age range: 3–18 years
No. of pupils: 585
Fees: Day £7,995–£17,025
FB £27,765–£37,455
🌐 Ⓐ 🏫 £ 🖉 ⒃

St Michael's Preparatory School
Otford Court, Row Dow, Otford,
Sevenoaks, Kent TN14 5RY
Tel: 01959 522137
Head: Mr Nik Pears
Age range: 2–13 years
🖉

Steephill School
Off Castle Hill, Fawkham,
Longfield, Kent DA3 7BG
Tel: 01474 702107
Head: Mrs Caroline Birtwell BSc, MBA, PGCE
Age range: 3–11
No. of pupils: 131
Fees: Day £9,750
£ 🖉

Sutton Valence Preparatory School
Chart Sutton, Maidstone,
Kent ME17 3RF
Tel: 01622 842117
Head: Miss C Corkran
Age range: 3–11
No. of pupils: 320
Fees: Day £3,000–£4,610
🖉

Sutton Valence School
North Street, Sutton
Valence, Kent ME17 3HL
Tel: 01622 845200
Headmaster: Mr James A Thomas MA (Cantab) MA (London) NPQH
Age range: 11–18 years
No. of pupils: 570
🌐 Ⓐ 🏫 £ 🖉 ⒃

The Granville School
2 Bradbourne Park Road,
Sevenoaks, Kent TN13 3LJ
Tel: 01732 453039
Headmistress: Mrs Louise Lawrance B. Prim. Ed. (Hons)
Age range: B3–4 G3–11
🏫 £ 🖉

The Junior King's School, Canterbury
Milner Court, Sturry,
Canterbury, Kent CT2 0AY
Tel: 01227 714000
Head: Emma Károlyi
Age range: 3–13
Fees: Day £11,475–£19,290
FB £26,475

The King's School, Canterbury
The Precincts, Canterbury,
Kent CT1 2ES
Tel: 01227 595501
Head: Mr Peter Roberts
Age range: 13–18
No. of pupils: 858 VIth385
Fees: Day £27,495 FB £38,955

The Mead School
16 Frant Road, Tunbridge
Wells, Kent TN2 5SN
Tel: 01892 525837
Headmaster: Mr Andrew Webster
Age range: 3–11
No. of pupils: 188
Fees: Day £4,536–£11,625

The New Beacon School
Brittains Lane, Sevenoaks,
Kent TN13 2PB
Tel: 01732 452131
Headmaster: Mr M Piercy BA(Hons)
Age range: B4–13 years

TONBRIDGE SCHOOL
For further details see p. 106
High Street, Tonbridge,
Kent TN9 1JP
Tel: 01732 304297
Email: admissions@
tonbridge-school.org
Website:
www.tonbridge-school.co.uk
Headmaster: Mr James Priory
MA (Oxon)
Age range: B13–18 years
No. of pupils: 798
Fees: Day £33,636 FB £44,835

Walthamstow Hall Pre-Prep and Junior School
Sevenoaks, Kent TN13 3LD
Tel: 01732 451334
Headmistress: Miss S Ferro
Age range: G2–11
No. of pupils: 218
Fees: Day £12,135–£15,300

Walthamstow Hall School
Sevenoaks, Kent TN13 3UL
Tel: 01732 451334
Headmistress: Miss S Ferro
Age range: G2–18
No. of pupils: 500 VIth80

Wellesley House
114 Ramsgate Road,
Broadstairs, Kent CT10 2DG
Tel: 01843 862991
Headmaster: Mr G D Franklin
Age range: 7–13
No. of pupils: 133
Fees: Day £12,231–£19,917 FB £26,331

Surrey

ABERDOUR SCHOOL
For further details see p. 86
Brighton Road, Burgh Heath,
Tadworth, Surrey KT20 6AJ
Tel: +44 (0)1737 354119
Email: enquiries@
aberdourschool.co.uk
Website:
www.aberdourschool.co.uk
Headmaster: Mr S. D. Collins
Age range: 2–11 years
No. of pupils: 343
Fees: Day £4,710–£16,272

ACS Cobham International School
Heywood, Portsmouth Road,
Cobham, Surrey KT11 1BL
Tel: +44 (0) 1932 867251
Head of School: Mr Barnaby
Sandow
Age range: 2–18

ACS Egham International School
Woodlee, London Road,
Egham, Surrey TW20 0HS
Tel: +44 (0) 1784 430 800
Head of School: Mr Jeremy Lewis
Age range: 4–18
Fees: Day £11,090–£25,870

Aldro School
Lombard Street, Shackleford,
Godalming, Surrey GU8 6AS
Tel: 01483 810266
Headmaster: Mr Chris Carlier
Age range: 7–13 years

Amesbury School
Hazel Grove, Hindhead,
Surrey GU26 6BL
Tel: 01428 604322
Head of School: Mr Jonathan
Whybrow
Age range: 2–13 years
No. of pupils: 360

Banstead Preparatory School
Sutton Lane, Banstead,
Surrey SM7 3RA
Tel: 01737 363601
Headteacher: Miss Vicky Ellis
Age range: 2–11
No. of pupils: 225

Barfield School
Guildford Road, Runfold,
Farnham, Surrey GU10 1PB
Tel: 01252 782271
Headmaster: Mr Andy Boyle
Age range: 2–11 years

Barrow Hills School
Roke Lane, Witley, Godalming,
Surrey GU8 5NY
Tel: +44 (0)1428 683639
Headmaster: Mr Philip Oldroyd
Age range: 2–13 years
No. of pupils: 216
Fees: Day £16,785

BELMONT SCHOOL
For further details see p. 87
Pasturewood Road, Holmbury St
Mary, Dorking, Surrey RH5 6LQ
Tel: 01306 730852
Email: admissions@
belmont-school.org
Website:
www.belmont-school.org
Headmistress: Mrs Helen Skrine
BA, PGCE, NPQH, FRSA
Age range: 3–16 years
No. of pupils: 200

Bishopsgate School
Bishopsgate Road, Englefield
Green, Egham, Surrey TW20 0YJ
Tel: 01784 432109
Headmaster: Mr R Williams
Age range: 3–13 years

Box Hill School
London Road, Mickleham,
Dorking, Surrey RH5 6EA
Tel: 01372 373382
Headmaster: Cory Lowde
Age range: 11–18 years
No. of pupils: 425
Fees: Day £20,820 WB £30,480

Cambridge Management College
4-8 Castle Street, Oakington,
Kingston upon Thames,
Surrey KT11SS
Tel: 08003166282
Principal: Dr Peter Holmes

Caterham School
Harestone Valley, Caterham,
Surrey CR3 6YA
Tel: 01883 343028
Head: Mr C. W. Jones MA(Cantab)
Age range: 11–18
No. of pupils: VIth321
Fees: Day £18,735–£19,620 WB
£30,936–£33,270 FB £36,795–£38,760

Charterhouse
Godalming, Surrey GU7 2DX
Tel: +44 (0)1483 291501
Head: Dr Alex Peterken
Age range: B13–18 years
G16–18 years
No. of pupils: 895

Chinthurst School
52 Tadworth Street, Tadworth,
Surrey KT20 5QZ
Tel: 01737 812011
Head: Miss Catherine Trundle
Age range: B3–11 years

City of London Freemen's School
Ashtead Park, Ashtead,
Surrey KT21 1ET
Tel: 01372 277933
Headmaster: Mr R Martin
Age range: 7–18
No. of pupils: 877 VIth213
Fees: Day £14,067–£19,194 WB
£29,784–£29,841 FB £30,780–£30,816

Claremont Fan Court School

Claremont Drive, Esher,
Surrey KT10 9LY
Tel: 01372 473780
Head: Mr William Brierly
Age range: 2 1/2–18 years
No. of pupils: 1010

Ⓐ Ⓔ 🖉 ⑯

Coworth Flexlands School

Valley End, Chobham,
Surrey GU24 8TE
Tel: 01276 855707
Head of School: Miss Nicola Cowell
Age range: B2.5–7 years
G2.5–11 years
No. of pupils: 120

🖉

Cranleigh Preparatory School

Horseshoe Lane, Cranleigh,
Surrey GU6 8QH
Tel: 01483 542058
Headmaster: Mr Neil Brooks
BA(Hons) (QTS)
Age range: 7–13 years

🏛

Cranleigh School

Horseshoe Lane, Cranleigh,
Surrey GU6 8QQ
Tel: +44 (0) 1483 273666
Headmaster: Mr Martin Reader
MA, MPhil, MBA
Age range: 7–18 years
(including Prep School)
No. of pupils: 683 VIth256
Fees: Day £33,510 FB £40,710

🏉 Ⓐ 🏛 Ⓔ 🖉 ⑯

Cranmore School

Epsom Road, West Horsley,
Surrey KT24 6AT
Tel: 01483 280340
Headmaster: Mr Barry Everitt
Age range: 2–13 years

🖉

Danes Hill School

Leatherhead Road, Oxshott,
Surrey KT22 0JG
Tel: 01372 842509
Age range: 3–13 years
No. of pupils: 725
Fees: Day £6,981–£20,340

Ⓔ 🖉

Danesfield Manor School

Rydens Avenue, Walton-on-
Thames, Surrey KT12 3JB
Tel: 01932 220930
Principal: Mrs Jo Smith
Age range: 2–11
No. of pupils: 170
Fees: Day £9,456–£10,098

🖉

Downsend School

1 Leatherhead Road,
Leatherhead, Surrey KT22 8TJ
Tel: 01372 372197
Headmaster: Mr Ian Thorpe
Age range: 2–16 years
No. of pupils: 792
Fees: Day £11,970–£17,985

🖉

Downsend School (Ashtead Pre-Prep)

Ashtead Lodge, 22 Oakfield
Road, Ashtead, Surrey KT21 2RE
Tel: 01372 385439
Head Teacher: Tessa Roberts
Age range: 2–6
No. of pupils: 66
Fees: Day £11,535

Downsend School (Epsom Pre-Prep)

Epsom Lodge, 6 Norman Avenue,
Epsom, Surrey KT17 3AB
Tel: 01372 385438
Head Teacher: Vanessa Conlan
Age range: 2–6
No. of pupils: 110
Fees: Day £11,535

🖉

Downsend School (Leatherhead Pre-Prep)

Leatherhead Lodge, Epsom Road,
Leatherhead, Surrey KT22 8ST
Tel: 01372 385437
Headteacher: Mrs Gill Brooks
Age range: 2–6
No. of pupils: 106
Fees: Day £11,535

Drayton House Pre-School and Nursery

35 Austen Road, Guildford,
Surrey GU1 3NP
Tel: 01483 504707
Headmistress: Mrs J Tyson-Jones
Froebel Cert.Ed. London University
Age range: 6 months–5 years
No. of pupils: 65
Fees: Day £4,420–£12,500

🖉

Duke of Kent School

Peaslake Road, Ewhurst,
Surrey GU6 7NS
Tel: 01483 277313
Head: Mrs Sue Knox BA(Hons) MBA
MEd
Age range: 3–16 years
No. of pupils: 316
Fees: Day £2,740–£6,540

🏉 Ⓔ 🖉

Dunottar School

High Trees Road, Reigate,
Surrey RH2 7EL
Tel: 01737 761945
Head of School: Mr Mark Tottman
Age range: 11–18
No. of pupils: 460
Fees: Day £18,621

Ⓐ Ⓔ ⑯

Edgeborough

84 Frensham Road, Frensham,
Farnham, Surrey GU10 3AH
Tel: 01252 792495
Headmaster: Mr Dan Thornburn
Age range: 2–13 years
No. of pupils: 370

🏛 Ⓔ 🖉

Emberhurst School

94 Ember Lane, Esher,
Surrey KT10 8EN
Tel: 020 8398 2933
Headmistress: Mrs P Chadwick BEd
Age range: 2–7
No. of pupils: 70

Epsom College

Epsom, Surrey KT17 4JQ
Tel: 01372 821000
Headmaster: Mr Jay A Piggot MA
Age range: 11–18
No. of pupils: 884
Fees: Day £19,611–£26,151
WB £35,034 FB £38,568

🏉 Ⓐ 🏛 Ⓔ 🖉 ⑯

Essendene Lodge School

Essendene Road, Caterham,
Surrey CR3 5PB
Tel: 01883 348349
Head Teacher: Mrs K Ali
Age range: 2–11
No. of pupils: 153
Fees: Day £3,315–£7,305

Ⓔ 🖉

Ewell Castle School

Church Street, Ewell, Epsom,
Surrey KT17 2AW
Tel: 020 8393 1413
Principal: Mr Silas Edmonds
Age range: 3–18 years
No. of pupils: 670
Fees: Day £5,382–£18,141

Ⓐ Ⓔ 🖉 ⑯

Feltonfleet School

Cobham, Surrey KT11 1DR
Tel: 01932 862264
Head of School: Mrs S Lance
Age range: 3–13 years
No. of pupils: 492

🏛 Ⓔ 🖉

Frensham Heights

Rowledge, Farnham,
Surrey GU10 4EA
Tel: 01252 792561
Head: Mr Rick Clarke
Age range: 3–18
No. of pupils: 497 VIth105
Fees: Day £7,110–£21,060
FB £27,450–£32,070

🏉 Ⓐ 🏛 Ⓔ 🖉 ⑯

Glenesk School

Ockham Road North, East
Horsley, Surrey KT24 6NS
Tel: 01483 282329
Headmistress: Mrs Sarah Bradley
Age range: 2–7 years
No. of pupils: 100
Fees: Day £11,658–£13,176

Ⓔ 🖉

Greenfield School

Old Woking Road, Woking,
Surrey GU22 8HY
Tel: 01483 772525
Headmistress: Mrs. Tania Botting
MEd
Age range: 6 months–11 years
No. of pupils: 335

Ⓔ 🖉

Guildford High School

London Road, Guildford,
Surrey GU1 1SJ
Tel: 01483 561440
Headmistress: Mrs F J Boulton BSc,
MA
Age range: G4–18
No. of pupils: 985
Fees: Day £11,400–£18,300

🏃 Ⓐ Ⓔ ⑯

Hall Grove School

London Road, Bagshot,
Surrey GU19 5HZ
Tel: 01276 473059
Headmaster: Mr Alastair Graham
Age range: 3–13
No. of pupils: 410
Fees: Day £10,800–£15,450

🏛

Halstead Preparatory School

Woodham Rise, Woking,
Surrey GU21 4EE
Tel: 01483 772682
Headmistress: Mrs P Austin
Age range: G3–11
No. of pupils: 220
Fees: Day £10,800–£15,210

🏃 Ⓔ 🖉

Hazelwood School

Wolf's Hill, Limpsfield,
Oxted, Surrey RH8 0QU
Tel: 01883 712194
Head: Mrs Lindie Louw
Age range: 2–13
No. of pupils: 399
Fees: Day £10,275–£16,380

Ⓔ 🖉

Hoe Bridge School

Hoe Place, Old Woking Road,
Woking, Surrey GU22 8JE
Tel: 01483 760018
Headmaster: Mr C Webster MA BSc
(Hons) PGCE
Age range: 2–13 years

Ⓔ 🖉

Hurtwood House

Holmbury St Mary, Dorking,
Surrey RH5 6NU
Tel: 01483 279000
Principal: Mr Cosmo Jackson
Age range: 16–18 years
No. of pupils: 360
Fees: Day £29,748 FB £44,622

⑯ Ⓐ 🏛

Kids Inc Day Nursery – Guildford
Railton Road, Queen Elizabeth Park, Guildford, Surrey GU2 9LX
Tel: 01483 237999

KING EDWARD'S WITLEY
For further details see p. 92
Petworth Road, Godalming, Surrey GU8 5SG
Tel: 01428 686735
Email: admissions@kesw.org
Website: www.kesw.org
Head: Mrs Joanna Wright
Age range: 11–18 years
No. of pupils: 420

Kingswood House School
56 West Hill, Epsom, Surrey KT19 8LG
Tel: 01372 723590
Headmaster: Mr Duncan Murphy BA (Hons), MEd, FRSA
Age range: 4–16 years
No. of pupils: 250

Lingfield College
Racecourse Road, Lingfield, Surrey RH7 6PH
Tel: 01342 832407
Headmaster: Mr R Bool B.A. Hons, MBA
Age range: 2–18
No. of pupils: 935
Fees: Day £11,250–£21,801

Longacre School
Hullbrook Lane, Shamley Green, Guildford, Surrey GU5 0NQ
Tel: 01483 893225
Head of School: Mr Matthew Bryan MA(Cantab.), MA(Oxon.), MSc, FRSA
Age range: 2–11 years
No. of pupils: 267
Fees: Day £11,355–£17,250

Lyndhurst School
36 The Avenue, Camberley, Surrey GU15 3NE
Tel: 01276 22895
Head: Mr A Rudkin BEd(Hons)
Age range: 3–11
No. of pupils: 126

Manor House School, Bookham
Manor House Lane, Little Bookham, Leatherhead, Surrey KT23 4EN
Tel: 01372 457077
Headteacher: Ms Tracey Fantham BA (Hons) MA NPQH
Age range: B2–4 years G2–16 years
No. of pupils: 300
Fees: Day £9,747–£18,315

Micklefield School
10 Somers Road, Reigate, Surrey RH2 9DU
Tel: 01737 224212
Head: Mr R Ardé
Age range: 3–11 years
No. of pupils: 210
Fees: Day £10,965–£13,935

Milbourne Lodge School
Arbrook Lane, Esher, Surrey KT10 9EG
Tel: 01372 462737
Head: Mrs Judy Waite
Age range: 4–13 years
No. of pupils: 276
Fees: Day £13,695–£17,205

New Life Christian Primary School
Cairo New Road, Croydon, Surrey CR0 1XP
Tel: 020 8680 7671 Ext:327

Notre Dame School
Cobham, Surrey KT11 1HA
Tel: 01932 869990
Head of Seniors: Mrs Anna King MEd, MA (Cantab), PGCE
Age range: 2–18
No. of pupils: 600

Oakhyrst Grange School
160 Stanstead Road, Caterham, Surrey CR3 6AF
Tel: 01883 343344
Headmaster: Mr Alex Gear
Age range: 4–11 years
No. of pupils: 152
Fees: Day £1,472–£3,414

OneSchool Global UK Hindhead Campus
Tilford Road, Hindhead, Surrey GU26 6SJ
Tel: 01428 601800
Age range: 7–18 years

OneSchool Global UK Kenley Campus
Victor Beamish Avenue, Kenley, Surrey CR3 5FX
Tel: 01883 338634
Age range: 7–18 years

Parkside School
The Manor, Stoke d'Abernon, Cobham, Surrey KT11 3PX
Tel: 01932 862749
Headteacher: Ms Nicole Janssen
Age range: B2–13 years G2–4 years
No. of pupils: 270

Prior's Field
Priorsfield Road, Godalming, Surrey GU7 2RH
Tel: 01483 810551
Head of School: Mrs Tracey Kirnig
Age range: G11–18
No. of pupils: 450
Fees: Day £18,900 FB £30,825

Reed's School
Sandy Lane, Cobham, Surrey KT11 2ES
Tel: 01932 869001
Headmaster: Mr Mark Hoskins BA MA MSc
Age range: B11–18 G16–18
No. of pupils: 650 VIth230
Fees: Day £20,430–£25,530 FB £27,225–£32,910

Reigate Grammar School
Reigate Road, Reigate, Surrey RH2 0QS
Tel: 01737 222231
Headmaster: Mr Shaun Fenton MA (Oxon) MEd (Oxon)
Age range: 11–18
No. of pupils: 969 VIth262
Fees: Day £19,140–£19,350

Reigate St Mary's Prep & Choir School
Chart Lane, Reigate, Surrey RH2 7RN
Tel: 01737 244880
Headmaster: Mr Marcus Culverwell MA
Age range: 2–11 years

RGS Prep
Maori Road, Guildford, Surrey GU1 2EL
Tel: 01483 880650
Head of School: Mr Toby Freeman-Day
Age range: B3–11 years
Fees: Day £15,999

Ripley Court School
Rose Lane, Ripley, Surrey GU23 6NE
Tel: 01483 225217
Headmistress: Ms Aislinn Clarke
Age range: 3–13

Rowan Preparatory School
6 Fitzalan Road, Claygate, Surrey KT10 0LX
Tel: 01372 462627
Headmistress: Mrs Susan Clarke BEd, NPQH
Age range: G2–11
No. of pupils: 317
Fees: Day £11,526–£15,294

Royal Grammar School, Guildford
High Street, Guildford, Surrey GU1 3BB
Tel: 01483 880600
Headmaster: Dr J M Cox BSc, PhD
Age range: B11–18
No. of pupils: 940
Fees: Day £19,035

Royal School of Needlework
Apartment 12A, Hampton Court Palace, East Molesey, Surrey KT8 9AU
Tel: 020 3166 6932

Rydes Hill Preparatory School
Rydes Hill House, Aldershot Road, Guildford, Surrey GU2 8BP
Tel: 01483 563160
Headmistress: Mrs Sarah Norville
Age range: B3 G3–11
No. of pupils: 180
Fees: Day £3,006–£4,565

Shrewsbury House Pre-Preparatory School
22 Milbourne Lane, Esher, Surrey KT10 9EA
Tel: 01372 462781
Head: Mr Jon Akhurst BA (Hons) PGCE
Age range: 3–7
Fees: Day £6,225–£13,740

Sir William Perkins's School
Guildford Road, Chertsey, Surrey KT16 9BN
Tel: 01932 574900
Head: Mr C C Muller
Age range: G11–18 years
No. of pupils: 600
Fees: Day £5,618

St Catherine's, Bramley
Station Road, Bramley, Guildford, Surrey GU5 0DF
Tel: 01483 899609
Headmistress: Alice Phillips
Age range: G4–18
Fees: Day £9,240–£18,885 FB £31,125

St Christopher's School
6 Downs Road, Epsom, Surrey KT18 5HE
Tel: 01372 721807
Headteacher: Mrs A C Thackray MA, BA(Hons)
Age range: 3–7
No. of pupils: 137
Fees: Day £10,485

St Edmund's School
Portsmouth Road, Hindhead, Surrey GU26 6BH
Tel: 01428 604808
Headmaster: Mr A J Walliker MA(Cantab), MBA, PGCE
Age range: 2–16 years

St George's College
Weybridge Road, Addlestone, Weybridge, Surrey KT15 2QS
Tel: 01932 839300
Headmistress: Mrs Rachel Owens
Age range: 11–18
No. of pupils: 909 VIth250
Fees: Day £17,655–£20,100

St George's Junior School
Thames Street, Weybridge,
Surrey KT13 8NL
Tel: 01932 839400
Head Master: Mr Antony Hudson
MA (CANTAB), PGCE, NPQH
Age range: 3–11 years
No. of pupils: 644
Fees: Day £5,640–£14,640
(£)(✎)

St Hilary's School
Holloway Hill, Godalming,
Surrey GU7 1RZ
Tel: 01483 416551
Headmistress: Mrs Jane
Whittingham BEdCert,
ProfPracSpLD
Age range: B2–11 G2–11
No. of pupils: 250
Fees: Day £10,092–£14,850
(£)(✎)

St Ives School
Three Gates Lane, Haslemere,
Surrey GU27 2ES
Tel: 01428 643734
Headteacher: Kay Goldsworthy
Age range: 2–11
No. of pupils: 149
Fees: Day £9,900–£13,950
(£)(✎)

St John's School
Epsom Road, Leatherhead,
Surrey KT22 8SP
Tel: 01372 373000
Head of School: Mrs Rowena Cole
Age range: 11–18
No. of pupils: 840
Fees: Day £19,785–£24,810
WB £25,035–£31,365
(🏇)(A)(⚑)(£)(✎)(16)

St Teresa's Effingham (Preparatory School)
Effingham, Surrey RH5 6ST
Tel: 01372 453456
Headmaster: Mr. Mike Farmer
Age range: B2–4 G2–11
No. of pupils: 100
Fees: Day £1,185–£14,685
WB £25,515 FB £28,665
(🏃)(⚑)(✎)

St Teresa's Effingham (Senior School)
Beech Avenue, Effingham,
Surrey RH5 6ST
Tel: 01372 452037
Executive Director: Mr Mike Farmer
Age range: G11–18
No. of pupils: 640 VIth90
Fees: Day £17,865–£18,465 WB
£28,875–£29,175 FB £30,795–£31,455
(🏃)(🏇)(A)(⚑)(£)(✎)(16)

St. Andrew's School
Church Hill House, Horsell,
Woking, Surrey GU21 4QW
Tel: 01483 760943
Headmaster: Mr D Fitzgerald
Age range: 3–13 years
No. of pupils: 300
Fees: Day £4,203–£16,545
(£)(✎)

Surbiton Preparatory School
3 Avenue Elmers, Surbiton,
Surrey KT6 4SP
Tel: 020 8390 6640
Principal: Mrs Rebecca Glover
Age range: B4–11 G4–11
No. of pupils: 135
Fees: Day £10,857–£13,974
(🏃)(🏇)(✎)

Tante Marie Culinary Academy
Woodham House, Carlton Road,
Woking, Surrey GU21 4HF
Tel: 01483 726957
Principal: Mr Andrew Maxwell
Age range: 16–60
No. of pupils: 72
Fees: Day £20,750
(16)(✎)(16)

TASIS The American School in England
Coldharbour Lane, Thorpe,
Surrey TW20 8TE
Tel: +44 (0)1932 582316
Head of School: Mr Bryan Nixon
Age range: 3–18
No. of pupils: 620
Fees: Day £12,280–
£26,375 FB £48,900
(🏇)(⚑)(IB)(16)

The Hawthorns School
Pendell Court, Bletchingley,
Redhill, Surrey RH1 4QJ
Tel: 01883 743048
Head of School: Mr Adrian Floyd
Age range: 2–13 years
(✎)

The Royal Junior School
Portsmouth Road, Hindhead,
Surrey GU26 6BW
Tel: 01428 607977
Principal: Mrs Anne J P Lynch
Age range: 6 weeks–11 years
Fees: Day £10,200–£11,955
(🏇)

The Royal School
Farnham Lane, Haslemere,
Surrey GU27 1HQ
Tel: 01428 605805
Head: Mrs Pippa Smithson
Age range: 11–18 years
Fees: Day £10,506–£18,507
WB £27,747 FB £31,557
(🏇)(A)(⚑)(£)(✎)(16)

Tormead School
27 Cranley Road, Guildford,
Surrey GU1 2JD
Tel: 01483 575101
Headmistress: Mrs Christina Foord
Age range: G4–18
No. of pupils: 760 VIth120
Fees: Day £8,385–£15,915
(🏃)(A)(£)(✎)(16)

Warlingham Park School
Chelsham Common,
Warlingham, Surrey CR6 9PB
Tel: 01883 626844
Headmaster: Mrs S S Buist
Age range: 2–11
No. of pupils: 96
Fees: Day £4,230–£8,565
(✎)

Weston Green School
Weston Green Road, Thames
Ditton, Surrey KT7 0JN
Tel: 020 8398 2778
Headteacher: Mrs Sarah Evans
Age range: 2–11
No. of pupils: 200
Fees: Day £3,389–£3,809
(✎)

Westward School
47 Hersham Road, Walton-
on-Thames, Surrey KT12 1LE
Tel: 01932 220911
Headmistress: Mrs Shelley
Stevenson
Age range: 3–12
No. of pupils: 140
Fees: Day £7,380–£8,235
(£)(✎)

Woldingham School
Marden Park, Woldingham,
Surrey CR3 7YA
Tel: 01883 349431
Head of School: Dr James
Whitehead
Age range: G11–18
No. of pupils: 611
Fees: Day £22,710–£24,750
FB £32,850–£40,710
(🏇)(🏇)(A)(⚑)(£)(✎)(16)

Woodcote House School
Snows Ride, Windlesham,
Surrey GU20 6PF
Tel: 01276 472115
Headmaster: Mr D.M.K. Paterson
Age range: B7–13 years
(🏃)(⚑)(✎)

World Federation of Hairdressing & Beauty Schools
PO Box 367, Coulsdon,
Surrey CR5 2TP
Tel: 01737 551355
(16)

Yehudi Menuhin School
Stoke Road, Stoke d'Abernon,
Cobham, Surrey KT11 3QQ
Tel: 01932 864739
Interim Head: Richard Tanner
Age range: 7–19
No. of pupils: 80 VIth36
Fees: FB £34,299
(🏇)(A)(⚑)(£)(✎)(16)

West Berkshire

Brockhurst & Marlston House Schools
Hermitage, Newbury, West
Berkshire RG18 9UL
Tel: 01635 200293
Headmaster: Mr David Fleming MA
(Oxon), MSc
Age range: 2 1/2–13 years
(🏃)(🏇)(⚑)(✎)

Cheam School
Headley, Newbury, West
Berkshire RG19 8LD
Tel: +44 (0)1635 268242
Headmaster: Mr Martin Harris
Age range: 3–13 years
(⚑)(✎)

Downe House School
Downe House, Cold Ash,
Thatcham, West Berkshire RG18 9JJ
Tel: +44 (0)1635 200286
Headmistress: Mrs Emma
McKendrick BA(Liverpool)
Age range: G11–18 years
No. of pupils: 590
Fees: Day £10,435 FB £14,030
(🏃)(🏇)(A)(⚑)(£)(✎)(16)

Horris Hill
Newtown, Newbury, West
Berkshire RG20 9DJ
Tel: 01635 40594
Headmaster: Dr S Bailey
Age range: B4–13 years
(🏃)(⚑)(✎)

Newbury Hall
Enborne Road, (corner of
Rockingham Road), Newbury,
West Berkshire RG14 6AD
Tel: +44 (0)1635 36879
(⚑)

St Gabriel's
Sandleford Priory, Newbury,
West Berkshire RG20 9BD
Tel: 01635 555680
Principal: Mr Richard Smith MA
(Hons), MEd, PGCE
Age range: B6 months–11
G6 months–18
No. of pupils: 469 VIth40
Fees: Day £10,668–£17,418
Ⓐ Ⓔ ✎ ⑯

St Michael's School
Harts Lane, Burghclere, Newbury,
West Berkshire RG20 9JW
Tel: 01635 278137
Headmaster: Rev. Fr. John Brucciani
Age range: B5–18 G5–11
Ⓐ 🏫 ✎

West Sussex

Ardingly College
College Road, Ardingly, Haywards
Heath, West Sussex RH17 6SQ
Tel: +44 (0)1444 893320
Headmaster: Mr Ben Figgis
Age range: 13–18
No. of pupils: 559
Fees: –£23,985 FB £35,865–£29,250
🏫 Ⓐ 🏫 Ⓔ ⒤Ⓑ ✎ ⑯

**Ardingly College
Preparatory School**
Haywards Heath, West
Sussex RH17 6SQ
Tel: 01444 893200
Head of Prep School: Mr Harry
Hastings
Age range: 2 1/2–13 years
🏫 ✎

Brambletye
Brambletye, East Grinstead,
West Sussex RH19 3PD
Tel: 01342 321004
Headmaster: Will Brooks
Age range: 2–13 years
🏫 ✎

Burgess Hill Girls
Keymer Road, Burgess Hill,
West Sussex RH15 0EG
Tel: 01444 241050
Head of School: Liz Laybourn
Age range: B2.5–4 years
G2.5–18 years
No. of pupils: 505 VIth70
Fees: Day £9,150–£20,850
FB £31,800–£36,750
🏫 🏫 Ⓐ 🏫 Ⓔ ✎ ⑯

**Chichester High
Schools Sixth Form**
Kingsham Road, Chichester,
West Sussex PO19 8AE
Tel: +44 1243 832 546

Christ's Hospital
Horsham, West Sussex RH13 0LJ
Tel: 01403 211293
Head Teacher: Mr Simon Reid
Age range: 11–18
No. of pupils: 900
Fees: Day £18,510–£23,310
FB £35,850
🏫 Ⓐ 🏫 Ⓔ ⒤Ⓑ ⑯

Conifers School
Egmont Road, Midhurst,
West Sussex GU29 9BG
Tel: 01730 813243
Headmistress: Mrs Emma Smyth
Age range: 2–13
No. of pupils: 104
Fees: Day £7,350–£9,750
Ⓔ ✎

Copthorne Prep School
Effingham Lane, Copthorne,
West Sussex RH10 3HR
Tel: 01342 712311
Headmaster: Mr Chris Jones
Age range: 2–13
No. of pupils: 340
Fees: Day £9,750–£16,740
WB £20,400 FB £25,500
🏫 Ⓔ ✎

Cottesmore School
Buchan Hill, Pease Pottage,
West Sussex RH11 9AU
Tel: 01293 520648
Head: T F Rogerson
Age range: 4–13
No. of pupils: 170
Fees: Day £3,199–£4,267 FB £9,095
🏫 Ⓔ ✎

Cumnor House Sussex
London Road, Danehill, Haywards
Heath, West Sussex RH17 7HT
Tel: 01825 792 006
Head of School: Mr Fergus Llewellyn
Age range: 2–13
No. of pupils: 385
Fees: Day £8,985–£19,530
WB £22,635 FB £23,250
🏫 Ⓔ ✎

Dorset House School
The Manor, Church Lane, Bury,
Pulborough, West Sussex RH20 1PB
Tel: 01798 831456
Headmaster: Mr Matt Thomas Med
BA Ed (Hons) (Exeter) FRGS
Age range: 4–13 years
No. of pupils: 140
Fees: Day £9,315–£18,945
WB £1,258–£4,488
🏫 Ⓔ ✎

Farlington School
Strood Park, Horsham,
West Sussex RH12 3PN
Tel: 01403 282573
Head of School: Mr James Passam
Age range: 4–18
No. of pupils: 311
Fees: Day £5,850–£18,300 WB
£29,100–£29,400 FB £30,450–£30,750
🏫 Ⓐ 🏫 Ⓔ ✎ ⑯

Great Ballard School
Eartham House, Eartham, Nr
Chichester, West Sussex PO18 0LR
Tel: 01243 814236
Head of School: Mr Matt King
Age range: 2.5–16 years
No. of pupils: 136
Fees: Day £8,580–£16,200
Ⓔ ✎

Great Walstead School
East Mascalls Lane,
Lindfield, Haywards Heath,
West Sussex RH16 2QL
Tel: 01444 483528
Headmaster: Mr Chris Calvey
Age range: 2.5–13 years
No. of pupils: 345
Fees: Day £2,895–£5,550
🏫 Ⓔ ✎

Handcross Park School
Handcross, Haywards Heath,
West Sussex RH17 6HF
Tel: 01444 400526
Headmaster: Mr Richard Brown
Age range: 2–13
No. of pupils: 339
Fees: Day £3,230–£6,360 WB
£5,370–£7,480 FB £6,030–£8,130
🏫 Ⓔ ✎

Hurstpierpoint College
College Lane, Hurstpierpoint,
West Sussex BN6 9JS
Tel: 01273 833636
Headmaster: Mr. T J Manly BA, MSc
Age range: 4–18
No. of pupils: 1156
Fees: Day £8,790–£22,860
WB £28,800
🏫 Ⓐ 🏫 Ⓔ ⑯

**Hurstpierpoint College
Prep School**
Hurstpierpoint, West Sussex BN6 9JS
Tel: 01273 834975
Head: Mr I D Pattison BSc
Age range: 4–13
No. of pupils: 360
Ⓔ ✎

Lancing College
Lancing, West Sussex BN15 0RW
Tel: 01273 452213
Head Master: Mr Dominic T Oliver
MPhil
Age range: 13–18
No. of pupils: 550 VIth255
Fees: Day £8,190 FB £11,995
🏫 Ⓐ 🏫 Ⓔ ✎ ⑯

Lancing Prep Worthing
Broadwater Road, Worthing,
West Sussex BN14 8HU
Tel: 01903 201123
Head: Mrs Heather Beeby
Age range: 2–13 years
✎

**Oakwood Preparatory
School**
Chichester, West Sussex PO18 9AN
Tel: 01243 575209
Headteacher: Mrs Clare Bradbury
Age range: 2.5–11 years
No. of pupils: 275
Fees: Day £3,170–£5,110
✎

Our Lady of Sion School
Gratwicke Road, Worthing,
West Sussex BN11 4BL
Tel: 01903 204063
Headmaster: Mr Steven Jeffery
Age range: 3–18
No. of pupils: 410
Fees: Day £8,640–£13,575
Ⓐ Ⓔ ⑯

Pennthorpe School
Church Street, Horsham,
West Sussex RH12 3HJ
Tel: 01403 822391
Headmistress: Alexia Bolton
Age range: 2–13
No. of pupils: 362
Fees: Day £2,070–£16,605
Ⓔ ✎

Rikkyo School in England
Guildford Road, Rudgwick,
Horsham, West Sussex RH12 3BE
Tel: 01403 822107
Headmaster: Mr Roger Munechika
Age range: 10–18
No. of pupils: 116
Fees: FB £15,000–£21,600

Seaford College
Lavington Park, Petworth,
West Sussex GU28 0NB
Tel: 01798 867392
Headmaster: J P Green MA BA
Age range: 6–18 years
No. of pupils: 903 VIth235
Fees: Day £3,665–£7,595 WB
£7,635–£10,290 FB £11,750

Shoreham College
St Julians Lane, Shoreham-by-
Sea, West Sussex BN43 6YW
Tel: 01273 592681
Headmaster: Mr R Taylor-West
Age range: 3–16 years
No. of pupils: 375
Fees: Day £9,750–£15,150

Slindon College
Slindon House, Slindon, Arundel,
West Sussex BN18 0RH
Tel: 01243 814320
Head Teacher: Mr Mark Birkbeck
Age range: B8–18 years

Sompting Abbotts Preparatory School
Church Lane, Sompting,
West Sussex BN15 0AZ
Tel: 01903 235960
Principal: Mrs P M Sinclair
Age range: 2–13 years

The Prebendal School
52-55 West Street, Chichester,
West Sussex PO19 1RT
Tel: 01243 772220
Headteacher: Mrs L Salmond Smith
Age range: 3–13
No. of pupils: 181
Fees: Day £8,160–£15,495 WB
£18,975–£20,100 FB £22,290

Westbourne House School
Coach Road, Chichester,
West Sussex PO20 2BH
Tel: 01243 782739
Headmaster: Mr Martin Barker
Age range: 2.5–13 years

Windlesham House School
London Road, Washington,
Pulborough, West Sussex RH20 4AY
Tel: 01903 874701
Head of School: Ben Evans
Age range: 4–13
No. of pupils: 280

Worth School
Paddockhurst Road, Turners Hill,
Crawley, West Sussex RH10 4SD
Tel: +44 (0)1342 710200
Head Master: Stuart McPherson
Age range: 11–18
No. of pupils: 580 VIth222
Fees: Day £15,960–£23,730
FB £21,210–£33,690

International Schools in London and the South-East

London

Central London

Accent London
12 Bedford Square,
London WC1B 3JA
Tel: 020 7813 7723
Head: Natasa Blecic
🌐 16+

CATS London
43-45 Bloomsbury Square,
London WC1A 2RA
Tel: 02078 411580
Principal: Mario Di Clemente
Age range: 15–24
🌐 Ⓐ 🏫 £ 16+

ÉCOLE JEANNINE MANUEL - LONDON
For further details see p. 49
43-45 Bedford Square,
London WC1B 3DN
Tel: 020 3829 5970
Email: admissions@
jmanuel.uk.net
Website: www.
ecolejeanninemanuel.org.uk
Head of School: Pauline Prévot
Age range: 3–18 years
No. of pupils: 585
Fees: Day £20,760
🌐 £ IB

North London

Dwight School London
6 Friern Barnet Lane,
London N11 3LX
Tel: 020 8920 0600
Head: Chris Beddows
Age range: 2–18 years
🌐 £ IB ✎ 16+

North-West London

Collège Français Bilingue de Londres
87 Holmes Road, Kentish
Town, , London NW5 3AX
Tel: 020 7993 7400
Head of School (from September 2021): Mr David Gassian
Age range: 3–15 years
No. of pupils: 700
🌐

ICS London
7B Wyndham Place,
London W1H 1PN
Tel: +44 (0)20 729 88800
Head of School: David Laird
Age range: 3–19 years
No. of pupils: 175
Fees: Day £19,650–£28,770
🌐 IB ✎ 16+

Mill Hill School
The Ridgeway, Mill Hill
Village, London NW7 1QS
Tel: 020 8959 1176
Head: Mrs Jane Sanchez BSc (Hons)
PGCE
Age range: 13–18 years
No. of pupils: 876 VIth312
Fees: Day £21,987 WB
£31,140 FB £36,900
🌐 Ⓐ 🏫 £ ✎ 16+

Southbank International School - Hampstead
16 Netherhall Gardens,
London NW3 5TH
Tel: 020 7243 3803
Principal: Shirley Harwood
Age range: 3–11 years
No. of pupils: 210
🌐 IB ✎

The American School in London
One Waverley Place,
London NW8 0NP
Tel: 020 7449 1221
Head: Robin Appleby
Age range: 4–18
No. of pupils: 1350
Fees: Day £27,050–£31,200
🌐 16+

The Mount, Mill Hill International
Milespit Hill, London NW7 2RX
Tel: +44 (0)20 3826 33
Head of School: Ms Sarah Bellotti
Age range: 13–17 years
No. of pupils: 80
Fees: Day £27,000 WB
£37,500 FB £44,250
🌐 🏫

South-East London

Bellerbys College London
Bounty House, Stowage,
Greenwich, London SE8 3DE
Tel: +44 (0)208 694 7000
Age range: 14–19 years
🌐 16+ Ⓐ 🏫

DLD College London
199 Westminster Bridge
Road, London SE1 7FX
Tel: +44 (0)20 7935 8411
Principal: Irfan H Latif BSc (Hons)
PGCE FRSA FRSC
No. of pupils: 426
Fees: Day £23,500–£29,950
FB £18,000–£28,000
🌐 16+ Ⓐ 🏫 £ ✎

Dulwich College
Dulwich Common, ,
London SE21 7LD
Tel: 020 8693 3601
Master: Dr J A F Spence
Age range: B0–18 years
Fees: Day £21,672 WB
£42,408 FB £45,234
🏃 🌐 Ⓐ 🏫 £ ✎ 16+

St Dunstan's College
Stanstead Road, London SE6 4TY
Tel: 020 8516 7200
Headmaster: Mr Nicholas Hewlett
Age range: 3–18
No. of pupils: 870
🌐 Ⓐ £ 16+

South-West London

Centre Academy London
92 St John's Hill, Battersea,
London SW11 1SH
Tel: 020 7738 2344
Headteacher: Rachel Maddison
Age range: 9–19
🌐 £ ✎ 16+

Ecole Charles De Gaulle - Wix
Clapham Common North
Side, London SW4 0AJ
Tel: +44 20 7738 0287
Headteacher: Mr Blanchard
Age range: 5–11
No. of pupils: 100
🌐

École Primaire Marie D'Orliac
60 Clancarty Road,
London SW6 3AA
Tel: +44 (0)20 7736 5863
Director: Mr Blaise Fenart
Age range: 4–11
🌐

Hill House
17 Hans Place, Chelsea,
London SW1X 0EP
Tel: 020 7584 1331
Headmaster: Mr Richard Townend
Age range: 4–13
No. of pupils: 600
Fees: Day £15,000–£18,600
🌐 £ ✎

King's College School
Southside, Wimbledon
Common, London SW19 4TT
Tel: 020 8255 5300
Acting Head: Ms Jude Lowson MA
Age range: B7–18 years
G16–18 years
No. of pupils: 1477 VIth419
🏃 🌐 Ⓐ £ IB 16+

L'ECOLE DE BATTERSEA
For further details see p. 52
Trott Street, Battersea,
London SW11 3DS
Tel: 020 7371 8350
Email: admin@
lecoledespetits.co.uk
Website:
www.lecoledespetits.co.uk
Principal: Mrs F Brisset
Age range: 3–11 years
No. of pupils: 250
Fees: Day £4,745
🌐

L'ECOLE DES PETITS
For further details see p. 53
2 Hazlebury Road, Fulham,
London SW6 2NB
Tel: 020 7371 8350
Email: admin@
lecoledespetits.co.uk
Website:
www.lecoledespetits.co.uk
Principal: Mrs F Brisset
Age range: 3–6 years
No. of pupils: 120
Fees: Day £4,615
🌐

LYCÉE FRANÇAIS CHARLES DE GAULLE DE LONDRES
For further details see p. 55
35 Cromwell Road,
London SW7 2DG
Tel: 020 7584 6322
Email: inscription@
lyceefrancais.org.uk
Website:
www.lyceefrancais.org.uk
Headteacher: Didier Devilard
Age range: 3–18 years
No. of pupils: 3450
Fees: Day £7,066–£14,782
🌐 £ ✎ 16+

St Paul's School
Lonsdale Road, Barnes,
London SW13 9JT
Tel: 020 8748 9162
High Master: Ms Sally-Anne Huang
Age range: B13–18 years
🏃 🌐 Ⓐ 🏫 £ ✎ 16+

Wandsworth Preparatory School
The Old Library, 2 Allfarthing
Lane, London SW18 2PQ
Tel: 0208 870 4133
Headteacher: Ms Jo Fife
Age range: 4–11
No. of pupils: 100
Fees: Day £4,710
🌐 £

Westminster School
Little Dean's Yard, Westminster,
London SW1P 3PB
Tel: 020 7963 1000
Head Master: Dr Gary Savage
Age range: B13–18 years
G16–18 years

West London

Bales College
742 Harrow Road, Kensal
Town, London W10 4AA
Tel: 020 8960 5899
Principal: William Moore
Age range: 11–19
No. of pupils: 90
Fees: Day £11,550–£12,750

Ecole Francaise
Jacques Prevert
59 Brook Green, London W6 7BE
Tel: 020 7602 6871
Headteacher: Delphine Gentil
Age range: 4–11

FULHAM SCHOOL
For further details see p. 51
1-3 Chesilton Road,
London SW6 5AA
Tel: 020 8154 6751
Email: senioradmin@
fulham.school
Website: fulham.school
Pre-Prep & Nursery Head: Di
Steven
Age range: 3–18 years
No. of pupils: 650
Fees: Day £18,420–£21,567

Godolphin and
Latymer School
Iffley Road, Hammersmith,
London W6 0PG
Tel: +44 (0)20 8741 1936
Head Mistress: Dr Frances Ramsey
Age range: G11–18 years
No. of pupils: 800
Fees: Day £23,085

Halcyon London
International School
33 Seymour Place, ,
London W1H 5AU
Tel: +44 (0)20 7258 1169
Headteacher: Mr Barry Mansfield
Age range: 11–18
No. of pupils: 195

Instituto Español Vicente
Cañada Blanch
317 Portobello Road,
London W10 5SZ
Tel: +44 (0) 20 8969 2664
Principal: Carmen Pinilla Padilla
Age range: 4–19
No. of pupils: 405

International School
of London (ISL)
139 Gunnersbury Avenue,
London W3 8LG
Tel: +44 (0)20 8992 5823
Principal: Mr Richard Parker
Age range: 3–18 years
No. of pupils: 500
Fees: Day £19,000–£26,300

King Fahad Academy
Bromyard Avenue, Acton,
London W3 7HD
Tel: 020 8743 0131
Director General: Dr Tahani Aljafari
Age range: 3–19

Southbank International
School - Kensington
36-38 Kensington Park
Road, London W11 3BU
Tel: +44 (0)20 7243 3803
Principal: Siobhan McGrath
Age range: 3–18 years

Southbank International
School - Westminster
63-65 Portland Place,
London W1B 1QR
Tel: 020 7243 3803
Principal: Dr Paul Wood
Age range: 11–19

Berkshire

Bradfield College
Bradfield, Berkshire RG7 6AU
Tel: 0118 964 4516
Headmaster: Dr Christopher
Stevens
Age range: 13–18 years
No. of pupils: 820
Fees: Day £32,280 FB £40,350

Eton College
Windsor, Berkshire SL4 6DW
Tel: +44 (0)1753 370 611
Head Master: Mr Simon Henderson
MA
Age range: B13–18 years
No. of pupils: 1342
Fees: FB £44,094

Heathfield School
London Road, Ascot,
Berkshire SL5 8BQ
Tel: 01344 898343
Head of School: Ms Sarah Wilson
Age range: G11–18 years
Fees: Day £7,840–£8,000
FB £12,650–£12,950

LEIGHTON PARK SCHOOL
For further details see p. 94
Shinfield Road, Reading,
Berkshire RG2 7ED
Tel: 0118 987 9600
Email: admissions@
leightonpark.com
Website:
www.leightonpark.com
Head: Mr Matthew L S Judd BA,
PGCE
Age range: 11–18 years
No. of pupils: 520

Luckley House School
Luckley Road, Wokingham,
Berkshire RG40 3EU
Tel: 0118 978 4175
Head: Mrs Areti Bizior
Age range: 11–18 years

LVS ASCOT
For further details see p. 96
London Road, Ascot,
Berkshire SL5 8DR
Tel: 01344 882770
Email: enquiries@lvs.
ascot.sch.uk
Website: www.lvs.ascot.sch.uk
Principal: Mrs Christine Cunniffe
BA (Hons), MMus, MBA
Age range: 4–18 years
No. of pupils: 800
Fees: Day £12,915–£19,335
FB £27,585–£33,975

Padworth College
Sopers Lane, Reading,
Berkshire RG7 4NR
Tel: 0118 983 2644
Principal: Lorraine Atkins
Age range: 14–19 years

Pangbourne College
Pangbourne, Reading,
Berkshire RG8 8LA
Tel: 0118 984 2101
Headmaster: Thomas J C Garnier
Age range: 11–18 years
No. of pupils: 458
Fees: Day £6,300–£8,540 WB
£8,210–£11,510 FB £9,050–£12,680

QUEEN ANNE'S SCHOOL
For further details see p. 98
6 Henley Road, Caversham,
Reading, Berkshire RG4 6DX
Tel: 0118 918 7300
Email: office@qas.org.uk
Website: www.qas.org.uk
Head: Ms Elaine Purves
Age range: G11–18 years
No. of pupils: 450
Fees: Day £8,370 FB £13,590

REDDAM HOUSE
BERKSHIRE
For further details see p. 100
Bearwood Road, Sindlesham,
Wokingham, Berkshire RG41 5BG
Tel: +44 (0)118 974 8300
Email: registrar@
reddamhouse.org.uk
Website:
www.reddamhouse.org.uk
Principal: Mr Rick Cross
Age range: 3 months–18 years
No. of pupils: 675
Fees: Day £11,490–£18,420
WB £27,981–£32,244 FB
£29,526–£33,789

St George's Ascot
Wells Lane, Ascot, Berkshire SL5 7DZ
Tel: 01344 629900
Headmistress: Mrs Liz Hewer MA
(Hons) (Cantab) PGCE
Age range: G11–18 years

St Mary's School Ascot
St Mary's Road, Ascot,
Berkshire SL5 9JF
Tel: 01344 296614
Headmistress: Mrs Danuta Staunton
Age range: G11–18 years

The Abbey School
Kendrick Road, Reading,
Berkshire RG1 5DZ
Tel: 0118 987 2256
Head: Mr Will le Fleming
Age range: G3–18 years
No. of pupils: 1000
Fees: Day £11,025–£18,885

The Oratory School
Woodcote, Reading,
Berkshire RG8 0PJ
Tel: 01491 683500
Head Master: Mr Joe Smith
BA(Hons), MEd, PGCE
Age range: 11–18 years

Wellington College
Duke's Ride, Crowthorne,
Berkshire RG45 7PU
Tel: +44 (0)1344 444000
Master: Mr James Dahl
Age range: 13–18 years
No. of pupils: 1090 VIth475
Fees: Day £31,140–£35,760
FB £42,630

Buckinghamshire

International School of Creative Arts (ISCA)
Framewood Road, Wexham,
Buckinghamshire SL2 4QS
Tel: +44 (0)1753 208820
Head of School: Mr Robert Hunter
Age range: 15–19 years

Teikyo School UK
Framewood Road, Wexham,
Buckinghamshire SL2 4QS
Tel: 01753 663711
Age range: 15–18 years

Thornton College
College Lane, Thornton, Milton
Keynes, Buckinghamshire MK17 0HJ
Tel: 01280 812610
Headteacher: Mrs Val Holmes
Age range: G3–18 years
(Boarding from age 7)
No. of pupils: 402
Fees: Day £10,545–£16,815 WB
£18,525–£23,445 FB £23,040–£28,575

Wycombe Abbey
Frances Dove Way, High Wycombe,
Buckinghamshire HP11 1PE
Tel: +44 (0)1494 520381
Headmistress: Mrs Jo Duncan MA
(St Andrews), PGCE (Cantab)
Age range: G11–18 years
No. of pupils: 663
Fees: Day £30,945 FB £41,250

East Sussex

Battle Abbey School
Battle, East Sussex TN33 0AD
Tel: 01424 772385
Headmaster: Mr D Clark BA(Hons)
Age range: 2–18
No. of pupils: 286 VIth48
Fees: Day £6,939–£16,914
FB £26,649–£31,932

Bede's School
The Dicker, Upper Dicker,
Hailsham, East Sussex BN27 3QH
Tel: +44 (0)1323843252
Head: Mr Peter Goodyer
Age range: 3 months–18
No. of pupils: 800 VIth295
Fees: Day £10,230–£17,400
FB £22,290–£25,650

Bellerbys College Brighton
1 Billinton Way, Brighton,
East Sussex BN1 4LF
Tel: +44 (0)1273 339333
Age range: 14–19 years

Brighton College
Eastern Road, Brighton,
East Sussex BN2 0AL
Tel: 01273 704200
Head Master: Richard Cairns MA
Age range: 3–18
No. of pupils: 950
Fees: Day £10,050–£24,540 WB
£33,390–£34,410 FB £37,470–£45,210

Buckswood School
Broomham Hall, Rye
Road, Guestling, Hastings,
East Sussex TN35 4LT
Tel: 01424 813 813
School Director: Mr Giles Sutton
Age range: 10–19
No. of pupils: 420

Eastbourne College
Old Wish Road, Eastbourne,
East Sussex BN21 4JX
Tel: 01323 452323 (Admissions)
Headmaster: Mr Tom Lawson MA
(Oxon)
Age range: 13–18
No. of pupils: 650 VIth312
Fees: Day £23,895–£24,375
FB £36,420–£36,975

Greenfields Independent Day & Boarding School
Priory Road, Forest Row,
East Sussex RH18 5JD
Tel: +44 (0)1342 822189
Executive Head: Mr. Jeff Smith
Age range: 2–19

MAYFIELD SCHOOL
For further details see p. 97
The Old Palace, Mayfield,
East Sussex TN20 6PH
Tel: 01435 874642
Email: registrar@
mayfieldgirls.org
Website: www.mayfieldgirls.org
Head: Ms Antonia Beary MA,
MPhil (Cantab), PGCE
Age range: G11–18 years
No. of pupils: 405
Fees: Day £7,750 FB £12,250

Michael Hall School
Kidbrooke Park, Priory Road,
Forest Row, East Sussex RH18 5JA
Tel: 01342 822275
Age range: 0 years–18 years
No. of pupils: VIth102
Fees: Day £9,245–£12,670

Roedean Moira House
Upper Carlisle Road, Eastbourne,
East Sussex BN20 7TE
Tel: 01323 644144
Headmaster: Mr Andrew Wood
Age range: G0–18
No. of pupils: 289

ROEDEAN SCHOOL
For further details see p. 101
Roedean Way, Brighton,
East Sussex BN2 5RQ
Tel: 01273 667500
Email: info@roedean.co.uk
Website: www.roedean.co.uk
Headmaster: Mr. Oliver Bond
BA(Essex), PGCE, NPQH
Age range: G11–18 years
No. of pupils: 630 VIth155
Fees: Day £5,670–£7,415
WB £10,030–£11,185 FB
£10,990–£13,305

Essex

Brentwood School
Middleton Hall Lane,
Brentwood, Essex CM15 8EE
Tel: 01277 243243
Headmaster: Mr Michael Bond
Age range: 3–18 years
No. of pupils: 1850
Fees: Day £20,598 FB £40,365

Chigwell School
High Road, Chigwell, Essex IG7 6QF
Tel: 020 8501 5700
Headmaster: Mr M E Punt M.A.
M.Sc. P.G.C.E.
Age range: 4–18
Fees: Day £4,250–£6,295 FB £10,995

Felsted School
Felsted, Great Dunmow,
Essex CM6 3LL
Tel: +44 (0)1371 822600
Headmaster: Mr Chris Townsend
Age range: 4–18 years

Gosfield School
Cut Hedge Park, Halstead Road,
Gosfield, Halstead, Essex CO9 1PF
Tel: 01787 474040
Headteacher: Mr Guy Martyn
Age range: 4–18
No. of pupils: VIth21
Fees: Day £6,690–£15,525

New Hall School
The Avenue, Boreham,
Chelmsford, Essex CM3 3HS
Tel: 01245 467588
Principal: Mrs Katherine Jeffrey MA,
BA, PGCE, MA(Ed Mg), NPQH
Age range: 1–18 years
No. of pupils: 1400
Fees: Day £9,621–£20,502 WB
£18,234–£28,026 FB £21,177–£32,472

Hampshire

Bedales School
Church Road, Steep, Petersfield,
Hampshire GU32 2DG
Tel: 01730 711733
Head of School: Magnus Bashaarat
Age range: 13–18
No. of pupils: 463
Fees: Day £28,515 FB £36,285

Brockwood Park & Inwoods School
Brockwood Park, Bramdean,
Hampshire SO24 0LQ
Tel: +44 (0)1962 771744
Principal: Mr Antonio Autor
Age range: 14–19
No. of pupils: 112 VIth39
Fees: Day £5,630–£6,400 FB £21,400

Embley
Embley Park, Romsey,
Hampshire SO51 6ZE
Tel: 01794 512206
Headteacher: Mr Cliff Canning
Age range: 2–18
No. of pupils: 500
Fees: Day £8,754–£31,338

Lord Wandsworth College
Long Sutton, Hook,
Hampshire RG29 1TB
Tel: 01256 862201
Head of School: Mr Adam Williams
Age range: 11–18 years
No. of pupils: 615
Fees: Day £21,240–£24,390
WB £29,400–£33,000 FB
£30,345–£34,650

Moyles Court School
Moyles Court, Ringwood,
Hampshire BH24 3NF
Tel: 01425 472856
Headmaster: Mr Richard Milner-Smith
Age range: 3–16
No. of pupils: 195
Fees: Day £6,885–£14,655
FB £21,246–£26,805

Rookwood School
Weyhill Road, Andover,
Hampshire SP10 3AL
Tel: 01264 325900
Headmaster: Mr A Kirk-Burgess BSc,
PGCE, MSc (Oxon)
Age range: 2–16
Fees: Day £9,360–£15,600
FB £23,250–£27,465

Sherfield School
South Drive, Sherfield-on-Loddon,
Hook, Hampshire RG27 0HU
Tel: 01256 884800
Headmaster: Mr Nick Brain
BA(Hons), PGCE, MA, NPQH
Age range: 3 months–18 years
No. of pupils: 450
Fees: Day £10,320–£17,085 WB
£18,960–£26,130 FB £22,125–£30,495

St John's College
Grove Road South, Southsea,
Portsmouth, Hampshire PO5 3QW
Tel: 023 9281 5118
Head of School: Mrs Mary Maguire
Age range: 4–18
No. of pupils: 560 VIth86
Fees: Day £9,975–£13,125
FB £28,500–£32,250

ST SWITHUN'S SCHOOL
For further details see p. 108
Alresford Road, Winchester,
Hampshire SO21 1HA
Tel: 01962 835700
Email: office@stswithuns.com
Website: www.stswithuns.com
Head of School: Jane Gandee
MA(Cantab)
Age range: G11–18 years
No. of pupils: 510
Fees: Day £21,918 FB £36,339

The Portsmouth Grammar School
High Street, Portsmouth,
Hampshire PO1 2LN
Tel: +44 (0)23 9236 0036
Headmistress: Dr Anne Cotton
Age range: 2–18
No. of pupils: 1556 VIth336
Fees: Day £10,233–£15,951

Winchester College
College Street, Winchester,
Hampshire SO23 9NA
Tel: 01962 621247
Headmaster: Dr. T R Hands
Age range: B13–18
No. of pupils: 690 VIth280
Fees: FB £39,912

Hertfordshire

Aldenham School
Elstree, Hertfordshire WD6 3AJ
Tel: 01923 858122
Head of School: Mr Andrew Williams
Age range: 3–18

BERKHAMSTED SCHOOL
For further details see p. 88
Overton House, 131 High Street, Berkhamsted, Hertfordshire HP4 2DJ
Tel: 01442 358001
Email: admissions@berkhamsted.com
Website: www.berkhamsted.com
Principal: Mr Richard Backhouse MA(Cantab)
Age range: 3–18 years
No. of pupils: 2001 VIth408
Fees: Day £10,830–£22,170 WB £29,850 FB £35,610

Bishop's Stortford College
10 Maze Green Road, Bishop's Stortford, Hertfordshire CM23 2PJ
Tel: 01279 838575
Headmaster: Mr Jeremy Gladwin
Age range: 13–18
No. of pupils: VIth249
Fees: Day £20,349–£20,532 WB £31,569–£31,917 FB £33,402–£33,930

Bishop's Stortford College Prep School
Maze Green Road, Bishop's Stortford, Hertfordshire CM23 2PQ
Tel: 01279 838583
Head of the Prep School: Mr Bill Toleman
Age range: 4–13 years

Haileybury
Haileybury, Hertford, Hertfordshire SG13 7NU
Tel: +44 (0)1992 706353
The Master: Mr Martin Collier MA BA PGCE
Age range: 11–18 years
No. of pupils: 915 VIth364
Fees: Day £18,240–£27,435 FB £23,610–£37,215

St Christopher School
Barrington Road, Letchworth, Hertfordshire SG6 3JZ
Tel: 01462 650 850
Head: Richard Palmer
Age range: 3–18
No. of pupils: 511 VIth78
Fees: Day £4,590–£18,075 WB £19,950–£24,675 FB £31,650

St Edmund's College & Prep School
Old Hall Green, Nr Ware, Hertfordshire SG11 1DS
Tel: 01920 824247
Headmaster: Mr Matthew Mostyn BA (Hons) MA (Ed)
Age range: 3–18
No. of pupils: 852
Fees: Day £9,882–£18,345 WB £24,165–£27,630 FB £28,302–£32,460

St Francis' College
Broadway, Letchworth Garden City, Hertfordshire SG6 3PJ
Tel: 01462 670511
Headmistress: Mrs B Goulding
Age range: G3–18
No. of pupils: 460 VIth75
Fees: Day £9,990–£16,980 WB £22,350–£26,475 FB £27,990–£31,995

St Margaret's School, Bushey
Merry Hill Road, Bushey, Hertfordshire WD23 1DT
Tel: +44 (0)20 8416 4400
Headteacher: Lara Péchard
Age range: 2–18 years
No. of pupils: 530

Stanborough School
Stanborough Park, Garston, Watford, Hertfordshire WD25 9JT
Tel: 01923 673268
Acting Head Teacher: Ms Eileen Hussey
Age range: 3–17
No. of pupils: 300
Fees: Day £6,630–£10,224 WB £10,350–£13,995

The Purcell School, London
Aldenham Road, Bushey, Hertfordshire WD23 2TS
Tel: 01923 331100
Headteacher: Dr Bernard Trafford
Age range: 10–18
No. of pupils: 180
Fees: Day £25,707 FB £32,826

The Royal Masonic School for Girls
Rickmansworth Park, Rickmansworth, Hertfordshire WD3 4HF
Tel: 01923 773168
Headmaster: Mr Kevin Carson M.Phil (Cambridge)
Age range: G4–18
No. of pupils: 930 VIth165
Fees: Day £11,475–£17,475 WB £20,115–£27,495 FB £21,225–£29,835

Tring Park School for the Performing Arts
Mansion Drive, Tring, Hertfordshire HP23 5LX
Tel: 01442 824255
Principal: Mr Stefan Anderson MA, ARCM, ARCT
Age range: 8–19 years
No. of pupils: 370 VIth171
Fees: Day £15,405–£24,885 FB £26,190–£37,605

Kent

Ashford School
East Hill, Ashford, Kent TN24 8PB
Tel: 01233 739030
Head: Mr Michael Hall
Age range: 3 months–18 years
No. of pupils: 916 VIth127
Fees: Day £10,815–£18,294 WB £26,775 FB £38,778

Ashgrove School
116 Widmore Road, Bromley, Kent BR1 3BE
Tel: 020 8460 4143
Principal: Dr Patricia Ash CertEd, BSc(Hons), PhD, CMath, FIMA
Age range: 3–11 years

Benenden School
Cranbrook, Kent TN17 4AA
Tel: 01580 240592
Headmistress: Mrs S Price
Age range: G11–18
No. of pupils: 550
Fees: FB £12,650

Bethany School
Curtisden Green, Goudhurst, Cranbrook, Kent TN17 1LB
Tel: 01580 211273
Headmaster: Mr Francie Healy BSc, HDipEd, NPQH
Age range: 11–18 years
No. of pupils: 356 VIth73
Fees: Day £17,910–£19,785 WB £27,810–£30,705 FB £29,985–£33,750

CATS Canterbury
68 New Dover Road, Canterbury, Kent CT1 3LQ
Tel: +44 (0)1227866540
Principal: Severine Collins
Age range: 14–21 years
No. of pupils: 450
Fees: Day £17,370–£27,990 FB £13,230–£19,140

COBHAM HALL SCHOOL
For further details see p. 89
Brewers Road, Cobham, Kent DA12 3BL
Tel: 01474 823371
Email: enquiries@cobhamhall.com
Website: www.cobhamhall.com
Headteacher: Mrs Wendy Barrett
Age range: G11–18
No. of pupils: 150
Fees: Day £6,804–£8,246 FB £10,279–£12,831

Dover College
Effingham Crescent,
Dover, Kent CT17 9RH
Tel: 01304 205969
Headmaster: Mr Gareth Doodes
MA (Hons)
Age range: 3–18
No. of pupils: 301
Fees: Day £7,725–£16,050 WB
£21,000–£25,500 FB £24,750–£31,500

Earlscliffe
29 Shorncliffe Road,
Folkestone, Kent CT20 2NB
Tel: +44 (0)1303 253951
Director: Mr Tim Fish
Age range: 15–19 years

Farringtons School
Perry Street, Chislehurst,
Kent BR6 6LR
Tel: 020 8467 0256
Head: Mr David Jackson
Age range: 3–18 years
No. of pupils: 700 VIth100
Fees: Day £16,260 WB
£27,120 FB £34,050

Kent College Pembury
Old Church Road, Pembury,
Tunbridge Wells, Kent TN2 4AX
Tel: +44 (0)1892 822006
Head of School: Miss Katrina
Handford
Age range: G3–18 years
No. of pupils: 500
Fees: Day £22,575 WB
£28,200 FB £35,700

Kent College, Canterbury
Whitstable Road, Canterbury,
Kent CT2 9DT
Tel: +44 (0)1227 763 231
Head: Mr Mark Turnbull
Age range: 0–18 years
(Boarding from 8)
No. of pupils: 800
Fees: Day £5,797–£6,665
FB £8,967–£12,339

King's Rochester
Satis House, Boley Hill,
Rochester, Kent ME1 1TE
Tel: 01634 888555
Principal: Mr B Charles
Age range: 13–18 years
No. of pupils: 600 VIth95
Fees: Day £20,700 FB £33,840

Rochester Independent College
254 St Margaret's Banks,
Rochester, Kent ME1 1HY
Tel: +44 (0)163 482 8115
Head of School: Mr Alistair
Brownlow
Age range: 11–18 years

Sevenoaks School
High Street, Sevenoaks,
Kent TN13 1HU
Tel: +44 (0)1732 455133
Head of School: Mr Jesse R Elzinga
AB MSt FCCT
Age range: 11–18 years
No. of pupils: 1172
Fees: Day £25,020–£28,413
FB £39,790–£42,084

ST EDMUND'S SCHOOL
For further details see p. 102
St Thomas Hill, Canterbury,
Kent CT2 8HU
Tel: 01227 475601
Email: admissions@
stedmunds.org.uk
Website: www.stedmunds.org.uk
Head: Mr Edward O'Connor MA
(Cantab), MPhil (Oxon), MEd
(Cantab)
Age range: 2–18 years
No. of pupils: 558

St Lawrence College
Ramsgate, Kent CT11 7AE
Tel: 01843 572931
Head of College: Mr Barney Durrant
Age range: 3–18 years
No. of pupils: 585
Fees: Day £7,995–£17,025
FB £27,765–£37,455

Sutton Valence School
North Street, Sutton
Valence, Kent ME17 3HL
Tel: 01622 845200
Headmaster: Mr James A Thomas
MA (Cantab) MA (London) NPQH
Age range: 11–18 years
No. of pupils: 570

The King's School, Canterbury
The Precincts, Canterbury,
Kent CT1 2ES
Tel: 01227 595501
Head: Mr Peter Roberts
Age range: 13–18
No. of pupils: 858 VIth385
Fees: Day £27,495 FB £38,955

TONBRIDGE SCHOOL
For further details see p. 106
High Street, Tonbridge,
Kent TN9 1JP
Tel: 01732 304297
Email: admissions@
tonbridge-school.org
Website:
www.tonbridge-school.co.uk
Headmaster: Mr James Priory
MA (Oxon)
Age range: B13–18 years
No. of pupils: 798
Fees: Day £33,636 FB £44,835

Middlesex

ACS Hillingdon International School
Hillingdon Court, 108 Vine
Lane, Hillingdon, Uxbridge,
Middlesex UB10 0BE
Tel: +44 (0) 1895 259 771
Head of School: Mr Martin Hall
Age range: 4–18

North London Collegiate School
Canons, Canons Drive,
Edgware, Middlesex HA8 7RJ
Tel: +44 (0)20 8952 0912
Headmistress: Mrs Sarah Clark
Age range: G4–18 years
No. of pupils: 1080
Fees: Day £5,956–£7,049

Radnor House
Pope's Villa, Cross Deep,
Twickenham, Middlesex TW1 4QG
Tel: +44 (0)20 8891 6264
Head: Mr Darryl Wideman MA
Oxon, PGCE
Age range: 9–18 years

St Helen's School
Eastbury Road, Northwood,
Middlesex HA6 3AS
Tel: +44 (0)1923 843210
Headmistress: Dr Mary Short BA,
PhD
Age range: G3–18
No. of pupils: VIth165

Surrey

ACS Cobham International School
Heywood, Portsmouth Road,
Cobham, Surrey KT11 1BL
Tel: +44 (0) 1932 867251
Head of School: Mr Barnaby
Sandow
Age range: 2–18

ACS Egham International School
Woodlee, London Road,
Egham, Surrey TW20 0HS
Tel: +44 (0) 1784 430 800
Head of School: Mr Jeremy Lewis
Age range: 4–18
Fees: Day £11,090–£25,870

Box Hill School
London Road, Mickleham,
Dorking, Surrey RH5 6EA
Tel: 01372 373382
Headmaster: Cory Lowde
Age range: 11–18 years
No. of pupils: 425
Fees: Day £20,820 WB £30,480

Caterham School
Harestone Valley, Caterham,
Surrey CR3 6YA
Tel: 01883 343028
Head: Mr C. W. Jones MA(Cantab)
Age range: 11–18
No. of pupils: VIth321
Fees: Day £18,735–£19,620 WB
£30,936–£33,270 FB £36,795–£38,760

Charterhouse
Godalming, Surrey GU7 2DX
Tel: +44 (0)1483 291501
Head: Dr Alex Peterken
Age range: B13–18 years
G16–18 years
No. of pupils: 895
🏫Ⓐ🏛️Ⓔ ⓘⒷ ✏️ ⓰

City of London Freemen's School
Ashtead Park, Ashtead,
Surrey KT21 1ET
Tel: 01372 822400
Headmaster: Mr R Martin
Age range: 7–18
No. of pupils: 877 VIth213
Fees: Day £14,067–£19,194 WB
£29,784–£29,841 FB £30,780–£30,816
🏫Ⓐ🏛️Ⓔ ✏️ ⓰

Cranleigh School
Horseshoe Lane, Cranleigh,
Surrey GU6 8QQ
Tel: +44 (0) 1483 273666
Headmaster: Mr Martin Reader
MA, MPhil, MBA
Age range: 7–18 years
(including Prep School)
No. of pupils: 683 VIth256
Fees: Day £33,510 FB £40,710
🏫Ⓐ🏛️Ⓔ ✏️ ⓰

Duke of Kent School
Peaslake Road, Ewhurst,
Surrey GU6 7NS
Tel: 01483 277313
Head: Mrs Sue Knox BA(Hons) MBA
MEd
Age range: 3–16 years
No. of pupils: 316
Fees: Day £2,740–£6,540
🏫Ⓔ✏️

Epsom College
Epsom, Surrey KT17 4JQ
Tel: 01372 821000
Headmaster: Mr Jay A Piggot MA
Age range: 11–18
No. of pupils: 884
Fees: Day £19,611–£26,151
WB £35,034 FB £38,568
🏫Ⓐ🏛️Ⓔ ✏️ ⓰

Frensham Heights
Rowledge, Farnham,
Surrey GU10 4EA
Tel: 01252 792561
Head: Mr Rick Clarke
Age range: 3–18
No. of pupils: 497 VIth105
Fees: Day £7,110–£21,060
FB £27,450–£32,070
🏫Ⓐ🏛️Ⓔ ✏️ ⓰

KING EDWARD'S WITLEY
For further details see p. 92
Petworth Road, Godalming,
Surrey GU8 5SG
Tel: 01428 686735
Email: admissions@kesw.org
Website: www.kesw.org
Head: Mrs Joanna Wright
Age range: 11–18 years
No. of pupils: 420
🏫Ⓐ🏛️Ⓔ ⓘⒷ ✏️ ⓰

MARYMOUNT LONDON
For further details see p. 83
George Road, Kingston upon
Thames, Surrey KT2 7PE
Tel: +44 (0)20 8949 0571
Email: admissions@
marymountlondon.com
Website:
www.marymountlondon.com
Headmistress: Mrs Margaret
Giblin
Age range: G11–18 years
No. of pupils: 258
Fees: Day £27,250 WB
£44,180 FB £46.130
🏃🏫🏛️Ⓔ ⓘⒷ ✏️ ⓰

Prior's Field
Priorsfield Road, Godalming,
Surrey GU7 2RH
Tel: 01483 810551
Head of School: Mrs Tracey Kirnig
Age range: G11–18
No. of pupils: 450
Fees: Day £18,900 FB £30,825
🏃🏫Ⓐ🏛️Ⓔ ✏️ ⓰

Reed's School
Sandy Lane, Cobham,
Surrey KT11 2ES
Tel: 01932 869001
Headmaster: Mr Mark Hoskins BA
MA MSc
Age range: B11–18 G16–18
No. of pupils: 650 VIth230
Fees: Day £20,430–£25,530
FB £27,225–£32,910
🏃🏫Ⓐ🏛️Ⓔ ✏️ ⓰

Royal Russell School
Coombe Lane, Croydon,
Surrey CR9 5BX
Tel: 020 8657 3669
Headmaster: Christopher
Hutchinson
Age range: 11–18
No. of pupils: 590 VIth180
Fees: Day £18,480 FB £36,525
🏫Ⓐ🏛️Ⓔ ✏️ ⓰

St Catherine's, Bramley
Station Road, Bramley,
Guildford, Surrey GU5 0DF
Tel: 01483 899609
Headmistress: Alice Phillips
Age range: G4–18
Fees: Day £9,240–£18,885 FB £31,125
🏃🏫Ⓐ🏛️Ⓔ ✏️ ⓰

St James Senior Boys School
Church Road, Ashford,
Surrey TW15 3DZ
Tel: 01784 266930
Headmaster: Mr David Brazier
Age range: B11–18
No. of pupils: 403 VIth65
Fees: Day £18,930
🏃🏫Ⓐ🏛️Ⓔ ✏️ ⓰

St John's School
Epsom Road, Leatherhead,
Surrey KT22 8SP
Tel: 01372 373000
Head of School: Mrs Rowena Cole
Age range: 11–18
No. of pupils: 840
Fees: Day £19,785–£24,810
WB £25,035–£31,365
🏫Ⓐ🏛️Ⓔ ✏️ ⓰

St Teresa's Effingham (Senior School)
Beech Avenue, Effingham,
Surrey RH5 6ST
Tel: 01372 452037
Executive Director: Mr Mike Farmer
Age range: G11–18
No. of pupils: 640 VIth90
Fees: Day £17,865–£18,465 WB
£28,875–£29,175 FB £30,795–£31,455
🏃🏫Ⓐ🏛️Ⓔ ✏️ ⓰

TASIS The American School in England
Coldharbour Lane, Thorpe,
Surrey TW20 8TE
Tel: +44 (0)1932 582316
Head of School: Mr Bryan Nixon
Age range: 3–18
No. of pupils: 620
Fees: Day £12,280–
£26,375 FB £48,900
🏫🏛️ⓘⒷ ⓰

The Royal Junior School
Portsmouth Road, Hindhead,
Surrey GU26 6BW
Tel: 01428 607977
Principal: Mrs Anne J P Lynch
Age range: 6 weeks–11 years
Fees: Day £10,200–£11,955
🏫

The Royal School
Farnham Lane, Haslemere,
Surrey GU27 1HQ
Tel: 01428 605805
Head: Mrs Pippa Smithson
Age range: 11–18 years
Fees: Day £10,506–£18,507
WB £27,747 FB £31,557
🏫Ⓐ🏛️Ⓔ ✏️ ⓰

Whitgift School
Haling Park, South Croydon,
Surrey CR2 6YT
Tel: +44 20 8633 9935
Headmaster: Mr Christopher
Ramsey
Age range: B10–18 years
No. of pupils: 1550
Fees: Day £21,240 WB
£34,260 FB £41,550
🏃🏫Ⓐ🏛️Ⓔ ⓘⒷ ✏️ ⓰

Woldingham School
Marden Park, Woldingham,
Surrey CR3 7YA
Tel: 01883 349431
Head of School: Dr James
Whitehead
Age range: G11–18
No. of pupils: 611
Fees: Day £22,710–£24,750
FB £32,850–£40,710
🏃🏫Ⓐ🏛️Ⓔ ✏️ ⓰

Yehudi Menuhin School
Stoke Road, Stoke d'Abernon,
Cobham, Surrey KT11 3QQ
Tel: 01932 864739
Interim Head: Richard Tanner
Age range: 7–19
No. of pupils: 80 VIth36
Fees: FB £34,299
🏫Ⓐ🏛️Ⓔ ✏️ ⓰

West Berkshire

Downe House School
Downe House, Cold Ash,
Thatcham, West Berkshire RG18 9JJ
Tel: +44 (0)1635 200286
Headmistress: Mrs Emma
McKendrick BA(Liverpool)
Age range: G11–18 years
No. of pupils: 590
Fees: Day £10,435 FB £14,030
ⓘ ⓖ Ⓐ ⓜ £ ✎ ⑯

West Sussex

Ardingly College
College Road, Ardingly, Haywards
Heath, West Sussex RH17 6SQ
Tel: +44 (0)1444 893320
Headmaster: Mr Ben Figgis
Age range: 13–18
No. of pupils: 559
Fees:–£23,985 FB £35,865–£29,250
ⓖ Ⓐ ⓜ £ ⓘⒷ ✎ ⑯

Burgess Hill Girls
Keymer Road, Burgess Hill,
West Sussex RH15 0EG
Tel: 01444 241050
Head of School: Liz Laybourn
Age range: B2.5–4 years
G2.5–18 years
No. of pupils: 505 VIth70
Fees: Day £9,150–£20,850
FB £31,800–£36,750
ⓘ ⓖ Ⓐ ⓜ £ ✎ ⑯

Christ's Hospital
Horsham, West Sussex RH13 0LJ
Tel: 01403 211293
Head Teacher: Mr Simon Reid
Age range: 11–18
No. of pupils: 900
Fees: Day £18,510–£23,310
FB £35,850
ⓖ Ⓐ ⓜ £ ⓘⒷ ⑯

Farlington School
Strood Park, Horsham,
West Sussex RH12 3PN
Tel: 01403 282573
Head of School: Mr James Passam
Age range: 4–18
No. of pupils: 311
Fees: Day £5,850–£18,300 WB
£29,100–£29,400 FB £30,450–£30,750
ⓖ Ⓐ ⓜ £ ✎ ⑯

Hurstpierpoint College
College Lane, Hurstpierpoint,
West Sussex BN6 9JS
Tel: 01273 833636
Headmaster: Mr. T J Manly BA, MSc
Age range: 4–18
No. of pupils: 1156
Fees: Day £8,790–£22,860
WB £28,800
ⓖ Ⓐ ⓜ £ ⑯

Lancing College
Lancing, West Sussex BN15 0RW
Tel: 01273 452213
Head Master: Mr Dominic T Oliver
MPhil
Age range: 13–18
No. of pupils: 550 VIth255
Fees: Day £8,190 FB £11,995
ⓖ Ⓐ ⓜ £ ✎ ⑯

Rikkyo School in England
Guildford Road, Rudgwick,
Horsham, West Sussex RH12 3BE
Tel: 01403 822107
Headmaster: Mr Roger Munechika
Age range: 10–18
No. of pupils: 116
Fees: FB £15,000–£21,600
ⓖ ⓜ

Seaford College
Lavington Park, Petworth,
West Sussex GU28 0NB
Tel: 01798 867392
Headmaster: J P Green MA BA
Age range: 6–18 years
No. of pupils: 903 VIth235
Fees: Day £3,665–£7,595 WB
£7,635–£10,290 FB £11,750
ⓖ Ⓐ ⓜ £ ✎ ⑯

Slindon College
Slindon House, Slindon, Arundel,
West Sussex BN18 0RH
Tel: 01243 814320
Head Teacher: Mr Mark Birkbeck
Age range: B8–18 years
ⓘ ⓖ Ⓐ ⓜ £ ✎

Worth School
Paddockhurst Road, Turners Hill,
Crawley, West Sussex RH10 4SD
Tel: +44 (0)1342 710200
Head Master: Stuart McPherson
Age range: 11–18
No. of pupils: 580 VIth222
Fees: Day £15,960–£23,730
FB £21,210–£33,690
ⓖ Ⓐ ⓜ £ ⓘⒷ ✎ ⑯

Specialist schools and sixth form colleges

London

Central London

CATS London
43-45 Bloomsbury Square,
London WC1A 2RA
Tel: 02078 411580
Principal: Mario Di Clemente
Age range: 15–24
(🌐) (A) (♿) (£) (16+)

City of London School
Queen Victoria Street,
London EC4V 3AL
Tel: 020 3680 6300
Head: Mr A R Bird MSc
Age range: B10–18 years
No. of pupils: 950 VIth250
Fees: Day £19,995
(♟) (A) (£) (🖊) (16+)

City of London School for Girls
St Giles' Terrace, Barbican,
London EC2Y 8BB
Tel: 020 7847 5500
Headmistress: Mrs E Harrop
Age range: G7–18
No. of pupils: 725
(♿) (A) (£) (🖊) (16+)

Italia Conti Academy of Theatre Arts
Italia Conti House, 23 Goswell
Road, London EC1M 7AJ
Tel: 020 7608 0047
Director: Chris White
Age range: 10–21
(16+) (A) (16+)

The College of Central London
Tower Bridge Business Centre, 46-48
East Smithfield, London E1W 1AW
Tel: +44 (0) 20 3667 7607
(16+) (16+)

East London

Forest School
College Place, Snaresbrook,
London E17 3PY
Tel: 020 8520 1744
Warden: Mr Cliff Hodges
Age range: 4–18
No. of pupils: 1355 VIth260
Fees: Day £13,095–£18,681
(A) (£) (🖊) (16+)

North London

Channing School
The Bank, Highgate, London N6 5HF
Tel: 020 8340 2328
Head: Mrs B M Elliott
Age range: G4–18
No. of pupils: 746 VIth108
Fees: Day £17,610–£19,410
(♿) (A) (£) (🖊) (16+)

Dwight School London
6 Friern Barnet Lane,
London N11 3LX
Tel: 020 8920 0600
Head: Chris Beddows
Age range: 2–18 years
(🌐) (£) (IB) (🖊) (16+)

Greek Secondary School of London
22 Trinity Road, London N22 8LB
Tel: +44 (0)20 8881 9320
Headteacher: Nikos Kazantzakis
Age range: 13–18
(A) (16+)

Highgate
North Road, Highgate,
London N6 4AY
Tel: 020 8340 1524
Head Master: Mr A S Pettitt MA
Age range: 3–18
No. of pupils: 1541 VIth312
Fees: Day £18,165–£20,970
(A) (£) (16+)

North-West London

Francis Holland School, Regent's Park, NW1
Clarence Gate, Ivor Place,
Regent's Park, London NW1 6XR
Tel: 020 7723 0176
Head: Mr C B Fillingham MA (King's
College London)
Age range: G11–18
No. of pupils: 495 VIth120
Fees: Day £19,260
(♿) (A) (£) (16+)

ICS London
7B Wyndham Place,
London W1H 1PN
Tel: +44 (0)20 729 88800
Head of School: David Laird
Age range: 3–19 years
No. of pupils: 175
Fees: Day £19,650–£28,770
(🌐) (IB) (16+)

Lakefield Catering & Educational Centre
Maresfield Gardens,
Hampstead, London NW3 5RY
Tel: 020 7794 5669
Course Director: Mrs Maria Brown
Age range: G16–24
No. of pupils: 16
Fees: FB £1,160
(♿) (16+) (♿) (£) (🖊) (16+) (🌐)

London Academy of Dressmaking and Design
18 Dobree Avenue, Willesden,
London NW10 2AE
Tel: 020 8451 7174
Principal: Mrs P A Parkinson MA
Age range: 13+
Fees: Day £2,650
(16+) (🖊) (16+) (🌐)

Mill Hill School
The Ridgeway, Mill Hill
Village, London NW7 1QS
Tel: 020 8959 1176
Head: Mrs Jane Sanchez BSc (Hons)
PGCE
Age range: 13–18 years
No. of pupils: 876 VIth312
Fees: Day £21,987 WB
£31,140 FB £36,900
(♿) (A) (♿) (£) (🖊) (16+)

NW5 Theatre School
14 Fortess Road, London NW5 2EU
Tel: 020 8340 1498
Age range: 16–30
(16+) (16+)

South Hampstead High School GDST
3 Maresfield Gardens,
London NW3 5SS
Tel: 020 7435 2899
Head of School: Mrs V Bingham
Age range: G4–18
No. of pupils: 900
Fees: Day £15,327–£18,654
(♿) (A) (£) (🖊) (16+)

The American School in London
One Waverley Place,
London NW8 0NP
Tel: 020 7449 1221
Head: Robin Appleby
Age range: 4–18
No. of pupils: 1350
Fees: Day £27,050–£31,200
(🌐) (16+)

The King Alfred School
Manor Wood, North End
Road, London NW11 7HY
Tel: 020 8457 5200
Head: Robert Lobatto MA (Oxon)
Age range: 4–18
No. of pupils: 650 VIth100
Fees: Day £15,531–£18,723
(A) (£) (🖊) (16+)

University College School Hampstead (UCS) Senior
Frognal, Hampstead,
London NW3 6XH
Tel: 020 7435 2215
Headteacher: Mr Mark J Beard
Age range: B11–18 years
G16–18 years
(♟) (A) (£) (🖊) (16+)

Wentworth College
6-10 Brentmead Place,
London NW11 9LH
Tel: 020 8458 8524/5
Principal: Manuel Guimaraes
Age range: 14–19
No. of pupils: 115
(16+) (A) (16+)

South-East London

Alleyn's School
Townley Road, Dulwich,
London SE22 8SU
Tel: 020 8557 1500
Head of School: Jane Lunnon
Age range: 4–18 years
(A) (£) (🖊) (16+)

Blackheath High School GDST
Vanbrugh Park, Blackheath,
London SE3 7AG
Tel: 020 8853 2929
Head: Mrs Carol Chandler-
Thompson BA (Hons) Exeter, PGCE
Exeter
Age range: G3–18
No. of pupils: 780
(♿) (A) (£) (🖊) (16+)

Colfe's School
Horn Park Lane, Lee,
London SE12 8AW
Tel: 020 8852 2283
Head: Mr R F Russell MA(Cantab)
Age range: 3–18
No. of pupils: 1120
(A) (£) (🖊) (16+)

Dulwich College
Dulwich Common, ,
London SE21 7LD
Tel: 020 8693 3601
Master: Dr J A F Spence
Age range: B0–18 years
Fees: Day £21,672 WB
£42,408 FB £45,234
(♟) (🌐) (A) (♿) (£) (🖊) (16+)

Eltham College
Grove Park Road, Mottingham,
London SE9 4QF
Tel: 0208 857 1455
Headmaster: Guy Sanderson
Age range: 7–18
No. of pupils: 911 VIth199
(A) (£) (🖊) (16+)

James Allen's Girls' School
144 East Dulwich Grove,
Dulwich, London SE22 8TE
Tel: 020 8693 1181
Head of School: Mrs Sally-Anne
Huang MA, MSc
Age range: G4–18
No. of pupils: 1075
(♿) (A) (£) (🖊) (16+)

St Dunstan's College
Stanstead Road, London SE6 4TY
Tel: 020 8516 7200
Headmaster: Mr Nicholas Hewlett
Age range: 3–18
No. of pupils: 870
(🌐) (A) (£) (16+)

Sydenham High School GDST
15 & 19 Westwood Hill, London SE26 6BL
Tel: 020 8557 7004
Headmistress: Mrs Katharine Woodcock
Age range: G4–18
No. of pupils: 665
🚶 👥 Ⓐ ⓔ ✏ 16·

South-West London

Centre Academy London
92 St John's Hill, Battersea, London SW11 1SH
Tel: 020 7738 2344
Headteacher: Rachel Maddison
Age range: 9–19
🚶 ⓔ ✏ 16·

Emanuel School
Battersea Rise, London SW11 1HS
Tel: 020 8870 4171
Headmaster: Mr Robert Milne
Age range: 10–18 years
No. of pupils: 1050
Fees: Day £20,145
Ⓐ ⓔ ✏ 16·

Francis Holland School, Sloane Square, SW1
39 Graham Terrace, London SW1W 8JF
Tel: 020 7730 2971
Head: Mrs Lucy Elphinstone MA(Cantab)
Age range: G4–18
No. of pupils: 520 VIth70
Fees: Day £17,760–£20,085
🚶 👥 Ⓐ ⓔ ✏ 16·

Harrodian
Lonsdale Road, London SW13 9QN
Tel: 020 8748 6117
Headmaster: Mr James R Hooke
Age range: 4–18 years
No. of pupils: 1023
Fees: Day £5,000–£8,000
Ⓐ ⓔ ✏ 16·

Ibstock Place School
Clarence Lane, London SW15 5PY
Tel: 020 8876 9991
Head of School: Mr Christopher Wolsey
Age range: 4–18 years
No. of pupils: 990
Fees: Day £5,870–£7,450
Ⓐ ⓔ 16·

King's College School
Southside, Wimbledon Common, London SW19 4TT
Tel: 020 8255 5300
Acting Head: Ms Jude Lowson MA
Age range: B7–18 years G16–18 years
No. of pupils: 1477 VIth419
🚶 👥 Ⓐ ⓔ ⒾⒷ 16·

LYCÉE FRANÇAIS CHARLES DE GAULLE DE LONDRES
For further details see p. 55
35 Cromwell Road, London SW7 2DG
Tel: 020 7584 6322
Email: inscription@lyceefrancais.org.uk
Website: www.lyceefrancais.org.uk
Headteacher: Didier Devilard
Age range: 3–18 years
No. of pupils: 3450
Fees: Day £7,066–£14,782
👥 ⓔ ✏ 16·

MORE HOUSE SCHOOL
For further details see p. 61
22-24 Pont Street, Knightsbridge, London SW1X 0AA
Tel: 020 7235 2855
Email: registrar@morehousemail.org.uk
Website: www.morehouse.org.uk
Head: Ms Faith Hagerty
Age range: G11–18 years
No. of pupils: 140
Fees: Day £7,250
🚶 Ⓐ ⓔ ✏ 16·

Putney High School GDST
35 Putney Hill, London SW15 6BH
Tel: 020 8788 4886
Headmistress: Mrs Suzie Longstaff BA, MA, PGCE
Age range: G4–18
No. of pupils: 976 VIth150
🚶 Ⓐ ⓔ ✏ 16·

Queen's Gate School
133 Queen's Gate, London SW7 5LE
Tel: 020 7589 3587
Principal: Mrs R M Kamaryc BA, MSc, PGCE
Age range: G4–18 years
No. of pupils: 500 VIth81
👥 Ⓐ ⓔ ✏ 16·

St Paul's School
Lonsdale Road, Barnes, London SW13 9JT
Tel: 020 8748 9162
High Master: Ms Sally-Anne Huang
Age range: B13–18 years
🚶 👥 Ⓐ 🏫 ✏ 16·

Streatham & Clapham High School GDST
42 Abbotswood Road, London SW16 1AW
Tel: 020 8677 8400
Headmaster: Dr Millan Sachania
Age range: G3–18
No. of pupils: 603 VIth70
Fees: Day £10,431–£19,743
🚶 Ⓐ ⓔ ✏ 16·

Swedish School
82 Lonsdale Road, London SW13 9JS
Tel: 020 8741 1751
Head of School: Ms. Jenny Abrahamsson
Age range: 3–18
No. of pupils: 300 VIth145
Fees: Day £8,600–£9,100
16·

Westminster School
Little Dean's Yard, Westminster, London SW1P 3PB
Tel: 020 7963 1000
Head Master: Dr Gary Savage
Age range: B13–18 years G16–18 years
🚶 👥 Ⓐ 🏫 ✏ 16·

Wimbledon High School GDST
Mansel Road, Wimbledon, London SW19 4AB
Tel: 020 8971 0900
Headmistress: Mrs Jane Lunnon
Age range: G4–18
No. of pupils: 900 VIth155
Fees: Day £14,622–£18,810
🚶 Ⓐ ⓔ ✏ 16·

West London

Alan D Hairdressing Education
4 West Smithfield, London EC1A 9JX
Tel: 020 7580 1030
Director of Education: Alan Hemmings
Fees: Day £200 FB £12,400
16· 16· 🌐

Blake College
162 New Cavendish Street, London W1W 6YS
Tel: 020 7636 0658
Course Director: D A J Cluckie BA, BSc
Fees: Day £4,720–£5,310
16· 🌐

David Game College
31 Jewry Street, London EC3N 2ET
Tel: 020 7221 6665
Principal: D T P Game MA, MPhil
Age range: 14–19
No. of pupils: 200 VIth150
Fees: Day £3,680–£30,630
16· Ⓐ ⓔ 16·

Ealing Independent College
83 New Broadway, Ealing, London W5 5AL
Tel: 020 8579 6668
Principal: Dr Ian Moores
Age range: 13–19
No. of pupils: 100 VIth70
Fees: Day £2,910–£18,120
16· Ⓐ ⓔ 16·

Godolphin and Latymer School
Iffley Road, Hammersmith, London W6 0PG
Tel: +44 (0)20 8741 1936
Head Mistress: Dr Frances Ramsey
Age range: G11–18 years
No. of pupils: 800
Fees: Day £23,085
🚶 👥 Ⓐ ⓔ ⒾⒷ ✏ 16·

International School of London (ISL)
139 Gunnersbury Avenue, London W3 8LG
Tel: +44 (0)20 8992 5823
Principal: Mr Richard Parker
Age range: 3–18 years
No. of pupils: 500
Fees: Day £19,000–£26,300
👥 ⒾⒷ ✏ 16·

King Fahad Academy
Bromyard Avenue, Acton, London W3 7HD
Tel: 020 8743 0131
Director General: Dr Tahani Aljafari
Age range: 3–19
🌐 Ⓐ ⓔ ⒾⒷ ✏ 16·

Latymer Upper School
King Street, Hammersmith, London W6 9LR
Tel: 020862 92024
Head: Mr D Goodhew MA(Oxon)
Age range: 11–18
No. of pupils: 1400
Fees: Day £6,945
Ⓐ ⓔ ✏ 16·

Notting Hill & Ealing High School GDST
2 Cleveland Road, West Ealing, London W13 8AX
Tel: (020) 8799 8400
Headmaster: Mr Matthew Shoults
Age range: G4–18
No. of pupils: 903 VIth150
Fees: Day £14,313–£18,561
🚶 Ⓐ ⓔ 16·

Queen's College
43-49 Harley Street, London W1G 8BT
Tel: 020 7291 7000
Principal: Mr Richard Tillet
Age range: G11–18
No. of pupils: 360 VIth90
🚶 Ⓐ ⓔ 16·

Ray Cochrane Beauty School
118 Baker Street, London W1U 6TT
Tel: 02033224738
Principal: Miss Baljeet Suri
Age range: 16–50
No. of pupils: 30
Fees: Day £650–£8,495
16· 16· 🌐

Southbank International School - Westminster
63-65 Portland Place, London W1B 1QR
Tel: 020 7243 3803
Principal: Dr Paul Wood
Age range: 11–19
🌐 ⒾⒷ ✏ 16·

St Augustine's Priory
Hillcrest Road, Ealing,
London W5 2JL
Tel: 020 8997 2022
Headteacher: Mrs Sarah Raffray
M.A., N.P.Q.H
Age range: B3–4 G3–18
No. of pupils: 485
Fees: Day £11,529–£16,398
(ﾟ)(A)(✏)(16)

ST BENEDICT'S SCHOOL
For further details see p. 70
54 Eaton Rise, Ealing,
London W5 2ES
Tel: 020 8862 2000
Email: admissions@
stbenedicts.org.uk
Website:
www.stbenedicts.org.uk
Headmaster: Mr A Johnson BA
Age range: 3–18 years
No. of pupils: 1073 VIth203
Fees: Day £13,995–£18,330
(A)(£)(✏)(16)

St James Senior Girls' School
Earsby Street, London W14 8SH
Tel: 020 7348 1777
Headmistress: Mrs Sarah Labram BA
Age range: G11–18
No. of pupils: 295 VIth67
Fees: Day £20,100
(ﾟ)(A)(£)(16)

St Paul's Girls' School
Brook Green, London W6 7BS
Tel: 020 7603 2288
High Mistress: Mrs Sarah Fletcher
Age range: G11–18 years
No. of pupils: 778
Fees: Day £25,887–£27,831
(ﾟ)(A)(£)(✏)(16)

Berkshire

Bradfield College
Bradfield, Berkshire RG7 6AU
Tel: 0118 964 4516
Headmaster: Dr Christopher Stevens
Age range: 13–18 years
No. of pupils: 820
Fees: Day £32,280 FB £40,350
(ﾟ)(A)(ﾟ)(£)(IB)(✏)(16)

Claires Court Nursery, Girls and Sixth Form
1 College Avenue, Maidenhead,
Berkshire SL6 6AW
Tel: 01628 327500
Head of Juniors: Ms Leanne Kirby
Age range: B16–18
years G4–18 years
(ﾟ)(A)(£)(✏)(16)

Claires Court Senior Boys
Ray Mill Road East, Maidenhead,
Berkshire SL6 8TE
Tel: 01628 327600
Head of Senior Boys: Mr James Wilding
Age range: B11–16 years
(ﾟ)(A)(£)(✏)(16)

Eton College
Windsor, Berkshire SL4 6DW
Tel: +44 (0)1753 370 611
Head Master: Mr Simon Henderson MA
Age range: B13–18 years
No. of pupils: 1342
Fees: FB £44,094
(ﾟ)(ﾟ)(A)(ﾟ)(£)(✏)(16)

Heathfield School
London Road, Ascot,
Berkshire SL5 8BQ
Tel: 01344 898343
Head of School: Ms Sarah Wilson
Age range: G11–18 years
Fees: Day £7,840–£8,000
FB £12,650–£12,950
(ﾟ)(ﾟ)(A)(ﾟ)(£)(✏)(16)

LEIGHTON PARK SCHOOL
For further details see p. 94
Shinfield Road, Reading,
Berkshire RG2 7ED
Tel: 0118 987 9600
Email: admissions@
leightonpark.com
Website: www.leightonpark.com
Head: Mr Matthew L S Judd BA,
PGCE
Age range: 11–18 years
No. of pupils: 520
(ﾟ)(A)(ﾟ)(£)(IB)(✏)(16)

Luckley House School
Luckley Road, Wokingham,
Berkshire RG40 3EU
Tel: 0118 978 4175
Head: Mrs Areti Bizior
Age range: 11–18 years
(ﾟ)(ﾟ)(A)(ﾟ)(£)(✏)(16)

LVS ASCOT
For further details see p. 96
London Road, Ascot,
Berkshire SL5 8DR
Tel: 01344 882770
Email: enquiries@lvs.
ascot.sch.uk
Website: www.lvs.ascot.sch.uk
Principal: Mrs Christine Cunniffe
BA (Hons), MMus, MBA
Age range: 4–18 years
No. of pupils: 800
Fees: Day £12,915–£19,335
FB £27,585–£33,975
(ﾟ)(A)(ﾟ)(£)(✏)(16)

Padworth College
Sopers Lane, Reading,
Berkshire RG7 4NR
Tel: 0118 983 2644
Principal: Lorraine Atkins
Age range: 14–19 years
(ﾟ)(A)(ﾟ)(£)(16)

Pangbourne College
Pangbourne, Reading,
Berkshire RG8 8LA
Tel: 0118 984 2101
Headmaster: Thomas J C Garnier
Age range: 11–18 years
No. of pupils: 458
Fees: Day £6,300–£8,540 WB
£8,210–£11,510 FB £9,050–£12,680
(ﾟ)(A)(ﾟ)(£)(✏)(16)

QUEEN ANNE'S SCHOOL
For further details see p. 98
6 Henley Road, Caversham,
Reading, Berkshire RG4 6DX
Tel: 0118 918 7300
Email: office@qas.org.uk
Website: www.qas.org.uk
Head: Ms Elaine Purves
Age range: G11–18 years
No. of pupils: G450
Fees: Day £8,370 FB £13,590
(ﾟ)(ﾟ)(A)(ﾟ)(£)(✏)(16)

Reading Blue Coat School
Holme Park, Sonning Lane, Sonning,
Reading, Berkshire RG4 6SU
Tel: 0118 944 1005
Headmaster: Mr Peter Thomas
Age range: B11–18 years
G16–18 years
(ﾟ)(A)(£)(✏)(16)

REDDAM HOUSE BERKSHIRE
For further details see p. 100
Bearwood Road, Sindlesham,
Wokingham, Berkshire RG41 5BG
Tel: +44 (0)118 974 8300
Email: registrar@
reddamhouse.org.uk
Website:
www.reddamhouse.org.uk
Principal: Mr Rick Cross
Age range: 3 months–18 years
No. of pupils: 675
Fees: Day £11,490–£18,420
WB £27,981–£32,244 FB
£29,526–£33,789
(ﾟ)(A)(ﾟ)(£)(✏)(16)

St George's Ascot
Wells Lane, Ascot, Berkshire SL5 7DZ
Tel: 01344 629900
Headmistress: Mrs Liz Hewer MA
(Hons) (Cantab) PGCE
Age range: G11–18 years
(ﾟ)(ﾟ)(A)(ﾟ)(£)(✏)(16)

St Joseph's College
Upper Redlands Road,
Reading, Berkshire RG1 5JT
Tel: 0118 966 1000
Head of School: Mrs Laura
Stotesbury
Age range: 3–18 years
(A)(£)(✏)(16)

St Mary's School Ascot
St Mary's Road, Ascot,
Berkshire SL5 9JF
Tel: 01344 296614
Headmistress: Mrs Danuta Staunton
Age range: G11–18 years
(ﾟ)(ﾟ)(A)(ﾟ)(£)(16)

The Abbey School
Kendrick Road, Reading,
Berkshire RG1 5DZ
Tel: 0118 987 2256
Head: Mr Will le Fleming
Age range: G3–18 years
No. of pupils: 1000
Fees: Day £11,025–£18,885
(ﾟ)(ﾟ)(A)(£)(IB)(✏)(16)

The Marist School
King's Road, Sunninghill,
Ascot, Berkshire SL5 7PS
Tel: 01344 624291
Principal: Ms Jo Smith
Age range: G2–18 years
(ﾟ)(A)(16)

The Oratory School
Woodcote, Reading,
Berkshire RG8 0PJ
Tel: 01491 683500
Head Master: Mr Joe Smith
BA(Hons), MEd, PGCE
Age range: 11–18 years
(ﾟ)(A)(ﾟ)(£)(16)

Wellington College
Duke's Ride, Crowthorne,
Berkshire RG45 7PU
Tel: +44 (0)1344 444000
Master: Mr James Dahl
Age range: 13–18 years
No. of pupils: 1090 VIth475
Fees: Day £31,140–£35,760
FB £42,630
(ﾟ)(A)(ﾟ)(£)(IB)(✏)(16)

Buckinghamshire

Pipers Corner School
Pipers Lane, Great
Kingshill, High Wycombe,
Buckinghamshire HP15 6LP
Tel: 01494 718 255
Headmistress: Mrs H J Ness-Gifford
BA(Hons), PGCE
Age range: G4–18 years
(♀)(A)(⚲)(£)(✑)(16·)(🐾)

St Mary's School
94 Packhorse Road, Gerrards
Cross, Buckinghamshire SL9 8JQ
Tel: 01753 883370
Head of School: Mrs Patricia Adams
Age range: G3–18 years
(♀)(A)(£)(✑)(16·)

Stowe School
Buckingham, Buckinghamshire
MK18 5EH
Tel: 01280 818000
Headmaster: Dr Anthony
Wallersteiner
Age range: 13–18 years
(⚲)(A)(⚲)(£)(✑)(16·)

Wycombe Abbey
Frances Dove Way, High Wycombe,
Buckinghamshire HP11 1PE
Tel: +44 (0)1494 520381
Headmistress: Mrs Jo Duncan MA
(St Andrews), PGCE (Cantab)
Age range: G11–18 years
No. of pupils: 663
Fees: Day £30,945 FB £41,250
(♀)(⚲)(A)(⚲)(£)(✑)(16·)

East Sussex

Battle Abbey School
Battle, East Sussex TN33 0AD
Tel: 01424 772385
Headmaster: Mr D Clark BA(Hons)
Age range: 2–18
No. of pupils: 286 VIth48
Fees: Day £6,939–£16,914
FB £26,649–£31,932
(⚲)(A)(⚲)(£)(✑)(16·)

Bede's School
The Dicker, Upper Dicker,
Hailsham, East Sussex BN27 3QH
Tel: +44 (0)1323843252
Head: Mr Peter Goodyer
Age range: 3 months–18
No. of pupils: 800 VIth295
Fees: Day £10,230–£17,400
FB £22,290–£25,650
(⚲)(A)(⚲)(£)(✑)(16·)(🐾)

Brighton College
Eastern Road, Brighton,
East Sussex BN2 0AL
Tel: 01273 704200
Head Master: Richard Cairns MA
Age range: 3–18
No. of pupils: 950
Fees: Day £10,050–£24,540 WB
£33,390–£34,410 FB £37,470–£45,210
(⚲)(A)(⚲)(£)(✑)(16·)

Brighton Girls GDST
Montpelier Road, Brighton,
East Sussex BN1 3AT
Tel: 01273 280280
Head: Jennifer Smith
Age range: G3–18
No. of pupils: 680 VIth70
Fees: Day £7,191–£14,421
(♀)(A)(£)(✑)(16·)

Buckswood School
Broomham Hall, Rye
Road, Guestling, Hastings,
East Sussex TN35 4LT
Tel: 01424 813 813
School Director: Mr Giles Sutton
Age range: 10–19
No. of pupils: 420
(⚲)(A)(⚲)(£)(IB)(✑)(16·)

Eastbourne College
Old Wish Road, Eastbourne,
East Sussex BN21 4JX
Tel: 01323 452323 (Admissions)
Headmaster: Mr Tom Lawson MA
(Oxon)
Age range: 13–18
No. of pupils: 650 VIth312
Fees: Day £23,895–£24,375
FB £36,420–£36,975
(⚲)(A)(⚲)(£)(✑)(16·)

Greenfields Independent Day & Boarding School
Priory Road, Forest Row,
East Sussex RH18 5JD
Tel: +44 (0)1342 822189
Executive Head: Mr. Jeff Smith
Age range: 2–19
(⚲)(A)(⚲)(✑)(16·)

Lewes Old Grammar School
High Street, Lewes, East
Sussex BN7 1XS
Tel: 01273 472634
Headmaster: Mr Robert Blewitt
Age range: 3–18
No. of pupils: 463 VIth50
Fees: Day £8,760–£14,625
(A)(£)(✑)(16·)

MAYFIELD SCHOOL
For further details see p. 97
The Old Palace, Mayfield,
East Sussex TN20 6PH
Tel: 01435 874642
Email: registrar@
mayfieldgirls.org
Website: www.mayfieldgirls.org
Head: Ms Antonia Beary MA,
MPhil (Cantab), PGCE
Age range: G11–18 years
No. of pupils: 405
Fees: Day £7,750 FB £12,250
(♀)(⚲)(A)(⚲)(£)(✑)(16·)

Michael Hall School
Kidbrooke Park, Priory Road,
Forest Row, East Sussex RH18 5JA
Tel: 01342 822275
Age range: 0 years–18 years
No. of pupils: VIth102
Fees: Day £9,245–£12,670
(⚲)(A)(⚲)(✑)(16·)

Roedean Moira House
Upper Carlisle Road, Eastbourne,
East Sussex BN20 7TE
Tel: 01323 644144
Headmaster: Mr Andrew Wood
Age range: G0–18
No. of pupils: 289
(♀)(⚲)(A)(⚲)(£)(✑)(16·)

ROEDEAN SCHOOL
For further details see p. 101
Roedean Way, Brighton,
East Sussex BN2 5RQ
Tel: 01273 667500
Email: info@roedean.co.uk
Website: www.roedean.co.uk
Headmaster: Mr. Oliver Bond
BA(Essex), PGCE, NPQH
Age range: G11–18 years
No. of pupils: 630 VIth155
Fees: Day £5,670–£7,415
WB £10,030–£11,185 FB
£10,990–£13,305
(♀)(⚲)(A)(⚲)(£)(✑)(16·)

Essex

Bancroft's School
High Road, Woodford
Green, Essex IG8 0RF
Tel: 020 8505 4821
Head: Mr Simon Marshall MA, PGCE
(Cantab), MA, MPhil (Oxon)
Age range: 7–18
No. of pupils: 1120 VIth247
(A)(£)(✑)(16·)

Brentwood School
Middleton Hall Lane,
Brentwood, Essex CM15 8EE
Tel: 01277 243243
Headmaster: Mr Michael Bond
Age range: 3–18 years
No. of pupils: 1850
Fees: Day £20,598 FB £40,365
(⚲)(A)(⚲)(£)(IB)(✑)(16·)

Chigwell School
High Road, Chigwell, Essex IG7 6QF
Tel: 020 8501 5700
Headmaster: Mr M E Punt M.A.
M.Sc. P.G.C.E.
Age range: 4–18
Fees: Day £4,250–£6,295 FB £10,995
(⚲)(A)(⚲)(£)(✑)(16·)

Felsted School
Felsted, Great Dunmow,
Essex CM6 3LL
Tel: +44 (0)1371 822600
Headmaster: Mr Chris Townsend
Age range: 4–18 years
(⚲)(A)(⚲)(£)(IB)(✑)(16·)

Gosfield School
Cut Hedge Park, Halstead Road,
Gosfield, Halstead, Essex CO9 1PF
Tel: 01787 474040
Headteacher: Mr Guy Martyn
Age range: 4–18
No. of pupils: VIth21
Fees: Day £6,690–£15,525

New Hall School
The Avenue, Boreham,
Chelmsford, Essex CM3 3HS
Tel: 01245 467588
Principal: Mrs Katherine Jeffrey MA,
BA, PGCE, MA(Ed Mg), NPQH
Age range: 1–18 years
No. of pupils: 1400
Fees: Day £9,621–£20,502 WB
£18,234–£28,026 FB £21,177–£32,472

Park School for Girls
20-22 Park Avenue,
Ilford, Essex IG1 4RS
Tel: 020 8554 2466
Head Teacher: Mrs Androulla
Nicholas BSc Hons (Econ) PGCE
Age range: G4–16
No. of pupils: 160
Fees: Day £2,375–£3,580

Hampshire

Alton School
Anstey Lane, Alton,
Hampshire GU34 2NG
Tel: 01420 82070
Head: Karl Guest
Age range: 0–18 years
No. of pupils: 400

Bedales School
Church Road, Steep, Petersfield,
Hampshire GU32 2DG
Tel: 01730 711733
Head of School: Magnus Bashaarat
Age range: 13–18
No. of pupils: 463
Fees: Day £28,515 FB £36,285

**Brockwood Park &
Inwoods School**
Brockwood Park, Bramdean,
Hampshire SO24 0LQ
Tel: +44 (0)1962 771744
Principal: Mr Antonio Autor
Age range: 14–19
No. of pupils: 112 VIth39
Fees: Day £5,630–£6,400 FB £21,400

Churcher's College
Petersfield, Hampshire GU31 4AS
Tel: 01730 263033
Headmaster: Mr Simon Williams ,
MA, BSc
Age range: 3–18 years
Fees: Day £10,830–£16,440

Embley
Embley Park, Romsey,
Hampshire SO51 6ZE
Tel: 01794 512206
Headteacher: Mr Cliff Canning
Age range: 2–18
No. of pupils: 500
Fees: Day £8,754–£31,338

Farnborough Hill
Farnborough Road, Farnborough,
Hampshire GU14 8AT
Tel: 01252 545197
Head: Mrs A Neil BA, MEd, PGCE
Age range: G11–18
No. of pupils: 550 VIth90
Fees: Day £14,796

King Edward VI School
Wilton Road, Southampton,
Hampshire SO15 5UQ
Tel: 023 8070 4561
Head Master: Mr N T Parker
Age range: 11–18 years
No. of pupils: 965
Fees: Day £17,631

Lord Wandsworth College
Long Sutton, Hook,
Hampshire RG29 1TB
Tel: 01256 862201
Head of School: Mr Adam Williams
Age range: 11–18 years
No. of pupils: 615
Fees: Day £21,240–£24,390
WB £29,400–£33,000 FB
£30,345–£34,650

**Portsmouth High
School GDST**
Kent Road, Southsea, Portsmouth,
Hampshire PO5 3EQ
Tel: 023 9282 6714
Headmistress: Mrs Jane Prescott
BSc NPQH
Age range: G3–18 years
No. of pupils: 500
Fees: Day £2,574–£4,800

Salesian College
Reading Road, Farnborough,
Hampshire GU14 6PA
Tel: 01252 893000
Headmaster: Mr Gerard Owens
Age range: B11–18 G16–18
No. of pupils: 650 VIth140
Fees: Day £11,961

Sherfield School
South Drive, Sherfield-on-Loddon,
Hook, Hampshire RG27 0HU
Tel: 01256 884800
Headmaster: Mr Nick Brain
BA(Hons), PGCE, MA, NPQH
Age range: 3 months–18 years
No. of pupils: 450
Fees: Day £10,320–£17,085 WB
£18,960–£26,130 FB £22,125–£30,495

St John's College
Grove Road South, Southsea,
Portsmouth, Hampshire PO5 3QW
Tel: 023 9281 5118
Head of School: Mrs Mary Maguire
Age range: 4–18
No. of pupils: 560 VIth86
Fees: Day £9,975–£13,125
FB £28,500–£32,250

ST SWITHUN'S SCHOOL
For further details see p. 108
Alresford Road, Winchester,
Hampshire SO21 1HA
Tel: 01962 835700
Email: office@stswithuns.com
Website: www.stswithuns.com
Head of School: Jane Gandee
MA(Cantab)
Age range: G11–18 years
No. of pupils: 510
Fees: Day £21,918 FB £36,339

**The Portsmouth
Grammar School**
High Street, Portsmouth,
Hampshire PO1 2LN
Tel: +44 (0)23 9236 0036
Headmistress: Dr Anne Cotton
Age range: 2–18
No. of pupils: 1556 VIth336
Fees: Day £10,233–£15,951

Winchester College
College Street, Winchester,
Hampshire SO23 9NA
Tel: 01962 621247
Headmaster: Mr T R Hands
Age range: B13–18
No. of pupils: 690 VIth280
Fees: FB £39,912

Hertfordshire

Aldenham School
Elstree, Hertfordshire WD6 3AJ
Tel: 01923 858122
Head of School: Mr Andrew Williams
Age range: 3–18

BERKHAMSTED SCHOOL
For further details see p. 88
Overton House, 131 High Street, Berkhamsted, Hertfordshire HP4 2DJ
Tel: 01442 358001
Email: admissions@berkhamsted.com
Website: www.berkhamsted.com
Principal: Mr Richard Backhouse MA(Cantab)
Age range: 3–18 years
No. of pupils: 2001 VIth408
Fees: Day £10,830–£22,170 WB £29,850 FB £35,610

Bishop's Stortford College
10 Maze Green Road, Bishop's Stortford, Hertfordshire CM23 2PJ
Tel: 01279 838575
Headmaster: Mr Jeremy Gladwin
Age range: 13–18
No. of pupils: VIth249
Fees: Day £20,349–£20,532 WB £31,569–£31,917 FB £33,402–£33,930

Champneys International College of Health & Beauty
Chesham Road, Wigginton, Tring, Hertfordshire HP23 6HY
Tel: 01442 291333
College Principal: Ms Pam Clegg
Age range: 16+
No. of pupils: 61
Fees: Day £3,000–£9,050

Haberdashers' Aske's School for Girls
Aldenham Road, Elstree, Borehamwood, Hertfordshire WD6 3BT
Tel: 020 8266 2300
Head of School: Ms Rose Hardy
Age range: G4–18
No. of pupils: 1190
Fees: Day £17,826–£19,311

Haileybury
Haileybury, Hertford, Hertfordshire SG13 7NU
Tel: +44 (0)1992 706353
The Master: Mr Martin Collier MA BA PGCE
Age range: 11–18 years
No. of pupils: 915 VIth364
Fees: Day £18,240–£27,435 FB £23,610–£37,215

Immanuel College
87/91 Elstree Road, Bushey, Hertfordshire WD23 4EB
Tel: 020 8950 0604
Headmaster: Mr Gary Griffin
Age range: 4–18
No. of pupils: 520 VIth127
Fees: Day £10,995

Mount House School
Camlet Way, Hadley Wood, Barnet, Hertfordshire EN4 0NJ
Tel: 020 8449 6889
Principal: Sarah Richardson
Age range: 11–18
No. of pupils: 230
Fees: Day £16,560

Queenswood
Shepherd's Way, Brookmans Park, Hatfield, Hertfordshire AL9 6NS
Tel: 01707 602500
Principal: Mrs Jo Cameron
Age range: G11–18
No. of pupils: 418
Fees: Day £7,115–£8,440 WB £7,325–10,615 FB £8,395–£11,810

Sherrardswood School
Lockleys, Welwyn, Hertfordshire AL6 0BJ
Tel: 01438 714282
Headmistress: Mrs Anna Wright
Age range: 2–18
No. of pupils: 357
Fees: Day £10,383–£16,113

St Albans High School for Girls
Townsend Avenue, St Albans, Hertfordshire AL1 3SJ
Tel: 01727 853800
Headmistress: Amber Waite
Age range: G4–18
No. of pupils: 940 VIth170

St Albans School
Abbey Gateway, St Albans, Hertfordshire AL3 4HB
Tel: 01727 855521
Headmaster: Mr JWJ Gillespie MA(Cantab), FRSA
Age range: B11–18 G16–18
No. of pupils: 870
Fees: Day £18,600

St Christopher School
Barrington Road, Letchworth, Hertfordshire SG6 3JZ
Tel: 01462 650 850
Head: Richard Palmer
Age range: 3–18
No. of pupils: 511 VIth78
Fees: Day £4,590–£18,075 WB £19,950–£24,675 FB £31,650

St Columba's College
King Harry Lane, St Albans, Hertfordshire AL3 4AW
Tel: 01727 892040
Head: Mr David Buxton
Age range: 4–18 years
No. of pupils: 780

St Edmund's College & Prep School
Old Hall Green, Nr Ware, Hertfordshire SG11 1DS
Tel: 01920 824247
Headmaster: Mr Matthew Mostyn BA (Hons) MA (Ed)
Age range: 3–18
No. of pupils: 852
Fees: Day £9,882–£18,345 WB £24,165–£27,630 FB £28,302–£32,460

St Francis' College
Broadway, Letchworth Garden City, Hertfordshire SG6 3PJ
Tel: 01462 670511
Headmistress: Mrs B Goulding
Age range: G3–18
No. of pupils: 460 VIth75
Fees: Day £9,990–£16,980 WB £22,350–£26,475 FB £27,990–£31,995

St Margaret's School, Bushey
Merry Hill Road, Bushey, Hertfordshire WD23 1DT
Tel: +44 (0)20 8416 4400
Headteacher: Lara Péchard
Age range: 2–18 years
No. of pupils: 530

Stanborough School
Stanborough Park, Garston, Watford, Hertfordshire WD25 9JT
Tel: 01923 673268
Acting Head Teacher: Ms Eileen Hussey
Age range: 3–17
No. of pupils: 300
Fees: Day £6,630–£10,224 WB £10,350–£13,995

The Haberdashers' Aske's Boys' School
Butterfly Lane, Elstree, Borehamwood, Hertfordshire WD6 3AF
Tel: 020 8266 1700
Headmaster: Mr Gus Lock MA (Oxon)
Age range: B5–18 years
No. of pupils: 1428
Fees: Day £15,339–£20,346

The Purcell School, London
Aldenham Road, Bushey, Hertfordshire WD23 2TS
Tel: 01923 331100
Headteacher: Dr Bernard Trafford
Age range: 10–18
No. of pupils: 180
Fees: Day £25,707 FB £32,826

The Royal Masonic School for Girls
Rickmansworth Park, Rickmansworth, Hertfordshire WD3 4HF
Tel: 01923 773168
Headmaster: Mr Kevin Carson M.Phil (Cambridge)
Age range: G4–18
No. of pupils: 930 VIth165
Fees: Day £11,475–£17,475 WB £20,115–£27,495 FB £21,225–£29,835

Tring Park School for the Performing Arts
Mansion Drive, Tring, Hertfordshire HP23 5LX
Tel: 01442 824255
Principal: Mr Stefan Anderson MA, ARCM, ARCT
Age range: 8–19 years
No. of pupils: 370 VIth171
Fees: Day £15,405–£24,885 FB £26,190–£37,605

Kent

Ashford School
East Hill, Ashford, Kent TN24 8PB
Tel: 01233 739030
Head: Mr Michael Hall
Age range: 3 months–18 years
No. of pupils: 916 VIth127
Fees: Day £10,815–£18,294
WB £26,775 FB £38,778
🌐Ⓐ🏛£✏️16+

Beckenham College
The Clockhouse Business Centre,
Unit 2, Thayers Farm Road,
Beckenham, Kent BR3 4LZ
Tel: 020 8650 3321
Principal: Mrs E Wakeling
Age range: 16+
Fees: Day £100–£3,500
16+ 16+ ♿

Beechwood Sacred Heart
12 Pembury Road, Tunbridge
Wells, Kent TN2 3QD
Tel: 01892 532747
Acting Head: Mrs Helen Rowe
Age range: 3–18
No. of pupils: 400 VIth70
Fees: Day £8,685–£17,385
WB £26,850 FB £29,850
Ⓐ🏛£✏️16+

Benenden School
Cranbrook, Kent TN17 4AA
Tel: 01580 240592
Headmistress: Mrs S Price
Age range: G11–18
No. of pupils: 550
Fees: FB £12,650
👤🌐Ⓐ🏛£✏️16+

Bethany School
Curtisden Green, Goudhurst,
Cranbrook, Kent TN17 1LB
Tel: 01580 211273
Headmaster: Mr Francie Healy BSc,
HDipEd, NPQH
Age range: 11–18 years
No. of pupils: 356 VIth73
Fees: Day £17,910–£19,785 WB
£27,810–£30,705 FB £29,985–£33,750
🌐Ⓐ🏛£✏️16+

Bishop Challoner School
228 Bromley Road, Shortlands,
Bromley, Kent BR2 0BS
Tel: 020 8460 3546
Headteacher: Mrs Paula Anderson
Age range: 3–18
No. of pupils: 340
Fees: Day £3,150–£4,500
Ⓐ£✏️16+

Bromley High School GDST
Blackbrook Lane, Bickley,
Bromley, Kent BR1 2TW
Tel: 020 8781 7000/1
Head: Mrs A M Drew BA(Hons), MBA
(Dunelm)
Age range: G4–18
👤Ⓐ£✏️16+

CATS Canterbury
68 New Dover Road,
Canterbury, Kent CT1 3LQ
Tel: +44 (0)1227866540
Principal: Severine Collins
Age range: 14–21 years
No. of pupils: 450
Fees: Day £17,370–£27,990
FB £13,230–£19,140
🌐16+ Ⓐ🏛IB 16+

COBHAM HALL SCHOOL
For further details see p. 89
Brewers Road, Cobham,
Kent DA12 3BL
Tel: 01474 823371
Email: enquiries@
cobhamhall.com
Website: www.cobhamhall.com
Headteacher: Mrs Wendy
Barrett
Age range: G11–18
No. of pupils: 150
Fees: Day £6,804–£8,246
FB £10,279–£12,831
👤🌐🏛✏️16+

Darul Uloom London
Foxbury Avenue, Perry Street,
Chislehurst, Kent BR7 6SD
Tel: 020 8295 0637
Principal: Mufti Mustafa
Age range: B11–18
No. of pupils: 160
Fees: FB £2,400
👤Ⓐ🏛16+

Dover College
Effingham Crescent,
Dover, Kent CT17 9RH
Tel: 01304 205969
Headmaster: Mr Gareth Doodes
MA (Hons)
Age range: 3–18
No. of pupils: 301
Fees: Day £7,725–£16,050 WB
£21,000–£25,500 FB £24,750–£31,500
🌐Ⓐ🏛£✏️16+

Farringtons School
Perry Street, Chislehurst,
Kent BR7 6LR
Tel: 020 8467 0256
Head: Mr David Jackson
Age range: 3–18 years
No. of pupils: 700 VIth100
Fees: Day £16,260 WB
£27,120 FB £34,050
🌐Ⓐ🏛£✏️16+

Kent College Pembury
Old Church Road, Pembury,
Tunbridge Wells, Kent TN2 4AX
Tel: +44 (0)1892 822006
Head of School: Miss Katrina
Handford
Age range: G3–18 years
No. of pupils: 500
Fees: Day £22,575 WB
£28,200 FB £35,700
👤🌐Ⓐ🏛£✏️16+

Kent College, Canterbury
Whitstable Road, Canterbury,
Kent CT2 9DT
Tel: +44 (0)1227 763 231
Head: Mr Mark Turnbull
Age range: 0–18 years
(Boarding from 8)
No. of pupils: 800
Fees: Day £5,797–£6,665
FB £8,967–£12,339
🌐Ⓐ🏛£IB✏️16+

King's Rochester
Satis House, Boley Hill,
Rochester, Kent ME1 1TE
Tel: 01634 888555
Principal: Mr B Charles
Age range: 13–18 years
No. of pupils: 600 VIth95
Fees: Day £20,700 FB £33,840
🌐Ⓐ🏛£✏️16+

Radnor House, Sevenoaks
Combe Bank Drive,
Sevenoaks, Kent TN14 6AE
Tel: 01959 563720
Head: Mr David Paton BComm
(Hons) PGCE MA
Age range: 2.5–18
No. of pupils: 250
Ⓐ£✏️16+ ♿

Sackville School
Tonbridge Rd, Hildenborough,
Tonbridge, Kent TN11 9HN
Tel: 01732 838888
Headmaster: Mr Justin Foster-
Gandey BSc (hons)
Age range: 11–18
No. of pupils: 160 VIth29
Fees: Day £15,750
Ⓐ£✏️16+ ♿

Sevenoaks School
High Street, Sevenoaks,
Kent TN13 1HU
Tel: +44 (0)1732 455133
Head of School: Mr Jesse R Elzinga
AB MSt FCCT
Age range: 11–18 years
No. of pupils: 1172
Fees: Day £25,020–£28,413
FB £39,790–£42,084
🌐Ⓐ🏛£IB✏️16+

ST EDMUND'S SCHOOL
For further details see p. 102
St Thomas Hill, Canterbury,
Kent CT2 8HU
Tel: 01227 475601
Email: admissions@
stedmunds.org.uk
Website: www.stedmunds.org.uk
Head: Mr Edward O'Connor MA
(Cantab), MPhil (Oxon), MEd
(Cantab)
Age range: 2–18 years
No. of pupils: 558
🌐Ⓐ🏛£✏️16+

St Lawrence College
Ramsgate, Kent CT11 7AE
Tel: 01843 572931
Head of College: Mr Barney Durrant
Age range: 3–18 years
No. of pupils: 585
Fees: Day £7,995–£17,025
FB £27,765–£37,455
🌐Ⓐ🏛£✏️16+

Sutton Valence School
North Street, Sutton
Valence, Kent ME17 3HL
Tel: 01622 845200
Headmaster: Mr James A Thomas
MA (Cantab) MA (London) NPQH
Age range: 11–18 years
No. of pupils: 570
🌐Ⓐ🏛£✏️16+

The King's School, Canterbury
The Precincts, Canterbury,
Kent CT1 2ES
Tel: 01227 595501
Head: Mr Peter Roberts
Age range: 13–18
No. of pupils: 858 VIth385
Fees: Day £27,495 FB £38,955
🌐Ⓐ🏛£✏️16+

TONBRIDGE SCHOOL
For further details see p. 106
High Street, Tonbridge,
Kent TN9 1JP
Tel: 01732 304297
Email: admissions@
tonbridge-school.org
Website:
www.tonbridge-school.co.uk
Headmaster: Mr James Priory
MA (Oxon)
Age range: B13–18 years
No. of pupils: 798
Fees: Day £33,636 FB £44,835
👤🌐Ⓐ🏛£✏️16+

Walthamstow Hall School
Sevenoaks, Kent TN13 3UL
Tel: 01732 451334
Headmistress: Miss S Ferro
Age range: G2–18
No. of pupils: 500 VIth80
👤Ⓐ£✏️16+

Middlesex

ACS Hillingdon International School
Hillingdon Court, 108 Vine Lane, Hillingdon, Uxbridge, Middlesex UB10 0BE
Tel: +44 (0) 1895 259 771
Head of School: Mr Martin Hall
Age range: 4–18

Halliford School
Russell Road, Shepperton, Middlesex TW17 9HX
Tel: 01932 223593
Head: Mr James Davies BMus (Hons) LGSM FASC ACertCM PGCE
Age range: B11–18 G16–18 years
No. of pupils: 445
Fees: Day £17,985

Hampton School
Hanworth Road, Hampton, Middlesex TW12 3HD
Tel: 020 8979 9273
Headmaster: Mr Kevin Knibbs MA (Oxon)
Age range: B11–18
No. of pupils: 1200
Fees: Day £6,390

Harrow School
5 High Street, Harrow on the Hill, Middlesex HA1 3HT
Tel: 020 8872 8000
Head Master: Mr Alastair Land
Age range: B13–18
No. of pupils: 830 VIth320
Fees: FB £40,050

KEW HOUSE SCHOOL
For further details see p. 82
Kew House, 6 Capital Interchange Way, London, Middlesex TW8 0EX
Tel: 0208 742 2038
Email: admissions@kewhouseschool.com
Website: www.kewhouseschool.com
Headmaster: Mr Will Williams
Age range: 11–18 years
No. of pupils: 576
Fees: Day £7,674

Lady Eleanor Holles
Hanworth Road, Hampton, Middlesex TW12 3HF
Tel: 020 8979 1601
Head of School: Mrs Heather Hanbury
Age range: G7–18
No. of pupils: 970
Fees: Day £21,738

Merchant Taylors' School
Sandy Lodge, Northwood, Middlesex HA6 2HT
Tel: 01923 820644
Head: Mr S J Everson MA (Cantab)
Age range: B11–18
No. of pupils: 865 VIth282
Fees: Day £19,998

North London Collegiate School
Canons, Canons Drive, Edgware, Middlesex HA8 7RJ
Tel: +44 (0)20 8952 0912
Headmistress: Mrs Sarah Clark
Age range: G4–18 years
No. of pupils: 1080
Fees: Day £5,956–£7,049

Northwood College for Girls GDST
Maxwell Road, Northwood, Middlesex HA6 2YE
Tel: 01923 825446
Head of School: Mrs Rebecca Brown
Age range: G3–18 years
No. of pupils: 844

Regent College London
Regent House, 167 Imperial Drive, Harrow, Middlesex HA2 7HD
Tel: +44 (0)20 3870 6666
Co-Principals: Dr Selva Pankaj & Mrs Tharshiny Pankaj
Age range: 14–24 years

St Helen's School
Eastbury Road, Northwood, Middlesex HA6 3AS
Tel: +44 (0)1923 843210
Headmistress: Dr Mary Short BA, PhD
Age range: G3–18
No. of pupils: VIth165

St. Catherine's School
Cross Deep, Twickenham, Middlesex TW1 4QJ
Tel: 020 8891 2898
Headmistress: Mrs Johneen McPherson MA
Age range: G4–18 years
No. of pupils: 449
Fees: Day £12,480–£16,125

St. John's Senior School
North Lodge, The Ridgeway, Enfield, Middlesex EN2 8BE
Tel: +44 (0)20 8366 0035
Head Teacher: Mr A Tardios
Age range: 11–18 years

The John Lyon School
Middle Road, Harrow on the Hill, Middlesex HA2 0HN
Tel: 020 8515 9443
Head: Miss Katherine Haynes BA, MEd, NPQH
Age range: B11–18 years
No. of pupils: 600

Surrey

ACS Cobham International School
Heywood, Portsmouth Road, Cobham, Surrey KT11 1BL
Tel: +44 (0) 1932 867251
Head of School: Mr Barnaby Sandow
Age range: 2–18

ACS Egham International School
Woodlee, London Road, Egham, Surrey TW20 0HS
Tel: +44 (0) 1784 430 800
Head of School: Mr Jeremy Lewis
Age range: 4–18
Fees: Day £11,090–£25,870

Box Hill School
London Road, Mickleham, Dorking, Surrey RH5 6EA
Tel: 01372 373382
Headmaster: Cory Lowde
Age range: 11–18 years
No. of pupils: 425
Fees: Day £20,820 WB £30,480

Cambridge Tutors College
Water Tower Hill, Croydon, Surrey CR0 5SX
Tel: 020 8688 5284/7363
Principal: Dr Chris Drew
Age range: 15–19
No. of pupils: 215 VIth200
Fees: Day £10,400–£22,995

Caterham School
Harestone Valley, Caterham, Surrey CR3 6YA
Tel: 01883 343028
Head: Mr C. W. Jones MA(Cantab)
Age range: 11–18
No. of pupils: VIth321
Fees: Day £18,735–£19,620 WB £30,936–£33,270 FB £36,795–£38,760

Charterhouse
Godalming, Surrey GU7 2DX
Tel: +44 (0)1483 291501
Head: Dr Alex Peterken
Age range: B13–18 years G16–18 years
No. of pupils: 895

City of London Freemen's School
Ashtead Park, Ashtead, Surrey KT21 1ET
Tel: 01372 277933
Headmaster: Mr R Martin
Age range: 7–18
No. of pupils: 877 VIth213
Fees: Day £14,067–£19,194 WB £29,784–£29,841 FB £30,780–£30,816

Claremont Fan Court School
Claremont Drive, Esher, Surrey KT10 9LY
Tel: 01372 473780
Head: Mr William Brierly
Age range: 2 1/2–18 years
No. of pupils: 1010

Cranleigh School
Horseshoe Lane, Cranleigh,
Surrey GU6 8QQ
Tel: +44 (0) 1483 273666
Headmaster: Mr Martin Reader
MA, MPhil, MBA
Age range: 7–18 years
(including Prep School)
No. of pupils: 683 VIth256
Fees: Day £33,510 FB £40,710

Croydon High School GDST
Old Farleigh Road, Selsdon,
South Croydon, Surrey CR2 8YB
Tel: 020 8260 7500
Headmistress: Mrs Emma Pattison
Age range: G3–18
No. of pupils: 580 VIth75

Dunottar School
High Trees Road, Reigate,
Surrey RH2 7EL
Tel: 01737 761945
Head of School: Mr Mark Tottman
Age range: 11–18
No. of pupils: 460
Fees: Day £18,621

Epsom College
Epsom, Surrey KT17 4JQ
Tel: 01372 821000
Headmaster: Mr Jay A Piggot MA
Age range: 11–18
No. of pupils: 884
Fees: Day £19,611–£26,151
WB £35,034 FB £38,568

Ewell Castle School
Church Street, Ewell, Epsom,
Surrey KT17 2AW
Tel: 020 8393 1413
Principal: Mr Silas Edmonds
Age range: 3–18 years
No. of pupils: 670
Fees: Day £5,382–£18,141

Frensham Heights
Rowledge, Farnham,
Surrey GU10 4EA
Tel: 01252 792561
Head: Mr Rick Clarke
Age range: 3–18
No. of pupils: 497 VIth105
Fees: Day £7,110–£21,060
FB £27,450–£32,070

Guildford High School
London Road, Guildford,
Surrey GU1 1SJ
Tel: 01483 561440
Headmistress: Mrs F J Boulton BSc,
MA
Age range: G4–18
No. of pupils: 985
Fees: Day £11,400–£18,300

KING EDWARD'S WITLEY
For further details see p. 92
Petworth Road, Godalming,
Surrey GU8 5SG
Tel: 01428 686735
Email: admissions@kesw.org
Website: www.kesw.org
Head: Mrs Joanna Wright
Age range: 11–18 years
No. of pupils: 420

Kingston Grammar School
70 London Rd, Kingston upon
Thames, Surrey KT2 6PY
Tel: 020 8546 5875
Head: Mr Stephen Lehec
Age range: 11–18

Lingfield College
Racecourse Road, Lingfield,
Surrey RH7 6PH
Tel: 01342 832407
Headmaster: Mr R Bool B.A. Hons,
MBA
Age range: 2–18
No. of pupils: 935
Fees: Day £11,250–£21,801

MARYMOUNT LONDON
For further details see p. 83
George Road, Kingston upon
Thames, Surrey KT2 7PE
Tel: +44 (0)20 8949 0571
Email: admissions@
marymountlondon.com
Website:
www.marymountlondon.com
Headmistress: Mrs Margaret
Giblin
Age range: G11–18 years
No. of pupils: 258
Fees: Day £27,250 WB
£44,180 FB £46,130

Notre Dame School
Cobham, Surrey KT11 1HA
Tel: 01932 869990
Head of Seniors: Mrs Anna King
MEd, MA (Cantab), PGCE
Age range: 2–18
No. of pupils: 600

Old Palace of John
Whitgift School
Old Palace Road, Croydon,
Surrey CR0 1AX
Tel: 020 8688 2027
Head: Mrs. C Jewell
Age range: G3–18 years
No. of pupils: 650
Fees: Day £3,300–£5,536

Prior's Field
Priorsfield Road, Godalming,
Surrey GU7 2RH
Tel: 01483 810551
Head of School: Mrs Tracey Kirnig
Age range: G11–18
No. of pupils: 450
Fees: Day £18,900 FB £30,825

Reed's School
Sandy Lane, Cobham,
Surrey KT11 2ES
Tel: 01932 869001
Headmaster: Mr Mark Hoskins BA
MA MSc
Age range: B11–18 G16–18
No. of pupils: 650 VIth230
Fees: Day £20,430–£25,530
FB £27,225–£32,910

Reigate Grammar School
Reigate Road, Reigate,
Surrey RH2 0QS
Tel: 01737 222231
Headmaster: Mr Shaun Fenton MA
(Oxon) MEd (Oxon)
Age range: 11–18
No. of pupils: 969 VIth262
Fees: Day £19,140–£19,350

Royal Grammar
School, Guildford
High Street, Guildford,
Surrey GU1 3BB
Tel: 01483 880600
Headmaster: Dr J M Cox BSc, PhD
Age range: B11–18
No. of pupils: 940
Fees: Day £19,035

Royal Russell School
Coombe Lane, Croydon,
Surrey CR9 5BX
Tel: 020 8657 3669
Headmaster: Christopher
Hutchinson
Age range: 11–18
No. of pupils: 590 VIth180
Fees: Day £18,480 FB £36,525

Sir William Perkins's School
Guildford Road, Chertsey,
Surrey KT16 9BN
Tel: 01932 574900
Head: Mr C C Muller
Age range: G11–18 years
No. of pupils: 600
Fees: Day £5,618

St Catherine's, Bramley
Station Road, Bramley,
Guildford, Surrey GU5 0DF
Tel: 01483 899609
Headmistress: Alice Phillips
Age range: G4–18
Fees: Day £9,240–£18,885 FB £31,125

St George's College
Weybridge Road, Addlestone,
Weybridge, Surrey KT15 2QS
Tel: 01932 839300
Headmistress: Mrs Rachel Owens
Age range: 11–18
No. of pupils: 909 VIth250
Fees: Day £17,655–£20,100

St James Senior
Boys School
Church Road, Ashford,
Surrey TW15 3DZ
Tel: 01784 266930
Headmaster: Mr David Brazier
Age range: B11–18
No. of pupils: 403 VIth65
Fees: Day £18,930

St John's School
Epsom Road, Leatherhead,
Surrey KT22 8SP
Tel: 01372 373000
Head of School: Mrs Rowena Cole
Age range: 11–18
No. of pupils: 840
Fees: Day £19,785–£24,810
WB £25,035–£31,365

St Teresa's Effingham
(Senior School)
Beech Avenue, Effingham,
Surrey RH5 6ST
Tel: 01372 452037
Executive Director: Mr Mike Farmer
Age range: G11–18
No. of pupils: 640 VIth90
Fees: Day £17,865–£18,465 WB
£28,875–£29,175 FB £30,795–£31,455

Surbiton High School
13-15 Surbiton Crescent, Kingston
upon Thames, Surrey KT1 2JT
Tel: 020 8546 5245
Principal: Mrs Rebecca Glover
Age range: B4–11 G4–18
No. of pupils: 1210 VIth186
Fees: Day £10,857–£17,142

Sutton High School GDST
55 Cheam Road, Sutton,
Surrey SM1 2AX
Tel: 020 8642 0594
Headmistress: Mrs Katharine
Crouch
Age range: G3–18
No. of pupils: 600 VIth60
Fees: Day £10,095–£17,043

Tante Marie Culinary
Academy
Woodham House, Carlton Road,
Woking, Surrey GU21 4HF
Tel: 01483 726957
Principal: Mr Andrew Maxwell
Age range: 16–60
No. of pupils: 72
Fees: Day £20,750

TASIS The American School in England
Coldharbour Lane, Thorpe,
Surrey TW20 8TE
Tel: +44 (0)1932 582316
Head of School: Mr Bryan Nixon
Age range: 3–18
No. of pupils: 620
Fees: Day £12,280–
£26,375 FB £48,900

The Royal School
Farnham Lane, Haslemere,
Surrey GU27 1HQ
Tel: 01428 605805
Head: Mrs Pippa Smithson
Age range: 11–18 years
Fees: Day £10,506–£18,507
WB £27,747 FB £31,557

Tormead School
27 Cranley Road, Guildford,
Surrey GU1 2JD
Tel: 01483 575101
Headmistress: Mrs Christina Foord
Age range: G4–18
No. of pupils: 760 VIth120
Fees: Day £8,385–£15,915

Trinity School
Shirley Park, Croydon,
Surrey CR9 7AT
Tel: 020 8656 9541
Head: Alasdair Kennedy MA (Cantab)
Age range: B10–18 G16–18
No. of pupils: 1007
Fees: Day £16,656

Whitgift School
Haling Park, South Croydon,
Surrey CR2 6YT
Tel: +44 20 8633 9935
Headmaster: Mr Christopher Ramsey
Age range: B10–18 years
No. of pupils: 1550
Fees: Day £21,240 WB
£34,260 FB £41,550

Woldingham School
Marden Park, Woldingham,
Surrey CR3 7YA
Tel: 01883 349431
Head of School: Dr James Whitehead
Age range: G11–18
No. of pupils: 611
Fees: Day £22,710–£24,750
FB £32,850–£40,710

Yehudi Menuhin School
Stoke Road, Stoke d'Abernon,
Cobham, Surrey KT11 3QQ
Tel: 01932 864739
Interim Head: Richard Tanner
Age range: 7–19
No. of pupils: 80 VIth36
Fees: FB £34,299

West Berkshire

Downe House School
Downe House, Cold Ash,
Thatcham, West Berkshire RG18 9JJ
Tel: +44 (0)1635 200286
Headmistress: Mrs Emma McKendrick BA(Liverpool)
Age range: G11–18 years
No. of pupils: 590
Fees: Day £10,435 FB £14,030

St Gabriel's
Sandleford Priory, Newbury,
West Berkshire RG20 9BD
Tel: 01635 555680
Principal: Mr Richard Smith MA (Hons), MEd, PGCE
Age range: B6 months–11
G6 months–18
No. of pupils: 469 VIth40
Fees: Day £10,668–£17,418

West Sussex

Ardingly College
College Road, Ardingly, Haywards Heath, West Sussex RH17 6SQ
Tel: +44 (0)1444 893320
Headmaster: Mr Ben Figgis
Age range: 13–18
No. of pupils: 559
Fees:–£23,985 FB £35,865–£29,250

Burgess Hill Girls
Keymer Road, Burgess Hill,
West Sussex RH15 0EG
Tel: 01444 241050
Head of School: Liz Laybourn
Age range: B2.5–4 years
G2.5–18 years
No. of pupils: 505 VIth70
Fees: Day £9,150–£20,850
FB £31,800–£36,750

Christ's Hospital
Horsham, West Sussex RH13 0LJ
Tel: 01403 211293
Head Teacher: Mr Simon Reid
Age range: 11–18
No. of pupils: 900
Fees: Day £18,510–£23,310
FB £35,850

Farlington School
Strood Park, Horsham,
West Sussex RH12 3PN
Tel: 01403 282573
Head of School: Mr James Passam
Age range: 4–18
No. of pupils: 311
Fees: Day £5,850–£18,300 WB
£29,100–£29,400 FB £30,450–£30,750

Hurstpierpoint College
College Lane, Hurstpierpoint,
West Sussex BN6 9JS
Tel: 01273 833636
Headmaster: Mr. T J Manly BA, MSc
Age range: 4–18
No. of pupils: 1156
Fees: Day £8,790–£22,860
WB £28,800

Lancing College
Lancing, West Sussex BN15 0RW
Tel: 01273 452213
Head Master: Mr Dominic T Oliver MPhil
Age range: 13–18
No. of pupils: 550 VIth255
Fees: Day £8,190 FB £11,995

Our Lady of Sion School
Gratwicke Road, Worthing,
West Sussex BN11 4BL
Tel: 01903 204063
Headmaster: Mr Steven Jeffery
Age range: 3–18
No. of pupils: 410
Fees: Day £8,640–£13,575

Seaford College
Lavington Park, Petworth,
West Sussex GU28 0NB
Tel: 01798 867392
Headmaster: J P Green MA BA
Age range: 6–18 years
No. of pupils: 903 VIth235
Fees: Day £3,665–£7,595 WB
£7,635–£10,290 FB £11,750

Worth School
Paddockhurst Road, Turners Hill,
Crawley, West Sussex RH10 4SD
Tel: +44 (0)1342 710200
Head Master: Stuart McPherson
Age range: 11–18
No. of pupils: 580 VIth222
Fees: Day £15,960–£23,730
FB £21,210–£33,690

Examinations and qualifications

Common Entrance

What is Common Entrance?

The Common Entrance examinations are used in UK independent schools (and some independent schools overseas) for transfer from junior to senior schools at the ages of 11+ and 13+. They were first introduced in 1904 and are internationally recognised as being a rigorous form of assessment following a thorough course of study. The examinations are produced by the Independent Schools Examinations Board and backed by HMC (Headmasters' and Headmistresses' Conference), GSA (Girls' Schools Association), and IAPS (Independent Association of Prep Schools) which together represent the leading independent schools in the UK, and many overseas.

Common Entrance is not a public examination as, for example, GCSE, and candidates may normally be entered only in one of the following circumstances:

a) they have been offered a place at a senior school subject to their passing the examination, or

b) they are entered as a 'trial run', in which case the papers are marked by the junior school concerned.

Candidates normally take the examination in their own junior or preparatory schools, either in the UK or overseas.

How does Common Entrance fit into the progression to GCSEs?

Rapid changes in education nationally and internationally have resulted in regular reviews of the syllabuses for all the Common Entrance examinations. Reviews of the National Curriculum, in particular, have brought about a number of changes, with the Board wishing to ensure that it continues to set high standards. It is also a guiding principle that Common Entrance should be part of the natural progression from 11-16, and not a diversion from it.

Common Entrance at 11+

At 11+, the examination consists of papers in English, mathematics and science. It is designed so that it can be taken by candidates either from independent preparatory schools or by candidates from schools in the maintained sector or overseas who have had no special preparation. The examination is normally taken in January for entrance to senior schools in the following September.

Common Entrance at 13+

At 13+, most candidates come from independent preparatory schools. The compulsory subjects are English, mathematics and science. Papers in French, geography, German, Classical Greek, history, Latin, religious studies and Spanish are also available and candidates usually offer as many subjects as they can. In most subjects, papers are available at more than one level to cater for candidates of different abilities. There are three examination sessions each year, with the majority of candidates sitting in the summer prior to entry to their senior schools in September.

Marking and grading

The papers are set centrally but the answers are marked by the senior school for which a candidate is entered. Mark schemes are provided by the Board but senior schools are free to set their own grade boundaries. Results are available within two weeks of the examinations taking place.

Pre-Testing and the ISEB Common Pre-Tests

A number of senior independent schools 'pre-test' pupils for entry, prior to them taking their main entrance examinations at a later date. Usually, these pre-tests take place when a pupil is in Year 6 or Year 7 of his or her junior school and will then be going on to sit Common Entrance in Year 8. The tests are designed to assess a pupil's academic potential and suitability for a particular senior school so that the child, the parents and the school know well in advance whether he/she is going to be offered a place at the school, subject to a satisfactory performance in the entrance examinations. The tests enable senior schools to manage their lists and help to ensure that pupils are not entered for examinations in which they are unlikely to be successful. In short, it reduces uncertainty for all concerned.

Pre-tests may be written specifically for the senior school for which the candidate is entered but a growing number of schools are choosing to use the Common Pre-Tests provided by the Independent Schools Examinations Board. These online tests are usually taken in the candidate's own junior school and one of their main advantages is that a pupil need sit the tests only once, with the results then made available to any senior school which wishes to use them. The multiple-choice tests cover verbal reasoning, non-verbal reasoning, English and mathematics, with the results standardised according to the pupil's age when they are taken. Further information is available on the ISEB website at www.iseb.co.uk.

Parents are advised to check the entrance requirements for senior schools to see if their child will be required to sit a pre-test.

Further information

Details of the Common Entrance examinations and how to register candidates are available on the ISEB website www.iseb.co.uk. Copies of past papers and a wide range of textbooks and other resources can be purchased from Galore Park Publishing Ltd at www.galorepark.co.uk. Support materials are also available from Hodder Education and other publishers; see the Resources section of the ISEB website for details.

Independent Schools Examinations Board
Endeavour House, Crow Arch Lane,
Ringwood, Hampshire BH24 1HP

Telephone: 01425 470555
Email: enquiries@iseb.co.uk
Web: www.iseb.co.uk

7+ Entrance Exams

What is the 7+?

The 7+ is the descriptive name given to the entrance exams set by an increasing number of independent schools for pupils wishing to gain admission into their Year 3.

7+ entrance exams may be simply for admission into a selective preparatory school, which will then prepare the child for Common Entrance exams to gain a place at senior school. Alternatively, the 7+ can be a route into a school with both prep and senior departments, therefore often effectively bypassing the 11+ or 13+ Common Entrance exams.

The Independent Schools Examinations Board provides Common Entrance examinations and assessments for pupils seeking entry to independent senior schools at 11+ and 13+, but there is as yet no equivalent for the 7+. The testing is largely undertaken by the individual schools, although some schools might commission the test from external agencies. Many schools in the incredibly competitive London area offer entrance exams at 7+ and some share specimen papers on their website to clarify what 7+ children will face.

Who sits the 7+?

The 7+ is sat by Year 2 children, who may be moving from a state primary school or a stand-alone pre-prep school to an independent prep school (although many prep schools now have their own pre-prep department, with a cohort of children poised to pass into Year 3 there).

Registration for 7+ entrance exams usually closes in the November of Year 2, with the exams then sat in January or February, for entry that September.

How is the 7+ assessed?

Written exam content will be primarily English and maths based, whilst spelling, dictation, mental arithmetic and more creative skills may be assessed verbally on a one-to-one basis. Group exercises are also sometimes used to look at a child's initiative and their ability to work with others.

Schools will not only be looking for academic potential, but also good citizens and a mixture of personalities to produce a well-rounded year group. For this reason, children are often asked to attend an interview. Some schools interview all candidates, whilst others may call back a limited number with good test results. They will be looking for a child's ability to look an adult in the eye and think on their feet, but also simply to show some spark and personality.

After the assessments, children will be told if they have been successful in gaining a firm place, or a place on a waiting list.

Further Information

As the 7+ is not centrally regulated, it is best for parents to seek accurate admissions and testing information direct from the schools in which they are interested. In addition to a school's facilities and ethos, choosing a school for admission at 7+ will probably also involve whether the school has a senior department and if not, the prep school's record in gaining its students places at target senior schools.

Experienced educational consultants may be able to help parents decide which independent prep school is best suited for their child, based on their personality, senior school ambitions and academic potential. Many parents enlist the help of tutors to prepare children for the 7+, if only to reduce the fear of the unknown in these very young children. This is achieved by teaching them the required curriculum, what to expect on their test and interview days, and giving them the opportunity to practice tackling the type of assessments they will face.

PSB

The Pre-Senior Baccalaureate (PSB) is a framework of study for children in junior and preparatory schools that was introduced in 2012, and focuses on the active development and assessment of 6 core skills: Communication, Collaboration, Leadership, Independence, Reviewing and Improving and Thinking and Learning. Member schools promote the core skills across all areas of school life, and provide guidance for pupils in progressing these skills, which are seen as essential for developing capable and balanced adults able to make the most of the opportunities of a fast-changing world. A strong but appropriate knowledge base compliments this, with the use of focused tutoring, pastoral care and Well Being programmes.

Schools do not work to a prescribed curriculum and the emphasis is upon promoting an independent approach which works for each individual school. There are subject INSET days for PSB school staff annually and these are supported by senior school colleagues, to ensure that work done in PSB schools compliments the demands of education at higher levels.

The PSB is a whole school initiative from Early Years to either Year 6 or Year 8, at which point the certificate is awarded at the time of matriculation to senior schools. An additional PSB Year 9 framework is being developed together with international membership.

The development of skills is now recognised as essential by the Independent Schools Inspectorate (ISI), and recent ISI reports on PSB schools highlight the excellent contribution the PSB has in schools achieving excellence.

Assessment

The PSB has a 10 point scale for all subjects studied with a compulsory spine covering: English, Maths, Science, Modern Languages, The Humanities, Art, Design Technology, Music, Sport and PE with each pupil additionally completing a cross curricular project. Optional subjects are agreed with schools but these must be supported by a scheme of work clearly identifying appropriate core skills which are assessed on a 5 point scale. There are distinction levels on both scales and the 10 point scale cross references both ISEB and National Curriculum assessment levels.

Pupils moving on to senior school do so via individual senior school pre-testing arrangements, the award of the PSB certificate, core ISEB papers or a combination of the above.

Membership categories

Partner membership is available to schools developing the PSB with support given from existing schools and the Communications director.

Full membership entitles schools to use the PSB matriculation certificate and join the PSB committee as voting members.

Affiliated membership is for schools that have developed their own skills based approach, in line with PSB principles; staff can participate in all training opportunities and the Heads of Affiliated Schools join committee meetings as non-voting guests.

Membership of the above categories is dependent upon strong ISI reports, the development of a skills based curriculum, with skills clearly identified in schemes of work and excellent teaching.

Associate membership is for senior schools that actively support the PSB in providing staff for subject meetings, hosting meetings, conferences and committee meetings and offer a valuable perspective on the demands of GCSE, A Level and the International Baccalaureate.

Further details

The PSB is an entirely independent charity overseen by a Board of Trustees who have expertise in both primary and secondary education. Details of the PSB can be found on the website – psbacc.org – and you can contact the PSB Administrator at rebecca.morris@psbacc.org and she will answer any questions you may have.

General Certificate of Secondary Education (GCSE)

What are the GCSE qualifications?

GCSE qualifications were first introduced in 1986 and are the principal means of assessment at Key Stage 4 across a range of academic subject areas. They command respect and have status not only in the UK but worldwide.

Main features of the GCSE

There are four unitary awarding organisations for GCSEs in England. WJEC and CCEA also offer GCSE qualifications in Wales and Northern Ireland. Each examining group designs its own specifications but they are required to conform to set criteria. For some aspects of the qualification system, the exam boards adopt common ways of working. When the exam boards work together in this way they generally do so through the Joint Council of Qualifications (JCQ). The award of a grade is intended to indicate that a candidate has met the required level of skills, knowledge and understanding.

New, reformed GCSEs have been introduced in recent years. New GCSEs in ancient languages (classical Greek, Latin), art and design, biology, chemistry, citizenship studies, combined science (double award), computer science, dance, drama, food preparation and nutrition, geography, history, modern foreign languages (French, German, Spanish), music, physics, physical education and religious studies were first taught in September 2016, with first results in summer 2018. Assessment in these reformed GCSEs consists primarily of formal examinations taken at the end of the student's two-year course. Other types of assessment, non-exam assessment (NEA), is used where there are skills and knowledge which cannot be assessed through exams. Ofqual have set the percentage of the total marks that will come from NEA.

The reformed GCSEs feature new and more demanding content, as required by the government and developed by the exam boards. Courses are designed for two years of study (linear assessment) and no longer divided into different modules.

Exams can only be split into 'foundation tier' and 'higher tier' if one exam paper does not give all students the opportunity to show their knowledge and their abilities. Such tiering is only available in maths, science and modern foreign languages; other subjects do not have tiers. Resit opportunities will only be available each

November in English language and maths, and then only for students who have turned 16 by the 31st of August in the year of the November assessment.

New GCSEs taught from September 2017: ancient history, astronomy, business, classical civilisation, design and technology, economics, electronics, engineering, film studies, geology, media studies, psychology, sociology, statistics, other (minority) foreign languages e.g. Italian, Polish.

New GCSEs taught from September 2018: ancient languages (biblical Hebrew) and modern foreign languages (Gujarati, Persian, Portuguese, Turkish).

Grading

The basic principle that exam boards follow when setting grade boundaries is that if the group of students (the cohort) taking a qualification in one year is of similar ability to the cohort in the previous year then the overall results (outcomes) should be comparable.

The reformed exams taken in summer 2017 were the first to show a new grading system, with the A* to G grades being phased out.

The new grading system is 9 to 1, with 9 being the top grade. Ofqual says this allows greater differentiation between students. It expects that broadly the same proportion of students will achieve a grade 4 and above as currently achieve a grade C and above, that broadly the same proportion of students will achieve a grade 7 and above as currently achieve a grade A and above. There are three anchor points between the new grading system and the old one: the bottom of the new 1 grade is the same as the bottom of the old G grade, the bottom of the new 4 grade is the bottom of the old C grade, and the bottom of the 7 grade is the same as the bottom of the old A grade. Grade 9 will be set using the tailored approach formula in the first award.

Grades 2, 3, 5 and 6 will be awarded arithmetically so that the grade boundaries are equally spaced in terms of marks from neighbouring grades.

The government's definition of a 'strong pass' will be set at grade 5 for reformed GCSEs. A grade 4 – or 'standard pass' – will continue to be a level 2 achievement. The DfE does not expect employers, colleges or universities to raise the bar to a grade 5 if a grade 4 would meet their requirements.

Can anyone take GCSE qualifications?

GCSEs are intended mainly for 16-year-old pupils, but are open to anyone of any age, whether studying full-time or part-time at a school, college or privately. There are no formal entry requirements.

Students normally study up to ten subjects over a two-year period. Short course GCSEs are available in some subjects (including PE and religious studies) – these include half the content of a full GCSE, so two short course GCSEs are equivalent to one full GCSE.

The English Baccalaureate

The English Baccalaureate (EBacc) is a school performance measure. It allows people to see how many pupils get a grade C or above (current grading) in the core academic subjects at Key Stage 4 in any government-funded school. The DfE introduced the EBacc measure in 2010.

Progress 8 and Attainment 8

Progress 8 aims to capture the progress a pupil makes from the end of primary school to the end of secondary school. It is a type of value added measure, which means that pupils' results are compared to the actual achievements of other pupils with the same prior attainment.

The new performance measures are designed to encourage schools to offer a broad and balanced curriculum with a focus on an academic core at Key Stage 4, and reward schools for the teaching of all their pupils, measuring performance across 8 qualifications. Every increase in every grade a pupil achieves will attract additional points in the performance tables.

Progress 8 will be calculated for individual pupils solely in order to calculate a school's Progress 8 score, and there will be no need for schools to share individual Progress 8 scores with their pupils. Schools should continue to focus on which qualifications are most suitable for individual pupils, as the grades pupils achieve will help them reach their goals for the next stage of their education or training.

Attainment 8 will measure the achievement of a pupil across 8 qualifications including mathematics (double weighted) and English (double weighted), 3 further qualifications that count in the English Baccalaureate (EBacc) measure and 3 further qualifications that can be GCSE qualifications (including EBacc subjects) or any other non-GCSE qualification on the DfE approved list.

General Certificate of Education (GCE) Advanced level (A level)

Typically, A level qualifications are studied over a two-year period. There are no lower or upper age limits. Schools and colleges usually expect students aged 16-18 to have obtained grades A*-C (grade 5 in the new criteria) in five subjects at GCSE level before taking an advanced level course. This requirement may vary between centres and according to which specific subjects are to be studied. Mature students may be assessed on different criteria as to their suitability to embark on the course.

GCE Qualifications

Over the past few years, AS level and A level qualifications have been in a process of reform. New subjects have been introduced gradually, with the first wave taught from September 2015. Subjects that have not been reformed are no longer available for teaching.

GCE qualifications are available at two levels: the Advanced Subsidiary (AS), which is generally delivered over one year and is seen as half an A level; and the A level (GCE). Nearly 70 titles are available, covering a wide range of subject areas, including humanities, sciences, language, business, arts, mathematics and technology.

One of the major reforms is that AS level results no longer count towards an A level (they previously counted for 50%). The two qualifications are linear, with AS assessments typically taking place after one year and A levels after two.

New-style AS and A levels were first taught from September 2015 for: art and design, biology, business studies, chemistry, computer studies, economics, English language, English language and literature, English literature, history, physics, psychology, and sociology.

Subjects first taught from September 2016 include: ancient languages such as Latin or Greek, dance, drama (theatre studies), geography, modern languages such as Spanish or French, music, physical education, religious studies.

Those introduced for first teaching from September 2017: accounting, design and technology, music technology, history of art, environmental science, philosophy, maths, further maths, archaeology, accounting, electronics, ancient history, law, classical civilisation, film studies, media studies, politics, geology, statistics, Chinese, Italian, Russian. In 2018 Biblical Hebrew, Modern Hebrew & languages such as Bengali, Polish and Urdu were available for first teaching.

Some GCE AS and A levels, particularly the practical ones, contain a proportion of coursework. All GCE A levels that contain one or more types of assessment will have an element of synoptic assessment that tests students' understanding of the whole specification. GCE AS are graded A-E and A levels are graded A*-E.

Overall the amount of coursework at A level has been reduced in the reforms. In some subjects, such as the sciences, practical work will not contribute to the final A level but will be reported separately in a certificate of endorsement. In the sciences, students will do at least 12 practical activities, covering apparatus and techniques. Exam questions about practical work will make up at least 15% of the total marks for the qualification and students will be assessed on their knowledge, skills and understanding of practical work.

Cambridge International AS & A Level

Cambridge International AS & A Level is an internationally benchmarked qualification, taught in over 130 countries worldwide. It is typically for learners aged 16 to 19 years who need advanced study to prepare for university. It was created specifically for an international audience and the content has been devised to suit the wide variety of schools worldwide and avoid any cultural bias.

Cambridge International A Level is typically a two-year course, and Cambridge International AS Level is typically one year. Some subjects can be started as a Cambridge International AS Level and extended to a Cambridge International A Level. Students can either follow a broad course of study, or specialise in one particular subject area.

Learners use Cambridge International AS & A Levels to gain places at leading universities worldwide, including the UK, Ireland, USA, Canada, Australia, New Zealand, India, Singapore, Egypt, Jordan, South Africa, the Netherlands, Germany and Spain. In places such as the US and Canada, good grades in carefully chosen Cambridge International A Level subjects can result in up to one year of university course credit.

Assessment options:

Cambridge International AS & A Levels have a linear structure with exams at the end of the course. Students can choose from a range of assessment options:

Option 1: take Cambridge International AS Levels only. The Cambridge International AS Level syllabus content is half a Cambridge International A Level.

Option 2: staged assessment, which means taking the Cambridge International AS Level in one exam session and the Cambridge International A Level at a later session. However, this route is not possible in all subjects.

Option 3: take all Cambridge International A Level papers in the same examination session, usually at the end of the course.

Grades and subjects

Cambridge International A Levels are graded from A* to E. Cambridge International AS Levels are graded from A to E.

Subjects: available in 55 subjects including accounting, Afrikaans, Afrikaans – first language (AS only), Afrikaans language (AS only), applied information and communication technology, Arabic, Arabic language (AS only), art and design, biology, business, chemistry, Chinese, Chinese language (AS only), classical

studies, computing, design and technology, design and textiles, digital media & design, divinity, economics, English language, English literature, environmental management, food studies, French, French language (AS only), French literature (AS only), general paper, geography, German, German language (AS only), Global Perspectives & Research, Hindi, Hindi language (AS only), Hindi literature (AS only), Hinduism, history, Islamic studies, Japanese language (AS only), English language and literature (AS only), law, Marathi, Marathi language (AS only), marine science, mathematics, further mathematics, media studies, music, physical education, physical science, physics, Portuguese, Portuguese language (AS only), Portuguese literature (AS only), psychology, sociology, Spanish, Spanish first language (AS only), Spanish language (AS only), Spanish literature (AS only), Tamil, Tamil language (AS only), Telugu, Telugu language (AS only), thinking skills, travel and tourism, Urdu, Urdu language (AS only).
Website: www.cambridgeinternational.org/alevel

Cambridge IGCSE

Cambridge IGCSE is the world's most popular international qualification for 14 to16 year olds. It develops skills in creative thinking, enquiry and problem solving, in preparation for the next stage in a student's education. Cambridge IGCSE is taken in over 150 countries, and is widely recognised by employers and higher education institutions worldwide.

Cambridge IGCSE is graded from A*-G. In the UK, Cambridge IGCSE is accepted as equivalent to the GCSE. It can be used as preparation for Cambridge International A & AS Levels, UK A and AS levels, IB or AP and in some instances entry into university. Cambridge IGCSE First Language English and Cambridge IGCSE English Language qualifications are recognised by a significant number of UK universities as evidence of competence in the language for university entrance.

Subjects: available in over 70 subjects including accounting, Afrikaans – first language, Afrikaans – second language, agriculture, Arabic – first language, Arabic – foreign language, art and design, Baha Indonesia, Bangladesh studies, biology, business studies, chemistry, child development, Chinese – first language, Chinese – second language, Chinese (Mandarin) – foreign language, computer studies, Czech – first language, design and technology, development studies, drama, Dutch – first language, Dutch – foreign language, economics, English – additional language , English – first language, English – literature, English – second language, enterprise, environmental management, food and nutrition, French – first language, French – foreign language, geography, German – first language, German – foreign language, global perspectives, Greek – foreign language, Hindi as a second language, Italian – foreign language, history, India studies, Indonesian – foreign language, information and communication technology, IsiZulu as a second language, Japanese – first language, Japanese – foreign language, Kazakh as a second language, Korean (first language), Latin, Malay – first language, Malay – foreign language, mathematics, mathematics – additional, international mathematics, music, Pakistan studies, physical education, physical science, physics, Portuguese – first language, Portuguese – foreign language, religious studies, Russian – first language, science – combined, sciences – co-ordinated (double), sociology, Spanish – first language, Spanish – foreign language, Spanish – literature, Thai – first language, travel and tourism, Turkish – first language, Urdu – second language, world literature.
Website: www.cambridgeinternational.org/igcse

Edexcel International GCSEs

Pearson's Edexcel International GCSEs are academic qualifications aimed at learners aged 14 to 16. They're equivalent to a UK General Certificate of Secondary Education (GCSE), and are the main requirement for Level 3 studies, including progression to GCE AS or A levels, BTECs or employment. International GCSEs are linear qualifications, meaning that students take all of the exams at the end of the course. They are available at Level 1 (grades 3-1) and Level 2 (grades 9-4). There are currently more than 100,000 learners studying Edexcel International GCSEs, in countries throughout Asia, Africa, Europe, the Middle East and Latin America. Developed by subject specialists and reviewed regularly, many of Pearson's Edexcel International GCSEs include specific international content to make them relevant to students worldwide.

Pearson's Edexcel International GCSEs were initially developed for international schools. They have since become popular among independent schools in the UK, but are not approved for use in UK state schools.

Free Standing Maths Qualifications (FSMQ)

Aimed at those students wishing to acquire further qualifications in maths, specifically additional mathematics and foundations of advanced mathematics (MEI). Further UCAS points can be earned upon completion of the advanced FSMQ in additional mathematics.

AQA Certificate in Mathematical Studies (Core Maths)

This Level 3 qualification has been available since September 2015. It is designed for students who achieved a Grade 4 or above at GCSE and want to continue studying Maths. The qualification carries UCAS points equivalent to an AS level qualification.

AQA Certificate in Further Maths

This level 2 qualification has been designed to provide stretch and challenge to the most able mathematicians. This will be best suited to students who either already have, or are expected to achieve the top grades in GCSE Mathematics and are likely to progress to A level Mathematics and Further Mathematics.

Scottish qualifications

Information supplied by the Scottish Qualifications Authority

In Scotland, qualifications are awarded by the Scottish Qualifications Authority (SQA), the national accreditation and awarding body. A variety of qualifications are offered in schools, including:

- National Qualifications (National Units, National Courses, Skills for Work Courses and Scottish Baccalaureates)

- National Qualification Group Awards (National Certificates and National Progression Awards)

- Awards

National Qualifications cover subjects to suit everyone's interests and skills – from Chemistry to Construction, History to Hospitality, and Computing to Care.

Qualifications in the Scottish qualifications system sit at various levels on the Scottish Credit and Qualifications Framework (SCQF). There are 12 levels on the SCQF and each level represents the difficulty of learning involved. Qualifications in schools span SCQF levels 1 to 7.

National Qualifications (NQ)

National Qualifications are among the most important types of qualification in Scotland.

National Qualifications range from SCQF levels 1 to 7 and include National Units, National Courses, Skills for Work Courses, Scottish Baccalaureates and National Qualification Group Awards.

They are taught in the senior phase of secondary school and they are also offered in colleges, and by some training providers.

They are designed to help young people to demonstrate the skills, knowledge and understanding they have developed at school or college and enable them to prepare for further learning, training and employment.

National Courses

National Courses are available in over 60 subjects, at the following levels: National 2 (SCQF level 2), National 3 (SCQF level 3), National 4 (SCQF level 4), National 5 (SCQF level 5), Higher (SCQF level 6), and Advanced Higher (SCQF level 7).

National 2, National 3 and National 4 courses consist of units and unit assessments, which are internally assessed

by teachers and lecturers, and quality assured by SQA. Students complete the unit assessments during class time. National 4 courses also include an Added Value Unit assessment that assesses students' performance across the whole course. This is usually in the form of an assignment, performance, practical activity or class test. National 2 to National 4 courses are not graded but are assessed as pass or fail.

National 5, Higher and Advanced Higher courses do not include units. They involve a course assessment that takes place at the end of the course. For most subjects, the course assessment is a combination of one or more formal exams and one or more coursework assessments (such as an assignment, performance, project or practical activity). SQA marks all exams and the majority of coursework. In some subjects, coursework is internally assessed by the teacher or lecturer and quality assured by SQA, while performances and practical activities may be subject to visiting assessment by an SQA examiner.

National 5, Higher and Advanced Higher courses are graded A to D or 'no award'.

National Units

National Units are the building blocks of National 2 to National 4 Courses and National Qualification Group Awards. They are also qualifications in their own right and can be done on an individual basis — such as National 1 qualifications, which are standalone units. Units are normally designed to take 40 hours of teaching to complete and each one is assessed by completing a unit assessment. Over 3500 National Units are available, including National Literacy and Numeracy Units, which assess students' literacy and numeracy skills.

Freestanding units are also available at SCQF levels 5, 6 and 7 and can be taken on an individual basis.

Skills for Work Courses

Skills for Work courses are designed to introduce students to the demands and expectations of the world of work. They are available in a variety of areas such as construction, hairdressing and hospitality. The courses involve a strong element of learning through involvement in practical and vocational activities, and develop knowledge, skills and experience that are related to employment. They consist of units and unit assessments, which are internally assessed by teachers and lecturers, and quality assured by SQA. Skills for Work courses are not graded but are assessed as pass or fail. They are available at National

4, National 5 and Higher levels (SCQF levels 4 to 6) and are often delivered in partnership between schools and colleges.

Scottish Baccalaureates

Scottish Baccalaureates consist of a coherent group of Higher and Advanced Higher qualifications, with the addition of an interdisciplinary project. They are available in four subject areas: Expressive Arts, Languages, Science and Social Sciences. The interdisciplinary project is marked and awarded at Advanced Higher level (SCQF level 7). It provides students with a platform to apply their knowledge in a realistic context, and to demonstrate initiative, responsibility and independent working. Aimed at high-achieving sixth year students, the Scottish Baccalaureate encourages personalised, in-depth study and interdisciplinary learning in their final year of secondary school.

National Qualification Group Awards

National Certificates (NCs) and National Progression Awards (NPAs) are referred to as National Qualification Group Awards. These qualifications provide students preparing for work with opportunities to develop skills that are sought after by employers. They are available at SCQF levels 2 to 6.

NCs prepare students for employment, career development or progression to more advanced study at HNC/HND level. They are available in a range of subjects, including: Sound Production, Technical Theatre, and Child, Health and Social Care.

NPAs develop specific skills and knowledge in specialist vocational areas, including Journalism, Architecture and Interior Design, and Legal Services. They link to National Occupational Standards, which are the basis of Scottish Vocational Qualifications (SVQs) and are taught in partnership between schools, colleges, employers and training providers.

Awards

SQA Awards provide students with opportunities to acquire skills, recognise achievement and promote confidence through independent thinking and positive attitudes, while motivating them to be successful and participate positively in the wider community.

A variety of different awards are offered at a number of SCQF levels and cover subjects including leadership, employability and enterprise. These awards are designed to recognise the life, learning and work skills that students gain from taking part in activities both in and out of school, such as sports, volunteering and fundraising.

For more information on SQA and its portfolio of qualifications, visit www.sqa.org.uk

Additional and Alternative

Cambridge Primary

Cambridge Primary is typically for learners aged 5 to 11 years. It develops learner skills and understanding in 10 subjects: English as a first or second language, mathematics, science, art & design, digital literacy, music, physical education, Cambridge Global Perspectives and ICT. The flexible curriculum frameworks include optional assessment tools to help schools monitor learners' progress and give detailed feedback to parents. At the end of Cambridge Primary, schools can enter students for Cambridge Primary Checkpoint tests which are marked in Cambridge.
Website: www.cambridgeinternational.org/primary

Cambridge ICT Starters introduces learners, typically aged 5 to 14 years, to the key ICT applications they need to achieve computer literacy and to understand the impact of technology on our daily lives. It can be taught and assessed in English or Spanish.

Cambridge Lower Secondary

Cambridge Lower Secondary is typically for learners aged 11 to 14 years. It develops learner skills and understanding in 10 subjects: English, English as a second language, mathematics, science, art & design, digital literacy, music, physical education, Cambridge Global Perspectives and ICT, and includes assessment tools. At the end of Cambridge Lower Secondary, schools can enter students for Cambridge Lower Secondary Checkpoint tests which are marked in Cambridge and provide an external international benchmark for student performance.
Website: www.cambridgeinternational.org/lowersecondary

European Baccalaureate (EB)

Not to be confused with the International Baccalaureate (IB) or the French Baccalaureate, this certificate is available in European schools and recognised in all EU countries.

To obtain the baccalaureate, a student must obtain a minimum score of 60%, which is made up from: coursework, oral participation in class and tests (40%); five written examinations (36%) – mother-tongue, first foreign language and maths are compulsory for all candidates; four oral examinations (24%) – mother tongue and first foreign language are compulsory (history or geography may also be compulsory here, dependant on whether the candidate has taken a written examination in these subjects).

Throughout the EU the syllabus and examinations necessary to achieve the EB are identical. The only exception to this rule is the syllabus for the mother tongue language. The EB has been specifically designed to meet, at the very least, the minimum qualification requirements of each member state.

Study for the EB begins at nursery stage (age four) and progresses through primary (age six) and on into secondary school (age 12).

Syllabus
Languages: Bulgarian, Czech, Danish, Dutch, English, Estonian, Finnish, Finnish as a second national language, French, German, Greek, Hungarian, Irish, Italian, Latvian, Lithuanian, Maltese, Polish, Portuguese, Romanian, Slovak, Slovenian, Spanish, Swedish, Swedish for Finnish pupils.

Literary: art education, non-confessional ethics, geography, ancient Greek, history, human sciences, Latin, music, philosophy, physical education.

Sciences: biology, chemistry, economics, ICT, integrated science, mathematics, physics.
For more information, contact:
Office of the Secretary-General of the European Schools, rue de la Science 23 – 2nd floor, B-1040 Bruxelles, Belgique
Tel: +32 (0)2 895 26 11
Website: www.eursc.eu

The International Baccalaureate (IB)

The International Baccalaureate (IB) offers four challenging and high quality educational programmes for a worldwide community of schools, aiming to develop internationally minded people who, recognizing their common humanity and shared guardianship of the planet, help to create a better, more peaceful world.

The IB works with schools around the world (both state and privately funded) that share the commitment to international education to deliver these programmes.

Schools that have achieved the high standards required for authorization to offer one or more of the IB programmes are known as IB World Schools. There are over half a million students attending almost 5000 IB World Schools in over 150 countries and this number is growing annually.

The Primary Years, Middle Years and Diploma Programmes share a common philosophy and common characteristics. They develop the whole student, helping students to grow intellectually, socially, aesthetically and culturally. They provide a broad and balanced education that includes science and the humanities, languages and mathematics, technology and the arts. The programmes teach students to think critically, and encourage them to draw connections between areas of knowledge and to use problem-solving techniques and concepts from many disciplines. They instil in students a sense of responsibility towards others and towards the environment. Lastly, and perhaps most importantly, the programmes give students an awareness and understanding of their own culture and of other cultures, values and ways of life.

A fourth programme called the IB Career-related Programme (CP) became available to IB World Schools from September 2012. All IB programmes include:

- A written curriculum or curriculum framework

- Student assessment appropriate to the age range

- Professional development and networking opportunities for teachers

- Support, authorization and programme evaluation for the school

The IB Primary Years Programme

The IB Primary Years Programme (PYP), for students aged three to 12, focuses on the development of the whole child as an inquirer, both in the classroom and in the world outside. It is a framework consisting of five essential elements (concepts, knowledge, skills, attitude, action) and guided by six trans-disciplinary themes of global significance, explored using knowledge and skills derived from six subject areas (language, social studies, mathematics, science and technology, arts, and personal, social and physical education) with a powerful emphasis on inquiry-based learning.

The most significant and distinctive feature of the PYP is the six trans-disciplinary themes. These themes are about issues that have meaning for, and are important to, all of us. The programme offers a balance between learning about or through the subject areas, and learning beyond them. The six themes of global significance create a trans-disciplinary framework that allows students to 'step up' beyond the confines of learning within subject areas:

- Who we are

- Where we are in place and time

- How we express ourselves

- How the world works

- How we organize ourselves

- Sharing the planet

The PYP exhibition is the culminating activity of the programme. It requires students to analyse and propose solutions to real-world issues, drawing on what they have learned through the programme. Evidence of student development and records of PYP exhibitions are reviewed by the IB as part of the programme evaluation process.

Assessment is an important part of each unit of inquiry as it both enhances learning and provides opportunities for students to reflect on what they know, understand and can do. The teacher's feedback to the students provides the guidance, the tools and the incentive for them to become more competent, more skilful and better at understanding how to learn.

The IB Middle Years Programme (MYP)

The Middle Years Programme (MYP), for students aged 11 to 16, comprises eight subject groups:

- Language acquisition

- Language and literature

- Individuals and societies

- Sciences

- Mathematics

- Arts

- Physical and health education

- Design

The MYP requires at least 50 hours of teaching time for each subject group in each year of the programme. In years 4 and 5, students have the option to take courses from six of the eight subject groups within certain limits, to provide greater flexibility in meeting local requirements and individual student learning needs.

Each year, students in the MYP also engage in at least one collaboratively planned interdisciplinary unit that involves at least two subject groups.

MYP students also complete a long-term project, where they decide what they want to learn about, identify what they already know, discovering what they will need to know to complete the project, and create a proposal or criteria for completing it.

The MYP aims to help students develop their personal understanding, their emerging sense of self and their responsibility in their community.

The MYP allows schools to continue to meet state, provincial or national legal requirements for students with access needs. Schools must develop an inclusion/special educational needs (SEN) policy that explains assessment access arrangements, classroom accommodations and curriculum modification that meet individual student learning needs.

The IB Diploma Programme (IBDP)

The IB Diploma Programme, for students aged 16 to 19, is an academically challenging and motivating curriculum of international education that prepares students for success at university and in life beyond studies.

DP students choose at least one course from six subject groups, thus ensuring depth and breadth of knowledge and experience in languages, social studies, the experimental sciences, mathematics, and the arts. With more than 35 courses to choose from, students have the flexibility to further explore and learn subjects that meet their interest. Out of the six courses required, at least three and not more than four must be taken at higher level (240 teaching hours), the others at standard level (150 teaching hours). Students can take examinations in English, French or Spanish.

In addition, three unique components of the programme – the DP core – aim to broaden students' educational experience and challenge them to apply their knowledge and skills. The DP core – the extended essay (EE), theory of knowledge (TOK) and creativity, activity, service (CAS) – are compulsory and central to the philosophy of the programme.

The IB uses both external and internal assessment to measure student performance in the DP. Student results are determined by performance against set standards, not by each student's position in the overall rank order. DP assessment is unique in the way that it measures the extent to which students have mastered advanced academic skills not what they have memorized. DP assessment also encourages an international outlook and intercultural skills, wherever appropriate.

The IB diploma is awarded to students who gain at least 24 points out of a possible 45 points, subject to certain minimum levels of performance across the whole programme and to satisfactory participation in the creativity, activity, and service requirement.

Recognized and respected by leading universities globally, the DP encourages students to be knowledgeable, inquiring, caring and compassionate, and to develop intercultural understanding, open-mindedness and the attitudes necessary to respect and evaluate a range of viewpoints.

The IB Career Related Programme (IBCP)

The IB Career-related Programme, for students aged 16 to 19, offers an innovative educational framework that combines academic studies with career-related learning. Through the CP, students develop the competencies they need to succeed in the 21st century. More importantly, they have the opportunity to engage with a rigorous study programme that genuinely interests them while gaining transferable and lifelong skills that prepares them to pursue higher education, apprenticeships or direct employment.

CP students complete four core components – language development, personal and professional skills, service learning and a reflective project – in order to receive the International Baccalaureate Career-related Programme Certificate. Designed to enhance critical thinking and intercultural understanding, the CP core helps students develop the communication and personal skills, as well as intellectual habits required for lifelong learning.

Schools that choose to offer the CP can create their own distinctive version of the programme and select career pathways that suit their students and local community needs. The IB works with a variety of CRS providers around the world and schools seeking to develop career pathways with professional communities can benefit from our existing collaborations. All CRS providers undergo a rigorous curriculum evaluation to ensure that their courses align with the CP pedagogy and meet IB quality standards. The flexibility to meet the needs, backgrounds and contexts of learners allows

CP schools to offer an education that is relevant and meaningful to their students.

Launched in 2012, there are 250 CP schools. Many schools with the IB Diploma Programme (DP) and the Middle Years Programme (MYP) have chosen the CP as an alternative IB pathway to offer students. CP schools often report that the programme has helped them raise student aspiration, increase student engagement and retention and encouraged learners to take responsibility for their own actions, helping them foster high levels of self-esteem through meaningful achievements.

For more information on IB programmes, visit: www.ibo.org

Africa, Europe, Middle East IB Global Centre,
Churchillplein 6, The Hague, 2517JW, The Netherlands
Tel: +31 (0)70 352 6000
Email: support@ibo.org

Pearson Edexcel Mathematics Awards

Pearson's Edexcel Mathematics Awards are small, stand-alone qualifications designed to help students to develop and demonstrate proficiency in different areas of mathematics. These Awards enable students to focus on understanding key concepts and techniques, and are available across three subjects, including: Number and Measure (Levels 1 and 2), Algebra (Levels 2 and 3) and Statistical Methods (Levels 1, 2 and 3).

Designed to build students' confidence and fluency; the Awards can fit into the existing programme of delivery for mathematics in schools and colleges, prepare students for GCSE and/or GCE Mathematics, and to support further study in other subjects, training or the workplace. They offer a choice of levels to match students' abilities, with clear progression between the levels. These small, 60-70 guided learning hour qualifications are assessed through one written paper per level. Each qualification is funded and approved for pre-16 and 16-18 year old students in England and in schools and colleges in Wales.

Projects

Extended Project Qualification (EPQ)

AQA, OCR, Pearson and WJEC offer the Extended Project Qualification, which is a qualification aimed at developing a student's research and independent learning skills. The EPQ can be taken as a stand-alone qualification, and it is equivalent to half an A level in UCAS points (but only a third of performance points).

Students complete a research based written report and may produce an artefact or a practical science experiment as part of their project.

Cambridge International Project Qualification (IPQ)

Cambridge International is offering a new standalone project-based qualification, which can be taken alongside Cambridge International AS & A levels. Students complete a 5000-word research project on a topic of their choice. The qualification is assessed by Cambridge International.

For more information, go to www.cambridgeinternational.org/advanced

Entry level and basic skills

Entry Level Qualifications

If you want to take GCSE or NVQ Level 1 but have not yet reached the standard required, then entry level qualifications are for you as they are designed to get you started on the qualifications ladder.

Entry level qualifications are available in a wide range of areas. You can take an entry level certificate in most subjects where a similar GCSE exists. There are also vocational entry level qualifications – some in specific areas like retail or catering and others where you can take units in different work-related subjects to get a taster of a number of career areas. Also available are entry level certificates in life skills and the basic skills of literacy and numeracy.

Anyone can take an entry level qualification – your school or college will help you decide which qualification is right for you.

Entry level qualifications are flexible programmes so the time it takes to complete will vary according to where you study and how long you need to take the qualification.

Subjects available include: Art and Design, Computer Science, English, Geography, History, Latin, Mathematics, Physical Education and Science.

Functional Skills

Functional Skills are qualifications in English and maths that equip learners with the basic practical skills required in everyday life, education and the workplace. They are available at Entry Level, Level 1 and Level 2. Functional Skills are identified as funded 'stepping stone' qualifications to English and maths GCSE for post-16 learners who haven't previously achieved a grade 3 in these subjects. There are part of apprenticeship completion requirements.

Vocational qualifications

Applied Generals/Level 3 Certificates

Applied General qualifications are available in Business and Science and are a practical introduction to these subjects, they are a real alternative to A level support progression to further study or employment aimed at students aged 16-18.

Developed together with teachers, schools, colleges and higher education institutions, they help learners to develop knowledge and skills.

A mixture of assessment types means learners can apply their knowledge in a practical way. An integrated approach creates a realistic and relevant qualification for learners.

AQA Technical Award

AQA's Technical Award is a practical, vocational Level 1/2 qualification for 14- to 16-year-olds to take alongside GCSEs.

The Technical Award in Performing Arts provides an introduction to life and work, equipping learners with the practical, transferable skills and core knowledge needed to progress to further general or vocational study, including Level 3 qualifications, employment or apprenticeships.

Learners are assessed on doing rather than knowing through the project-based internal assessments, where they can apply their knowledge to practical tasks. There are two internally assessed units worth 30% each, and an externally assessed exam worth 40%.

The last time schools can enter for this qualification will be summer 2023, and there will be no resit opportunity.

BTECs

BTEC Level 2 First qualifications

ie BTEC Level 2 Diplomas, BTEC Level 2 Extended Certificates, BTEC Level 2 Certificates and BTEC Level 2 Award.

BTEC Firsts are Level 2 introductory work-related programmes covering a wide range of vocational areas including business, engineering, information technology, health and social care, media, travel and tourism, and public services.

Programmes may be taken full or part-time. They are practical programmes that provide a foundation for the knowledge and skills you will need in work. Alternatively, you can progress onto a BTEC National qualification, Applied GCE A level or equivalent.

There are no formal entry requirements and they can be studied alongside GCSEs. Subjects available include: Agriculture, Animal Care, Applied Science, Art and Design, Business, Children's Care, Learning and Development, Construction, Countryside and the Environment, Engineering, Fish Husbandry, Floristry, Health and Social care, Horse Care, Horticulture, Hospitality, IT, Land-based Technology, Business, Creative Media Production, Music, Performing Arts, Public Services, Sport, Travel and Tourism, and Vehicle Technology.

BTEC Foundation Diploma in Art and Design (QCF)

For those students preparing to go on to higher education within the field of art and design. This diploma is recognised as one of the best courses of its type in the UK, and is used in preparation for degree programmes. Units offered include researching, recording and responding in art and design, media experimentation, personal experimental studies, and a final major project.

BTEC Nationals

ie BTEC Level 3 Extended Diplomas (QCF), BTEC Level 3 Diplomas (QCF), BTEC Level 3 Subsidiary Diplomas (QCF), BTEC Level 3 Certificates (QCF)

BTEC National programmes are long-established vocational programmes. They are practical programmes that are highly valued by employers. They enable you to gain the knowledge and skills that you will need in work, or give you the choice to progress on to a BTEC Higher National, a Foundation Degree or a degree programme.

BTEC Nationals, which hold UCAS points cover a range of vocationally specialist sectors including child care, children's play, learning and development, construction, art and design, aeronautical engineering, electrical/electronic engineering, IT, business, creative and media production, performing arts, public services, sport, sport and exercise sciences and applied science. The programmes may be taken full- or part-time, and can be taken in conjunction with NVQs and/or functional skills units at an appropriate level.

There are no formal entry requirements, but if you have any of the following you are likely to be at the right level to study a BTEC national qualification.

- a BTEC Level 2 First qualification
- GCSEs – at grades A*-C in several subjects
- Relevant work experience

There are also very specialist BTEC Nationals, such as Pharmaceutical Science and Blacksmithing and Metalworking.

BTEC Higher Nationals

Known as HNDs and HNCs – ie BTEC Level 5 HND Diplomas (QCF) and BTEC Level 4 HNC Diplomas (QCF)

BTEC HNDs and HNCs are further and higher education qualifications that offer a balance of education and vocational training. They are available in over 40 work-related subjects such as Graphic Design, Business, Health and Social Care, Computing and Systems Development, Manufacturing Engineering, Hospitality Management, and Public Services.

BTEC higher national courses combine study with hands-on work experience during your course. Once completed, you can use the skills you learn to begin your career, or continue on to a related degree course.

HNDs are often taken as a full-time course over two years but can also be followed part-time in some cases.

HNCs are often for people who are working and take two years to complete on a part-time study basis by day release, evenings, or a combination of the two. Some HNC courses are done on a full-time basis.

There are no formal entry requirements, but if you have any of the following you are likely to be at the right academic level:

- at least one A level
- a BTEC Level 3 National qualification
- level 3 NVQ

BTEC specialist and professional qualifications

These qualifications are designed to prepare students for specific and specialist work activities. These are split into two distinct groups:

- Specialist qualifications (entry to Level 3)
- Professional qualifications (Levels 4-7)

Cambridge Nationals

Cambridge Nationals are vocationally-related qualifications that take an engaging, practical and inspiring approach to learning and assessment.

They are industry-relevant, geared to key sector requirements and very popular with schools and colleges because they suit such a broad range of learning styles and abilities.

Cambridge Nationals are available in: Child Development, Creative iMedia, Engineering Design, Engineering Manufacture, Enterprise and Marketing, Health and Social Care, ICT, Information Technologies, Principles in Engineering and Engineering Business, Sport Science, Sport Studies, Systems Control in Engineering. They are joint Level 1 and 2 qualifications aimed at students aged 14-16 in full-time study.

Cambridge Technicals

OCR's Cambridge Technicals are practical and flexible vocationally-related qualifications, offering students in-depth study in a wide range of subjects, including business, health and social care, IT, sport, art and design, digital media, applied science, performing arts and engineering.

Cambridge Technicals are aimed at young people aged 16-19 who have completed Key Stage 4 of their education and want to study in a more practical, work-related way.

Cambridge Technicals are available at Level 2 and Level 3, and carry UCAS points at Level 3.

NVQs

NVQs reward those who demonstrate skills gained at work. They relate to particular jobs and are usefully taken while you are working. Within reason, NVQs do not have to be completed in a specified amount of time. They can be taken by full-time employees or by school and college students with a work placement or part-time job that enables them to develop the appropriate skills. There are no age limits and no special entry requirements.

NVQs are organised into levels, based on the competencies required. Levels 1-3 are the levels most applicable to learners within the 14-19 phase. Achievement of Level 4 within this age group will be rare. See the OCR website for further information.

Occupational Studies (Northern Ireland)

Targeted at learners working towards and at Level 1 and 2 in Key Stage 4 within the Northern Ireland curriculum. For further information see the CCEA website.

OCR Vocational Qualifications

These are available at different levels and different sizes. Levels 1-3 are the levels most applicable to learners within the 14-19 phase. The different sizes are indicated with the use of Award, Certificate and Diploma in the qualification title and indicate the number of hours it typically takes to complete the qualification.

Vocational qualifications are assessed according to each individual specification, but may include practical assessments and/or marked assessments. They are designed to provide evidence of a student's relevant skills and knowledge in their chosen subject. These qualifications can be used for employment or as a path towards further education. See the OCR website for further details.

SVQs (Scotland)

Scottish Vocational Qualifications (SVQs) are based on national standards, which are drawn up by people from industry, commerce and education. They are studied in the workplace, in college or with training providers. Some schools offer them in partnership with colleges and employers. SVQs are available in many subject areas, from forestry to IT, management to catering, and journalism to construction.

Each unit of an SVQ defines one aspect of a job or work role and what it is to be competent in that aspect of the job.

SVQs are available at SCQF Levels 4-11 and Levels 4-7 are most applicable to learners aged 16-18.

Awarding organisations and examination dates

Awarding organisations

In England there are four awarding organisations, each offering GCSEs, AS and A levels (Eduqas offers only reformed qualifications in England, whereas WJEC offers in England, Wales, Northern Ireland and independent regions). There are separate awarding organisations in Wales (WJEC) and Northern Ireland (CCEA). The awarding organisation in Scotland (SQA) offers equivalent qualifications.

This information was supplied by the awarding bodies and was accurate at the time of going to press. It is intended as a general guide only for candidates in the United Kingdom. Dates are subject to variation and should be confirmed with the awarding organisation concerned.

AQA

Qualifications offered:
GCSE
AS and A level
Foundation Certificate of Secondary Education (FCSE)
Entry Level Certificate (ELC)
Foundation and Higher Projects
Extended Project Qualification (EPQ)
Applied Generals/AQA Level 3 Certificates and Extended Certificates
Functional Skills
AQA Certificate
Technical Award

Other assessment schemes:
Unit Award Scheme (UAS)

Contact:
Email: eos@aqa.org.uk
Website: www.aqa.org.uk
Tel: 0800 197 7162 (8am–5pm Monday to Friday)
+44 161 696 5995 (Outside the UK)

Devas Street, Manchester M15 6EX
Stag Hill House, Guildford, Surrey GU2 7XJ
Windsor House, Cornwall Road, Harrogate, HG1 2PW
2nd Floor, Lynton House, 7–12 Tavistock Square, London, WC1H 9LT

CCEA – Council for the Curriculum, Examinations and Assessment

Qualifications offered:
GCSE
GCE AS/A level
Key Skills (Levels 1-4)
Entry Level Qualifications
Occupational Studies (Levels 1 & 2)
QCF Qualifications
Applied GCSE and GCE

Contact:
Email: info@ccea.org.uk
Website: www.ccea.org.uk

29 Clarendon Road, Clarendon Dock, Belfast, BT1 3BG
Tel: (028) 9026 1200

Eduqas

Eduqas, part of WJEC, offers Ofqual reformed GCSEs, AS and A levels to secondary schools and colleges. Our qualifications are available in England, Channel Islands, Isle of Man, Northern Ireland and to the independent sector in Wales (restrictions may apply).

Qualifications offered:
GCSE (9-1)
AS
A level
Level 3

Contact:
Email: info@wjec.co.uk
Website: www.eduqas.co.uk

Eduqas (WJEC CBAC Ltd),
245 Western Avenue, Cardiff, CF5 2YX
Telephone: 029 2026 5000

IB – International Baccalaureate

Qualification offered:
IB Diploma
IB Career-related Certificate

Contact:
Email: support@ibo.org
Website: www.ibo.org

IB Global Centre, The Hague, Churchillplein 6, 2517 JW, The Hague, The Netherlands
Tel: +31 70 352 60 00

IB Global Centre, Washington DC, 7501 Wisconsin Avenue, Suite 200 West Bethesda, Maryland 20814, USA
Tel: +1 301 202 3000

IB Global Centre, Singapore, 600 North Bridge Road, #21-01 Parkview Square, Singapore 188778
Tel: +65 6 579 5000

IB Global Centre, Cardiff, Peterson House, Malthouse Avenue, Cardiff Gate, Cardiff, Wales, CF23 8GL, UK
Email: reception@ibo.org
Tel: +44 29 2054 7777

International Baccalaureate Foundation Office, Route des Morillons 15, Grand-Saconnex, Genève, CH-1218, Switzerland
Tel: +41 22 309 2540

OCR – Oxford Cambridge and RSA Examinations – and Cambridge International

Qualifications offered by OCR or sister awarding organisation Cambridge Assessment International Education (Cambridge International) include:
GCSE
GCE AS/A level
IGCSE
International AS/A level
Extended Project
Cambridge International Project Qualification
Cambridge Pre-U
Cambridge Nationals
Cambridge Technicals
Functional Skills
FSMQ – Free Standing Maths Qualification
NVQ

Contact:
OCR
OCR Head Office, The Triangle Building, Shaftesbury Road, Cambridge, CB2 8EA
Website: www.ocr.org.uk
Tel: +44 1223 553998

Cambridge International
Website: www.cambridgeinternational.org
Email: info@cambridgeinternational.org
Tel: +44 1223 553554

Pearson

Qualifications offered:

Pearson's qualifications are offered in the UK but are also available through their international centres across the world. They include:

DiDA, CiDA
GCE A levels
GCSEs
Functional Skills
International GCSEs and Edexcel Certificates
ESOL (Skills for Life)
BTEC Enterprise qualifications
BTEC Entry Level, Level 1 and Level 1 Introductory
BTEC Firsts
BTEC Foundation Diploma in Art and Design
BTEC Industry Skills
BTEC International Level 3
BTEC Level 2 Technicals
BTEC Level 3 Technical Levels in Hospitality
BTEC Nationals
BTEC Specialist and Professional qualifications
BTEC Tech Awards
Higher Nationals
T Levels

Contact:
190 High Holborn, London WC1V 7BH
See website for specific contact details:
qualifications.pearson.com

SQA – Scottish Qualifications Authority

Qualifications offered:

National Qualifications (NQs): National 1 to National 5; Higher; Advanced Higher
Skills for Work; Scottish Baccalaureates
National Certificates (NCs)
National Progression Awards (NPAs)
Awards
Core Skills
Scottish Vocational Qualifications (SVQs)
Higher National Certificates and Higher National Diplomas (HNCs/HNDs)*

*SQA offers HNCs and HNDs to centres in Scotland. Outside of Scotland, the equivalent qualifications are the SQA Advanced Certificate and SQA Advanced Diploma.

*Examination dates for summer 2022: 26 April – 1 June***

**The 2022 exams will take place if it is safe to do so. SQA is continuing to follow public health advice and is preparing for a range of scenarios, with associated contingencies, to acknowledge the possibility of further disruption and to help ensure the safe delivery of National 5, Higher and Advanced Higher courses this year.

Contact:
Email: customer@sqa.org.uk Tel: 0345 279 1000
Website: www.sqa.org.uk
Glasgow – The Optima Building, 58 Robertson Street, Glasgow, G2 8DQ
Dalkeith – Lowden, 24 Wester Shawfair, Dalkeith, Midlothian, EH22 1FD

WJEC

With over 65 years' experience in delivering qualifications, WJEC is the largest provider in Wales and a leading provider in England and Northern Ireland.

Qualifications offered:
GCSE
GCE A/AS
Functional Skills
Entry Level
Welsh Baccalaureate Qualifications
Essential Skills Wales
Wider Key Skills
Project Qualifications Principal Learning
Other general qualifications such as Level 1 and Level 2 Awards and Certificates including English Language, English Literature, Latin Language, Latin Language & Roman Civilisation and Latin Literature
QCF Qualifications

Contact:
Email: info@wjec.co.uk
Website: www.wjec.co.uk

245 Western Avenue, Cardiff, CF5 2YX
Tel: 029 2026 5000

Educational organisations

Educational organisations

Artsmark

Arts Council England's Artsmark was set up in 2001, and rounds are held annually.

All schools in England can apply for an Artsmark – primary, middle, secondary, special and pupil referral units, maintained and independent – on a voluntary basis. An Artsmark award is made to schools showing commitment to the full range of arts – music, dance, drama and art and design.

Tel: 0161 934 4317
Email: artsmark@artscouncil.org.uk
Website: www.artsmark.org.uk

Association for the Education and Guardianship of International Students (AEGIS)

AEGIS brings together schools and guardianship organisations to ensure and promote the welfare of international students. AEGIS provides accreditation for all reputable guardianship organisations.

AEGIS, The Wheelhouse, Bond's Mill Estate, Bristol Road, Stonehouse, Gloucestershire GL10 3RF.
Tel: 01453 821293
Email: info@aegisuk.net
Website: www.aegisuk.net

The Association of American Study Abroad Programmes (AASAP)

Established in 1991 to represent American study abroad programmes in the UK.

Contact: Kalyn Franke, AASAP/UK,
University of Maryland in London, Connaught Hall,
36-45 Tavistock Square, London WC1H 9EX
Email: info@aasapuk.org
Website: www.aasapuk.org

The Association of British Riding Schools (ABRS)

An independent body of proprietors and principals of riding establishments, aiming to look after their interests and those of the riding public and to raise standards of management, instruction and animal welfare.

The Association of British Riding Schools, Unit 8, Bramble Blenheim Business Centre, Smithers Hill Ln, Horsham RH13 8PP. Tel: 01403 790294
Email: office@abrs-info.org
Website: www.abrs-info.org

Association of Colleges (AOC)

Created in 1996 to promote the interest of further education colleges in England and Wales.

2-5 Stedham Place, London WC1A 1HU
Tel: 0207 034 9900
Email: enquiries@aoc.co.uk
Website: www.aoc.co.uk

Association of Governing Bodies of Independent Schools (AGBIS)

AGBIS supports and advises governing bodies of schools in the independent sector on all aspects of governance.

Registered charity No. 1108756
Association of Governing Bodies of Independent Schools,
3 Codicote Road, Welwyn, Hertfordshire AL6 9LY
Tel: 01438 840730
Email: enquiries@agbis.org.uk
Website: www.agbis.org.uk

Association of Employment and Learning Providers (AELP)

AELP's purpose is to influence the education and training agenda. They are the voice of independent learning providers throughout England.
Association of Employment and Learning Providers,
2nd Floor, 9 Apex Court, Bradley Stoke, Bristol, BS32 4JT
Tel: 0117 986 5389
Email: enquiries@aelp.org.uk
Website: www.aelp.org.uk

The Association of School and College Leaders (ASCL)

Formerly the Secondary Heads Association, the ASCL is a professional association for secondary school and college leaders.
2nd Floor, Peat House, 1 Waterloo Way, Leicester LE1 6LP
Tel: 0116 299 1122
Fax: 0116 299 1123
Email: info@ascl.org.uk
Website: www.ascl.org.uk

Boarding Schools' Association (BSA)

For information on the BSA see editorial on page 30

The British Accreditation Council (BAC)

The British Accreditation Council (BAC) has now been the principal accrediting body for the independent further and higher education and training sector for nearly 30 years. BAC-accredited institutions in the UK now number more than 300, offering everything from website design to yoga to equine dentistry, as well as more standard qualifications in subjects such as business, IT, management and law. As well as our accreditation of institutions offering traditional teaching, BAC has developed a new accreditation scheme for providers offering online, distance and blended learning. Some students may also look to study outside the UK at one of the institutions holding BAC international accreditation.
Wax Chandlers' Hall 1st Floor, 6 Gresham Street, London EC2V 7AD
Tel: 0300 330 1400
Email: info@the-bac.org
Website: www.the-bac.org

The British Association for Early Childhood Education (BAECE)

Promotes quality provision for all children from birth to eight in whatever setting they are placed. Publishes booklets and organises conferences for those interested in early years education and care. Registered charity Nos. 313082; SC039472
Fountain Court, 2 Victoria Square, St Albans AL1 3T
Tel: 01727 884925
Email: office@early-education.org.uk
Website: www.early-education.org.uk

The Choir Schools' Association (CSA)

Represents 44 schools attached to cathedrals, churches and college chapels, which educate cathedral and collegiate choristers.
CSA Information Officer, 39 Bournside Road, Cheltenham, Gloucestershire GL51 3AL
Tel: 07903 850597
Email: ian.jones@choirschools.org.uk
Website: www.choirschools.org.uk

CIFE

CIFE is the professional association for independent sixth form and tutorial colleges accredited by the British Accreditation Council (BAC), the Independent Schools Council or the DfE (Ofsted). Member colleges specialise in preparing students for GCSE and A level (AS and A2) in particular and university entrance in general.

The aim of the association is to provide a forum for the exchange of information and ideas, and for the promotion of best practice, and to safeguard adherence to strict standards of professional conduct and ethical propriety. Further information can be obtained from CIFE:
Tel: 0208 767 8666
Email: enquiries@cife.org.uk
Website: www.cife.org.uk

Council of British International Schools (COBIS)

COBIS is a membership association of British schools of quality worldwide and is committed to a stringent process of quality assurance for all its member schools. COBIS is a member of the Independent Schools Council (ISC) of the United Kingdom.
COBIS, 55–56 Russell Square, Bloomsbury,
London WC1B 4HP
Tel: 020 3826 7190
Email: pa@cobis.org.uk
Website: www.cobis.org.uk

Council of International Schools (CIS)

CIS is a not-for-profit organisation committed to supporting its member schools and colleges in achieving and delivering the highest standards of international education. CIS provides accreditation to schools, teacher and leader recruitment and best practice development. CIS Higher Education assists member colleges and universities in recruiting a diverse profile of qualified international students.
Schipholweg 113, 2316 XC Leiden, The Netherlands.
Tel: +31 71 524 3300
Email: info@cois.org
Website: www.cois.org

Dyslexia Action (DA)

A registered, educational charity (No. 268502), which has established teaching and assessment centres and conducts teacher-training throughout the UK. The aim of the institute is to help people with dyslexia of all ages to overcome their difficulties in learning to read, write and spell and to achieve their potential.
Dyslexia Action Training and Guild, Centurion House,
London Road, Staines-upon-Thames TW18 4AX
Tel: 01784 222 304
Email: trainingcourses@dyslexiaaction.org.uk
Website: www.dyslexiaaction.org.uk

European Association for International Education (EAIE)

A not-for-profit organisation aiming for internationalisation in higher education in Europe. It has a membership of over 1800.
PO Box 11189, 1001 GD Amsterdam, The Netherlands
Tel: +31 20 344 5100
Fax: +31 20 344 5119
Email: info@eaie.org
Website: www.eaie.org

ECIS (European Collaborative for International Schools)

ECIS is a membership organisation which provides services to support professional development, good governance and leadership in international schools.
24 Greville Street,
London, EC1N 8SS
Tel: 020 7824 7040
Email: ecis@ecis.org
Website: www.ecis.org

The Girls' Day School Trust (GDST)

The Girls' Day School Trust (GDST) is one of the largest, longest-established and most successful groups of independent schools in the UK, with 4000 staff and over 20,000 students between the ages of 3 and 18. As a charity that owns and runs a family of 25 schools in England and Wales, it reinvests all its income into its schools for the benefit of the pupils. With a long history of pioneering innovation in the education of girls, the GDST now also educates boys in some of its schools, and has two coeducational sixth form colleges. Registered charity No. 306983

10 Bressenden Place, London, SW1E 5DH
Tel: 020 7393 6666
Email: info@wes.gdst.net
Website: www.gdst.net

Girls' Schools Association (GSA)

For information on the GSA see editorial on page 31

The Headmasters' and Headmistresses' Conference (HMC)

For information on the HMC see editorial on page 32

Human Scale Education (HSE)

An educational reform movement aiming for small education communities based on democracy, fairness and respect. Registered charity No. 1000400
Email: contact@hse.org.uk
Website: www.humanscaleeducation.com

The Independent Association of Prep Schools (IAPS)

For further information about IAPS see editorial on page 34

The Independent Schools Association (ISA)

For further information about ISA see editorial on page 36

The Independent Schools' Bursars Association (ISBA)

Exists to support and advance financial and operational performance in independent schools. The ISBA is a charitable company limited by guarantee.
Company No. 6410037; registered charity No. 1121757
Bluett House, Unit 11–12 Manor Farm, Cliddesden, nr Basingstoke, Hampshire RG25 2JB
Tel: 01256 330369
Email: office@theisba.org.uk
Website: www.theisba.org.uk

The Independent Schools Council (ISC)

The Independent Schools Council exists to promote choice, diversity and excellence in education; the development of talent at all levels of ability; and the widening of opportunity for children from all backgrounds to achieve their potential. Its 1280 member schools educate more than 500,000 children at all levels of ability and from all socioeconomic classes. Nearly a third of children in ISC schools receive help with fees. The Governing Council of ISC contains representatives from each of the eight ISC constituent associations listed below.
See also page 44.

Members:
Association of Governing Bodies of Independent Schools (AGBIS)
Girls' Schools Association (GSA)
Headmasters' and Headmistresses' Conference (HMC)
Independent Association of Prep Schools (IAPS)
Independent Schools Association (ISA)
Independent Schools Bursars' Association (ISBA)
The Society of Heads
The council also has close relations with the BSA, COBIS, SCIS and WISC.

First Floor, 27 Queen Anne's Gate, London, SW1H 9BU
Tel: 020 7766 7070
Fax: 020 7766 7071
Email: research@isc.co.uk
Website: www.isc.co.uk

The Independent Schools Examinations Board (ISEB)

Details of the Common Entrance examinations are obtainable from:
Independent Schools Examinations Board,
Endeavour House, Crow Arch Lane, Ringwood BH24 1HP
Tel: 01425 470555
Email: enquiries@iseb.co.uk
Website: www.iseb.co.uk
Copies of past papers can be purchased from Galore Park: www.galorepark.co.uk

International Baccalaureate (IB)

For full information about the IB see full entry on page 191.

International Schools Theatre Association (ISTA)

International body of teachers and students of theatre, run by teachers for teachers. Registered charity No. 1050103
Lakeside Offices, The Old Cattle Market, Coronation Park, Helston, Cornwall TR13 0SR
Tel: 01326 560398
Email: office@ista.co.uk
Website: www.ista.co.uk

Maria Montessori Institute (MMI)

Authorised by the Association Montessori Internationale (AMI) to run their training course in the UK. Further information is available from:
26 Lyndhurst Gardens, Hampstead, London NW3 5NW
Tel: 020 7435 3646
Email: info@mariamontessori.org
Website: www.mariamontessori.org

The National Association of Independent Schools & Non-Maintained Schools (NASS)

A membership organisation working with and for special schools in the voluntary and private sectors within the UK.
Registered charity No. 1083632
PO Box 705, York YO30 6WW
Tel/Fax: 01904 624446
Email: krippon@nasschools.org.uk
Website: www.nasschools.org.uk

National Day Nurseries Association (NDNA)

A national charity that aims to promote quality in early years. Registered charity No. 1078275
NDNA, National Early Years Enterprise Centre,
Longbow Close, Huddersfield, West Yorkshire HD2 1GQ
Tel: 01484 407070
Fax: 01484 407060
Email: info@ndna.org.uk
Website: www.ndna.org.uk

NDNA Cymru, Office 3, Crown House, 11 Well Street,
Ruthin, Denbighshire LL15 1AE
Tel: 01824 707823
Email: wales@ndna.org.uk

NDNA Scotland, The Mansfield Traquair Centre,
15 Mansfield Place, Edinburgh EH3 6BB
Tel: 0131 516 6967
Email: scot@ndna.org.uk

National Foundation for Educational Research (NFER)

NFER is the UK's largest independent provider of research, assessment and information services for education, training and children's services. Its clients include UK government departments and agencies at both national and local levels. NFER is a not-for-profit organisation and a registered charity No. 313392
Head Office, The Mere, Upton Park,
Slough, Berkshire SL1 2DQ
Tel: 01753 574123
Fax: 01753 691632
Email: enquiries@nfer.ac.uk
Website: www.nfer.ac.uk

Potential Plus UK

Potential Plus UK is an independent charity that supports the social, emotional and learning needs of children with high learning potential of all ages and backgrounds. Registered charity No. 313182
The Open University, Vaughan Harley Building Ground Floor, Walton Hall, Milton Keynes MK7 6AA
Tel: 01908 646433
Email: amazingchildren@potentialplusuk.org
Website: www.potentialplusuk.org

Round Square

An international group of schools formed in 1967 following the principles of Dr Kurt Hahn, the founder of Salem School in Germany, and Gordonstoun in Scotland. The Round Square, named after Gordonstoun's 17th century circular building in the centre of the school, now has more than 100 member schools. Registered charity No. 327117
Round Square, First Floor, Morgan House, Madeira Walk, Windsor SL4 1EP
Tel: 01474 709843
Website: www.roundsquare.org

Royal National Children's SpringBoard Foundation

On 1 July 2017 the Royal National Children's Foundation (RNCF) merged with The SpringBoard Bursary Foundation to create the Royal National Children's SpringBoard Foundation ('Royal SpringBoard'). The newly merged charity gives life-transforming bursaries to disadvantaged and vulnerable children from across the UK.
6th Floor, Minster House, 42 Mincing Lane,
London, EC3R 7A
Tel: 01932 868622
Email: admin@royalspringboard.org.uk
Website: www.royalspringboard.org.uk

School Fees Independent Advice (SFIA)

For further information about SFIA, see editorial page 38

Schools Music Association of Great Britain (SMA)

The SMA is a national 'voice' for music in education. It is now part of the Incorporated Society of Musicians Registered charity No. 313646
Website: www.ism.org/sma

Scottish Council of Independent Schools (SCIS)

Representing more than 70 independent, fee-paying schools in Scotland, the Scottish Council of Independent Schools (SCIS) is the foremost authority on independent schools in Scotland and offers impartial information, advice and guidance to parents. Registered charity No. SC018033
1, St Colme Strreet, Edinburgh EH3 6AA
Tel: 0131 556 2316
Email: info@scis.org.uk
Website: www.scis.org.uk

Society of Education Consultants (SEC)

The Society is a professional membership organisation that supports management consultants who specialise in education and children's services. The society's membership includes consultants who work as individuals, in partnerships or in association with larger consultancies.
SEC, Bellamy House, 13 West Street, Cromer NR27 9HZ
Tel: 0330 323 0457
Email: administration@sec.org.uk
Website: www.sec.org.uk

The Society of Heads

For full information see editorial on page 35

State Boarding Forum (SBF)

For full information about the SBF see editorial on page 30

Steiner Waldorf Schools Fellowship (SWSF)

Representing Steiner education in the UK and Ireland, the SWSF has member schools and early years centres in addition to interest groups and other affiliated organisations. Member schools offer education for children within the normal range of ability, aged 3 to 18. Registered charity No. 295104
Steiner Waldorf Schools Fellowship® Ltd, 35 Park Road, London NW1 6XT
Tel: 0204 5249933
Email: admin@steinerwaldorf.org
Website: www.steinerwaldorf.org

Support and Training in Prep Schools (SATIPS)

SATIPS aims to support teachers in the independent and maintained sectors of education. Registered charity No. 313688
West Routengill, Walden, West Burton, Leyburn, North Yorkshire, DL8 4LF
Website: www.satips.org

The Tutors' Association

The Tutors' Association is the professional body for tutoring and wider supplementary education sector in the UK. Launched in 2013, they have over 850 members, including Individual and Corporate Members representing some 30,000 tutors throughout the UK.
Tel: 01628 306108
Email: info@thetutorsassociation.org.uk
Website: www.thetutorsassociation.org.uk

UCAS (Universities and Colleges Admissions Service)

UCAS is the organisation responsible for managing applications to higher education courses in England, Scotland, Wales and Northern Ireland. Registered charity Nos. 1024741 and SC038598
Rosehill, New Barn Lane,
Cheltenham, Gloucestershire GL52 3LZ
Tel: 0371 468 0 468
Website: www.ucas.com

UKCISA – The Council for International Student Affairs

UKCISA is the UK's national advisory body serving the interests of international students and those who work with them. Registered charity No. 1095294
Website: www.ukcisa.org.uk

United World Colleges (UWC)

UWC was founded in 1962 and their philosophy is based on the ideas of Dr Kurt Hahn (see Round Square Schools). Registered charity No. 313690.
UWC International, Third Floor, 55 New Oxford Street, London, WC1A 1BS, UK
Tel: 020 7269 7800
Fax: 020 7405 4374
Email: info@uwcio.uwc.org
Website: www.uwc.org

World-Wide Education Service of CfBT Education Trust (WES)

A leading independent service which provides home education courses worldwide.
Waverley House, Penton,
Carlisle, Cumbria CA6 5QU
Tel: 01228 577123
Email: office@weshome.com
Website: www.weshome.com

Glossary

Glossary

ACETS	Awards and Certificates in Education	COBIS	Council of British International)
AEA	Advanced Extension Award	CSA	The Choir Schools' Association
AEB	Associated Examining Board for the General Certificate of Education	CST	The Christian Schools' Trust
		DfE	Department for Education (formerly DfES and DCFS)
AEGIS	Association for the Education and Guardianship of International Students	DipEd	Diploma of Education
AGBIS	Association of Governing Bodies of Independent Schools	DipTchng	Diploma of Teaching
		EAIE	European Association for International Education
AHIS	Association of Heads of Independent Schools	ECIS	European Council of International Schools
AJIS	Association of Junior Independent Schools	EdD	Doctor of Education
ALP	Association of Learning Providers	Edexcel	GCSE Examining group, incorporating Business and Technology Education Council (BTEC) and University of London Examinations and Assessment Council (ULEAC)
ANTC	The Association of Nursery Training Colleges		
AOC	Association of Colleges		
AP	Advanced Placement		
ASCL	Association of School & College Leaders	EFL	English as a Foreign Language
ASL	Additional and Specialist Learning	ELAS	Educational Law Association
ATI	The Association of Tutors Incorporated	EPQ	Extended Project qualification
AQA	Assessment and Qualification Alliance/ Northern Examinations and Assessment Board	ESL	English as a Second Language
		FCoT	Fellow of the College of Teachers (TESOL)
BA	Bachelor of Arts	FEFC	Further Education Funding Council
BAC	British Accreditation Council for Independent Further and Higher Education	FRSA	Fellow of the Royal Society of Arts
		FSMQ	Free-Standing Mathematics Qualification
BAECE	The British Association for Early Childhood Education	GCE	General Certificate of Education
		GCSE	General Certificate of Secondary Education
BD	Bachelor of Divinity	GDST	Girls' Day School Trust
BEA	Boarding Educational Alliance	GNVQ	General National Vocational Qualifications
BEd	Bachelor of Education	GOML	Graded Objectives in Modern Languages
BLitt	Bachelor of Letters	GSA	Girls' Schools Association
BPrimEd	Bachelor of Primary Education	GSVQ	General Scottish Vocational Qualifications
BSA	Boarding Schools' Association	HMC	Headmasters' and Headmistresses' Conference
BSc	Bachelor of Science		
BTEC	Range of work-related, practical programmes leading to qualifications equivalent to GCSEs and A levels awarded by Edexcel	HMCJ	Headmasters' and Headmistresses' Conference Junior Schools
		HNC	Higher National Certificate
Cantab	Cambridge University	HND	Higher National Diploma
CATSC	Catholic Association of Teachers in Schools and Colleges	IAPS	Independent Association of Prep Schools
		IB	International Baccalaureate
CCEA	Council for the Curriculum, Examination and Assessment	ICT	Information and Communication Technology
		IFF	Inspiring Futures Foundation (formerly ISCO)
CDT	Craft, Design and Technology	IGCSE	International General Certificate of Secondary Education
CE	Common Entrance Examination		
CEAS	Children's Education Advisory Service	INSET	In service training
CertEd	Certificate of Education	ISA	Independent Schools Association
CIE	Cambridge International Examinations	ISBA	Independent Schools' Bursars' Association
CIFE	Conference for Independent Education	ISCis	Independent Schools Council information service
CIS	Council of International Schools		
CISC	Catholic Independent Schools' Conference	ISC	Independent Schools Council
CLAIT	Computer Literacy and Information Technology	ISEB	Independent Schools Examination Board
		ISST	International Schools Sports Tournament
CNED	Centre National d'enseignement (National Centre of long distance learning)	ISTA	International Schools Theatre Association

ITEC	International Examination Council
JET	Joint Educational Trust
LA	Local Authority
LISA	London International Schools Association
MA	Master of Arts
MCIL	Member of the Chartered Institute of Linguists
MEd	Master of Education
MIoD	Member of the Institute of Directors
MLitt	Master of Letters
MSc	Master of Science
MusD	Doctor of Music
MYP	Middle Years Programme
NABSS	National Association of British Schools in Spain
NAGC	National Association for Gifted Children
NAHT	National Association of Head Teachers
NAIS	National Association of Independent Schools
NASS	National Association of Independent Schools & Non-maintained Special Schools
NDNA	National Day Nurseries Association
NEASC	New England Association of Schools and Colleges
NFER	National Federation of Educational Research
NPA	National Progression Award
NQ	National Qualification
NQF	National Qualifications Framework
NQT	Newly Qualified Teacher
NVQ	National Vocational Qualifications
OCR	Oxford, Cambridge and RSA Examinations
OLA	Online Language Assessment for Modern Languages
Oxon	Oxford
PGCE	Post Graduate Certificate in Education
PhD	Doctor of Philosophy
PL	Principal Learning
PNEU	Parents' National Education Union
PYP	Primary Years Programme
QCA	Qualifications and Curriculum Authority
QCF	Qualifications and Credit Framework
RSIS	The Round Square Schools
SAT	Scholastic Aptitude Test
SATIPS	Support & Training in Prep Schools/Society of Assistant Teachers in Prep Schools
SBSA	State Boarding Schools Association
SCE	Service Children's Education
SCIS	Scottish Council of Independent Schools
SCQF	Scottish Credit and Qualifications Framework
SEC	The Society of Educational Consultants
SEN	Special Educational Needs
SFCF	Sixth Form Colleges' Forum
SFIA	School Fees Insurance Agency Limited
SFIAET	SFIA Educational Trust

SMA	Schools Music Association
SoH	The Society of Heads
SQA	Scottish Qualifications Authority
STEP	Second Term Entrance Paper (Cambridge)
SVQ	Scottish Vocational Qualifications
SWSF	Steiner Waldorf Schools Fellowship
TABS	The Association of Boarding Schools
TISCA	The Independent Schools Christian Alliance
TOEFL	Test of English as a Foreign Language
UCAS	Universities and Colleges Admissions Service for the UK
UCST	United Church Schools Trust
UKLA	UK Literacy Association
UKCISA	The UK Council for International Education
UWC	United World Colleges
WISC	World International Studies Committee
WJEC	Welsh Joint Education Committee
WSSA	Welsh Secondary Schools Association

Index

Index

Index

Index

Index